North Biscay

Brest to Bordeaux

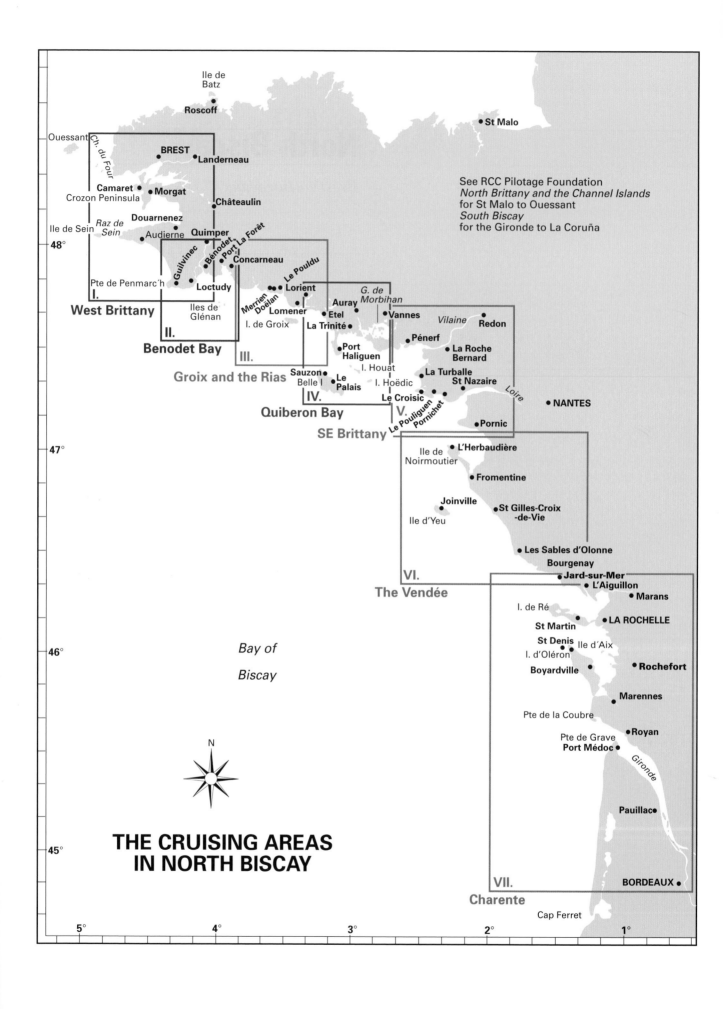

Ile de
Batz
Roscoff

• St Malo

Ouessant   Ch. du Four

BREST
Landerneau

See RCC Pilotage Foundation
North Brittany and the Channel Islands
for St Malo to Ouessant
South Biscay
for the Gironde to La Coruña

Camaret •   • **Morgat**
Crozon Peninsula   **Châteaulin**

Douarnenez
Ile de Sein   *Raz de Sein*   Audierne   **Quimper**

48°

Port La Forêt
Bénodet
Concarneau
Guilvinec
Pte de Penmarc'h   **Loctudy**
I.
West Brittany
Iles de Glénan
II.
Benodet Bay

Le Pouldu
Lorient
Merrien
Doëlan
Lomener
I. de Groix   **La Trinité**
III.
Groix and the Rias

Auray
Etel
G. de Morbihan

Vannes
Vilaine   **Redon**
Pénerf
Port
Haliguen
**La Roche
Bernard**
I. Houat
La Turballe
I. Hoëdic   **St Nazaire**
Sauzon
Belle I   **Le Palais**
Le Croisic
IV.
Quiberon Bay
V.
SE Brittany
Le Pouliguen
Pornichet
Loire   **• NANTES**
Pornic

47°

Ile de
Noirmoutier   **L'Herbaudière**
Fromentine
Joinville
Ile d'Yeu   **St Gilles-Croix
-de-Vie**
VI.
The Vendée
Les Sables d'Olonne
Bourgenay
Jard-sur-Mer
L'Aiguillon
Marans
I. de Ré
St Martin   **• LA ROCHELLE**
St Denis   Ile d'Aix
I. d'Oléron
Boyardville   **• Rochefort**
Marennes
Pte de la Coubre
Royan
Pte de Grave
Port Médoc
VII.
Charente

Bay of

46°

Biscay

N

45°

**THE CRUISING AREAS
IN NORTH BISCAY**

Gironde

Pauillac

BORDEAUX
Cap Ferret

5°   4°   3°   2°   1°

North Biscay
Brest to Bordeaux

ROYAL CRUISING CLUB PILOTAGE FOUNDATION

Mike and Gill Barron

Imray Laurie Norie & Wilson Ltd

Published by
Imray Laurie Norie & Wilson Ltd
Wych House The Broadway St Ives Cambridgeshire PE27 5BT
England
☎ +44 (0)1480 462114 Fax +44 (0) 1480 496109
email ilnw@imray.com
www.imray.com
2005

Partly based on *Harbours and Anchorages Vols I* and *II* by K Adlard Coles, first published in 1959 and 1960.

As *North Biscay Pilot* published by Adlard Coles Ltd
Revised by Professor A N Black
Second edition 1977
Reprinted with amendments 1978
Third edition 1982
Revised by the RCC Pilotage Foundation
Reprinted with amendments 1985
Reprinted with amendments 1987
Fourth edition 1990
Sixth edition 2000
Seventh edition 2005

ISBN 0 85288 702 7

British Library Cataloguing in Publication Data.
A catalogue record for this title is available from the British Library.

The last input of technical information was October 2004

Printed in Great Britain at The Bath Press

CORRECTIONAL SUPPLEMENTS

This pilot book will be amended at intervals by the issue of correctional supplements. These are published on the internet at our web site www.imray.com and may be downloaded free of charge. Printed copies are also available on request from the publishers at the above address.

CAUTION

Whilst every care has been taken to ensure that the information contained in this book is accurate, the RCC Pilotage Foundation, the authors and the publishers hereby formally disclaim any and all liability for any personal injury, loss and/or damage howsoever caused, whether by reason of any error, inaccuracy, omission or ambiguity in relation to the contents and/or information contained within this book. The book contains selected information and thus is not definitive. It does not contain all known information on the subject in hand and should not be relied on alone for navigational use: it should only be used in conjunction with official hydrographic data. This is particularly relevant to the plans which should not be used for navigation.

The RCC Pilotage Foundation, the authors and publishers believe that the information which they have included is a useful aid to prudent navigation, but the safety of a vessel depends ultimately on the judgment of the navigator, who should assess all information, published or unpublished.

WAYPOINTS

This latest guide to North Biscay includes the introduction of waypoints. The RCC PF consider a waypoint to be a position likely to be helpful for navigation if entered into some form of electronic navigation system for use in conjunction with GPS. In this pilot they have been derived from electronic charts, paper charts or by actual observation. All waypoints given are to datum WGS 84 and every effort has been made to ensure their accuracy. Nevertheless, for each individual boat, the standard of onboard equipment, aerial position, datum setting, correct entry of data and operator skill all play a part in their effectiveness and safety. In particular, if plotting a GPS position on a chart then it is vital for the navigator to note the datum of the chart in use and apply the necessary correction.

Our use of the term 'waypoint' does not imply that all vessels can safely sail directly over those positions at all times – indeed some may be placed on readily identifiable features ashore. Some – as in this pilot – may be linked to form recommended routes under the appropriate conditions. However, skippers should be aware of the risk of collision with another vessel which is plying the exact reciprocal course. Verification by observation, or use of radar to check the accuracy of a waypoint, may sometimes be advisable and reassuring. This particularly applies to waypoints which are close inshore or near to dangers where the risk associated with errors is obviously greater. Such waypoints are included for the benefit of those who find them useful but they are not intended to be used as the prime means of navigating in such waters.

We emphasise that we regard waypoints as an aid to navigation for use as the navigator or skipper decides. We hope that the waypoints in this pilot will help ease that navigational load.

PLANS

The plans in this guide are not to be used for navigation – they are designed to support the text and should always be used together with navigational charts. Even so, every effort has been made to locate harbour and anchorage plans adjacent to the relevant text.

It should be borne in mind that the characteristics of lights may be changed during the life of the book, and that in any case notification of such changes is unlikely to be reported immediately. Each light is identified in both the text and where possible on the plans (where it appears in red) by its international index number, as used in the *Admiralty List of Lights*, from which the book may be updated when no longer new.

All bearings are given from seaward and refer to true north. Scales may be taken from the scales of latitude. Symbols are based on those used by the British Admiralty – users are referred to *Symbols and Abbreviations (NP 5011)*.

Foreword

The origin of this pilotage book goes back many years. The first to cover these waters was *Sailing Tours – Falmouth to the Loire* by Frank Cowper at the end of the nineteenth century and this present book is the seventh in line from Adlard Coles' 1959 *Biscay Harbours and Anchorages*, the copyright of which was donated to the Pilotage Foundation.

Mike and Gill Barron have sailed the North Biscay coast for many years and have completely revised the structure and presentation of the pilotage information for this edition. Additional detailed visits by land in 2003 were followed by re-sailing the coast this year to ensure the information given here is as accurate as is practicable to October 2004. To the traditional information have been added waypoints to WGS 84. They are offered as an aid to navigation and the attention of skippers is drawn to the note opposite.

We hope this modern pilot book will help yachtsmen to enjoy fully the fascinating coastline, harbours and anchorages of North Biscay. As always we welcome feedback through our publishers, Imray.

C D Power
Chairman, RCC Pilotage Foundation
October 2004

Preface

Perhaps the most important acknowledgement in a seventh edition is to the authors of the previous editions. We should particularly like to thank Gavin McLaren, author of the 6th edition, for providing us with such an excellent starting point.

An equally important acknowledgement is due to John Lawson, author of the companion volumes *North Brittany and Channel Islands* and *South Biscay*. John's superb pilots overlap *North Biscay* by a short distance in the north and by a much greater distance in the south. John has generously allowed us to use his material in both areas. *South Biscay* covers the Gironde in great detail and the brief coverage of the major ports in this volume is extensively based on John's research.

Another big thank-you is due to Patrick Roach who took the aerial photographs that are such an important feature of this book. The authors took the majority of the sea-level photos but we should like to thank Sally Muir and Mike Saunders for additional photos.

While compiling this volume, we have been given help and advice by so many yachtsmen, harbourmasters, marina staff and local people that we are unable to thank them individually. Thus we must simply thank all the friendly, helpful people who cruise and live in North Biscay and who make cruising there such a pleasure.

Some people have given us so much help and local knowledge that their contribution needs to be recognised individually. These include Chris Austin (*Lady Beth*), Christopher and Sally Buckley (*Wandering Moon III*), Tony Boas (*Bold Warrior*), David Darbyshire (*Eleanor Mary*), Michael and Jennifer Forster (*Border Rival*), Sally Muir and Martin Nash (*Arabesque*), Mike and Liz Redfern (*Dafony*). Robin Markes drew our attention to a number of fascinating and historically important naval battles that took place in North Biscay.

David Darbyshire, Michael Grubb, Ros Hogbin, John Lawson, John Palmer, Francis Walker and Martin Walker took on the vital but tedious task of proofreading. In the process they made many valuable contributions that have helped to make this book clearer and more accurate.

Last but not least we must thank the unsung heroes at Imray and the RCC Pilotage Foundation who turned our notes into a book.

Mike and Gill Barron
October 2004

THE RCC PILOTAGE FOUNDATION

In 1976 an American member of the Royal Cruising Club, Dr Fred Ellis, indicated that he wished to make a gift to the Club in memory of his father, the late Robert E Ellis, of his friends Peter Pye and John Ives and as a mark of esteem for Roger Pinckney. An independent charity known as the RCC Pilotage Foundation was formed and Dr Ellis added his house to his already generous gift of money to form the Foundation's permanent endowment. The Foundation's charitable objective is 'to advance the education of the public in the science and practice of navigation', which is at present achieved through the writing and updating of pilot books covering many diffent parts of the world.

The Foundation is extremely grateful and privileged to have been given the copyrights to books written by a number of distinguished authors and yachtsmen including the late Adlard Coles, Robin Brandon and Malcolm Robson. In return the Foundation has willingly accepted the task of keeping the original books up to date and many yachtsmen and women have helped (and are helping) the Foundation fulfil this commitment. In addition to the titles donated to the Foundation, several new books have been created and developed under the auspices of the Foundation. The Foundation works in close collaboration with three publishers – Imray Laurie Norie and Wilson, Adlard Coles Nautical and On Board Publications – and in addition publishes in its own name short run guides and pilot books for areas where limited demand does not justify large print runs. Several of the Foundation's books have been translated into French, German and Italian.

The Foundation runs its own website at www.rccpf.org.uk which not only lists all the publications but also contains free downloadable pilotage information.

The overall management of the Foundation is entrusted to trustees appointed by the Royal Cruising Club, with day-to-day operations being controlled by the Director. All these appointments are unpaid. In line with its charitable status, the Foundation distributes no profits; any surpluses are used to finance new books and developments and to subsidise those covering areas of low demand.

M R Walker
Director, RCC Pilotage Foundation

PUBLICATIONS OF THE RCC PILOTAGE FOUNDATION

Imray
The Baltic Sea
North Brittany and
 the Channel Islands
Faroe, Iceland and
 Greenland
Isles of Scilly
South Biscay
Atlantic Islands
Atlantic Spain & Portugal

Mediterranean Spain
 Costas del Azahar,
 Dorada & Brava
Mediterranean Spain
 Costas del Sol & Blanca
Islas Baleares
Corsica and North
 Sardinia
North Africa
Chile

Adlard Coles Nautical
Atlantic Crossing Guide
Pacific Crossing Guide
On Board Publications
South Atlantic Circuit
Havens and Anchorages for the South American Coast
The RCC Pilotage Foundation
Cruising Guide to West Africa
Supplement to Falkland Island Shores
RCC Website www.rccpf.org.uk
Supplements
Passage planning guides

Contents

Introduction

OVERVIEW OF NORTH BISCAY

The coast from Brest to Bordeaux is over 300 miles long with almost 100 ports and a similar number of anchorages. It comprises seven fairly distinct areas. Each has its own character and is big enough and interesting enough to be a cruising area in its own right.

West Brittany

The Chenal du Four and the Raz de Sein are two of Europe's nastier tidal races. As a result, many skippers like to pass through West Brittany as quickly as possible. This is a pity because it is a splendid cruising ground with lots of nice places to visit.

Camaret is a favourite first or last stop. The Oceanopolis aquarium next to Brest Marina is a perfect spot in bad weather. However, the Aulne is the real treasure of the Rade de Brest and a trip to Port Launay and Châteaulin will be a high point in any cruise. Outside the Rade, there is excellent sailing round the high cliffs of the Crozon peninsula and the spectacular beaches of Douarnenez bay. If weather permits, a visit to Ile de Sein offers challenging pilotage and a unique unspoilt island.

Bénodet Bay

Bénodet Bay is classic South Brittany. Bénodet and Loctudy are both delightful and somehow just right for messing about in boats. The Odet river from Bénodet to Quimper is possibly the most attractive river in North Biscay and has a number of peaceful anchorages. The Iles de Glénan, on a sunny day, could be mistaken for the Caribbean. Then there is the fascinating Ville Close at Concarneau, right next to the visitors' pontoon. Those who need a marina, will like the large modern one at Port-La-Forêt.

Groix and the Rias

The mainland opposite Groix has a series of flooded valleys that make interesting and attractive ports. Shallow draught boats can visit Pont Aven, where Gauguin worked, and see the fine art gallery and masses of artists' studios. The Belon River, home of the famous Belon oyster, is a pretty river where it is possible to combine peace and quiet with good walking and serious gastronomy.

Lorient is a big city with several marinas. There is plenty to do and a good waterbus for getting about. Etel is famous, or infamous, for having a very dangerous bar. It is necessary to call the pilot for entry instructions, which of course makes entry very easy. Once inside there is a nice town, a spectacular beach and an inland sea not much smaller than the Morbihan.

Quiberon Bay

Quiberon Bay is one of Europe's prime yacht racing centres. There are three large marinas - Haliguen, Trinité and Crouesty - and a dinghy-racing centre at Carnac. In addition, the Morbihan inland sea, which opens into Quiberon Bay, offers yet more good cruising.

It is said that the Morbihan has an island for every day of the year and the tides run so fast they can strip the galvanizing from an anchor chain. Neither statement is true, but there certainly are a lot of islands and the tide does run extremely fast, which makes the pilotage great fun but quite challenging. The Morbihan also has two very attractive medieval towns, Vannes and Auray. Vannes is particularly popular because it has a marina in the heart of town.

The chain of islands that protects Quiberon Bay also offers good cruising. Belle-Ile, the 'beautiful island', is the largest with a couple of proper harbours and lots of anchorages; one of these has been described as the most beautiful in all France. The little islands of Houat and Hoëdic are also very attractive and perfect spots to anchor in good weather.

Southeast Brittany

Brittany is generally considered to end at the Loire but some towns south of the Loire, such as Pornic, consider themselves to be Breton. However, well before the Loire the character of the ports and the coastline becomes much softer and more southern than true Brittany.

The jewel in this area is the Vilaine which was turned into a huge boating lake when a barrage was built near its mouth. It has 20 miles of non-tidal water, dozens of riverside anchorages and two delightful historic towns, La Roche Bernard and Redon.

South of the Vilaine, the granite hills of Brittany give way to the flat salt country around Guérande. There are several attractive places to stay. Piriac is a pretty holiday town with a new marina; Croisic is a fascinating old salt and sardine port that is still surrounded by active salt ponds. La Baule has two marinas for those who need a spectacular beach, some posh shopping and a visit to the casino.

Vendée

South of the Loire, the smart holiday resort of Pornic is well worth visiting, as are the two lovely islands of Noirmoutier and Yeu. The former is flat and sandy with lots of salt ponds. The latter is rocky with good walking, a modern marina and the best tuna steaks in France.

The attractive fishing port and beach resort of Saint-Gilles and France's premier yachting port, Les Sables d'Olonne, are on the mainland just south of Ile d'Yeu.

Charente

The Charente feels like the real south. There are sunflowers everywhere and the crew start complaining about sunburn and heatstroke instead of frostbite and mildew.

The area is centred on the two holiday islands of Ile d'Oleron and Ile de Ré. Both have north coast harbours that make good bases for biking and walking. On the mainland, the historic city of La Rochelle is a must and a trip up the River Charente to Rochefort is likely to be the high point of a cruise in this area. Both La Rochelle and Rochefort have good marinas.

The more adventurous can take the canal to Marans and visit the marshes of the Marais Poitevin or perhaps visit the River Seudre to see industrial scale oyster farming around Marennes. The oysters themselves can be sampled almost anywhere.

The Gironde is strictly outside the Charente and is covered in the companion volume *South Biscay*. However, the main ports of Royan, Port Médoc and Pauillac are covered briefly.

GETTING THERE

Short hops or a long leg?

From the Solent, it is about 210 miles to Camaret, 260 to Bénodet, 310 to Crouesty and 410 to La Rochelle. In a modern cruising yacht, in good weather, that means about 36 hours to Camaret, less than two days to Bénodet and not much more to Crouesty. Even La Rochelle should take less than 3 days.

In summer, it is not hard to find a weather window of a couple of days but much harder to guarantee any more, at least in the English Channel. Hence there is a lot to be said for going as far south as possible as quickly as possible. Furthermore, both the tide and the wind usually make West Brittany and the English Channel easier on the way back. On the other hand, the passage home through N Biscay will usually be against the wind.

The best route

The best route obviously depends on the starting point and personal preference. From the Solent there are essentially two choices: the French route and the English route. The straight-line route is not an option because it cuts diagonally through the traffic separation zone near Alderney.

The shortest route is to head towards Alderney, cross the shipping lanes E of the separation zone and approach the Four along the French coast. This has the great attraction of meeting almost no shipping after Alderney and having no tidal gates until the Four. There are also plenty of ports of refuge.

The alternative is to go north of the separation zone, perhaps with a stop at Dartmouth, and then cross to the Four. This is only 20 miles further but will require long hours in the shipping lanes and must take account of the tide gates at Portland and Start Point.

The route via Falmouth is 50 miles further than the Alderney route. It has some tidal advantages and provides the option of going outside Ushant and Ile de Sein. However, from the Solent, it only makes sense if the boat can be delivered to Falmouth in advance of the cruise.

Keeping the boat in France

An increasingly popular option is to keep the boat in a French marina. There are many excellent ones where a boat can be kept or over-wintered. Most are significantly cheaper than UK marinas.

TIDES

Tide times

Tide times for the majority of North Biscay are based on Brest. Those in the Charente are based on Pointe de Grave (PdG), which is only about 10 minutes later than Brest at springs and about 20 minutes later at neaps. Brest HW is at about 0600 and 1800 BST at springs and about 1200 and 2400 BST at neaps. Except in the Morbihan and some rivers, local HW is usually within 30 minutes of Brest. Thus, for planning purposes, the whole coast can be assumed to have midday highs at neaps and midday lows at springs.

Unfortunately, the exact differences from Brest vary quite a bit between springs and neaps. In this book, differences from Brest or Pointe de Grave are given to the nearest quarter of an hour for every port. French lock-keepers and French tidal atlases use Concarneau, Port Tudy, Port Navalo, St-Nazaire, Les Sables d'Olonne and La Rochelle as additional standard ports. Tide tables for these places are published in French almanacs and given away free in marinas. It is best to use them where possible, particularly for lock opening times.

Official tidal predictions for French ports, in this area, are based on UTC –1. This means they are already adjusted to British Summer Time (BST) but need to have an hour added to convert them to French Summer Time (FST). Free tide tables and lock opening times must be checked carefully because they may be in BST, FST or even UTC.

Tidal heights

Mean tidal heights are given in the data box for each chapter. Accurate calculations of depth of water should be made whenever it matters. However, the sequence 12345 works moderately well for most of the coast. This says there will be roughly 1m of water at MLWS, 2m at MLWN, 3m at half tide, 4m at MHWN and 5m at MHWS. Unfortunately the MLWS figure of 1m is often a bit optimistic and 0.7m is closer to the average.

In West Brittany and the Charente, above half tide, there is more water than the simple rule would suggest. Perhaps it needs to be stressed that the 12345 rule is useful for planning purposes but must never be used when the exact depth of water matters.

All depths and drying heights in this book relate to Lowest Astronomical Tide (LAT) chart datum. Above water rocks, clearances under bridges and the height of lighthouses or hills relate to MHWS.

French tide tables and therefore French harbourmasters use a tidal coefficient to quantify the changing tidal range between springs and neaps. An average tide has a coefficient of 70, mean springs have a coefficient of 95 and mean neaps a coefficient of 45.

Tidal streams

Tidal streams in North Biscay are less intuitive than those in the English Channel. They flow towards and away from the coast as much as they flow along it. They are also unpredictable in direction and significantly influenced by the wind. However, in some places, such as the Raz de Sein or the Teignouse passage, they are strong enough to be potentially dangerous. In most rivers and harbour mouths they are also very strong and sometimes dangerous. Thus, it is important to take tidal streams seriously.

Tidal stream information is available from many sources. This book provides a number of simplified tidal charts and there is a summary of key tidal stream data for those ports where it matters. More detail is provided in the tidal stream atlas *NP 265 France West Coast* published by the UK Hydrographic Office and the SHOM tidal atlases, *560-UJA Goulven to Penmarc'h*, *558-UJA Penmarc'h to Noirmoutier* and *559-UJA St Nazaire – Royan*. The latter are very detailed and highly recommended. However, note that French tidal atlases for La Rochelle are based on the time of low water not high water.

WINDS AND WEATHER

Winds

North Biscay is frequently under the influence of either the Azores high or lows passing along the English Channel. This causes the prevailing winds in summer to be W in the northern part and NW in the southern part. However, other pressure systems are common and changeable Atlantic weather is the norm.

In addition to winds driven by large-scale weather systems, local sea breeze effects are very important. North Biscay is well supplied with all the features necessary to generate a big sea breeze during the day. As a rule of thumb, a clear sky and a line of fluffy clouds along the line of the coast indicates that a sea breeze is developing and the afternoon wind will blow freshly onto the shore from the SW gradually veering to the W. Quiberon Bay and Pertuis d'Antioch are both famous for the strength and complexity of their sea breezes.

There is a reverse phenomenon that is particularly important when anchoring for the night. A land breeze, know as the *vent solaire*, can develop from about midnight and blow freshly from the NE. This breeze can be particularly strong if it blows down cliffs or along rivers. Ile de Groix is a good example. A night breeze blowing down the valleys and rivers in Lorient will blow directly from the NE into the harbour at Port Tudy with very uncomfortable results.

Sunshine and rain

The weather in the southern part of North Biscay is quite a bit better than the north. On average, there is less rain, about 2 hours a day more sunshine, temperatures are about 5°C higher and humidity is 10% lower.

However, when fronts cross southern Brittany or further south they can result in a few days of unsettled weather. One of the attractions of North Biscay as a cruising area is that there is always a protected inland waterway close at hand. The Rade de Brest, Lorient, the Morbihan, the Vilaine and the Charente are all protected and each has an interesting town so it is possible to get away from any unpleasant sea conditions.

Visibility

Fog, mist or haze can be frequent in the summer. On average, visibility is less than 5 miles on one day in five. Real fog, with visibility of less than ½ mile, averages one day in twenty. The coast is so well marked by beacons and towers that navigation in poor visibility is possible, particularly with the help of GPS and radar. However, fog can be particularly unpleasant in narrow tidal waters and rivers.

Swell

Swell is generated by storms and winds of Force 6 and above. With persistent winds of Force 8 or more, large waves are created that can take a few days to die down and will radiate out into areas that were never affected by the strong winds.

A large swell will break heavily on bars and in shallow water and can make some entrances, such as Belon, Etel and the Vilaine, dangerous even in fine weather. If swell enters a narrowing inlet, it tends to increase in height and steepness and funnel up the entrance to make anchorages uncomfortable or even untenable. In open water it can break intermittently and dangerously on rocks that rise from deep water, even if the depth over them is apparently safe.

In North Biscay swell occurs mainly on the NW and W coasts of Brittany, particularly in the vicinity of Ouessant and NE of Le Four. It is less frequent in the Bay of Biscay. However, any anchorages that are open to the Atlantic, such as those on the W and S side of Ile de Groix, Belle-Ile and Ile d'Yeu should only be used in settled weather. Before using such an anchorage, it is worth checking that there have been no recent disturbances in the Atlantic that could generate a sudden swell.

French weather forecasts include swell predictions (la houle).

Weather forecasts

North Biscay is very well served for weather forecasts. The many available sources are summarised in an excellent, 30 page Météo France booklet called *Le Guide Marine*. This is available free in every port office. It also contains an invaluable lexicon of meteorological terms in French and English.

Navtex forecasts are available from CROSS Corsen on 518kHz (A) and 490kHZ (E). The latter provides more local detail but in French. In the northern part of the area, less detailed forecasts can also be received from Niton on 518kHz (E) and in the southern part from La Coruña on 518KHz (D).

CROSS Corsen and CROSS Etel transmit area forecasts on VHF several times a day. These are detailed and generally accurate. They are in French but, with the aid of the Météo France lexicon mentioned above, even non-French speakers should be able to understand them. The times and frequencies vary from place to place and are shown in the table below.

Area	Ch	Local times
Le Stiff	79	0503, 0715, 1115[1], 1545, 1915
Pte du Raz	79	0445, 0703, 1103[1], 1533, 1903
Penmarc'h	80	0703, 1533, 1903
Ile de Groix	80	0715, 1545, 1915
Belle Ile	80	0733, 1603, 1933
St Nazaire	80	0745, 1615, 1945
Ile d'Yeu	80	0803, 1633, 2003
Sables	80	0815, 1645, 2015
Chassiron	79	0703, 1533, 1903
Soulac	79	0715, 1545, 1915

1. 1 May to 30 Sept

Most marinas display a daily forecast and quite detailed forecasts are published in the local newspapers.

Mobile phone coverage is excellent throughout the area so internet and phone forecasts can also be used.

SEAMANSHIP

North Biscay harbours

North Biscay is a splendid cruising ground for yachts and powerboats of all types. However, smaller marinas and most local harbours are designed around the needs of local boats. These are typically quite small and many dry out on every tide: small fishing boats are ubiquitous and shallow draught sailing boats under 9m are very common. As a result, the room to manoeuvre and berth a 12m deep-keeled yacht will often be quite limited. There are plenty of deep-water ports and anchorages that can handle larger boats but a 10m bilge-keeler will

certainly get to places that larger boats cannot reach.

Berthing space is scarce so rafting is very common. This may be on a visitors' pontoon or using bow and stern buoys or in a daisy round a central buoy. In all cases, long warps and plenty of fenders are needed. Mooring buoys rarely have a pick-up rope so a threading boat-hook is a great help.

Most anchorages are full of local moorings and sometimes it is possible to borrow one rather than anchor. In general, visitors' buoys are a distinctive colour or are labelled with a 'V', 'PL' or the word *Visiteur*. In popular harbours, such as the Morbihan, it is possible to phone the harbourmaster and officially borrow a private buoy. Otherwise it may be necessary to borrow one unofficially. This is always tricky because it is hard to tell whether the mooring is strong enough and whether the owner is about to return. There is no simple advice except to check the ground tackle as well as possible, never leave a boat unattended on a private mooring and be prepared to leave immediately if the owner returns.

Search and rescue

Search and rescue and navigational surveillance are handled by the Centres Régionaux Opérationnels de Surveillance et de Sauvetage (CROSS). CROSS Corsen covers the coast from Mont St Michel to Pointe de Penmarc'h; CROSS Etel from Pointe de Penmarc'h to the Spanish border.

Either station can be contacted on VHF 16 or VHF 70 (DSC). Their telephone numbers are:

CROSS Corsen   *t* 02 98 89 31 31
CROSS Etel   *t* 02 97 55 35 35.

CROSS Etel also provides urgent medical advice. The relevant telephone number depends on the area, as follows:

Brest	*t* 02 98 46 11 33
Vannes	*t* 02 97 54 22 11
Nantes	*t* 02 40 08 37 77
La Rochelle	*t* 05 46 27 32 15
Bordeaux	*t* 05 56 96 70 70

Fishing hazards

There are many fishermen's buoys round the coast and sometimes well out to sea. They present a hazard, especially under power at night, and a constant lookout is necessary. The buoys are often laid in pairs, each with a flag. If the pair can be identified, it is advisable not to pass between them.

South of Lorient a different method of fishing is used and a line of very small floats is often run between the larger buoys. It is particularly important not to pass between these buoys.

Much of the area is used for shellfish farming. Mussels are grown on ropes attached to stout stakes driven into the seabed. They are extremely dangerous because the stakes cover at high water. Oysters are grown in metal baskets supported on racks. They also cover at high water and are dangerous. Shellfish beds are usually shown on large-scale charts and are usually marked with buoys

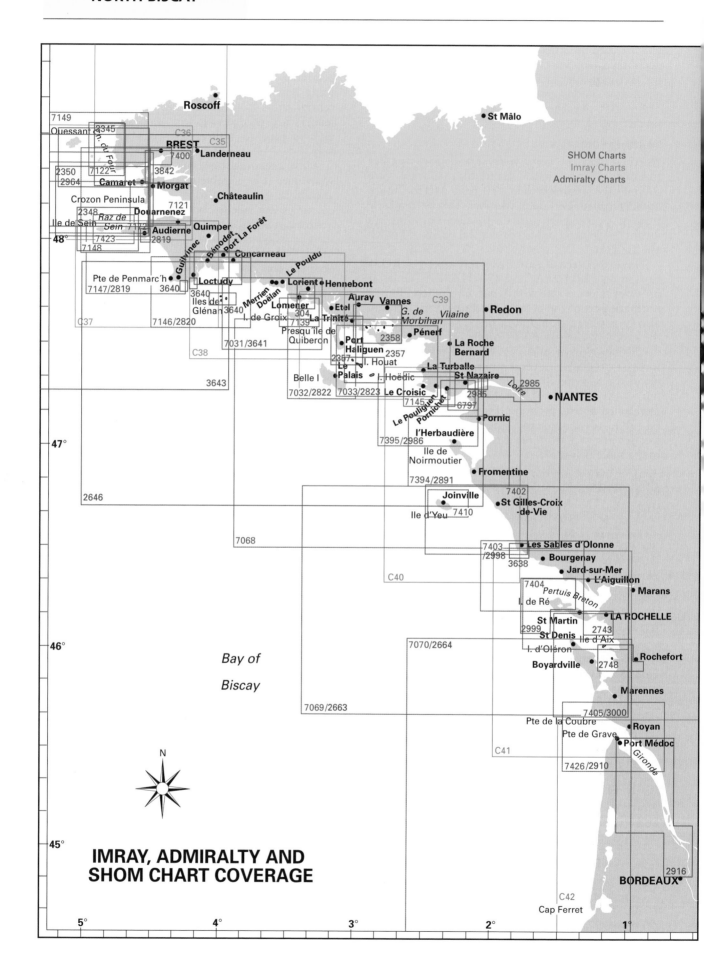

SHOM Charts
Imray Charts
Admiralty Charts

**IMRAY, ADMIRALTY AND
SHOM CHART COVERAGE**

International port traffic signals

MAIN MESSAGE		
1 ●●●	Flashing	Serious emergency - all vessels to stop or divert according to instructions
2 ●●●		Vessels shall not proceed
3 ●●●	Fixed or slow occulting	Vessels may proceed; One way traffic
4 ●●○		Vessels may proceed; Two way traffic
5 ●○●		A vessel may proceed only when it has received specific orders to do so
EXEMPTION SIGNALS AND MESSAGES		
2a ○●●●	Fixed or slow occulting	Vessels shall not proceed, except that vessels which navigate outside the main channel need not comply with the main message
5a ○●○●		A vessel may proceed only when it has received specific orders to do so, except that vessels which navigate outside the main channel need not comply with the main message
AUXILIARY SIGNALS		
		Auxiliary signals can be added, as required, normally to the right of the column carrying the main message and normally utilising only white or yellow lights. Such auxiliary signals could, for example, be added to message no. 5 to give information about the situation of traffic in the opposite direction, or to warn of a dredger operating in the channel

or withies. However, the marks are sometimes a bit patchy, particularly in areas that do not get many visitors.

Some fishing harbours do not wish to receive visiting yachtsmen. These harbours have not been covered in this book and should not be visited except in an emergency. With the decline of fishing, attitudes are changing and some of these harbours are becoming more welcoming. If planning to visit a non-yacht harbour, seek local advice.

Port signals
The French authorities use two systems of signals to control the traffic into harbours. These are best explained by means of the diagram above.

By day and night three green lights one above the other signify that the port is open but that there are obstructions in the channel and vessels must navigate with caution. The traffic signals are not usually hoisted for yachts, and they should be regarded more as a signal to keep out of the way of large vessels.

NAVIGATION

Charts
British Admiralty charts of North Biscay at 1:50,000 or larger scale are copies of French SHOM charts. The SHOM originals use the same international symbols as British charts and the recent ones have explanatory text in English as well as French. The 'L' series are on good quality thin paper and folded to A4. They are convenient to use, good value and very widely available in chandlers, book stores and even newsagents. They are not updated by the retailer, so watch out for old stock.

Most navigation will be done using the 1:50,000 series but larger scale charts are necessary for some areas such as the Iles de Glénan and the Morbihan. In most cases, identical large-scale charts are available from the British Admiralty and SHOM but there are some important gaps in the Admiralty coverage. Thus it makes sense to stick to SHOM large-scale charts and buy them in France as needed.

The most useful British Admiralty (BA) and SHOM charts are listed below. They are classified into three groups: planning charts (1:200,000), passage charts (1:50,000) and large-scale charts. In each list, the charts are sorted from north to south. Where no exactly equivalent chart exists, 'NA' replaces the number.

In addition to the following list, the text-box for each chapter includes the relevant chart numbers. In the text-boxes, the scale is abbreviated by omitting the thousands; thus 1:50,000 is shown as (50).

	BA	SHOM	Scale
Planning charts – North to South			
Ile d'Ouessant to Pointe de Penmarc'h	2643	(NA)	1:200,000
Pointe de Penmarc'h to Ile d'Yeu	2646	(NA)	1:200,000
Ile d'Yeu to Pointe de La Coubre	2663	(7069)	1:200,000
Pointe de la Coubre to Pointe d'Arcachon	2664	(7070)	1:200,000
Passage charts – North to South			
Le Four to Goulet de Brest	2694	(7149)	1:50,000
Pointe de Saint-Mathieu to Chaussée de Sein	2350	(7172)	1:50,000
Chaussée de Sein to Pointe de Penmarc'h	2819	(7147)	1:50,000
Pointe de Penmarc'h to Pointe de Trevignon	2820	(7146)	1:50,000
Ile de Penfret to Plateaux des Birvideaux	2821	(7031)	1:50,000

Ile de Groix to Belle Ile	2822	(7032)	1:50,000
Quiberon to Croisic	2823	(7033)	1:50,000
Approaches to La Loire	2986	(7395)	1:50,000
Pointe de St Gildas to Goulet de Fromentine	2981	(7394)	1:50,000
Les Sables d'Olonne to Ile de Ré	2998	(7403)	1:50,000
Pointe du Grouin du Cou to Pointe de Chassiron	2999	(7404)	1:50,000
La Rochelle to Pointe de la Coubre	3000	(7405)	1:50,000
Approaches to La Gironde	2910	(7426)	1:50,000
La Gironde	2916	(NA)	1:50,000
Large scale charts – North to South			
Chenal du Four	3345	(NA)	1:25,000
Approaches to Brest	3427	(7401)	1:22,500
Rade de Brest	3429	(7400)	1:22,500
Baie de Douarnenez	2349	(7121)	1:30,000
Raz de Sein	2348	(7423)	1:20,000
Harbours of the W Coast of France	3640	(NA)	Various
Loctudy to Concarneau	3641	(NA)	1:20,000
Cours de l'Odet – De Bénodet à Quimper	NA	(6679)	1:20,000
Iles de Glénan, partie Sud	NA	(6648)	1:20,000
Ports et mouillages en Bretagne Sud	NA	(7138)	Various
Ile de Groix	NA	(7139)	1:20,000
Passes et Rade de Lorient	304	(7140)	1:10,000
Belle-Ile	NA	(7142)	1:25,000
Abords des Iles de Houat et de Hoëdic	2835	(7143)	1:20,000
Golfe de Morbihan	2358	(7034)	1:25,000
La Baie de Pont-Mahé to Piriac-sur-Mer	NA	(7136)	1:15,000
La Turballe to Pornichet	NA	(7145)	1:25,000
Ile d'Yeu	NA	(7410)	1:20,000
La Charente Ile d'Aix to Tonnay-Charente	2748	(7415)	1:20,000

Imray charts provide an excellent and much cheaper alternative, particularly to supplement a chart plotter. They provide a passage chart, at a scale between 1:77,000 and 1:100,000, plus large-scale plans of most harbours. The latest Imray charts also show the key waypoints used in this book, which simplifies passage-planning.

Imray Charts for North Biscay

C18 Western Approaches to the English Channel and Biscay 1:1,000,000

C35 Baie de Morlaix to L'Aber-Ildut
Plans Approaches to L'Aber-Wrac'h and L'Aber-Benoît, Argenton, Port du Pontusval, Moguériec, Portsall, L'Aber-Ildut, Port de Morlaix 1:75,000

C36 Ile d'Ouessant to Raz de Sein
Plans Port du Conquet, Port de Brest and Marina du Moulin Blanc, Port de Morgat, Port de Camaret-sur-Mer, Baie de Lampaul (Ouessant), Port Douarnenez, l'Elorn (Continuation to Landerneau) 1:80,000

C37 Raz de Sein to Bénodet
Plans Lesconil, La Guilvinec, Bénodet, Audierne, Loctudy, St Guénole, L'Odet Fleuve, Ile de Sein 1:80,000

C38 Anse de Bénodet to Presqu'île de Quiberon
Plans Port-La-Forêt, Concarneau, Lorient, Lorient Yacht Harbour, Port Tudy, Étel,

Brigneau & Merrien, Port Manech, Doëlan, Iles de Glénan (North) 1:80,000

C39 Lorient to Le Croisic
Plans Sauzon, Le Palais, Port Haliguen, La Trinité-sur-Mer, Port de Crouesty, Piriac-sur-Mer, La Turballe, Le Croisic, Baie de Pouliguen
Inset Continuation of la Vilaine 1:80,000

C40 Le Croisic to Les Sables d'Olonne
Plans Joinville, Pornic, St-Nazaire, Goulet de Fromentine, St-Gilles-Croix de Vie, Les Sables d'Olonne, Le Croisic, L'Herbaudière 1:109,000

C41 Les Sables d'Olonne to La Gironde
Plans Jard-sur-Mer, Bourgenay, Ars-en-Ré, St-Martin-de-Ré, La Flotte-en-Ré, Rochefort, Douhet, St-Denis d'Oléron, Rade de Pallice, Boyardville, La Rochelle and Port des Minimes, Royan 1:109,400

C42 Embouchure de la Gironde to Bordeaux and Arcachon
Plans Royan, Pauillac, Port Bloc, Bordeaux, Arcachon, La Garonne to Bordeaux, La Dordogne to Libourne 1:127,000

GPS warning

GPS is a wonderful aid to navigation with one serious shortcoming. Unlike all other forms of navigation, it uses invisible satellites and mathematics to produce a position on a chart. There is no link to the real world; hence not much to trigger the navigator's common sense when something goes wrong. Fortunately, modern GPS sets are accurate and reliable and, at least in North Biscay, the charts are accurate, so what could go wrong? The answer is three types of human error, one of which appears to be horribly common.

An enormous amount of care has gone into checking the waypoints in this book. Nevertheless, it would be naïve to imagine that there are no errors. Thus every waypoint must be treated as suspect until it has been plotted on a paper chart or chart plotter and the bearing and distance to the next waypoint in a route has been checked. That should deal with the authors' human error.

The second human error comes when waypoints are entered into the GPS or plotter. It is easy to type wrong numbers, easy to miss a crucial waypoint from a route and, on a plotter, easy to click a waypoint into a position relative to the wrong headland. Again double-checking is essential as well as a careful look at the resulting track on the chart to ensure that it does not pass over or close to dangers.

The third and most common human error is failure to set the GPS datum correctly. Paper charts for North Biscay are particularly confusing because some use the French datum ED50 while others use the International datum WGS84. All waypoints in this book are based on WGS84. If these are used on an ED50 chart, without adjustment, they could be very dangerous. The difference is about 150m, which in several places would be a large enough error to be very dangerous.

Chart plotters normally work in WGS84 and expect waypoints in WGS84. Thus the waypoints in this book need no adjustment for chart plotters and the visual position of waypoints on the charts and plans in the book should match the plotter.

The problem arises when paper charts are used. Most, particularly older ones, are based on ED50, so WGS84 waypoints must be converted to ED50 before they can be plotted. In North Biscay, this requires adding 0'·06 to the latitude and subtracting about 0'·08 from the longitude. Many GPS sets can handle the conversion automatically by separately specifying the datum of the waypoint and the datum of the chart.

The very real risk of human error makes it vital to regularly check the position on the chart against the actual position. Formally plotting the position on a paper chart at regular intervals is good practice. But so is taking every opportunity to confirm the position with informal fixes such as the depth of water, buoys, objects in line, the distance and bearing to radar targets and so forth.

In several chapters, waypoints are provided to supplement intricate visual pilotage. It is obviously essential not to use the GPS as a substitute for visual pilotage but using the two in parallel can work very well.

Navigation and pilotage with GPS

There are three main ways to use GPS to keep off the rocks. First and most obvious is to enter a series of waypoints as a route and monitor the GPS off-track error to remain close to the route. It is often necessary to be a long way off track, particularly going to windward or in tidal waters, so it is always important to know how far off-track either side of the route is safe.

Most GPS sets can display the bearing to the next waypoint and this can often be used as a clearing bearing. In other words, off-track error is considered safe until the bearing to the next waypoint reaches a certain critical value.

All GPS sets display latitude and longitude. This can often be used directly to set horizontal and vertical clearing lines. For example, the dangerous rocks off the southwest side of Douarnenez Bay are all safely south of 48°06'·00N.

In this book, dangers close to routes are often mentioned. In these cases, it is particularly important to monitor the cross-track error near the danger. Not all dangers are mentioned, so it is necessary to check every route.

A good technique is to have a deck slate showing a list of waypoints, a summary of any dangers between them and a note of any clearing lines or clearing bearings. Since most GPS sets display the distance to the next waypoint, this can be used to specify the start and end of the danger zone.

Waypoints in this book

In this book, all waypoints are based on the WGS84 datum. They are shown on area charts and harbour plans using the waypoint symbol (⊕) followed by the waypoint's number. At the back of the book there is an appendix containing a complete list of all waypoints. In the text and the appendix, waypoints are referred to by both a name and a number. To maintain the clarity of the plans, some waypoints have been plotted slightly out of position. Their exact position is shown in the waypoint list and in the waypoint appendix.

The pilotage section of almost all chapters contains a section headed **By GPS**. This provides one or more routes based on the waypoints. Where relevant, dangers close to the route are mentioned.

Passage waypoints and port approach waypoints are shown on the area chart at the beginning of each section of the book. Entrance waypoints are shown on the harbour plans. However, note that for a number of ports the approach waypoint is too far away to show on the harbour plan.

Navigating among rocks

Rocky areas are rarely as bad as they look on the chart. At any moment, many rocks are either below the keel or showing above water; only those in between are dangerous. Suppose a boat with a 2.5m draught (including 0.5m for safety) is entering the Iles des Glénan at half tide in a calm sea. The height of tide will be about 2.9m so all rocks drying more than 2.9m will be visible above the surface. The boat only needs 2.5m so rocks drying 0.4m or less will be safely below the keel. Therefore, only rocks drying between 0.4m and 2.9m are dangerous. In the Iles de Glénan, there are surprisingly few.

In swell or bad weather, rocks much deeper than the keel of the boat can cause unpleasant or even dangerous seas and are best given a wide berth.

Bearings

All bearings are expressed in degrees true and measured from the boat. In 2004, variation was approximately 4°W in the north and 2°W in the south of the area.

Lights

The height of lights is given in metres (m), and the range of visibility is given in nautical miles (M). Where a light has sectors, the limits of the sectors are usually shown on the plan.

The distance at which a light may be seen depends on its brightness and its height. Although its loom may be visible from a very long way off, a light itself cannot be seen when it is below the observer's horizon. Tables at which lights of various heights can be seen from different heights of eye are given in most almanacs.

The distance at which a light is visible also depends on the clarity of the atmosphere at the time. A 'nominal' range can be calculated for each light; this is the range its rays will reach if the meteorological visibility is 10M. It is this nominal range (given in Admiralty light lists) that is quoted in this book. On a clear night it may shine further and on a hazy night less far. Lights with a range of less than 10M will often merge into other lights on the shore.

The characteristics referred to in the text are for 2004, and are liable to alterations. These will be shown on chart corrections and in the current *Admiralty List of Lights* Volumes A and D.

The general practice is for coloured sectors to indicate dangers and white sectors safe passages. However, this is not universal and should not be assumed. Generally, if a light shows a white safe sector with red and green sectors on each side, the green sector is to starboard and the red to port, at least in the principal channel. This rule is not universal and should be checked for each light. Narrow intensified sectors usually, but not always, fall within the safe width of the channel.

Lights are often 'directional'; that is, they show brightly over a very narrow sector and sometimes faintly outside the sector.

Beacons

In bad weather, the offshore marks on the North Biscay coast suffer damage that may not be repaired for some months. Beacons and beacon towers can lose their topmarks or even be totally destroyed. In this case, they may be replaced by a small buoy, with the appropriate marking, until they are repaired.

Beacons are commonly painted to conform with the cardinal or lateral buoyage systems and often have the appropriate topmarks. The heads of breakwaters, forming a harbour entrance, are often marked with white paint, and may have a green triangle or red square indicating the side on which to pass them. Bridges often have similar marks to indicate the appropriate channel.

ASHORE

Formalities

EU countries, including the UK but not the Channel Islands, no longer require yachts travelling from one EU country to another to report their departure or arrival, unless dutiable or prohibited goods are carried, or non-EU nationals are on board. Only boats arriving from non-EU countries or the Channel Islands should fly a Q flag and report to customs on arrival.

It is essential to carry on board evidence that VAT has been paid on the vessel, and all yachts visiting France must carry a Certificate of Registry. Either full or small ships registration is acceptable. Documents must be originals and not photocopies. Heavy, on the spot, fines are imposed on defaulters.

All members of the ship's company should carry personal passports. In practice they are likely to be required only for identification, for independent return to the UK by public transport and, in the case of the owner, for dealing with the Customs.

It is not unusual to be boarded by customs even when underway. During a visit ask for *une fiche*; if the officers are satisfied, you will be given one to show that the vessel has been cleared. Should you be approached at a later date, it may only be necessary to show *la fiche* to satisfy the officials.

It is no longer forbidden for one skipper to hand over to another in French waters, but owners must be aware of, and abide by, European VAT regulations and the French regulations for chartering.

Provisions

It is convenient to think about on board provisions in three categories. There are foods with a long-shelf life, those items that keep a few days like meat, cheese or fresh vegetables, and those required on a daily basis, like fish and bread.

Provisions with a long shelf life can be stowed on board before departure or can be purchased from a French supermarket. These wonderful big shops with their wide range of useful long-life provisions have mostly moved to the outskirts of towns, close to the resident population, and are rarely convenient for marinas. Chateaulin and Crouesty both have excellent supermarkets close by but in most cases a special expedition will be required.

Larger towns like Audierne, Vannes, Pornic and Rochefort have specialist shops selling cheese, meat or vegetables and will often have a daily covered market. Smaller towns make use of the touring markets. These move to a different village each day and serve the vast temporary population of holidaymakers. Piriac has a market three times a week, in Pornic and Vannes the market stalls are set up in the old winding streets and at La Rochelle and Rochefort the quality of the food on sale is second to none. Where possible market days have been included in the chapters.

Most small holiday villages have bread shops and many have fishmongers selling the local catch. These are often closed from lunchtime until late afternoon and invariably there are long queues just before lunch.

When the text refers to 'all shops' it implies at least bread, grocer, butcher and cooked meats.

Telephones

Most public telephones require cards that can be bought in tobacconists, bars and post offices as well as other shops. GSM mobile phone coverage is generally excellent but sometimes patchy on the islands, particularly when screened by cliffs.

Water

Water is generally available on marina or pontoon berths. At other places, water may only be available in cans. On a harbour wall, the water supply may be of a size more suitable for a large fishing boat than for a yacht.

If water is not for drinking, it will be labelled *non potable*. Water taps rarely have hoses so it is best to carry one, along with a set of threaded adapters obtainable from British garden centres. If piped water is available it can be assumed that it is safe to drink, but it should be left to run for a while as there may be stagnant water in the pipes. As dogs often frequent French marinas it is as well to give the tap a good wash before use.

Fuel

Diesel and petrol are available at the waterside in many places. In France, it is illegal to use duty-free diesel for leisure craft and occasionally there will only be a duty-free pump for fishermen.

Marina diesel pumps are often 24-hour self-service, operated by a 'chip and pin' credit card. UK 'chip and pin' cards work usually but not always. (In which case it will be necessary to find a marina attendant or a friendly local who can be persuaded to operate the pump for cash.)

Yacht clubs

There are yacht clubs and sailing schools in most French harbours; they are invariably hospitable to visitors. Assistance or advice is always given readily, and showers are often available.

Facilities

Not all facilities are listed for every harbour and common sense must be used. 'All shops' in a city like Brest clearly means something different from 'All shops' in a small fishing port. In both cases, it means all the shops that would be expected in a town of that type. If there is a marina it may be assumed to have water and electricity available on the pontoons, showers and toilets and a displayed weather forecast. Only the absence of these facilities is normally mentioned. The official number of visitors' berths is not given because these are frequently allocated to long-term visitors and are not available for short-term visitors. The few ports where space is a real problem are mentioned in the text.

Bicycles

Most long-term cruisers in North Biscay carry bicycles. In many places, the best shops and particularly the big supermarkets are beyond easy walking distance. However, the benefits of bikes go well beyond shopping.

All the islands are perfect for biking. They are fairly flat, have lots of bike tracks and are too big to explore on foot but perfect on a bike. The mainland is slightly less bike-friendly but there are still a great many places that can be explored on a bike but would be too far on foot.

On the islands, bike hire is easy and it is even possible to hire a decent bike. On the mainland, bike hire is usually possible but often requires a long walk to pick up and return the bike and the quality of bikes is a bit variable.

REFERENCE

Using the port chapters

The description of each port is set out in a standard form. At the start of the chapter is a box containing the key data that a skipper is likely to need. Some abbreviations are used and these are explained below under abbreviations.

The body of the chapter provides a brief description of the port followed by pilotage notes and finally a description of the facilities ashore. The aerial and sea-level photographs are an integral part of the chapter and information is often provided in the captions that is not provided elsewhere in the chapter.

In pilotage information a draught of 3m or less is assumed and depths greater than this are either not mentioned or described as deep. Also air draught is considered to be that of a masted yacht. Motorboats will often be able to go beyond bridges that are described as the limit of navigation. In most cases, passage speed should not make too much difference but the authors must confess that they cruise in a sailing yacht and may sometimes overlook the special needs of high-speed navigation.

ABBREVIATIONS

BA	British Admiralty
ECM	East cardinal mark
HW	high water
HW+2$\frac{1}{2}$	two and a half hours after HW
HWN	high water at neaps
HWS	high water at springs
IDM	isolated danger mark
IGN	Institut Geographic National
kts	knots
LW	low water
LWN	low water at neaps
LWS	low water at springs
m	metres
M	nautical miles
NCM	North cardinal mark
PdG	Pointe de Grave
PHM	Port-hand mark
SCM	South cardinal mark
SHM	starboard-hand mark
SHOM	French hydrographic office
SWM	safe water mark
WCM	West cardinal mark

Key to plans

Where possible, the plans follow the international conventions used on British Admiralty and SHOM charts.

Most plans have been subdivided along the left-hand and bottom margins into tenths of a minute of latitude and longitude. The use of identical units in each plan should give an immediate indication of the scale. Alternatively, in some large-scale plans, a scale of metres is shown on the plan.

THE BRETON LANGUAGE

To those unused to Celtic languages, Breton place names seem strange and hard to remember. Many can be translated quite easily and once understood become entirely appropriate and much easier to remember. The wonderfully named Kareg Kreiz, for example, simply means middle rock.

Breton pronunciation is more like English than French, with the final consonants sounded. The letters c'h represent the final sound of Scottish loch or Irish lough (but not English lock); there is indeed a word *loc'h*, meaning a lake or pool; ch is pronounced as sh in shall. The French books and charts do not always distinguish between these, and there may be some errors in this book in consequence. In France, as in England, mobility and the radio/TV are killing regional differences. Thus Raz is now usually pronounced Rah; Penmarc'h, pronounced Penmargh a generation ago, is now often Painmar, and Bénodet has gone from Benodette to Bainoday and collected an accent in the process. The most misleading example is *porz*, which means an open anchorage but is often wrongly changed to the French word port.

A Breton glossary is hard to use because initial letters are often mutated into others, following complicated rules and depending on the preceding word. To cope with this, likely mutations are given after certain letters. For example, I. er Gazek is a common name for a small island. There is no word *gazek* in the glossary, but under G it says 'try K'; *kazek* means 'mare' and mutates into *gazek* after er. Mutations of final letters also occur, but these do not usually cause any difficulty.

Ports of registration

The following letters identify the port of registration of fishing vessels and pleasure boats:

AD	Audierne
AY	Auray
BR	Brest
BX	Bordeaux
CC	Concarneau
CM	Camaret
DZ	Douarnenez
GV	Le Guilvinec
IO	Ile d'Oléron
LO	Lorient
LS	Les Sables d'Olonne
MN	Marennes
NA	Nantes
NO	Noirmoutier
SN	Saint Nazaire
VA	Vannes
YE	Ile d'Yeu

Breton	English
aber	estuary
anaon	the dead
al, an, ar	the
arvor	seaside
aven	river
B (try P)	
balan, banal	broom
bann, benn	hilltop
barr	summit, top
baz	shoal
beg	point, cape
beniget	cut, slit
benven, bosven	above-water rock
bian, bihan	small
bili, vili	shingle
bir, vir	needle, point
bran	crow
bras, braz	large
bre, brenn	small hill
breiz	Brittany
bri, brienn	cliff
C (try K)	
D (try T)	
daou	two
don, doun	deep
dour	water
du	black
ell	rock, shallow
enez	island
er a, an	the

Breton	English
fank	mud
froud, fred	strong current
freu	river
G (try K)	
garo, garv	rough
gavr	goat
glas	green
goban	shallow
gromell, gromilli	roaring
gwenn	white, pure
hir	long
hoc'h, houc'h	pig
iliz	church
izel	shallow
inis	island
kan(iou), kanal	channel
karn	cairn
kareg	rock
kastel	castle
kazek	mare
kein	shoal
kel(ou)	large rock
ker	house, hamlet
kern	summit, sharp peak
kleuz(iou)	hollow, deep
koad, goad	wood
kornog	shoal
koz	old
kreiz	middle
kriben	crest

Breton	English
lan, lann	monastery
marc'h	horse
melen	yellow
men	rock
mor, vor	sea, seawater
nevez	new
penn	head, point
plou, plo	parish
porz, porzig	anchorage
poul	pool, anchorage
raz	strait, tide race
roc'h	rock
ros	wooded knoll
ruz	red
ster	river, inlet
stiv, stiff	fountain, spring
teven, tevenneg	cliff, dune
toull	hole, deep place
trez, treaz	sand, beach
V (try B, M)	
W (try Gw)	
yoc'h	group of rocks

Le Four lighthouse

I. West Brittany

Les Vieux Moines

Men Brial, Ile de Sein

La Vieille and La Plate, Raz de Sein

Ile de Sein lighthouse

Petit Minou lighthouse

Le Conquet lighthouse

Ile de Sein

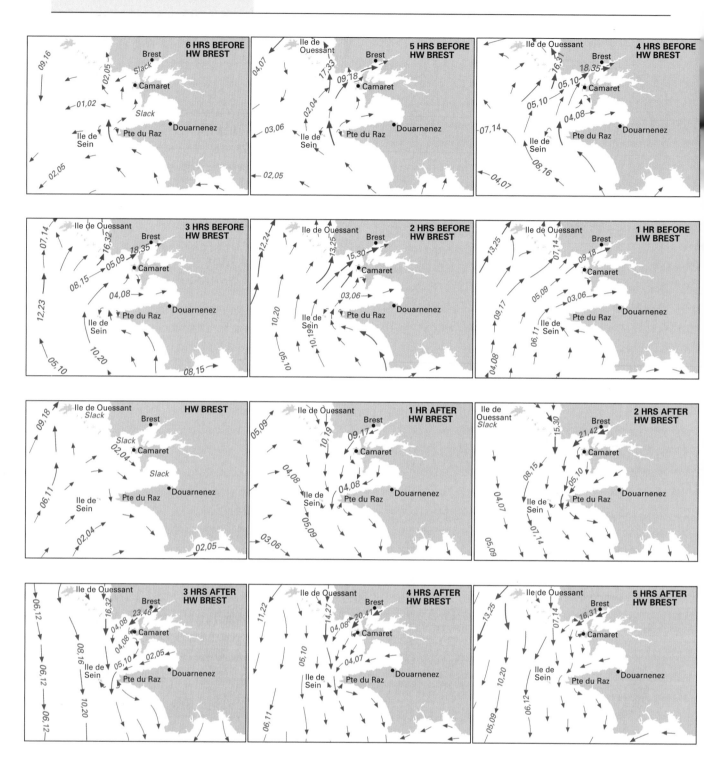

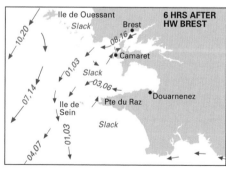

WEST BRITTANY TIDAL STREAMS

Chart IA

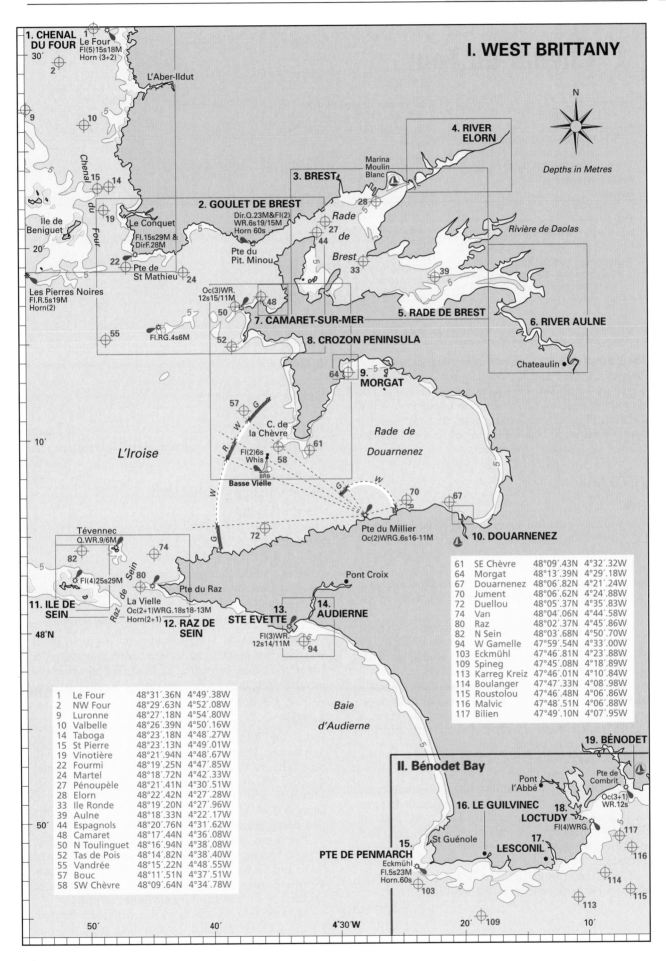

1. CHENAL DU FOUR

1 Le Four
Fl(5)15s18M
Horn (3+2)

2

L'Aber-Ildut

I. WEST BRITTANY

N

Depths in Metres

4. RIVER ELORN

Marina Moulin Blanc

3. BREST

28

2. GOULET DE BREST
Dir.Q.23M&Fl(2)
WR.6s19/15M
Horn 60s

27
44

Rade de Brest

Rivière de Daolas

9

33

39

5. RADE DE BREST

6. RIVER AULNE

Chateaulin

Ile de Beniguet

19

15 14

Le Conquet
Fl.15s29M &
DirF.28M

22

Pte de St Mathieu

24

Pte du Pit. Minou

Oc(3)WR.
12s15/11M

48

50

7. CAMARET-SUR-MER

8. CROZON PENINSULA

Les Pierres Noires
Fl.R.5s19M
Horn(2)

55

Fl.RG.4s6M

52

64

9. MORGAT

L'Iroise

57 G

C. de la Chèvre

W

R

Fl(2)6s
Whis

61

58

Rade de Douarnenez

BRB
Basse Viélle

W

70

67

Pte du Millier
Oc(2)WRG.6s16-11M

10. DOUARNENEZ

72

Tévennec
Q.WR.9/6M

74

82

80

Pont Croix

St-Guénolé

11. ILE DE SEIN

Fl(4)25s29M

Raz de Sein

Pte du Raz

La Vielle
Oc(2+1)WRG.18s18-13M
Horn(2+1)

12. RAZ DE SEIN

13. STE EVETTE

14. AUDIERNE

Fl(3)WR.
12s14/11M

94

48°N

50′

1	Le Four	48°31′.36N	4°49′.38W
2	NW Four	48°29′.63N	4°52′.08W
9	Luronne	48°27′.18N	4°54′.80W
10	Valbelle	48°26′.39N	4°50′.16W
14	Taboga	48°23′.18N	4°48′.27W
15	St Pierre	48°23′.13N	4°49′.01W
19	Vinotière	48°21′.94N	4°48′.67W
22	Fourmi	48°19′.25N	4°47′.85W
24	Martel	48°18′.72N	4°42′.33W
27	Pénoupèle	48°21′.41N	4°30′.51W
28	Elorn	48°22′.42N	4°27′.28W
33	Ile Ronde	48°19′.20N	4°27′.96W
39	Aulne	48°18′.33N	4°22′.17W
44	Espagnols	48°20′.76N	4°31′.62W
48	Camaret	48°17′.44N	4°36′.08W
50	N Toulinguet	48°16′.94N	4°38′.08W
52	Tas de Pois	48°14′.82N	4°38′.40W
55	Vandrée	48°15′.22N	4°48′.55W
57	Bouc	48°11′.51N	4°37′.51W
58	SW Chèvre	48°09′.64N	4°34′.78W

61	SE Chèvre	48°09′.43N	4°32′.32W
64	Morgat	48°13′.39N	4°29′.18W
67	Douarnenez	48°06′.82N	4°21′.24W
70	Jument	48°06′.62N	4°24′.88W
72	Duellou	48°05′.37N	4°35′.83W
74	Van	48°04′.06N	4°44′.58W
80	Raz	48°02′.37N	4°45′.86W
82	N Sein	48°03′.68N	4°50′.70W
94	W Gamelle	47°59′.54N	4°33′.00W
103	Eckmühl	47°46′.81N	4°23′.88W
109	Spineg	47°45′.08N	4°18′.89W
113	Karreg Kreiz	47°46′.01N	4°10′.84W
114	Boulanger	47°47′.33N	4°08′.98W
115	Roustolou	47°46′.48N	4°06′.86W
116	Malvic	47°48′.51N	4°06′.88W
117	Bilien	47°49′.10N	4°07′.95W

Baie d'Audierne

19. BÉNODET

II. Bénodet Bay

Pont l'Abbé

Pte de Combrit

16. LE GUILVINEC

18. LOCTUDY

Oc(3+1)
WR.12s

Fl(4)WRG.

117

17. LESCONIL

15. PTE DE PENMARCH

St Guénole

116

Eckmühl
Fl.5s23M
Horn.60s

103

114

115

113

109

50′ 40′ 4°30′W 20′ 10′

1 Chenal du Four

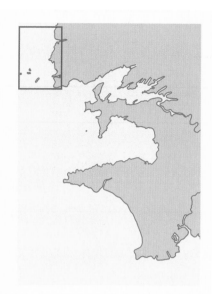

Location
48°22′N 4°49′W

Hazards
Strong tide over uneven seabed; complex tidal streams; well marked rocks and shallow patches; fog

Night passage Well lit

HW time
Brest HW

Mean height of tide (m)

	HWS	HWN	LWN	LWS
Le Conquet	6.8	5.3	2.5	1.0

Tidal stream Le Four light
N – Brest HW–5½ to +1½ (2.2kts)
S – Brest HW+1½ to –5½ (1.6 kts)

Tidal stream Chenal du Four
N – Brest HW–6 to –½ (3.4kts)
S – Brest HW–½ to +6 (4.0kts)

Charts
BA 2694 (50), 3345 (30)
SHOM 7149 (50), 7122 (25)
Imray C36 (77)

Radio
CROSS Corsen VHF 16, 70 (DSC), 79 (MSI)
Le Conquet VHF 16, 12
Direction finding VHF 16, 11, 67

Telephone
CROSS Corsen *t* 02 98 89 31 31
St-Mathieu *t* 02 98 89 01 59
Le Conquet HM *t* 02 98 89 08 07

Exposed NW corner of Brittany

The Chenal du Four is the shortest route between the English Channel and the Biscay ports. It avoids the larger seas and heavy traffic outside Ouessant. The channel is wide and deep and the navigation is not difficult. However, the strong tides and exposure to the Atlantic swell often result in steep seas, and the visibility is frequently poor.

PILOTAGE

Tidal strategy

The roughest seas occur in the N approaches, not in the Chenal du Four itself. N winds can bring a considerable swell to the area N of Le Four and wind against tide conditions produce steep seas. These reduce as soon as the tide turns. Also, Ouessant and the inner islands provide some shelter from W winds in the Chenal du Four.

With a fair wind, aim to go through the Four when the tide is favourable. If the wind is ahead, go through the narrow part, off St-Mathieu, at slack water because the stream there runs very hard.

The tide turns at St-Mathieu earlier than it does N of Le Four. Southbound, this is a nuisance because several hours of S stream run to waste. However, S of St-Mathieu the stream is much less strong and will have turned fair by the time the Raz de Sein is reached. Northbound, the tidal lag is a benefit and provides a few extra hours of fair tide.

Navigating in poor visibility requires special care. Once the narrows are reached, it is difficult to turn back. Speed over the ground is likely to be high so the buoys themselves become a hazard. In very bad visibility it may be better to avoid the area altogether.

The Chenal de la Helle is W of the Chenal du Four and is preferable in rough weather.

Chenal du Four

By GPS

From the NE
Aim for ⊕1-Le Four.

From the N or NW
Aim for ⊕2-NW Four.

Continue using ⊕10-Valbelle, ⊕14-Taboga, ⊕19-Vinotière.

For Brest use
⊕23-St-Mathieu, ⊕24-Martel.

For the Raz use
⊕22-Fourmi, ⊕55-Vandrée.

For Camaret use
⊕23-St-Mathieu, ⊕48-Camaret.

Note that ⊕22-Fourmi is close to the unlit Fourmi buoy so care is required at night.

It is possible to omit ⊕14-Taboga but this short-cut passes very close to the unlit Saint-Pierre buoy.

The Chenal du Four is wide and deep. In good weather, it is possible to deviate a long way from the suggested route, providing care is taken to avoid the isolated dangers. In bad weather it is best to stay close to the recommended route.

By day

From the NE, pass at least ¼M from Le Four lighthouse. Then take care to avoid Les Linioux and especially the Plateau des Fourches. Enter the Chenal du Four NE of Les Plâtresses. The lighthouses of St-Mathieu and Kermorvan should be in transit, bearing 158°. Continue on this course until Pointe de Corsen bears 012°.

Turn onto 192° and use Pointe de Corsen 012° as a back-bearing to pass between Rouget starboard buoy and Grand Vinotière. About ½M S of Grande Vinotière turn onto 160° to leave Tournon et Lochrist buoy and Les Vieux Moines to port.

Arriving late on the tide, the worst of the foul stream can be avoided by standing into the bay

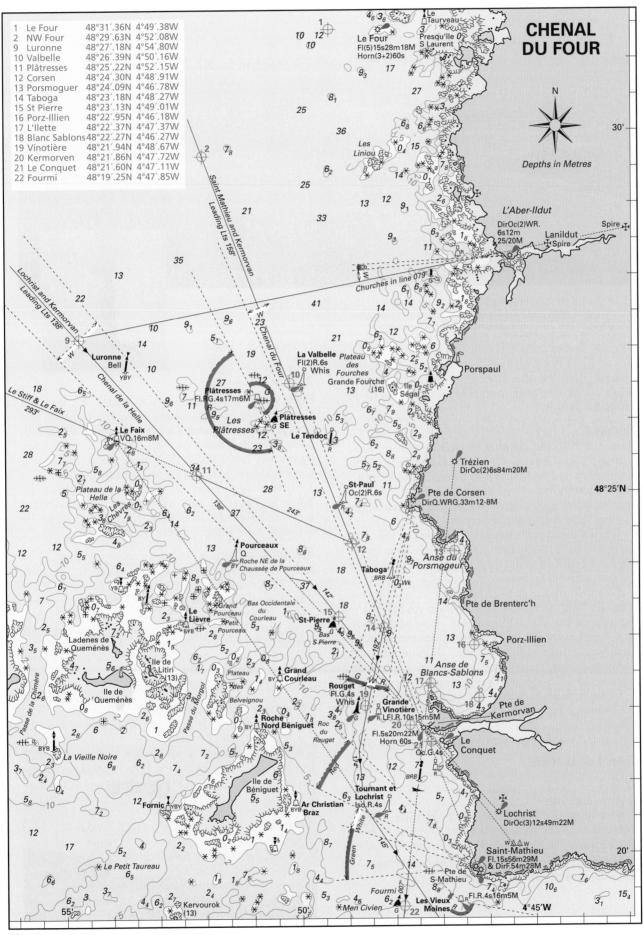

CHENAL DU FOUR

1	Le Four	48°31´.36N	4°49´.38W
2	NW Four	48°29´.63N	4°52´.08W
9	Luronne	48°27´.18N	4°54´.80W
10	Valbelle	48°26´.39N	4°50´.16W
11	Plâtresses	48°25´.22N	4°52´.15W
12	Corsen	48°24´.30N	4°48´.91W
13	Porsmoguer	48°24´.09N	4°46´.78W
14	Taboga	48°23´.18N	4°48´.27W
15	St Pierre	48°23´.13N	4°49´.01W
16	Porz-Illien	48°22´.95N	4°46´.18W
17	L'Ilette	48°22´.37N	4°47´.37W
18	Blanc Sablons	48°22´.27N	4°46´.27W
19	Vinotière	48°21´.94N	4°48´.67W
20	Kermorven	48°21´.86N	4°47´.72W
21	Le Conquet	48°21´.60N	4°47´.11W
22	Fourmi	48°19´.25N	4°47´.85W

Depths in Metres

Le Four
Fl(5)15s28m18M
Horn(3+2)60s

L'Aber-Ildut
DirOc(2)WR.
6s12m
25/20M

Lanildut
Spire

Churches in line 079°

La Valbelle
Fl(2)R.6s
Whis

Plâtresses
Fl.R.G.4s17m6M

Les
Plâtresses

Plâtresses
SE

Le Tendoc

Luronne
Bell

Le Faix
VQ.16m8M

Plateau de la
Helle

Les
Chèvres

Porspaul

Ile de
Ségal

Trézien
DirOc(2)6s84m20M

Pte de Corsen
DirQ.WRG.33m12-8M

St-Paul
Oc(2)R.6s

Anse du
Porsmoguer

Taboga
BRB

Pourceaux
Q
Roche NE de la
Chaussée de Pourceaux

Pte de Brenterc'h

Porz-Illien

Bas Occidentale
du
Courleau

Le
Lièvre

Grand
Pourceau
Petit
Pourceau

St-Pierre
Bas
S Pierre

Anse de
Blancs-Sablons

Ladenes de
Quéménès

Ile de
Litiri
(13)

Plateau
des
Iles

Grand
Courleau

Rouget
Fl.G.4s
Whis

Grande
Vinotière
Fl.I.R.10s15m5M

Pte de
Kermorven

Ile de
'Quéménès

Belveignou

Roche
Nord Béniguet

Roc
du
Rouget

Fl.5s20m22M
Horn 60s

Le Conquet

Oc.G.4s

Passe de la Chimère

La Vieille Noire

Passe du Morgol

Ile de
Béniguet

Tournant et
Lochrist
Iso.R.4s

Lochrist
DirOc(3)12s49m22M

Fornic

Ar Christian
Braz

Saint-Mathieu
Fl.15s56m29M
& DirF.54m28M

Le Petit Taureau

Pte de
S-Mathieu

Fl.R.4s16m5M

Kervourok
(13)

Men Civien

Fourmi

Les Vieux
Moines

Plan 1

1.1 Le Chenal du Four looking S.
Le Four lighthouse (inset) marks the extent of the Roches d'Argenton. The inner islands just visible on the horizon provide some shelter from the prevailing westerly winds

towards the Anse des Blancs Sablons, and the bay south of Le Conquet, but care must be taken to avoid the dangers.

By night

From the NE, the channel is well lit and in good weather the navigation is easy. Steer with Kermorvan and St-Mathieu in transit, bearing 158°. St-Mathieu shows a fixed white directional light in a narrow sector each side of this transit, as well as the flashing light that shows all round.

When Corsen turns white steer in this sector, with the light astern. As soon as the auxiliary light on St-Mathieu becomes red, make good 174°, and enter the red sector of Corsen.

When Tournant et Lochrist buoy is abeam, the auxiliary light on St-Mathieu will turn white and the red light on Les Vieux Moines will open. Make good 145° until Kermorvan is brought in transit with Trézien, bearing 007° astern. Be sure to get Kermorvan and Trézien in transit before leaving the green sector of St-Mathieu auxiliary.

Going S, keep E of the 007° transit until clear of the unlit La Fourmi buoy, which lies close to the transit.

Going E or SE, leave Les Vieux Moines to port.

Chenal de la Helle

By GPS

Southbound, use
⊕9-Luronne, ⊕15-St Pierre, ⊕19-Vinotière, then continue as in the Chenal du Four. At night, note that Luronne, St Pierre and Fourmi buoys are unlit.

For Porsmagour or Blancs Sablonnes anchorages, leave the channel at ⊕11-Plâtresses.

By day

Bring Kermorvan lighthouse to bear 138°, between the first and second houses from the right of five similar houses forming Le Conquet radio station. In good weather steer on this transit until Corsen lighthouse bears 012°, then make good 192° using Corsen bearing 012° as a stern bearing. Note that Kermorvan/Le Conquet transit leads across the Basse St Pierre (4.5m) leaving St Pierre starboard buoy to port. In bad weather the shoal can be avoided, by leaving the buoy to starboard.

By night

Keep Kermorvan in transit with Lochrist, bearing 138°. To avoid the Basse St Pierre, if necessary, leave this alignment when Le Stiff light on Ouessant comes in transit with Le Faix, bearing 293°, and make good 113° on this stern transit to join the Four channel.

1.2 Kermorvan lighthouse looking N

Northbound, take care not to leave the Lochrist/Kermorvan transit before the unlit Luronne buoy has been passed.

ANCHORAGES

Ouessant and the inner islands are well worth exploring in settled weather. They are covered in the companion volume *North Brittany and the Channel Islands* and require a detailed chart.

The following anchorages on the mainland are available under suitable conditions:

⚓ L'Aber-Ildut

This attractive little harbour is described in *North Brittany and the Channel Islands* and not in this volume. It should not be entered without a detailed chart as there are rocks in the approach.

⊕4-Aber Ildut (48°28'.09N 4°48'.14W)

⚓ Porspaul

Sheltered from NE to SE and slightly sheltered from other directions by the Plateau des Fourches. Porspaul is a drying harbour with an outer anchorage that can be used in fine weather and no swell. The entrance through the Plateau des Fourches requires a large-scale chart.

Identify Grande Fourche, about 1¼M E of La Valbelle, and approach it above half tide from the direction of Valbelle. Avoid the dangers of Plateau des Fourches, which are about ¼M NW of Grande Fourche. Pass about 200–300m N of Grande Fourche (⊕7-Porspaul). Steer towards Basse de Porspaul green beacon tower on 095° and round it by about 200m (⊕8-Porspaul 1). Anchor in about 200m ENE of the beacon. Boats that can take the ground can dry out in the harbour on firm sand clear of local moorings.

⊕7-Porspaul (48°26'.58N 4°48'.08W)

⚓ Anse de Porsmoguer

Sheltered from N through E, this pretty bay is about 1M S of Pointe de Corsen. There is good holding in sand with depths shoaling from 6m.

The beach is popular for bathing and there is a village, without shops, about ½M to the north.

⊕13-Porsmoguer (48°24'.09N 4°46'.78W)

⚓ Anse des Blancs Sablons

Sheltered from the SE through SW, this wide sandy bay is 3M S of Pointe de Corsen. It is free from dangers except off the headlands on each side. The anchorage is anywhere, in from 9m to 1m on a sandy shelving bottom. The bay dries out nearly ¼M from the shore, except on the W side, where there is 3m close to the rocks off Kermorvan. There is often some swell.

This is a good place to wait out a foul tide. Slip round L'Ilette (the small islet just N of Kermorvan) when the stream becomes fair but watch out for the rock, awash at datum, that lies 200m E of L'Ilette.

⊕18-Blanc Sablons (48°22'.27N 4°46'.27W)

⚓ Porz-Illien

When the wind is from the N or E, better shelter may be found in this little bay in the NE corner of Anse des Blancs Sablons.

⊕16-Porz-Illien (48°22'.95N 4°46'.18W)

⚓ Le Conquet

Sheltered from NW through SE, there is a good, though often crowded, anchorage in the inlet south of Pointe de Kermorvan. Leave the red La Louve tower to port and go in as far as depth permits. For a full description see *North Brittany and the Channel Islands*.

⊕21-Le Conquet (48°21'.60N 4°47'.11W)

1.3 The fishing town of Le Conquet looking N. Pointe Ste-Barbe at the foot of the breakwater in Le Conquet has superb views at sunset when the lights from all the lighthouses from Le Four to Ile de Sein can be seen. To the N is the anchorage of Anse des Blancs Sablons and, beyond that, the next sandy bay and anchorage is Anse de Porsmoguer

2 Goulet de Brest

Location
48°20'N 4°34'W
Hazards
Strong tide in the narrows; well marked rocks in mid-channel
Night passage Well lit
HW time
Brest HW
Mean height of tide (m)

	HWS	HWN	LWN	LWS
Brest	6.9	5.4	2.6	1.0

Tidal streams Goulet de Brest (Chart 1c)
NE – Brest HW–5½ to –½ (3.9kts)
Slack – Brest HW–½ to +½
SW – Brest HW+½ to –5½ (4.0kts)

South side stream is weaker
Counter current in S side +5½ to –5½
Charts
BA 2694 (50)
SHOM 7149 (50)
Imray C36 (77)
Radio
CROSS Corsen VHF 16, 70 (DSC), 79 (MSI)
Le Conquet VHF 16, 12
Telephone
CROSS Corsen *t* 02 98 89 31 31
St-Mathieu *t* 02 98 89 01 59

Entrance to the Rade de Brest

The Goulet de Brest is the passage between the Chenal du Four and the Rade de Brest. At the narrowest point, it is 1M wide and the tide in the narrows is fierce.

There are cliffs on either side but they are steep to. In mid-channel there is a chain of well marked rocks called Plateau des Fillettes. The navigation is not difficult.

PILOTAGE

Rade de Brest approaches

By GPS

From the Chenal du Four use ⊕23-St-Mathieu, ⊕24-Martel.

From the Chenal du Toulinget use ⊕50-N Toulinguet, ⊕46-Kerviniou, ⊕45-Robert.

From Camaret use ⊕47-Capucins, ⊕46-Kerviniou, ⊕45-Robert.

Then for Brest and the Elorn use ⊕27-Pénoupèle; for the Aulne use ⊕44-Espagnols.

The channel is wide and the dangers well marked so there is no need to stick slavishly to a GPS track.

By day

From the Chenal du Four, round Pointe de St-Mathieu and leave Les Vieux Moines tower, Le Coq buoy and Charles Martel buoy all to port. The transit for the Goulet is the twin white towers of Le Petit Minou in line with Pointe du Portzic grey octagonal tower on 068°.

The rocky Plateau des Fillettes is in mid-channel. Fillettes WCM marks the W end and Roche Mengam BRB beacon tower, ¼M to the NE, marks the E end. A line between them marks the S edge of the N channel.

2.1 Pointe de St-Mathieu looking N.
Apart from the lighthouse, the buildings on the headland include those of a large Benedictine abbey church that was founded in the 6th century. It has been abandoned since the French revolution. The red beacon (inset) is Les Vieux Moines which should be left to port when approaching the Goulet de Brest

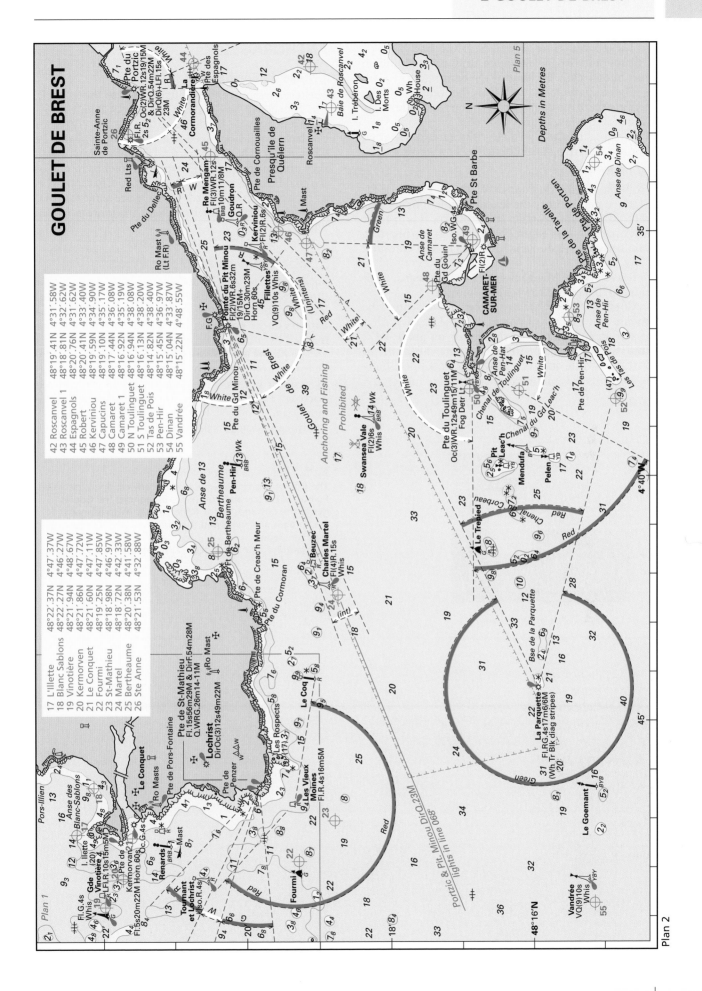

GOULET DE BREST

42	Roscanvel	48°19′.41N	4°31′.58W
43	Roscanvel 1	48°18′.81N	4°32′.62W
44	Espagnols	48°20′.76N	4°31′.62W
45	Robert	48°20′.41N	4°33′.40W
46	Kerviniou	48°19′.59N	4°34′.90W
47	Capucins	48°19′.10N	4°35′.17W
48	Camaret	48°17′.44N	4°35′.85W
49	Camaret 1	48°16′.92N	4°35′.19W
50	N Toulinguet	48°16′.94N	4°38′.08W
51	S Toulinguet	48°16′.13N	4°38′.20W
52	Tas de Pois	48°14′.82N	4°38′.40W
53	Pen-Hir	48°15′.45N	4°36′.97W
54	Dinan	48°15′.04N	4°33′.87W
55	Vandrée	48°15′.22N	4°48′.55W

17	L'Illette	48°22′.37N	4°47′.37W
18	Blanc Sablons	48°22′.27N	4°46′.27W
19	Vinotière	48°21′.94N	4°48′.67W
20	Kermorven	48°21′.86N	4°47′.72W
21	Le Conquet	48°21′.60N	4°47′.11W
22	Fourmi	48°19′.25N	4°47′.85W
23	St-Mathieu	48°18′.98N	4°46′.97W
24	Martel	48°18′.72N	4°42′.33W
25	Bertheaume	48°20′.38N	4°41′.58W
26	Ste Anne	48°21′.53N	4°32′.88W

Plan 2

The plateau extends well S of the line between Fillettes and Roche Mengam and two additional port buoys mark the limit of the danger.

The S passage is useful if the tide is ebbing because there is a counter-current on the S side of the Goulet in the last hours of the ebb.

When using the S passage, take care to avoid La Cormorandière just off Pointe des Espagnols.

By night

From the Chenal du Four or W, round Pointe de St-Mathieu and identify the leading lights (068°) of Le Petit Minou and Portzic and steer on this transit. Once past Charles Martel buoy bear to starboard to pass between Pte du Petit Minou light and Goudron buoy.

Leave Roche Mengam tower to starboard, steer about 070° towards Pénoupèle buoy.

Coming from Camaret, steer N to enter the intense white sector of Portzic (Q(6)+LFl.15s). Alter to starboard and keep in this sector on about 047° until Roche Mengam tower is abaft the beam to port, then turn onto 065° towards Pénoupèle buoy as above.

ANCHORAGES

⚓ Anse de Bertheaume

Sheltered from N and W, but exposed to the S and E, this convenient bay is about 3M east of Pointe de St-Mathieu. Fort de Bertheaume, on the SW corner of the bay, should be given a good berth to avoid Le Chat rocks. These are particularly hazardous when they are covered near HW springs. Anchor in one of the two bays immediately north of Le Chat, going in as far as possible for shelter. There are some visitors' moorings. Further north and east the bottom is foul with rocks.

⊕25-Bertheaume (48°20´.38N 4°41´.58W)

⚓ Sainte-Anne de Portzic

Sheltered from the N and E and with a mole that provides some protection from the W, this is a small local harbour just W of Pte de Portzic. There are no dangers in the approach but there is an isolated rock marked by a beacon on the E side of the harbour.

The pier is used by survey vessels from the nearby Oceanographic research centre and must not be used by visiting yachts. However, it may be possible to borrow a mooring or to anchor outside the moorings.

⊕26-Ste-Anne (48°21´.53N 4°32´.88W)

2.2 The Goulet de Brest looking E.
The Goulet is only 1M wide at its narrowest point, between Pointe de Portzic and Pointe des Espagnols. The Goulet marks the entrance to the Rade de Brest with its many anchorages and rivers and the sprawling city of Brest at the N of the Rade
Inset are the twin lighthouses at Pointe de Petit Minou

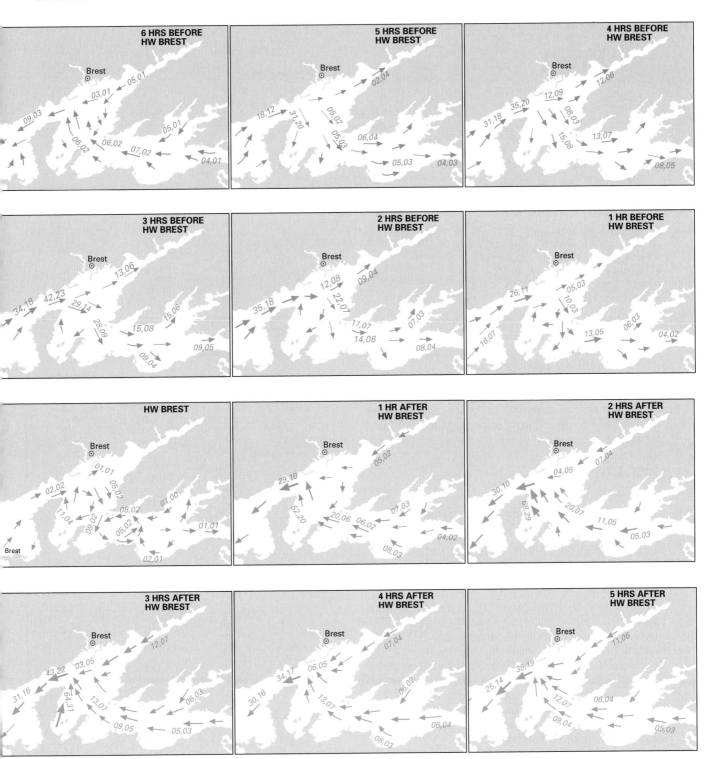

Chart IC

GOULET DE BREST TIDAL STREAMS

3 Brest

Location
48°23'N 4°26'W

Shelter
Excellent in Moulin Blanc Marina

Depth restrictions
1.5m in approach to marina

Night entry
Well lit to the marina

HW time
Brest HW

Mean height of tide (m)

	HWS	HWN	LWN	LWS
Brest	6.9	5.4	2.6	1.0

Berthing
Visitors' pontoon

Fuel
S side of Moulin Blanc N basin

Marina facilities All services

Charts
BA 3429 (22.5)
SHOM 7400 (22.5), 7397, 7398 (12.5)
Imray C36 (Various)

Radio
Moulin Blanc Marina VHF 09
Brest port VHF 08, 16

Telephone
Moulin Blanc Marina *t* 02 98 02 20 02
Customs *t* 02 98 44 35 20
Tourist Office *t* 02 98 44 24 96

Modern city with large marina

Brest is a modern city with a busy port. Visitors are not welcome in the Port du Commerce but there is a large and well-equipped marina.

The Océanopolis oceanographic centre, a major tourist attraction, is very close to the marina. Transport by bus, train and air (twice daily to Paris) is good so Moulin Blanc is convenient for changing crews.

PILOTAGE

(See Plan 5)

Goulet de Brest to Moulin Blanc marina

By GPS

Use ⊕27-Pénoupèle, ⊕28-Elorn, ⊕29-Moulin Blanc, ⊕30-Moulin Blanc 1

By day

From Pointe du Portzic steer about 065° and look for the curved arches of the Albert-Louppe Bridge over the River Elorn. In the foreground a line of PH channel buoys lead past the breakwater of the commercial port. Beyond is the conspicuous white roof of the Océanopolis centre. To its right is the breakwater of Moulin Blanc marina.

Leave Moulin Blanc buoy 200m astern before turning into the dredged marina channel, which is marked by small, lateral buoys.

Enter the marina between MB4 and MB3. Then leave MBA, marking the extremity of the central pier, to port. The visitors' pontoon is immediately to port.

By night

Leaving Pénoupèle close to port, steer 065° to follow the buoyed channel to Moulin Blanc buoy. Leave it to port and continue for about 200m before altering to about 005° to locate the lights marking the narrow dredged channel. When MB1 and MB2 have been identified, steer between them on 007° to the marina entrance.

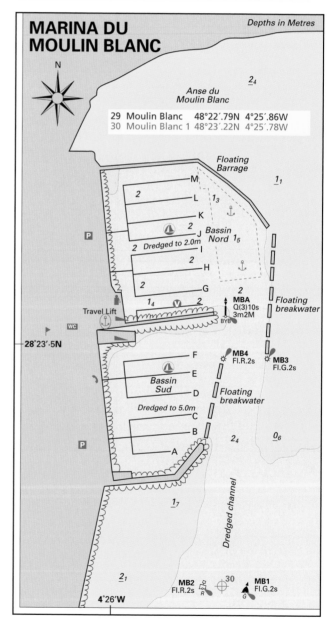

Plan 3A

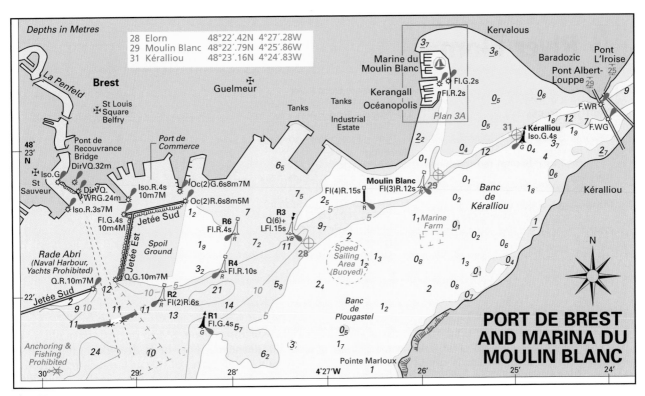

Plan 3B

BERTHS

Moulin Blanc Marina

The marina is well equipped and the staff are helpful. In 2003 many of the pontoons were extended to increase the existing 1200 boat capacity. The marina office produces an excellent guide with maps, charts and details of the facilities available. Almost all repairs can be carried out, as there are chandlers, sail makers and a shipyard with marine engineer near to the Port de Commerce.

Close by is a launderette, as well as bars, restaurants and a small beach.

ASHORE IN BREST

Facilities

A supermarket in Rue de Verdun, NW of the marina, will return you and your shopping to the marina free of charge. The bus service into Brest is frequent and the city has all the usual facilities of a modern city.

Places to visit near the Marina

Océanopolis is a marine scientific centre. The distinctive white concrete and glass building is shaped in the form of a crab and has a large amount of exhibition space and three big aquaria. One aquarium houses the grey seal collection.

The Conservatoire Botanique National is in the Stang Alar valley one mile N of Moulin Blanc. It is dedicated to the preservation of endangered plant species many of which come from the Brittany peninsula. The gardens cover 40 acres and contain plants native to five continents.

3.1 The visitors' pontoon at Moulin Blanc marina

4 River Elorn

Location
48°22'N 4°20'W

Depth restrictions
Dries above St Jean
2m to Landerneau at MHWN

Night passage
Lit to St Jean but not recommended

HW time
Brest HW

Mean height of tide (m)

	HWS	HWN	LWN	LWS
Brest	6.9	5.4	2.6	1.0

Tidal stream Elorn River
Slack – Brest HW–5½ to –4½
Flood – Brest HW–4½ to –½
Slack – Brest HW–½ to +½
Ebb – Brest HW+½ to –5½

Berthing
Anchorages
Drying quay at Landerneau

Charts
BA 3429 (22.5) (to St Jean)
SHOM 7400 (22.5) (to St Jean)
Imray C36 (large scale)

Telephone
Lifting bridge *t* 06 11 03 31 20

Tidal river to historic town

The Elorn is an attractive tidal river with several peaceful anchorages. At all states of the tide, it is navigable to St Jean, which is about 4M beyond Moulin Blanc marina. The remainder of the river dries but it is possible to visit the historic town of Landerneau on the tide.

PILOTAGE

Moulin Blanc to Landerneau

By GPS

This route requires visual pilotage. The following waypoints may be of assistance in the first section
⊕29-Moulin Blanc, ⊕31-Kéraliou,
⊕32-Camfrout.

By day

The River Elorn leads 8M to the attractive old town of Landerneau. For deep-draught yachts it is navigable at all states of tide as far as St Jean. Above St Jean the river dries but is navigable, near high water, for boats drawing up to 2m.

From Moulin Blanc buoy (see plan 3B), pass under Albert-Louppe Bridge. Follow the channel markers and the deep-water moorings. It is possible to anchor on either side of the river or find a vacant mooring as far up as St Jean.

4.1 The River Elorn looking NE.
The anchorage at Le Passage is on the S bank at the bottom of the picture. An alternative anchorage offering more protection from the SW is at Anse Saint-Nicolas. This is a little further up river on the N side. At Saint Jean the river narrows and bends to the N. More anchorages are available above Saint Jean

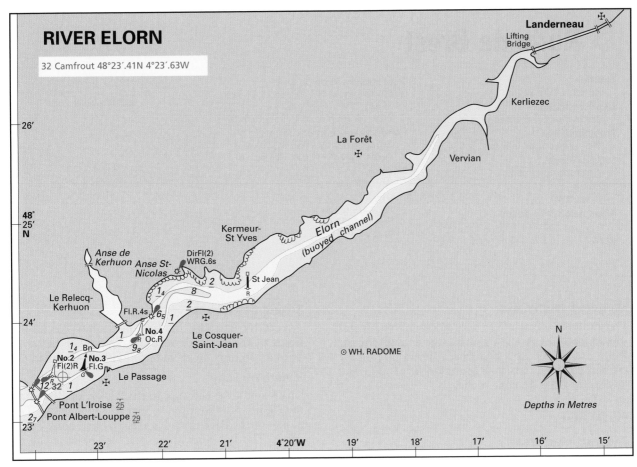

RIVER ELORN

32 Camfrout 48°23′.41N 4°23′.63W

Landerneau

Lifting Bridge

Kerliezec

La Forêt

Vervian

Kermeur-St Yves

Elorn (buoyed channel)

Anse de Kerhuon

Anse St-Nicolas

DirFl(2) WRG.6s

St Jean

Le Relecq-Kerhuon

Fl.R.4s

Le Cosquer-Saint-Jean

WH. RADOME

No.4 Oc.R

Bn

No.2 Fl(2)R

No.3 Fl.G

Le Passage

Pont L'Iroise

Pont Albert-Louppe

N

Depths in Metres

Plan 4

At Kerhuon there is a slip, marked by a beacon with an orange top. A wharf marks the eastern end of Kerhuon where the river curves north and then east for the last stretch before St Jean.

Above St Jean, rather small and widely spaced green and red buoys and the yacht moorings mark the channel. 3½M above St Jean there is a lifting bridge which will be opened on request or by telephoning in advance (06 11 03 31 20).

Follow the canal to Landerneau, pass the large sand-barge wharf, and tie up against the wall on the port side.

By night

The Elorn is only lit as far as Anse Saint-Nicolas and night passage is not recommended.

BERTHS AND ANCHORAGES

Landerneau

Landerneau is attractive and has all the facilities of a fair-sized town. Market days are Monday, Tuesdays, Fridays and Saturdays. It is on the Morlaix-Brest railway line.

It may be possible to dry out on the port side against a short length of wall with a slipway where the bottom is hard and flat. There is 3m at HW neaps. There is water and electricity on the quay on the port side.

⚓ Le Passage

Although somewhat exposed to the SW, there is an attractive anchorage about ¾M above the Albert-Louppe Bridge on the S side of the river near Le Passage. The bottom may be foul so buoy the anchor.

⊕32 Camfrout (48°23′.41N 4°23′.63W)

⚓ Anse Saint-Nicolas

Anse Saint-Nicolas is better sheltered from the SW than Le Passage. It is in a bay on the N side of the river, about 1¾M above Albert-Louppe Bridge.

⚓ Kerhuon

Good shelter from all directions can be found in the stretch of river between Anse de Kerhuon and about ¼M NE of Saint Jean beacon tower.

4.2 The drying wall and slipway at Landerneau

5 Rade de Brest

Location
48°19′N 4°25′W

Depth restrictions
None in main channel

Prohibited area
Near Ile Longue in SW

Night passage
Not recommended

HW time
Brest HW

Mean height of tide (m)

	HWS	HWN	LWN	LWS
Brest	6.9	5.4	2.6	1.0

Tidal streams Rade de Brest
Flood – Brest HW–5½ to –½ (1.5kts)
Slack – Brest HW–½ to +½
Ebb – Brest HW+½ to +5½ (1.0kts)

Flood stream counter-currents
Espagnols Brest HW –4½ to –½
Armorique Brest HW –3½ to –½

Berthing
Anchorages

Charts
BA 3429 (22.5)
SHOM 7400 (22.5)
Imray C36 (77)

Sheltered sailing area

The Rade de Brest offers very good sailing. It has shelter from the Atlantic but is large enough for the wind not to be too disturbed. There are many anchorages for boats that can take the ground and several for deep draught yachts.

PILOTAGE

The restricted areas

There is a restricted area in the SW of the Rade. Roscanvel on the W of Ile Longue Military Port and Le Fret on the E can be visited. However, there are areas where navigation is restricted and anchoring prohibited. In particular, entry is prohibited within 500m of the shore around Ile Longue.

The Naval College beyond Pen-ar-Vir has a restricted zone marked by the NCM and yellow buoys. Anchoring is not allowed in this area and entry may also be prohibited without warning. Boats may also be refused access to a rectangular area N of the Naval College marked by yellow buoys.

Goulet de Brest to Traverse de l'Hôpital

By GPS

Use ⊕44-Espagnols, ⊕33-Ile Ronde, ⊕39-Aulne, ⊕40-Hôpital.

By day

From the Goulet de Brest steer 120° to Le Renard WCM. Leave Ile Ronde and the two rectangular concrete dolphins 300m to port.

A course of 104° will lead to the outer PHM No 4, about 1M W of the Ile du Bindy.

The succeeding channel buoys No 6 and No 8 are also red. After No 8 the numbered buoys are closer together and easier to see. Note that port buoys are conical although painted red.

By night

Night passage is not recommended.

Rivière de l'Hôpital

The pretty entrance of this small river lies to the north of the entrance to the Aulne. Since the river dries it can only be visited around HW (see plan 6).

Rivière du Faou

Upstream of the entrance to the Rivière de l'Hôpital, the Aulne turns south into a large double bend. The mouth of the Rivière du Faou is on the E bank of the curve. The bar dries 0.6m and lies between Ile de Tibidy and the charming little islet of Arun. North of this islet is a pool with 0.4m. Beyond the pool the river dries but, at springs, it is possible to go up to the substantial village of Le Faou (see plan 6).

ANCHORAGES

⚓ Roscanvel

Sheltered from N through W to SE, the E coast of Presqu'île de Quélern offers good protection. Between Pte des Espagnols and the village of Roscanvel there are several small bays with yacht moorings. There is a welcoming yacht club at Roscanvel, which may loan a mooring on request.

Roscanvel is a small holiday village. It has a double slipway, one running out east and the other south. Anchor off the slips clear of the moorings. The E slip dries at LW and there are obstructions outside it. If landing at the S slip towards LW approach from the south and use the inside only.

Watch out for the stream in the Baie de Roscanvel. There is a counter-current on the flood from about Brest HW–3 to HW but no counter-current on the ebb. This means the stream only runs S for a couple of hours after LW.

⊕43-Roscanvel 1 (48°18′.8N 4°32′.2W)

⚓ Anse de l'Auberlac'h

Sheltered from all directions except SW, the picturesque hamlet of L'Auberlach lies at the head of a bay running NE from Ile Ronde. It is rather

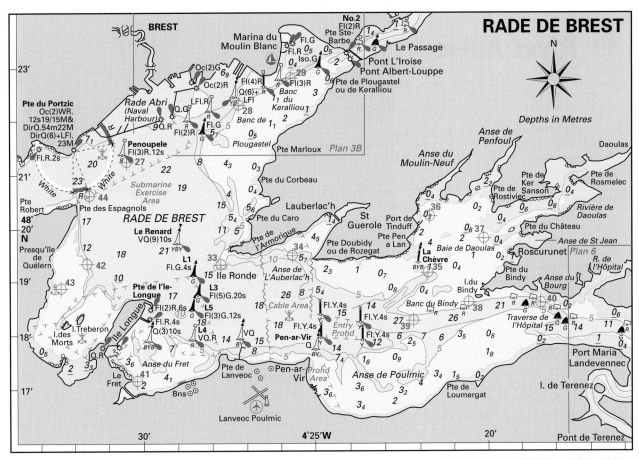

Plan 5

27 Pénoupèle	48°21′.41N	4°30′.51W
28 Elorn	48°22′.42N	4°27′.28W
29 Moulin Blanc	48°22′.79N	4°25′.86W
33 Ile Ronde	48°19′.21N	4°27′.96W
34 Auberlac'h	48°19′.55N	4°25′.48W
35 La Chèvre	48°19′.41N	4°21′.89W
36 Tinduff	48°20′.27N	4°21′.85W
37 Daoulas	48°19′.99N	4°19′.57W
38 Bindy	48°18′.69N	4°20′.64W
39 Aulne	48°18′.33N	4°22′.17W
40 Hôpital	48°18′.63N	4°18′.72W
41 Le Fret	48°17′.12N	4°30′.17W
42 Roscanvel	48°19′.41N	4°31′.58W
43 Roscanvel 1	48°18′.81N	4°32′.62W
44 Espagnols	48°20′.76N	4°31′.62W

crowded with moorings, but there are three or four white visitors' buoys. There may be space to anchor but beyond the pier the bay shoals rapidly.

⊕34-Auberlac'h (48°19′.55N 4°25′.48W)

⚓ Le Fret

Sheltered from all directions except NW, the Anse du Fret provides a pleasant anchorage SE of Ile Longue. A course of 215° from Ile Ronde will lead into the anchorage clear of the exclusion zone. There is space to anchor with good holding on sand/mud. From the pier, fast ferries go to Brest and buses go to Camaret.

⊕41-Le Fret (48°17′.12N 4°30′.17W)

⚓ Tinduff

Sheltered from W and N, Tinduff is a small harbour on the W side of the shallow Baie de Daoulas, ½M to the north of Pointe de Pen a Lan. Keep at least ¼M from the point to avoid the shoals and La Chèvre rock (dries 4.7m), which is marked by an ECM. There is another rock (drying 4.2m) closer inshore and a third unmarked isolated rock, drying 0.7m, about 300m WSW of the beacon.

The bay is shallow and can only be entered with sufficient rise of tide but there is a 2m pool off the end of the pier. There are many moorings but there is room to anchor, with good holding. At neaps, it is possible to go further into the bay where there is better shelter. Keep clear of the fish farm, marked by small, unlit yellow buoys.

⊕36-Tinduff (48°20′.27N 4°21′.85W)

⚓ Rivière de Daoulas

Sheltered from all directions, this shallow river runs into the NE corner of the Baie de Daoulas. The bay can only be entered with sufficient rise of tide as there is a bar at the entrance. The deepest water is found by keeping Pte du Château on a bearing of 070°. The Pointe is not easy to distinguish against the land but can be identified by the conspicuous large grey shed with houses above and to the right. Almost the entire river is taken up with moorings and there is little space left to anchor. There may be space about ¾M upriver off the second slip, in 1.8m (mud). The river to Daoulas dries 4.5m.

⊕37-Daoulas (48°19′.99N 4°19′.57W)

6 River Aulne

Location
48°18′N 4°16′W

Depth restrictions
6m to Pte de Térénez
2.5m at MHWN to the Guily Glaz
2.7m beyond the lock

Height restrictions 23m

Guily Glaz lock
Brest HW −2 to +2 (0600 to 2200)

HW time
Brest HW

Mean height of tide (m)

	HWS	HWN	LWN	LWS
Brest	6.9	5.4	2.6	1.0

Tidal streams Landevennec
Flood – Brest HW−5½ to −½
Slack – Brest HW−½ to +½
Ebb – Brest HW+½ to −5½

Berthing
Quay at Port Launay
Visitors' pontoon at Châteaulin
Anchorages

Fuel
Châteaulin hypermarket

Facilities
Water at Port Launay and
Châteaulin
Hypermarket at Châteaulin

Charts
BA 3429 (22.5)
SHOM 7400 (22.5)
Imray C36 (large scale)
IGN TOP25 sheet 0518

Telephone
Guily Glaz lock *t* 02 98 86 03 21

Gateway to the Brest Canal

The Aulne is a beautiful sheltered river in the southern part of the Rade de Brest. It it navigable on the tide to Guily Glaz lock where the Aulne joins the old Nantes-Brest canal. Beyond Guily Glaz there is the pretty canal village of Port Launay and the market town of Châteaulin. Perhaps surprisingly, Châteaulin is a good place for provisioning because the visitors' pontoon is very close to a hypermarket.

Major construction work is being carried out on Guily Glaz lock which may put it out of action during the 2005 season. Telephone the lock-keeper on 02 98 86 03 21.

PILOTAGE

Traverse de l'Hôpital to Châteaulin

There is no chart of the river above Pont de Térénez. Sheet 0518 *Châteaulin-Douarnenez* in the IGN TOP 25 series of maps is the best alternative and shows the line of deepest water. However, Plan 6 provides sufficient detail for the passage.

Apart from a 6m patch at Traverse de l'Hôpital there is 10m as far as Pont de Térénez. From there to within about a mile of the lock, there is at least 4m at half tide. In the last mile to the lock, depth is reduced in some places to 2.5m at MHWN. In the upper reaches the bottom is generally very soft mud. Beyond the lock at Guily Glaz there is between 2.7m and 3m. The overhead clearance below bridges and power lines is 27m or more. The power line above the viaduct at Guily Glaz is 23m.

6.1 The River Aulne looking N.
The river curves around the village at Port Maria and the ruined Abbey at Landevennec. The Abbey and the site museum can be visited from the drying jetty at Port Maria at the W of the curve or from Port Styvel in the SW corner. The Abbey is the oldest holy place in Brittany and was probably founded in the 5th century

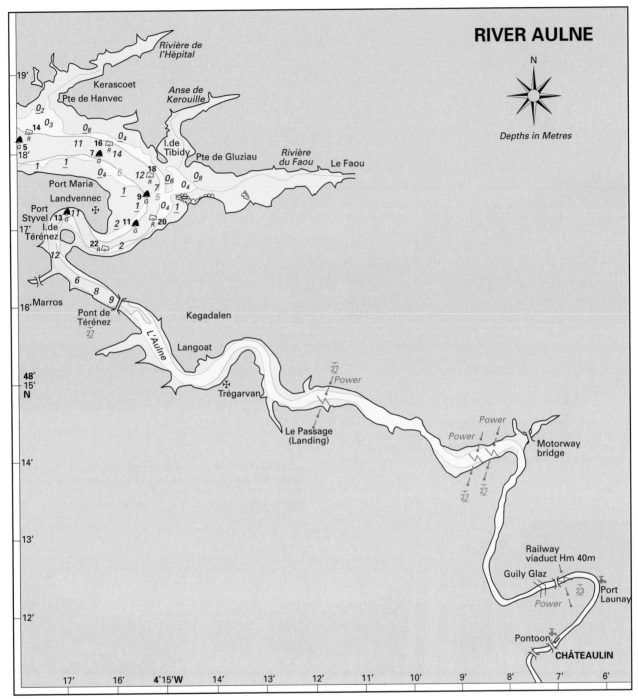

RIVER AULNE

N

Depths in Metres

Rivière de l'Hèpital

Kerascoet
Pte de Hanvec

Anse de Kerouille

I.de Tibidy

Pte de Gluziau

Rivière du Faou

Le Faou

0_2
0_3
14
0_6
0_4

G 5
18'
11 16 0_4
7 14
1
1
0_4 5 12 18
7
Port Maria
Landvennec
0_6 0_4 0_8
1
9
5
Port Styvel 13 11
17' I.de Térénez
2 11 20
0_4 1
22 2
12
6
8 9

16' Marros

Pont de Térénez
27

Kegadalen

L'Aulne

Langoat

48°
15'
N

Trégarvan
27
Power

Le Passage (Landing)

Power
Power
Power

Motorway bridge

27 27

14'

13'

Railway viaduct Hm 40m

Guily Glaz

23 Port Launay

Power

12'

Pontoon

CHÂTEAULIN

17' 16' 4°15'W 14' 13' 12' 11' 10' 9' 8' 7' 6'

Plan 6

From Traverse de l'Hôpital to Port Styvel there are mud banks on both sides of the river and it is best to keep to the buoyed channel. At Port Styvel the channel marker buoys end. Continue to the bridge, keeping to the outside of bends and to the middle where the river narrows. From the bridge it is 12M to the lock at Guily Glaz.

At Trégarvan, about two miles above Pont de Térénez, the river bends N and then S and the banks become lower. With luck you may see kingfishers and egret in the reed beds. The river passes very close to the dual carriageway just before turning S again. This is the shallowest part of the trip and the deepest water is close in to the N bank.

The flower-covered lock is a surprise after the peace of the river. It evokes an earlier age when barges travelled from Brest to Nantes and pleasure boats from Camaret came up to Port Launay for the day.

Beautiful Port Launay is 1M above the lock. The village has a long curve of grass-covered quays backed by old houses under high tree-covered hills. To carry on to Châteaulin, leave Port Launay and pass the hotel De Bon Accueil on the port side. (You can tie up if you are staying for supper.) Opposite the hotel there are two green markers that indicate a rocky patch on the starboard side. Generally, the

6.2 Above Trégarvan the banks become lower and kingfishers and egrets may be seen in the reed beds. Just ahead is the dual carriageway that briefly disturbs the peace before the river turns away to starboard

6.3 Guily Glaz lock at the start of the old Brest to Nantes canal. Bonaparte started to build the canal in 1804 in order to escape the blockade of Brest by using canals to get to Nantes; sadly the canal is no longer continuous

deepest water from this point to Châteaulin is on the SE side of the river. At the town there is a visitors' pontoon on the N bank.

BERTHS AND ANCHORAGES

Port Launay

Port Launay has a long stone quay that runs alongside the main street. Once it must have been full of barges waiting for the tide but today there is plenty of room for visiting yachts. Water and electricity is neatly concealed in the shrubs. There are showers (key from the town hall), a few small food shops, a restaurant and a number of cafés.

Châteaulin

Châteaulin has a visitors' pontoon with water and electricity. There are toilets and showers at the N end of the quay. The shower key is obtainable on deposit from the tourist office by the road bridge. Modest berthing fees are also payable at the tourist office.

Ashore it has a visitor centre dedicated to salmon. It has all the facilities of a medium-sized town with markets on Thursdays and Sundays. The hypermarket and fuel station is a short walk from the visitors' pontoon.

⚓ Port Maria at Landevennec

Sheltered from the SW and SE, Port Maria is a drying jetty on the south bank just inside SHM No. 7. From here you can walk to the attractive village of Landevennec.

⚓ Ile de Térénez to Pont de Térénez

There are several, well sheltered, anchorages between Port Styvel and Pont de Térénez.

The bottom is rocky away from the banks but it is possible to anchor at Port Styvel (buoy the anchor because this used to be a naval graveyard). From here it is possible to land and follow a path through the woods to Landevennec, where there are shops, a hotel and the famous Abbaye de Saint-Guénolé.

Anchoring may be possible at the mouth of either of the drying creeks SW of Ile de Térénez or on the E side of the river SW of Ile de Térénez. On the starboard side of the bank between Port Styvel and Pont de Térénez there are several very small inlets where it may be possible to anchor.

⚓ Trégarvan

Trégarvan, 2M upstream of Pont de Térénez, provides a reasonable anchorage; there are several moorings and a slip. There is another landing at Le Passage about 2M further up.

6.4 Port Launay is 17M into inland Brittany

6.5 The berthing is easy and the village is charming

6.6 The visitors' pontoon at Châteaulin. The large grey roof beyond the houses belongs to the hypermarket

7 Camaret-sur-Mer

Location
48°17′N 4°35′W

Shelter
Good except from NE

Depth restrictions
3m in outer harbour
2m shoaling to 0.4m in inner
harbour

Night entry Well lit

HW time
Brest HW–¼

Mean height of tide (m)

	HWS	HWN	LWN	LWS
Camaret	6.6	5.1	2.5	1.0

Tidal streams
Weak in the bay

Berthing
Two marinas
Visitors' moorings

Fuel
Port Vauban wave breaker

Facilities
Some repair facilities, many shops,
bars and restaurants

Charts
BA 2350 (50), 3427 (22.5)
SHOM 7401 (22.5)
Imray C36 (large scale)

Radio
Camaret port VHF 09

Telephone
Capitainerie *t* 02 98 27 89 31
Tourist Office *t* 02 98 27 93 60

Attractive fishing port with excellent facilities

Camaret is an ideal stopover when bound north or south through the Chenal du Four. It is an attractive fishing port that has successfully transformed itself into a yachting and tourist centre. There are shops, seafood restaurants, excellent coast path walking, good beaches and some history.

PILOTAGE

(See Plan 8)

Camaret approach and entrance

By GPS

From the Chenal du Four use
⊕23-St-Mathieu, ⊕48-Camaret,
⊕49-Camaret 1;

From Brest use
⊕47-Capucins, ⊕49-Camaret 1

From the Chenal du Toulinguet use
⊕50-N Toulinguet, ⊕48-Camaret,
⊕49-Camaret 1.

By day

From the W, the coast between Pointe de Toulinguet and Pointe de Grand Gouin is steep-to and has no dangers more than 200m from the above-water rocks.

The approach is clear of dangers except for the shallow, rocky bay between Pointe de Grand Gouin and the old green lighthouse. Identify the north mole that extends E from the old green lighthouse and steer for the green-topped white light structure at its E end.

By night

Approach in the white sector of the light on the N mole and round it at a reasonable distance. There is a large fish farm, lit by N and W cardinal buoys, and

7.1 At Port Vauban in Camaret three new pools have been created. There is plenty of room to manoeuvre and when necessary boats raft alongside each other in the pools

there are mooring buoys in the bay to the southeast of the outer marina. The shore lights usually provide enough illumination to avoid them.

BERTHS

Port Vauban

Visitors with larger boats are expected to use the outer marina which has pontoons connected to the south side of the N mole. This is exposed to the NE and, in the past, has been uncomfortable or even dangerous in strong winds between N and E. A new wave breaker, installed in 2004, has improved the protection. The outside of the wave breaker is for ferries and for the fuel dock; visitors go inside.

The Port Vauban harbour office is by the old green lighthouse; showers and toilets are by the Vauban tower.

Port du Notic

Port du Notic marina has visitors' berths for smaller boats and is in the inner harbour much closer to the town. Anchoring is forbidden in the inner harbour. The Capitainerie and the showers and toilets are on the quay opposite the entrance to the marina.

Visitors' moorings

In the bay SE of the N mole there are moorings in 3m or more, including some white ones for visitors. Anchoring is not allowed in the harbour and channel and the bottom is reported to be foul.

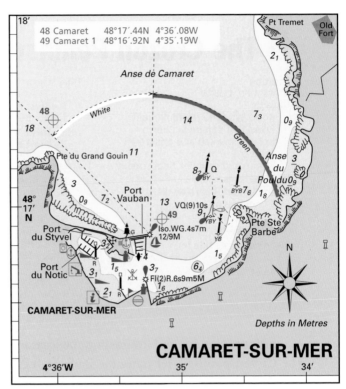

Plan 7

Port du Styvel

This marina, just N of Port du Notic, has no places for visitors.

ASHORE IN CAMARET

Facilities

Camaret has chandlers, a shipbuilder, a sailmaker, supermarkets, launderettes, restaurants, bars and a wide variety of leisure shops.

There is a bus service to Le Fret, from where there is a fast ferry to Brest.

Leisure

A walk in Camaret is likely to take you along the breakwater to or from Sillon Point.

The rotting fishing boats are much photographed but the more enduring buildings are also interesting. The church with the broken tower is Notre-Dame de Rocamadour. It is so called because pilgrims from Ireland and Britain used to disembark at Camaret and set out overland to Rocamadour. The church has some fine wooden statues as well as a collection of votive offerings. Sailors brought these, in thanks for narrow escapes at sea.

The rugged Vauban Tower was built just in time to successfully repulse an Anglo-Dutch landing attempt at the end on the 17th Century. There are another two forts near Camaret, one at the Pointe de Toulinguet and the other at Pointe du Grand Gouin. They are not accessible but on a fine day the walking is wonderful.

7.2 The inner harbour, Port du Styvel Marina, looking across to the Vauban tower

8 The Crozon Peninsula

Location
48°15′N 4°38′W

Hazards
Rocks W of Pte du Toulinguet
Rocks S of Cap de la Chèvre
Isolated marked and unmarked rocks
Strong and complex tidal streams

Night passage
Toulinguet is partially lit
S Chèvre is lit

HW time
Brest HW–¼

Mean height of tide (m)

	HWS	HWN	LWN	LWS
Camaret	6.6	5.1	2.5	1.0

Tidal stream Toulinguet
N – Brest HW–5½ to +½ (1.7kts)
S – Brest HW+½ to +5½ (1.7kts)
Slack – Brest HW+5½ to –5½

Tidal stream W Cap de la Chèvre
E – Brest HW–4½ to –1½ (0.7kts)
Slack – Brest HW–1½ to +½
SW – Brest HW+½ to +2½ (0.3kts)
NW – Brest HW+2½ to +5½ (0.4kts)
NE – Brest HW+5½ to –4½ (0.5kts)

Tidal stream E of Cap de la Chèvr
NE – Brest HW–5½ to –1½ (0.4kts)
Slack – Brest HW–1½ to +1½
SW – Brest HW+1½ to +5½ (0.3kts)
Slack – Brest HW+5½ to –5½

Charts
BA 2350 (50), 2349 (30)
SHOM 7172 (50), 7121 (30)
Imray C36 (77)

Magnificent scenery and interesting navigation

The Crozon peninsula separates the Rade de Brest from the Bay of Douarnenez. Its granite cliffs rise from 50m in the N at Camaret to 100m in the S at Cap de la Chèvre. There are many off lying rocks. Some like the Rochers du Toulinguet and Les Tas de Pois are more than 30m high; others are less spectacular but more dangerous. Careful navigation is required but it is well rewarded by the magnificent scenery.

There are two main dangers. In the N, rocks extend W from Point du Toulinguet for nearly 4 miles. There are several passages through the rocks. The Chenal du Toulinguet is the innermost and saves a good many miles when going between the Rade de Brest and the Bay of Douarnenez or the Raz de Sein.

The second danger is the southern tip of the Crozon Peninsula where several lines of rocks extend like fangs from the Cap de la Chèvre.

PILOTAGE

Chenal du Toulinguet

By GPS

Southbound for the Raz de Sein use
⊕50-N Toulinguet, ⊕51-S Toulinguet,
⊕80-Raz.
Southbound for Cap de la Chèvre use
⊕50-N Toulinguet, ⊕52-Tas de Pois.

These routes need not be followed precisely. The only danger is a 4.9m shallow patch near La Louve beacon (unlit).

By day

The W side of the channel is marked by the Roches du Toulinguet, which rise to 30m. Le Pohen (height 8m) is nearest to the channel and is steep-to. La Louve tower marks the E side of the channel.

Keep to the middle of the channel. The depth is at least 4.9m and the channel is ¼M wide.

By night

The passage is partially lit. From the S use Le Toulinguet light and Petit Minou light; from the N use Le Portzic light. However, night passage without GPS is not recommended.

Chenal du Petit Leac'h

By GPS

From the SW use
⊕56-Basse du Lis, ⊕50-N Toulinguet.

By day or night

From the SW, leave Petit Leac'h beacon SCM (unlit) to the W and Pelen beacon SCM and Basse Mendufa NCM (both unlit) to the E.

At night Le Portzic light can be held on a constant bearing of 043°.

The channel is 600m wide with a depth of more than 10m. The tide sets strongly.

Les Tas de Pois

Les Tas de Pois are 5 magnificent rocks extending out to sea from the Pointe de Pen-Hir. On a calm day you may feel tempted to pass between them. Numbering from seaward, the rocks are:

1. Tas de Pois Ouest, height 47m.
2. La Fourche, height 10m.
3. La Dentelé, height 35m.
4. Le Grand Tas de Pois, height 64m.
5. Le Tas de Pois de Terre, height 58m.

Between 1 and 2, the channel is about 200m wide. There is a rock, drying 0.5m, about 50m NE of 1 and another drying rock close to 2. Near LW keep to mid-channel, if anything closer to 2.

Between 2 and 3 the channel is about 100m and clean.

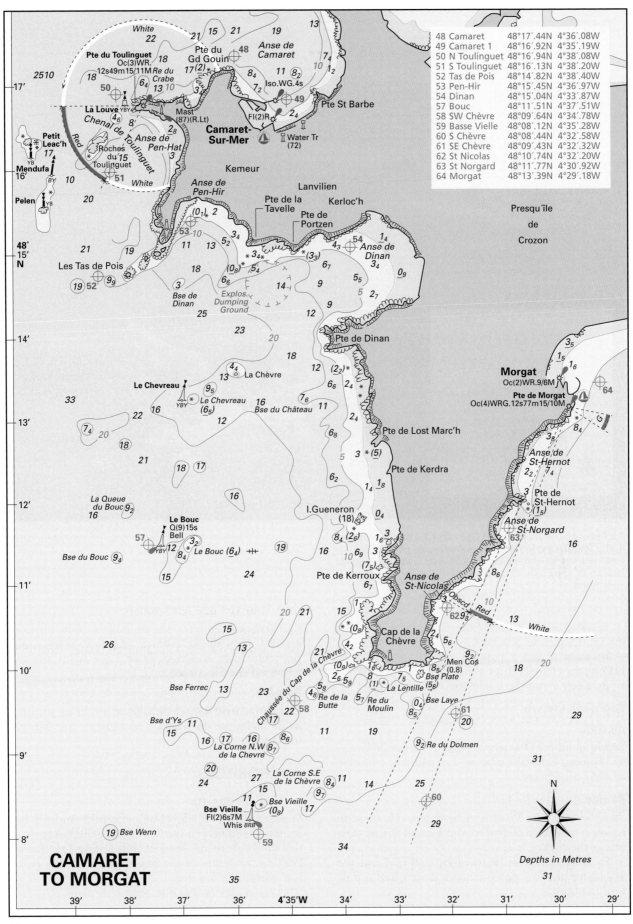

48	Camaret	48°17´.44N 4°36´.08W
49	Camaret 1	48°16´.92N 4°35´.19W
50	N Toulinguet	48°16´.94N 4°38´.08W
51	S Toulinguet	48°16´.13N 4°38´.20W
52	Tas de Pois	48°14´.82N 4°38´.40W
53	Pen-Hir	48°15´.45N 4°36´.97W
54	Dinan	48°15´.04N 4°33´.87W
57	Bouc	48°11´.51N 4°37´.51W
58	SW Chèvre	48°09´.64N 4°34´.78W
59	Basse Vieille	48°08´.12N 4°35´.28W
60	S Chèvre	48°08´.44N 4°32´.58W
61	SE Chèvre	48°09´.43N 4°32´.32W
62	St Nicolas	48°10´.74N 4°32´.20W
63	St Norgard	48°11´.77N 4°30´.92W
64	Morgat	48°13´.39N 4°29´.18W

**CAMARET
TO MORGAT**

Plan 8

8.1 Chenal du Toulinguet and Camaret-sur-Mer looking E. In the foreground the Roches du Toulinguet rise to 30m and mark the W of the channel. The inset is La Louve (unlit) beacon on the E side of the channel at the Pointe du Toulinguet

Between 3 and 4 keep closer to 3; there is a rock drying 0.6m close NW of 4.

Between 4 and 5 passage is only possible near HW as the channel dries almost right across.

Between 5 and the land there is no passage.

Cap de la Chèvre

By GPS

Southbound for Douarnenez use ⊕52-Tas de Pois, ⊕57-Bouc, ⊕58-SW Chèvre. For Morgat, continue to ⊕61-SE Chèvre.

By day

Southbound, pass W of Le Chevreaux. The beacon has been partially destroyed and a small WCM now marks the rock.

Le Bouc rocks are marked by a WCM but the associated shallow patch extends nearly half a mile E of the buoy.

There are dangers up to half a mile offshore around Cap de la Chèvre. At low water, take particular care to avoid Basse Laye 0.4m shallow patch off the SE corner.

By night

The dangers off Cap de la Chèvre are lit by sectored lights at Pointe du Milier and Morgat. See Morgat for details.

ANCHORAGES

⚓ Anse de Pen-Hir

Sheltered from all directions except S and SE but sometimes subject to swell. This snug anchorage is in the sandy Anse de Pen-Hir, just inside Les Tas de Pois. In the centre of the bay, there is a rocky patch just within the 5m line.

⊕53-Pen-Hir (48°15´.45N 4°36´.97W)

8.2 Les Tas de Pois looking N.
The boat is passing between No 4 (64m high) and No 3 (35m high). Keep closer to No 3 as there is a rock drying 0.6m close NW of No 4

⚓ Anse de Dinan

Sheltered from the N and E but exposed to wind or swell from the W and SW. This wide, shallow bay is 3M E of Les Tas de Pois. Enter from SW taking care to avoid the rock 400m S of Pointe de la Tavelle and the rock 200m E of Pointe de Portzen. The best anchorage is in the NE corner of the bay.

⊕54-Dinan (48°15´.04N 4°33´.87W)

⚓ Anse de Saint-Nicolas

Sheltered from the NW, this is a rugged but attractive anchorage about 1M N of Cap de la Chèvre. Approach from the SE to avoid the dangers of Cap de la Chèvre.

⊕62-St-Nicolas (48°10´.74N 4°32´.20W)

⚓ Anse de Saint-Norgard

Sheltered from the W and NW, this rocky bay is about 2M S of Morgat. Approach from the SE to avoid the drying rocks off Pointe de Saint-Hernot.

⊕63-St-Norgard (48°11´.77N 4°30´.92W)

8.3 Cap de la Chèvre

8.4 Les Rochers du Toulinguet looking N

8.5 Les Tas de Pois looking S

9 Morgat

Location
48°13'N 4°32'W

Shelter
Reasonable except from N and W
Swell sometimes enters the marina

Depth restrictions
1.5m in dredged channel
0.6m to 1.8m in the marina

Yachts >12m Must anchor

Night entry
Lit but care is required

HW time
Brest HW −¼

Mean height of tide (m)

	HWS	HWN	LWN	LWS
Morgat	6.5	5.0	2.4	0.9

Tidal streams
Weak in the bay

Berthing
Marina
Anchorage and some mooring buoys

Fuel
Base of visitors' pontoon

Facilities
Limited facilities, more shops in Crozon

Charts
BA 2349 (30)
SHOM 7121 (30)
Imray C36 (large scale)

Radio
Marina VHF 09

Telephone
Marina & HM *t* 02 98 27 01 97

Nineteenth century seaside resort

Morgat is a pretty seaside resort in the NW corner of Douarnenez Bay.

The marina is not piled and can be uncomfortable but it is well protected by floating concrete wave breakers and a rocky breakwater. Beyond the breakwater is a small sandy beach, protected from the SW by the Pointe de Morgat. There is another larger beach a short walk from the marina in Morgat village.

Yachts greater than 12m LOA are officially required to anchor but this rule does not appear to be enforced.

PILOTAGE

Morgat approach and entrance

By GPS

From the NW use ⊕58-SW Chèvre, ⊕61-SE Chèvre, ⊕64-Morgat. There are dangers off Cap de la Chèvre, Pointe de Saint-Hernot and Point de Morgat.

From Douarnenez use ⊕67-Douarnenez, ⊕64-Morgat. The rocks near La Pierre Profonde, are unlit and less than ½M E of this route.

From the Raz de Sein use ⊕80-Raz, ⊕74-Van, ⊕73-Basse Jaune, ⊕59-Basse Vieille, ⊕61-SE Chèvre, ⊕64-Morgat.

There are dangers close to ⊕74-Van, ⊕73-Basse Jaune and ⊕59-Basse Vieille and NW of the leg between ⊕61-SE Chèvre and ⊕64-Morgat. The track from ⊕74-Van to ⊕61-SE Chèvre is a straight line but the additional waypoints make it easier to identify the dangers.

By day

Pointe de Morgat is a bold headland with a red and white square tower lighthouse in the trees at the top

9.1 The red and white lighthouse on the top of the cliff at Pointe de Morgat

of the cliff. Two conspicuous above-water rocks at the foot of the headland are steep-to and can be passed within 50m.

The breakwater of the new harbour lies just to the north of the two rocks, but watch out for the concrete obstruction in the intervening bay. Continue north to the end of the breakwater where Morgat port buoy marks the safe ground. Leave this to port before entering the harbour or going to the anchorage.

Approaching from Douarnenez, or the beautiful beaches in the E of the bay, there is a rocky patch ¾M SSW of Rocher L'Aber and 2M ESE of Morgat. It consists of 3 groups of rocks. The largest is Les Verrès with a partially drying wreck to its NE. SW of Les Verrès is La Pierre Profonde with Le Taureau, the third group, to the N

By night

The dangers south of Cap de la Chèvre can be cleared by keeping in one of the two white sectors of

9.2 The visitors' pontoon at Morgat is on the W side of the harbour near the fishing boats

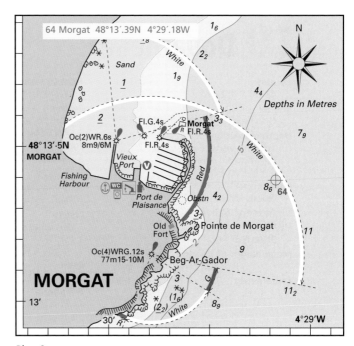

Plan 9

Pointe du Millier light until Pointe de Morgat light turns from red to white. Steer towards Pointe de Morgat light, keeping in the white sector until the 10m depth contour is reached. Turn to run along the coast on a course of about 035° crossing the green sector of Pointe de Morgat light. Keep a lookout for unlit mooring buoys. The light on the old harbour breakwater will open red, seen over the new breakwater. When it turns from red to white, alter course to leave the harbour entrance buoy to port. There are flashing green and red lights marking the entrance between the wave breakers.

BERTHS AND ANCHORAGES

Morgat marina and anchorage

Visitors' berth alongside the pontoon with the large *Visiteurs* sign in the SW corner of the harbour. The outer pontoon floating wave breakers may also be offered but are uncomfortable in easterlies. Yachts may anchor in 2m N and NE of the wave breakers. Anchoring is not permitted in the area enclosed by the breakwater and the wave breakers.

⚓ Ile de l'Aber

Sheltered from the NW to the NE, this attractive anchorage behind Ile de l'Aber is about 2M E of Morgat.

Coming from Morgat, leave Rocher de l'Aber close to port and turn NNE into the anchorage.

Coming from Cap de la Chèvre or Douarnenez, approach from the S to pass E of Les Vèrres and the nearby drying wreck.

⊕65-Ile de l'Aber (48°13′.42N 4°25′.81W)

ASHORE IN MORGAT

The marina has all the facilities of a substantial marina and fishing port.

Morgat was originally developed by the founder of the Peugeot car company as a place to send his executives for their holidays; consequently there are some fine hotels and villas. There are modest shops, bars and restaurants on the beachfront but the nearest large town is Crozon, which is 1½M away and a steep climb.

In calm weather it is great fun to take a dinghy trip into the caves at the foot of Pointe de Morgat. The largest cave is like a cathedral and is 300 feet long and 33 feet high with brightly coloured walls. For walkers, the cliff path starts close to the lighthouse and leads all the way to Cap de la Chèvre.

9.3 The beachfront at Morgat

10 Douarnenez

Location
48°06'N 4°20'W

Shelter
Good except in strong NW winds

Depth restrictions
1.5m on visitors' pontoon
Port Rhu sill dries 1.1m
3m in Port Rhu

Port Rhu lock
Opens HW±1

Night entry Well lit

HW time
Brest HW −½

Mean height of tide (m)

	HWS	HWN	LWN	LWS
Douarnenez	6.4	4.9	2.3	0.9

Tidal streams
Weak in the bay

Berthing
Visitors' pontoon and moorings
Port Rhu marina and anchorages

Fuel
NW side of Tréboul marina

Facilities
Some repair facilities, good shops
and restaurants

Charts
BA 2349 (30)
SHOM 7121 (30)
Imray C36 (large scale)

Radio
Marina VHF 09

Telephone
Port Rhu t 02 98 92 00 67

Fishing port and maritime heritage

Douarnenez, in the sheltered SW corner of Douarnenez Bay, is really two towns. The River Pouldavid, with Ile Tristan at its mouth, splits the fishing port of Douarnenez from the beach resort of Tréboul.

Visiting yachts use the pontoons and buoys near the river entrance or go further upstream. At Port Rhu a barrage with a lock has been built across the river to form a basin. This contains a visitors' pontoon, a large floating maritime museum and a marina for local boats.

PILOTAGE

Douarnenez approach and entrance

By GPS

From the Cap de la Chèvre use ⊕58-SW Chèvre, ⊕67-Douarnenez.

10.1 Douarnenez looking SE.
The Grande Passe leads to the visitors' pontoon on the starboard side at Tréboul. Further upstream, above the barrage, is Port Rhu where there is also a visitors' pontoon. The Passe de Guet, between Ile Tristan and Douarnenez, shows clearly. The harbour to the E is Rosmeur fishing harbour

From Morgat use ⊕64-Morgat, ⊕67-Douarnenez. La Pierre Profonde and its adjacent rocks lie less than ½M NE of this track.

From the Raz de Sein use ⊕80-Raz, ⊕74-Van, ⊕72-Duellou, ⊕70-Jument, ⊕67-Douarnenez. There are dangers off Pointe de Van, Basse Jaune and near ⊕72-Duellou.

For the final approach to Tréboul use ⊕67-Douarnenez, ⊕68-Douarnenez 1. This route leaves Basse Neuve 2.2m shallow patch just to port.

By day

From Pointe de la Jument (3M W of Douarnenez) there is a safe route clear of the rocky coast by keeping Pointe du Millier lighthouse open of Pointe de la Jument.

Douarnenez is easy to locate from seaward and easy to enter. Ile Tristan, with its lighthouse, is in the foreground with Rosmeur harbour mole E of the island and the Grande Passe and Tréboul marina to the W.

Leave Ile Tristan to port to enter the river or to starboard to approach the anchorage.

A clearing transit that clears any shallow patches in the entrance is Douarnenez belfry and Ploaré church, at the back of town, both in line with Ile Tristan lighthouse. Keep Ploaré church to the right of Ile Tristan for Tréboul or to the left for the anchorage at Rade du Gouet.

By night

Ile Tristan light has a red sector covering Basse Veur and Basse Neuve so keep in the white sector until the inner lights are picked up. For the anchorage at Port de Rosmeur, round the breakwaters a reasonable distance off, keeping a good lookout for the numerous unlit mooring buoys. For the visitors' pontoon in the Grande Passe, or Tréboul Marina, leave Pointe Biron light close to starboard. The sectored light at the head of the basin at Port Rhu leads into the Grande Passe and on to the gate in the barrage.

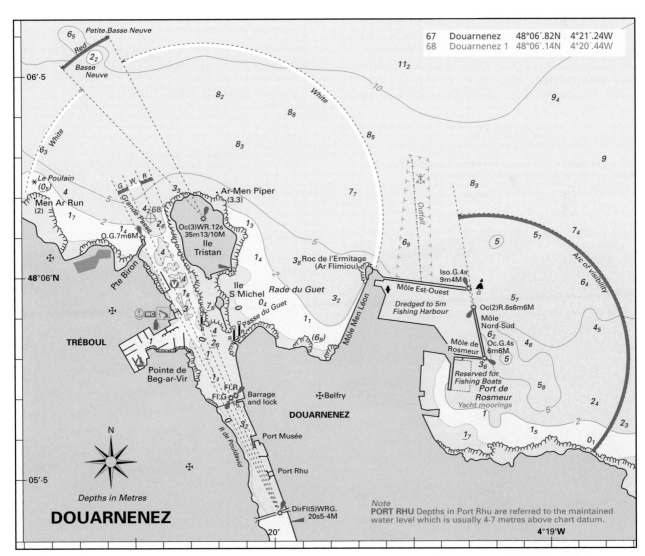

| 67 | Douarnenez | 48°06′.82N | 4°21′.24W |
| 68 | Douarnenez 1 | 48°06′.14N | 4°20′.44W |

Plan 10

BERTHS AND ANCHORAGES

Tréboul

There is a long visitors' pontoon on the W side of the river and a second, smaller, visitors' pontoon with finger berths in the channel just before the turn to starboard into the marina. Tréboul basin is dredged to 1.5m. The marina is crowded and no longer has space allocated for visitors. There is not much room to manoeuvre so call by radio or visit the port office before entering the basin.

The fuelling pontoon is just inside the marina on the starboard side.

Port Rhu

This was once the drying commercial port. In 1992 a barrage was built across the river to create a large wet basin for the Maritime Museum. Additional vessels are housed in the museum building on the E bank. In front of the barrage the bottom dries 3m (mud and sand). There is a visitors' pontoon on the port side immediately after passing through the lock. In summer, Port Rhu is the venue for open-air concerts and similar tourist events.

⚓ Rade du Guet

Sheltered from W through S to SE but exposed to swell from the W, this bay lies between Ile Tristan and the mole leading to Rocher de l'Ermitage. In offshore winds it is a good anchorage, with a convenient dinghy landing at the slip in Passe du Guet. It is quieter than Port de Rosmeur. The depths decrease steadily towards the SW from 3m. Go in as far as draught and tide permit to get as much shelter as possible.

The Passe du Guet, leading from the anchorage to the river, dries 3.5m, the best water is on the S side near the port beacons marking the slip. When the base of the first beacon is just covered there should be 1.5m in the Passe.

Fishing harbour

Visitors may not use this harbour.

⚓ Port de Rosmeur

Protected by the land and the breakwater from all directions except the E, Port de Rosmeur lies to the E of Douarnenez. The NW half of the harbour is for fishing boats and there are many yacht moorings and a fish farm in the remainder of the bay. Anchor in around 5m outside the moorings. There is good holding in mud. Inshore the depths vary irregularly and once the 3m line is crossed they shoal quickly in places.

In settled weather at neaps it is possible to anchor just beyond Port de Rosmeur on the W side of Anse du Ris. This is reasonably sheltered from W through S to E.

⚓ Rocher le Coulinec

Sheltered from the S, there is a fine-weather anchorage off Plage des Sables Blanc about 300m SE of Rocher le Coulinec.

⊕69-Coulinec. (48°06′.32N 4°21′.05W)

10.2 The Maritime Museum in the wet basin at Port Rhu. Many of these floating exhibits can be visited

10.3 The Bureau du Port at Port Rhu is moored just inside the lock gate on the E side of the entrance. The visitors' pontoon is just beyond it, also on the E side of the basin

⚓ Porz Péron

Sheltered from the SW through S to E, this rocky little bay is about 1¼M W of Pointe de Milier. Approach from the N, leaving the 9m rock Karreg Toull to starboard.

⊕71-Porz Péron (48°05′.38N 4°29′.35W)

10.4 Looking NW to Ile Tristan at LW. The Grande Passe entrance is W of the island. The drying Passe du Guet is to the E

ASHORE IN DOUARNENEZ

At Tréboul there is a fuel berth, repair facilities, a 6-tonne crane, launderette, cafés, restaurants and shops. Market day is Wednesday.

Douarnenez has all the usual facilities of a substantial town including a daily covered market. The Maritime Museum is well worth a visit.

11 Ile de Sein

Location
  48°02'N 4°51'W
Shelter
  Fair from S or SW but may be swell
Hazards
  Many marked and unmarked rocks
Depth restrictions
  0.8m beyond Nerroth
  1.8m in anchorage
Night entry
  Lit but not recommended
HW time
  Brest HW
Mean height of tide (m)

	HWS	HWN	LWN	LWS
Ile de Sein	6.2	4.8	2.4	0.9

Tidal streams N approach
  S – Brest HW–5½ to + 3½ (0.6kts)
  Slack – Brest HW+3½ to –5½
Berthing
  Limited room to anchor
Facilities
  Bars and restaurants but very
  limited shopping
Charts
  BA 2819 (50), 2348 (20, 10)
  SHOM 7147 (50), 7423 (20, 10)
  Imray C37 (large scale)
Radio
  Pte du Raz VHF 16

Tiny island surrounded by rocks

Ile de Sein is tiny but well worth a visit. The only town, Port de Sein, is a mass of painted houses and narrow streets. The island itself is so low-lying that the sea has occasionally covered it. There are no trees, or even bushes; just old fields surrounded by dry stone walls. However, the real attraction is the ever-present Atlantic and the huge Breton sky.

PILOTAGE

Warning

A large-scale chart is essential.

The navigation is intricate so slack tide at neaps is best for a first visit. Neap tides have the additional benefit of increasing the available anchoring space. Navigating in the area around Ile de Sein is not as difficult as it appears from the chart. The entrance channels are clearly marked. The tidal streams are not nearly as strong as in the Raz. Also the plateau is compact on the NE and E sides and the fringes are clearly marked.

Identifying Nerroth is the key. It forms the E side of the entrance to the harbour and looks like a flattish, rocky island at low water and three very large flat rocks at high water (see 11.1 and 11.2). Two white masonry beacons on the N and S ends of Nerroth are important day marks.

The north channel

This is the principal channel and the easiest for a stranger.

By GPS

This passage requires careful visual pilotage but ⊕82-N Sein, ⊕83-Vouzerez, ⊕84-Men Brial may provide some assistance.

11.1 Nerroth from the W at low water. The starboard beacon is Guernic

11.2 Nerroth from the SW at high water

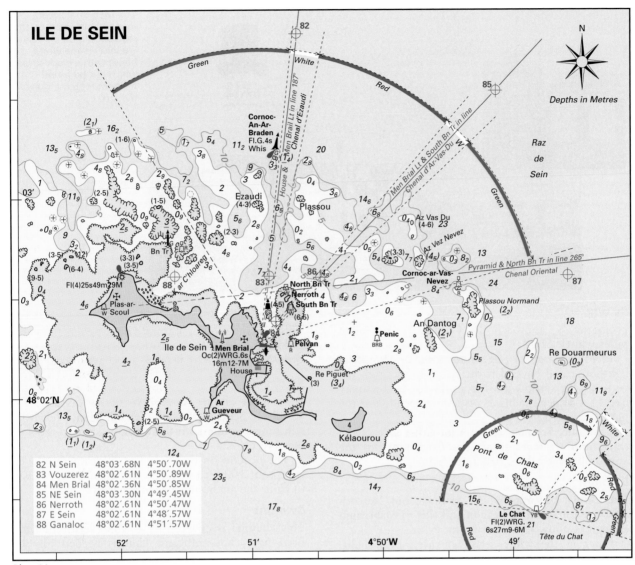

ILE DE SEIN

Plan 11

82	N Sein	48°03´.68N	4°50´.70W
83	Vouzerez	48°02´.61N	4°50´.89W
84	Men Brial	48°02´.36N	4°50´.85W
85	NE Sein	48°03´.30N	4°49´.45W
86	Nerroth	48°02´.61N	4°50´.47W
87	E Sein	48°02´.61N	4°48´.57W
88	Ganaloc	48°02´.61N	4°51´.57W

11.3 Port de Sein looking E.
The rocky island of Nerroth is situated on the left of the picture. The anchorage near Men Brial lighthouse and the lifeboat slip is in the centre. The whole harbour dries near the quays and in the bay on the right. Only the tip of the quay near Men Brial has sufficient water for the ferry at low tide

11.4 Men Brial green-topped lighthouse on the seafront at Port de Sein. The inset is the white house with a black stripe which can be found further along the quay to the left

By day

From the N, approach the Cornoc-An-Ar-Braden pillar whistle SHM.

Identify the green and white tower of Men Brial lighthouse and beyond it the white house with the vertical black stripe, third from the left by the quay (see 11.4). Keep the black stripe just open left of the lighthouse on 187°.

Continue, keeping within 50m either side of the track until Nerroth is abeam. Continue into the anchorage using the instructions below.

By night

There must be enough light to make out Nerroth and Guernic concrete beacon and tide must be high enough to allow some margin for error.

Enter in the white sector of Men Brial light, bearing 187° and leave Cornoc-An-Ar-Braden SHM to starboard. When Nerroth N beacon is abeam follow the instructions below for the entry into the anchorage.

Nerroth to the anchorage

By day

With Nerroth abeam, enter the harbour using Pelvan red concrete beacon in line with the E end of the E breakwater on 155°. At low water the breakwater is obscured so just steer 155° for Pelvan.

After passing Guernic tower SHM, nudge a bit to starboard of the transit to avoid a shoal patch.

When Men Brial lighthouse bears 220° alter course to the SW and aim for the anchorage.

By night

When Nerroth N beacon is abeam, alter course to 160° and enter the red sector of Men Brial, leaving Guernic tower 60m to starboard. When the other white sector of Men Brial is entered it is safe to steer for the anchorage.

The northeast channel

Coming from the E or NE this channel is a easier than the E channel.

By GPS

This passage requires careful visual pilotage but ⊕85-NE Sein, ⊕86-Nerroth, ⊕83-Vouzerez, ⊕84-Men Brial may provide some assistance.

By day

Start from about 300m NW of Ar-Vas-Du rock (⊕85-NE Sein). Approach Nerroth using Men Brial lighthouse in line with the white beacon on the S of Nerroth on 224°.

The beacon on the N end of Nerroth should be left about 100m to port so turn when it bears 265° to enter the anchorage as described above.

By night

This channel is covered by a white sector of Men Brial light, but sufficient light is needed for the deviation round Nerroth and into the harbour.

The east channel

By GPS

This passage requires careful visual pilotage but ⊕87-E Sein, ⊕83-Vouzerez, ⊕84-Men Brial may provide some assistance.

By day

From the Raz de Sein, keep the Cornoc-ar-Vas-Nevez beacon bearing less than 290° to avoid the rocks to the S.

Start from a position 100m N of the beacon. Approach Nerroth using the N end of Nerroth in line with the pyramid tower with a fluorescent top just S of the Ile de Sein main lighthouse on 265° (see 11.5). Carreg ar C'hloareg above-water rock and the a Cross of Lorraine monument are on virtually the same line. This transit must be held closely because Ar Vas Nevez (dries 5.0m) is close to the N of the line and another rock (dries 1.0m) is close to the S.

The beacon on the N end of Nerroth should be left about 100m to port so turn when it bears 265° to enter the anchorage as described above.

ANCHORAGES

⚓ Port de Sein

Sheltered from the S and W but exposed to the E above half tide, the anchorage is immediately off the lifeboat slip, SE of the Men Brial lighthouse. There is 1.8m off the lifeboat slip and 1m further to the SE. The bottom is mud over rock.

The whole harbour dries near the quays and S of them. The fishing fleet enters the harbour in the evening, and is often there by day. Its position indicates the best water. The round red buoys belong to the fishermen and there is not much room to anchor between them and the slip so it may be necessary to anchor E of them. Permission can sometimes be obtained to use a buoy.

Swell enters if the wind goes into the N and the anchorage would be dangerous in strong winds from any northerly direction.

Yachts that can take the ground may use the bay S of the slips and can find 1.5m in places at LW neaps. The bottom is mainly sand but there are some weed-covered stony patches.

⚓ Ile de Sein lighthouse

Sheltered from the S and SW, there is a small bay about 400m ESE of Ile de Sein lighthouse. Approach it from a point just N of Nerroth (⊕83-Vouzerez). Bring the lighthouse onto 270° and hold this course until due S of Roche Ganaloc red beacon tower (⊕88-Ganaloc). Now come round onto 230° and edge in carefully towards the beach as far as draught permits.

⊕88-Ganaloc (48°02′.61N 4°51′.57W)

ASHORE ON ILE DE SEIN

Facilities

Ship and engine repairs can be arranged and chandlery can be obtained from the fishermen's co-op. There are several small shops, bars and restaurants. Water is scarce but bread is delivered from the mainland although it must be ordered the night before.

History

Ile de Sein is an island of heroes. The entire male population left to join the Free French during the Second World War and their exploits are commemorated in an interesting little museum. A large number of the lifeboat men of West Brittany come from Ile de Sein.

11.5 The East Channel approach. Identify the white beacon on the N end of Nerroth (inset top right) and a pyramid tower with a fluorescent top just S of the Ile de Sein main lighthouse (inset top left). Bring these in line on 265°. If the Pyramid is hard to identify, look for the Cross of Lorraine monument which is just S of a large rock, Karreg ar C'hloareg, which never covers

12 Raz de Sein

Location
48°03′N 4°46′W

Hazards
Dangerous tide race; unmarked rocks SW of Tévennec and W of Pte du Van

Night passage Well lit

HW time
Brest HW

Mean height of tide (m)

	HWS	HWN	LWN	LWS
Ile de Sein	6.2	4.8	2.4	0.9

Tidal stream Raz de Sein
S – Brest HW –¼ to +4¼ (5.9kts)
Slack – Brest HW +4¼ to +4¾ (5.7kts)

N – Brest HW +4¾ to –¾
Slack – Brest HW –¾ to –¼

Koummoudog counter current
E – Brest HW–2½ to –½ (1.0kts)
W – Brest HW +½ to +4½ (1.0 kts)

Charts
BA 2819 (50), 2348 (20)
SHOM 7147 (50), 7423 (20)
Imray C36 (77)

Radio
Pte du Raz VHF 16, 70 (DSC)

Rocky SW corner of Brittany

The Raz de Sein is the short passage between the Pointe du Raz on the mainland and the Ile de Sein. It has a justifiably bad reputation but under reasonable conditions, it presents no great difficulties.

12.1 La Vieille and La Plate lighthouses

PILOTAGE

Tidal strategy

Timing is important and when possible, the Raz should be taken at slack water. Even in moderate conditions, with wind and tide, it can be rough. With light winds, neap tides and no swell, it is passable at any time.

The Raz is temperamental and the seas vary considerably but, with strong wind against tide, the overfalls are dangerous.

The Raz de Sein from the N

(See Plan 8)

By GPS

From the Chenal du Four use
⊕55-Vandrée, ⊕80-Raz. This route is safe but

goes slightly outside the area marked by the safe sectors of the lights.
By night
⊕55-Vandrée, ⊕75-E Tévennec, ⊕78-NW Raz, ⊕80-Raz may be preferred.
From the Chenal du Toulinguet use
⊕51-S Toulinguet, ⊕80-Raz.
By night
⊕51-S Toulinguet, ⊕78-NW Raz, ⊕80-Raz remains in the safe sectors of the lights.
From Morgat or Douarnenez use
⊕74-Van, ⊕80-Raz
Or by night ⊕74-Van, ⊕78-NW Raz, ⊕80-Raz.

By day

From the N make for La Vieille lighthouse on 180°, which puts La Vieille midway between Pointe du Van and Tévennec.

When ½M off La Vieille, bear to starboard to pass W of La Plate yellow and black tower WCM. There may be overfalls W of La Plate but the sea will moderate once it is passed.

Going S keep Pointe du Van in transit with Gorle Greiz, (the large rock between Pointe du Raz and La Vieille), bearing 041°. This leads between Kornog Bras and Masklou Greiz which can be rough in bad weather.

Going SE towards Penmarc'h, steer with Tévennec bearing 324° astern, open to the left of La Plate.

By night

Make good 180° in the white sector of Tévennec. When Le Chat turns from green to white, steer 115° until the directional flashing light on Tévennec opens. Then steer 150° past La Vieille and Le Chat.

Going S use the white sector of La Vieille, on 205°.

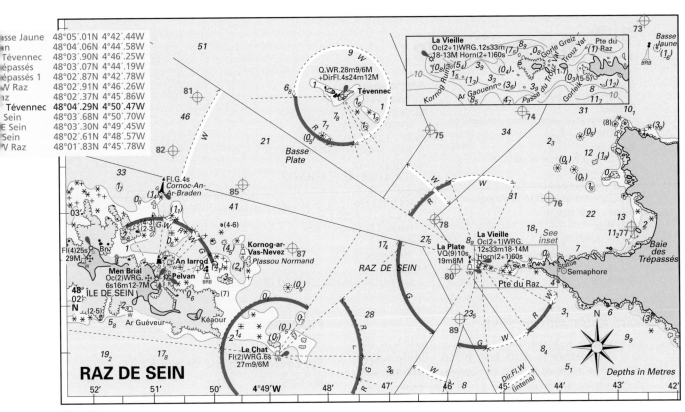

Plan 12

Going SE towards Penmarc'h use the directional sector of Tévennec until clear. The southern dangers are clear as soon as Le Chat turns from green to red, bearing 286°.

The Raz de Sein from the NW

By GPS
Use ⊕81-W Tévennec, ⊕80-Raz. Basse Plat is ½M N of this track.

By day
Avoid the dangers of Basse Plate, ½M to the SW of Tévennec by keeping La Vieille in transit with the southern limit of the cliffs SE of the Pointe du Raz, on 112°. When ½M off La Vieille alter course to leave La Plate to port.

By night
Make good 190° in the white sector of Men Brial light on Ile de Sein. When La Vieille turns from red to white, steer 120° until the directional isophase light on Tévennec opens. Then proceed as from the N.

The Raz de Sein from the S

By GPS
From Audierne use ⊕90-Koummoudog, ⊕80-Raz.

From the Pointe de Penmarc'h use ⊕103-Eckmühl, ⊕80-Raz.

From the SW use ⊕89-SW Raz, ⊕80-Raz to ensure an approach in the white sector of La Vieille. There is rough water in 3.6 and 8m about ½M S of ⊕89-SW Raz.

At night, these are cleared using the white sector of La Vieille.

By day
From the S or SW keep the steep island of Tévennec open to the W of La Plate on a bearing of 327°. Pass La Plate leaving it ½M to starboard.

Going N keep the back-bearing on La Vieille between 160° and 200° to clear the dangers off Pte du Van and Tévennec.

Going NW make 295° from La Plate keeping in the middle of the channel between Tévennec and Ile de Sein.

By night
Keep in the directional Fl.4s sector of Tévennec light until it bears 330° and La Plate bears 110°. A track of 020° will then lead N clear of the Raz. A track of 295° leads NW between Tévennec and Ile de Sein.

ANCHORAGE

⚓ Baie des Trépassés
Sheltered between NE and SE but exposed to swell from the W, there is a fair-weather anchorage in the Baie des Trépassés, ENE of the Pointe de Raz. To avoid the dangers SW of Pointe du Van, approach from due W. The bay is sandy and shelving so anchor in the most suitable depth. The best position is either in the centre, facing the valley or in the NE corner about 200m SE of Gravendeileg. Expect some swell.

⊕77-Trépassés 1 (48°02′.87N 4°42′.78W)

13 Sainte Evette

Location
48°00′N 4°33′W

Shelter
Reasonable except from strong E or SE wind

Hazards
Marked wreck and rocks in approach

Depth restrictions
2.2m in approach to moorings

Night entry Well lit

HW time
Brest HW −½

Mean height of tide (m)

	HWS	HWN	LWN	LWS
Audierne	5.2	4.1	2.0	0.8

Tidal streams
Weak in the bay

Berthing
Visitors' buoys

Fuel
Base of Ste Evette slip (cans)

Facilities
Good facilities in Audierne

Charts
BA 2819 (50,12.5), 3640 (24)
SHOM 7147 (50,12.5)
Imray C37 (large scale)

Radio
Ste Evette VHF 9

Telephone
Ste Evette HM *t* 02 98 70 00 28

Beach resort with moorings

Ste Evette is a small holiday resort situated in the outer approaches to Audierne. It has all-tide access and a large number of visitors' buoys. These are well sheltered, except from the E and S. The buoys are a little too close for comfort and often crowded but they provide a convenient overnight stop. There is some room to anchor.

Ste Evette has few facilities but it is a pleasant walk along the river bank to Audierne.

PILOTAGE

(See Plan 14)

Ste Evette from the W and S

By GPS

From the Raz de Sein use
⊕80-Raz, ⊕90-Koummoudog,
⊕94-W Gamelle, ⊕95-St Evette.

La Gamelle shallow patch (dries 0.8m) is about ¼M E of the track a little N of ⊕94-W Gamelle (see plan 14).

From the SW or S
⊕94-W Gamelle or ⊕98-E Gamelle can be approached directly. The continuation from ⊕94-W Gamelle is described above. The continuation from ⊕98-E Gamelle is described below in approaches from the SE.

13.1 The moorings at Ste Evette looking NE. The long breakwater protects the bay from the SW but not from strong winds from the E or S. There are two slipways just N of the breakwater. One is for the lifeboats while the more northerly of the two is marked by an inconspicuous E Cardinal at its end (see inset)

13.2 The moorings at Ste Evette

By day

From the Raz de Sein, the entrance to Sainte Evette is ½M W of Gamelle West whistle buoy WCM (⊕94-W Gamelle).

Identify two white, red-topped lighthouses to the N of the bay. Kergadec is on the skyline and is easy to spot. Below it, the old lighthouse of Trescadec is less easy to locate. Look for it in a gap between the houses. Line up the two lighthouses on 006°.

There are rocky patches either side of the channel, one at Le Sillon on the W of the harbour and the other is La Gamelle to the E of the channel. If there is a swell the seas break on La Gamelle. At low water, also note the shoal patch depth 2.2m on the leading line E of Ste Evette.

For Ste Evette moorings, leave the leading line and steer for the mole head when it bears 315°. Take care to avoid the rocks on the N edge of the mole.

By night

Enter the narrow white sector of Kergadec quick flashing light (006°). When the light on the Ste Evette mole head bears NW alter course for the Ste Evette anchorage.

Ste Evette from the SE

By GPS

From the Pointe de Penmarc'h use ⊕103-Eckmühl, ⊕98-E Gamelle, ⊕97-NE Gamelle, ⊕95-St Evette.

There is a wreck (dries 1.5m) on the E side of La Gamelle shallow patch about 400m W of the track between ⊕98-E Gamelle and ⊕97-NE Gamelle.

By day

From the SE the channel between La Gamelle to the W and the land to the E is wide and the least depth on the leading line is 2.5m. Gamelle East bell buoy should be left well to port.

The transit is Kergadec lighthouse, white with a red top on the skyline, with the Raoulic Jetty light tower on 331°. When Ste Evette breakwater head bears 293° it is safe to steer for the moorings.

By night

Approach with Raoulic light and Kergadec light in line on 331°. Pte de Lervily light has a red sector covering La Gamelle. When this light turns from red to white, it is safe to steer for Ste Evette.

BERTHS AND ANCHORAGES

Ste Evette moorings and anchorage

The Ste Evette anchorage is sheltered from W and N by the land and from the S by the breakwater. Some swell enters if there is S in the wind and this may be considerable if the wind is strong. The depths are 2.5m or more north of the end of the mole, decreasing steadily towards the shore. The moorings are tightly packed and not suitable for boats over 10m. A charge is collected for their use.

There may be room to anchor E of the moorings, with less shelter from the S. The holding is not very good and there are a few rocky patches. It is best to tuck in behind the breakwater as far as depth allows to get out of the swell.

The bay contains two hazards. First, the more northerly of the two slips extends a long way and has an inconspicuous ECM at its end (see 13.1). Second, there is a rock ledge, La Petite Gamelle marked by a beacon SCM, in the northern part of the anchorage. The bay is shallow N of the beacon.

⚓ Anse du Loc'h

Sheltered from all directions except SE to SW, this sandy bay is 3M W of Pointe de Lervily. Enter it on 030° to avoid the rocks on the E side.

⊕92-Anse du Loc'h (48°01′.44N 4°38′.29W)

⚓ Anse du Cabestan

Sheltered from N through E, this wide sandy bay is 3M W of Audierne. Approach from the SW to avoid two rocks. Basse du Loc'h (dries 1.9m) between Anse du Loc'hg and Anse du Cabestan and Roche de Porz-Tarz at the NW end of Anse du Cabestan.

⊕93-Cabestan (48°00′.56N 4°35′.91W)

⚓ Pors-Poulhan

Protected from the NE, this tiny harbour is 3M SE of Audierne. The harbour itself is very small and dries but there is an outside anchorage that can be used in settled weather.

⊕99-Pors-Poulhan (47°59′.00N 4°27′.80W)

ASHORE IN STE EVETTE

Facilities

Land at the ferry slip, at either Raoulic jetty or the little pier in the NW corner of the bay. Both the latter dry at LW. Fuel is available in cans close to the pier and there is a launderette and a few shops at the ferry pier. Audierne has all facilities and is only about a mile away.

A ferry goes to Ile de Sein from Ste Evette. The tourist ferry, Biniou II, takes a rock-hopping route and is to be recommended.

14 Audierne

Location
48°01'N 4°32'W
Shelter
Good in marina
Hazards
Audierne channel in strong S wind
Marked wreck and rocks in approach
Depth restrictions
Audierne channel dredged 1m
Marina 2m on pontoons D–G
Night entry
Lit but not recommended
HW time
Brest HW–½
Mean height of tide (m)

	HWS	HWN	LWN	LWS
Audierne	5.2	4.1	2.0	0.8

Tidal streams
Weak in the bay but strong in the river and marina
Berthing
Marina
Facilities
Some repair facilities, good shops and restaurants
Charts
BA 2819 (50,12.5), 3640 (24)
SHOM 7147 (50,12.5)
Imray C37 (large scale)
Radio
Audierne Marina VHF 09, 16
Telephone
Audierne Marina t 02 98 75 04 93

Attractive fishing port with marina

Audierne is an attractive port. It is 1M inland, accessed by a dredged channel (depth 1m). The small marina was extended in 2001 and has some space for visitors on the hammerheads.

PILOTAGE

Warning

The mouth of the Audierne channel is dangerous in strong S winds.

Audierne from W or S

By GPS

From the Raz de Sein use ⊕80-Raz, ⊕90-Koummoudog, ⊕94-W Gamelle, ⊕96-Audierne.
La Gamelle is about ¼M E of the track a little N of ⊕94-W Gamelle.
From the SW or S, ⊕94-W Gamelle or ⊕98-E Gamelle can be approached directly.

By day

From the Raz de Sein, arrive at a point about ½M W of Gamelle West whistle buoy WCM (⊕94-W Gamelle).

Line up Kergadec and Trescadec red-topped lighthouses on 006° to avoid the rocky patches either side of the channel. Deep draught vessels should also note the shoal patch of 2.2m on the leading line E of Ste Evette.

Continue on 006° until the end of Raoulic Jetty bears 034°. Then bring St Julien Church (on a grassy knoll on the E of the river) in line with the end of Raoulic Jetty bearing 034°.

Pilotage from the end of the jetty is given below.

By night

Partially lit but not recommended.

Audierne from SE

By GPS

From the Pointe de Penmarc'h use ⊕103-Eckmühl, ⊕98-E Gamelle, ⊕96-Audierne.

There is a wreck (dries 1.5m) on the E side of La Gamelle shallow patch 2 cables W of the track between ⊕98-E Gamelle and ⊕96-Audierne.

By day

Leave Gamelle East buoy well to port and come in using Kergadec red-topped lighthouse in line with the Raoulic Jetty light tower on 331°.

By night

Partially lit but not recommended.

The dredged channel to Audierne

By day

The channel is dredged 1m but at low water there is not much room for error so it is best to make a first visit above half tide.

There are two leading lines marked with pairs of red and white chevron boards and they are not easy to see. The first is on the Raoulic Jetty on 359°. The second is on 043° alongside a white patch on the fish market. This lines up with a grey cottage on the hill behind on the same bearing (see 14.2 and 14.3).

At the fish market the channel turns through 090° and runs along the quays to the marina.

By night

Partially lit but not recommended.

BERTHS AND ANCHORAGE

Audierne marina

The marina has been extended recently and there is now some space for visitors on the hammerheads. Pontoons A–C have been dredged 2m on the

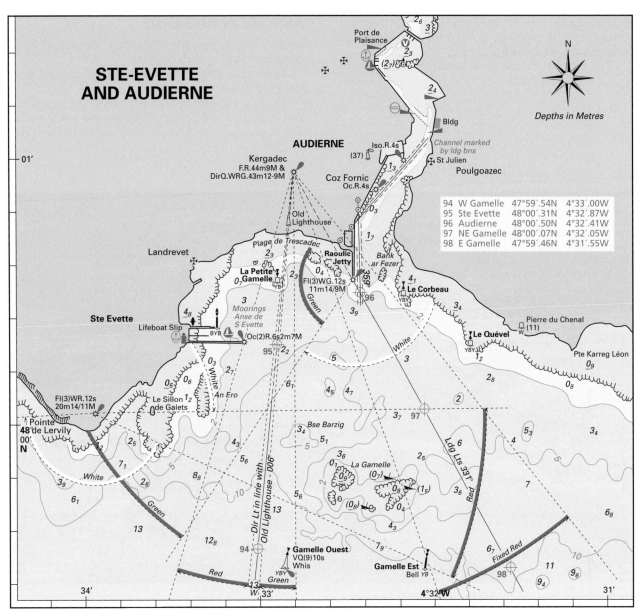

STE-EVETTE AND AUDIERNE

AUDIERNE

Kergadec
F.R.44m9M &
DirQ.WRG.43m12-9M

Port de Plaisance

Coz Fornic
Oc.R.4s

Iso.R.4s

Channel marked by ldg bns

Bldg

St Julien

Poulgoazec

Depths in Metres

94	W Gamelle	47°59′.54N	4°33′.00W
95	Ste Evette	48°00′.31N	4°32′.87W
96	Audierne	48°00′.50N	4°32′.41W
97	NE Gamelle	48°00′.07N	4°32′.05W
98	E Gamelle	47°59′.46N	4°31′.55W

Old Lighthouse

Plage de Trescadec

Landrevet

Raoulic Jetty

Bank ar Fezer

La Petite Gamelle

Fl(3)WG.12s 11m14/9M

Le Corbeau

Pierre du Chenal (11)

Ste Evette

Lifeboat Slip

Moorings Anse de S Evette

Le Quével

Pte Karreg Léon

(Oc(2)R.6s2m7M

Fl(3)WR.12s 20m14/11M

Le Sillon de Galets

An Ero

Pointe de Lervily

Bse Barzig

La Gamelle

Ldg Lts 331°

Dir Lt in line with Old Lighthouse - 006°

Gamelle Ouest
VQ(9)10s
Whis

Gamelle Est
Bell

Fixed Red

Plan 14

14.1 Raoulic Jetty light in line with the red top of Kergadec lighthouse

14.2 Raoulic Jetty transit

14.3 The fish market transit

hammerheads, D–G are reported to have 2m throughout. If possible, avoid F & G because the tide sets across them.

The channel to the new berths is marked with green starboard posts.

ASHORE IN AUDIERNE

Audierne is a pleasant town that has successfully combined fishing with tourism.

There is a shipyard as well as mechanical and electrical engineers.

The main shopping area is close to the pontoons and there is a wide range of shops and restaurants. The supermarket is a short walk upstream past the bridge.

14.4 The river to Audierne with the deeper water showing clearly in the channel. At the fish market on the right-hand side of the picture, the channel turns through 90° and continues past the quays to the marina

14.5 The marina and the waterfront shops at Audierne

II. Bénodet Bay

Les Perdrix, Loctudy

Ville Close, Concarneau

Ile Tudy

River Odet

Le Guilvinec

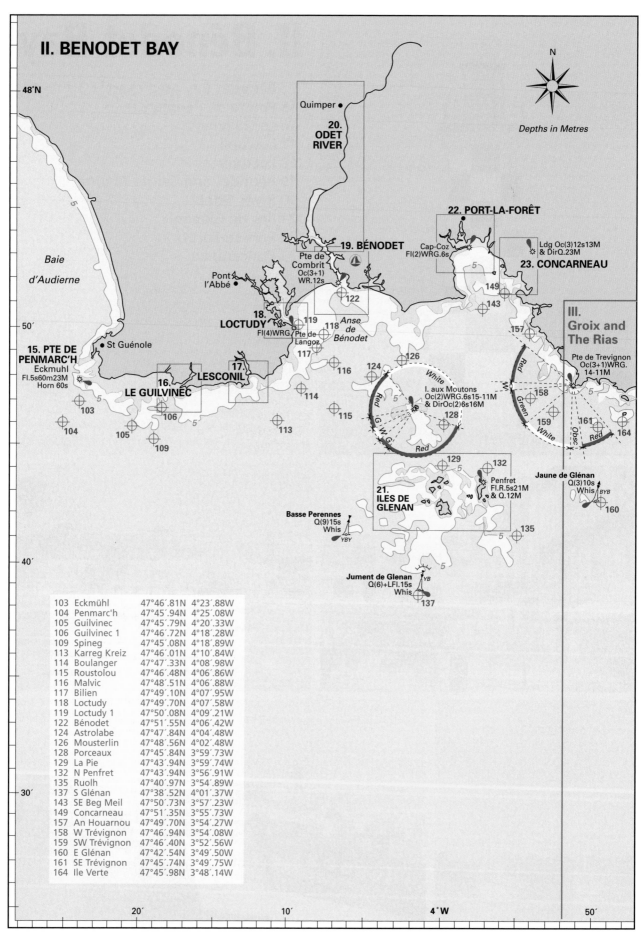

II. BENODET BAY

48°N

Baie
d'Audierne

Quimper •

**20.
ODET
RIVER**

N

Depths in Metres

22. PORT-LA-FORÊT

19. BÉNODET

Pte de
Combrit
Oc(3+1)
WR.12s

Cap-Coz
Fl(2)WRG.6s

Ldg Oc(3)12s13M
& DirQ.23M

23. CONCARNEAU

149

143

Pont
l'Abbé •

122

**III.
Groix and
The Rias**

50'

**18.
LOCTUDY**
Fl(4)WRG

119

Pte de
Langoz

118

*Anse
de
Bénodet*

157

Pte de Trevignon
Oc(3+1)WRG.
14-11M

117

• St Guénole

**15. PTE DE
PENMARC'H**
Eckmuhl
Fl.5s60m23M
Horn 60s

126

124

White

I. aux Moutons
Oc(2)WRG.6s15-11M
& DirOc(2)6s16M

158

**16.
LE GUILVINEC**

**17.
LESCONIL**

116

Red

G W G

5

128

W

Green

White

159

Obsc

161

Red

164

103

106

5

114

115

G
W G

Red

129

132

Penfret
Fl.R.5s21M
& Q.12M

Jaune de Glénan
Q(3)10s
Whis

BYB

104

105

109

113

**21.
ILES DE
GLENAN**

5

160

135

Basse Perennes
Q(9)15s
Whis

YBY

5

40'

Jument de Glenan
Q(6)+LFl.15s
Whis

YB

137

103	Eckmühl	47°46'.81N	4°23'.88W
104	Penmarc'h	47°45'.94N	4°25'.08W
105	Guilvinec	47°45'.79N	4°20'.33W
106	Guilvinec 1	47°46'.72N	4°18'.28W
109	Spineg	47°45'.08N	4°18'.89W
113	Karreg Kreiz	47°46'.01N	4°10'.84W
114	Boulanger	47°47'.33N	4°08'.98W
115	Roustolou	47°46'.48N	4°06'.86W
116	Malvic	47°48'.51N	4°06'.88W
117	Bilien	47°49'.10N	4°07'.95W
118	Loctudy	47°49'.70N	4°07'.58W
119	Loctudy 1	47°50'.08N	4°09'.21W
122	Bénodet	47°51'.55N	4°06'.42W
124	Astrolabe	47°47'.84N	4°04'.48W
126	Mousterlin	47°48'.56N	4°02'.48W
128	Porceaux	47°45'.84N	3°59'.73W
129	La Pie	47°43'.94N	3°59'.74W
132	N Penfret	47°43'.94N	3°56'.91W
135	Ruolh	47°40'.97N	3°54'.89W
137	S Glénan	47°38'.52N	4°01'.37W
143	SE Beg Meil	47°50'.73N	3°57'.23W
149	Concarneau	47°51'.35N	3°55'.73W
157	An Houarnou	47°49'.70N	3°54'.27W
158	W Trévignon	47°46'.94N	3°54'.08W
159	SW Trévignon	47°46'.40N	3°52'.56W
160	E Glénan	47°42'.54N	3°49'.50W
161	SE Trévignon	47°45'.74N	3°49'.75W
164	Ile Verte	47°45'.98N	3°48'.14W

30'

20'   10'   4° W   50'

Chart II

15 Pointe de Penmarc'h

Location
47°48′N 4°23′W

Hazards
Well marked rocks
Complex tidal streams that are much affected by the wind

Night passage Well lit

HW time
Brest HW– ¼ neaps, –½ springs

Mean height of tide (m)

	HWS	HWN	LWN	LWS
Guilvinec	5.1	4.0	2.0	0.9

Tidal streams Pte de Penmarc'h
SE – Brest HW–2½ to +2½ (1.0kts)
NW – Brest HW+2½ to –2½ (1.0kts)

St Guenole
St Guenole is a commercial fishing port that does not welcome yachtsmen. Entry is hazardous except in very good conditions

Charts
BA 2819 (50), 2820 (50)
SHOM 7147 (50), 7146 (50)
Imray C37 (77)

Gateway to the Sun

Eckmühl lighthouse marks the start of S Brittany so passing it eastbound is always a pleasure. In good weather at sunrise or sunset it is a magical place.

The Pointe de Penmarc'h is a low headland with a very high octagonal lighthouse (Eckmühl). Reefs extend, in all directions from the headland. These are well marked and, in good weather, it is possible to round close, using the various beacon towers. In poor weather or on passage S it is better to stay a few miles offshore.

PILOTAGE

Rounding Penmarc'h

By GPS

For Loctudy or Bénodet use
⊕103-Eckmühl, ⊕109-Spineg, ⊕113-Karreg Kreiz, ⊕115-Roustolou, ⊕116-Malvic. This route can be used at all states of the tide but it passes close to a number of well marked dangers so care is required.
⊕116-Malvic lies directly between two unlit buoys, which is a bit scary at night. The shortcut ⊕113-Karreg Kreiz, ⊕114-Boulanger, ⊕117-Bilien has a least depth of 2.2m but keeps well away from unlit buoys.
For Port-La-Forêt or Concarneau, use
⊕103-Eckmühl, ⊕109-Spineg,
⊕113-Karreg Kreiz, ⊕115-Roustolou,
⊕124-Astrolabe. The last leg has a least depth of 2.3m and passes between two unlit beacon towers.
For the SE use
⊕104-Penmarc'h, ⊕137-S Glénan. In good weather, ⊕103-Eckmühl can be substituted for ⊕104-Penmarc'h. This shortcut passes close S of Men-Hir and Spineg; both are lit.

By day

Give Men-Hir a good berth as the reef on which it stands extends over 200m to the W. Otherwise there are no hazards outside the lines joining the buoys.

15.1 Eckmühl Lighthouse was built in 1892 and has a range of 33.5 miles. From its gallery it is possible to see from the Raz de Sein in the W to the Iles de Glénan in the E. Alongside are the old lighthouse, a small chapel and the signal station

However, there is often a heavy swell in the vicinity of Pointe de Penmarc'h and in these circumstances, or in poor visibility, it is safest to stay at least 3M off shore.

By night

Use the white sector of Men-Hir to keep clear of the rocks off the Pointe of Penmarc'h. After that, the principal buoys are lit although care should be taken to keep well S of the unlit Ar Guisty S of Guilvinec.

16 Le Guilvinec

Location
47°48'N 4°17'W

Shelter Good

Hazards
1.8m shallow patch on leading line

Depth restrictions
3m in harbour

Night entry Well lit

Other restrictions
Total priority to fishing vessels
No entry or exit 1600–1830

HW time
Brest HW–¼ neaps, –½ springs

Mean height of tide (m)

	HWS	HWN	LWN	LWS
Guilvinec	5.1	4.0	2.0	0.9

Berthing
Two small visitors' pontoons and visitors' buoys

Facilities
As of a busy fishing port

Charts
BA 2820 (50), 3640 (15)
SHOM 7146 (50), 6646 (15)
Imray C37 (large scale)

Radio
Harbourmaster VHF 12

Telephone
Harbourmaster t 02 98 58 05 67
Tourist Office t 02 98 58 29 29

Colourful fishing port

Le Guilvinec is a commercial fishing port 4M E of Penmarc'h. The harbour is sheltered and the entrance is straightforward, providing care is taken to avoid outlying rocks. Le Guilvinec has recently made an effort to be more welcoming to visitors. There is not much room but there are two small visitors' pontoons and some visitors' buoys.

PILOTAGE

Guilvinec main channel

By GPS

From the W use
⊕103-Eckmühl, ⊕105-Guilvinec,
⊕106-Guilvinec 1, ⊕107-Guilvinec 2,
⊕108-Guilvinec 3. There is a 1.8m shallow patch on the leading line, which ⊕106-Guilvinec 1 avoids. With enough rise of tide, this waypoint can be omitted.
From the E use
⊕109-Spineg, ⊕105-Guilvinec.

By day

From the W keep well clear of Les Etocs above-water and drying rocks and make for Névez SHM, 900m S of Raguen tower.

Le Guilvinec is difficult to see among all the white houses with grey roofs. Look for the long white fish market, a red-topped lighthouse on the north mole and the massive blue travel-lift. The conspicuous leading marks, two large red cylinders on orange-red columns, will be in transit (053°).

The leading line crosses a 1.8m shallow patch, Basse aux Herbes. Near low water, especially in rough weather, it is best to move 150m to starboard when the Penmarc'h light tower is in line with Locarec tower (292°).

Follow the leading line and pass Men Du port beacon, Capelan SHM, Rousse ar Men Du port beacon and Le Groaik starboard tower.

Enter the harbour between the outer S mole and the N mole head and spur.

16.1 The harbour at Le Guilvinec looking NE. The visitors' pontoons are at the far end, one to starboard and one to port

From the E leave Basse Spinec SCM to starboard to make for the Névez SHM and enter as above.

By night

The synchronised leading lights are easy to identify. If entering at low water, avoid Basse aux Herbes by keeping 150m to starboard of the leading lights when in the red sector of Locarec light 1½M to the WNW. If the unlit beacon towers and Capelan SHM cannot be seen, stay on the leading line until the S mole light bears 030° distant 200m; it will then be safe to turn to port and head for the harbour entrance.

Guilvinec S channel

By GPS

From the W use
⊕109-Spineg, ⊕110-S Guilvinec,
⊕107-Guilvinec 2, ⊕108-Guilvinec 3.

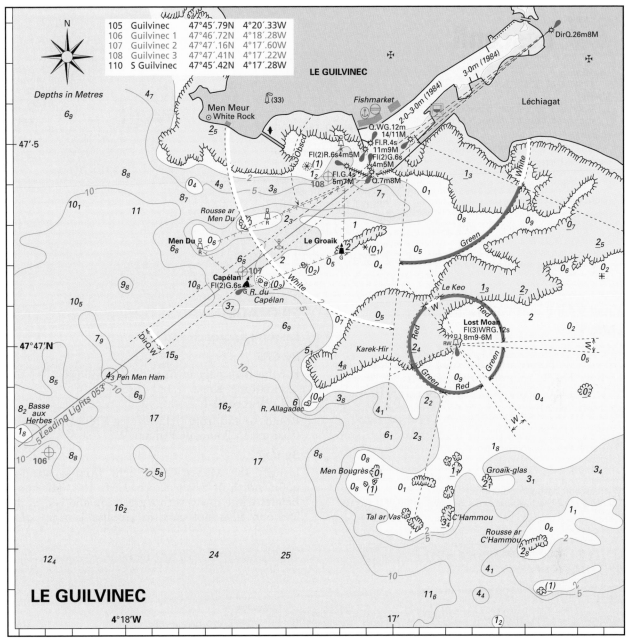

105	Guilvinec	47°45´.79N	4°20´.33W
106	Guilvinec 1	47°46´.72N	4°18´.28W
107	Guilvinec 2	47°47´.16N	4°17´.60W
108	Guilvinec 3	47°47´.41N	4°17´.22W
110	S Guilvinec	47°45´.42N	4°17´.28W

LE GUILVINEC

4°18´W

Plan 16

From the E use
⊕113-Karreg Kreiz, ⊕110-S Guilvinec.

By day

This route should only be used if the marks can be identified with certainty. Start near ⊕110-S Guilvinec, between Ar Guisty S cardinal tower and Spinec SCM. Les Fourches rocks 800m NE of this position never cover. Identify the Men Meur white-painted rock, at the W end of the Guilvinec waterfront, and bring it into transit with a slender pyramid with large diamond topmark a mile further inland, bearing 352°. Follow this transit for 1¾M to the Capelan SHM and enter as above.

By night

Not recommended.

BERTHS AND ANCHORAGES

Le Guilvinec harbour

Le Guilvinec is very busy and visitors must not secure to a quay or a fishing boat except in an emergency.

Yachting facilities have been improved and there is a small visitors' pontoon in the NE corner of the harbour and another on the SE side. There are also a few visitors' moorings close to the SE pontoon.

ASHORE IN LE GUILVINEC

The harbour is packed with brightly painted fishing boats and busy with fishing activity. The main part of town is on the N side of harbour. There are all the normal facilities and many seafood restaurants. Market day is Tuesday.

17 Lesconil

Location
47°47'N 4°12'W

Shelter
Good in harbour; anchorage sheltered from W through N to E

Hazards
Do not enter in strong S wind

Depth restrictions
2.6m in approach
1.5m in harbour entrance

Night entry Well lit

Other restrictions
Yachts not welcome in harbour
No entry or exit 1630–1830

HW time
Brest HW+¼ neaps, +½ springs

Mean height of tide (m)

	HWS	HWN	LWN	LWS
Lesconil	5.0	4.0	2.0	0.9

Berthing
Anchorage outside harbour

Facilities
As of a busy fishing port

Charts
BA 2820 (50), 3640 (15)
SHOM 7146 (50), 6646 (15)
Imray C37 (large scale)

Radio
Harbourmaster VHF 12

Telephone
Harbourmaster *t* 02 98 82 22 97

Small fishing port with restricted access for visitors

Lesconil is an attractive fishing port that is less crowded and more attractive than Le Guilvinec. The harbour has no room for visiting boats but there is an anchorage outside. Access is easy except in strong southerly winds.

17.1 Lesconil harbour looking E.
The W side of the harbour with the rows of small boats is drying

PILOTAGE

Lesconil approach and entrance

By GPS

For the anchorage in Anse de Lesconil use
⊕113-Kareg Kreiz, ⊕111-Lesconil,
⊕112-Lesconil 1.

Routes to and from ⊕113-Kareg Kreiz are given in Chapter 15 Pointe de Penmarc'h.

By day

Identify the Men-ar-Groas light from a position 600m north of Kareg Kreiz ECM. The light has a slender white tower with a green top and is E of the harbour. It is not easy to see but is right of a

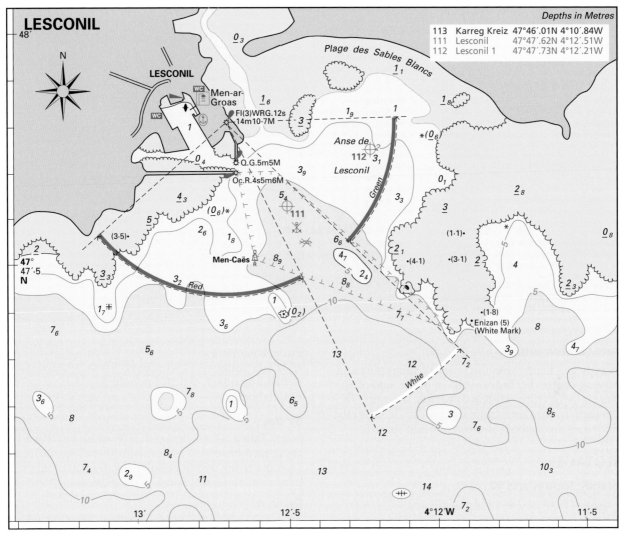

Plan 17

conspicuous white gable end with a large diamond shaped window and left of a long grey roof. The belfry of Lesconil church will be just open to the left when the light bears 325°.

Follow 325° passing the white mark on Enizan 400m to starboard and Men-Caës red beacon tower to port. Turn to port to enter the harbour between the breakwater lights.

Within the harbour red and green unlit buoys mark the deep water.

By night

From Kareg Kreiz ECM buoy steer 325° for Men-ar-Groas remaining in the white sector.

BERTHS AND ANCHORAGES

Lesconil harbour

Except in an emergency, visitors are not permitted to enter or leave between 1630 and 1830, when the fishing fleet returns. Neither may they lie alongside the quays. If obliged to do so, they should consult the harbourmaster to be allocated a berth. A boat that can take the ground may find room to anchor in the western part of the harbour.

⚓ Anse de Lesconil

Sheltered from the W through N to NE, there is a fair weather anchorage in the Anse de Lesconil immediately to the E of the harbour entrance. Enter from the SE to avoid the extensive rocks on the E side of the bay.

⊕112-Lesconil 1 (47°47′.73N 4°12′.21W)

ASHORE IN LESCONIL

Water can be obtained from the fish market, or standpipes on the quays. Fuel is available in cans. There is a launderette, a few modest shops and some bars.

18 Loctudy

Location
47°50'N 4°10'W

Shelter
Excellent except in strong ESE

Hazards
Bar and unmarked shallow patches
Strong tide in harbour

Depth restrictions
0.9m in the approach; 1.5m in marina

Night entry Partially lit

HW time
Brest HW–¼ neaps, –½springs

Mean height of tide (m)

	HWS	HWN	LWN	LWS
Loctudy	5.0	3.9	1.9	0.8

Tidal stream Loctudy entrance
Flood – Brest HW –5 to –2½ (3.0kts)
Slack – Brest HW –2½ to +2½

Ebb – Brest HW +2½ to +4½ (3.0kts)
Slack – Brest HW +4½ to –5

Berthing
Marina, visitors' buoys and anchorages

Fuel
Marina wave breaker

Facilities
All facilities

Charts
BA 2820 (50), 3641 (20)
SHOM 7146 (50), 6649 (15)
Imray C37 (large scale)

Radio
Harbourmaster VHF 9, 12

Telephone
Marina t 02 98 87 51 36

Pretty Breton estuary

Loctudy is a happy combination of fishing port and yachting centre. Ile Tudy on the opposite side of the river is a picture postcard Breton village. The approach is sheltered from the prevailing westerly winds and the harbour is attractive and secure.

PILOTAGE

Loctudy from N and W

By GPS

From Penmarc'h follow the route to ⊕116-Malvic or ⊕117-Bilien as described in Chapter 15 Pointe de Penmarc'h. Then use ⊕118-Loctudy, ⊕119-Loctudy 1, ⊕120-Loctudy 2, ⊕121-Loctudy 3. It is possible to omit ⊕118-Loctudy at high water.

From Bénodet use
⊕122-Bénodet, ⊕118-Loctudy,
⊕119-Loctudy 1, ⊕120-Loctudy 2,
⊕121-Loctudy 3.

By day

From Bilien ECM proceed NW until Les Perdrix chequered beacon is in line with the white Château Durumain on 289°. Follow this transit along the buoyed channel to approach the marina.

By night

From Bilien buoy ECM. Steer NW to enter the white sector of Langoz. Follow this until Karek-Saoz PHM beacon and Karek Croisic PHM buoy are identified. Leave these to port and then enter the river leaving the two green SHM buoys to starboard. The

18.1 Loctudy fishing harbour and marina looking NW.
The inset is the distinctive Les Perdrix beacon. Ile Tudy just comes into the picture on the right. From the marina there is a regular ferry that goes to Ile Tudy and the beach

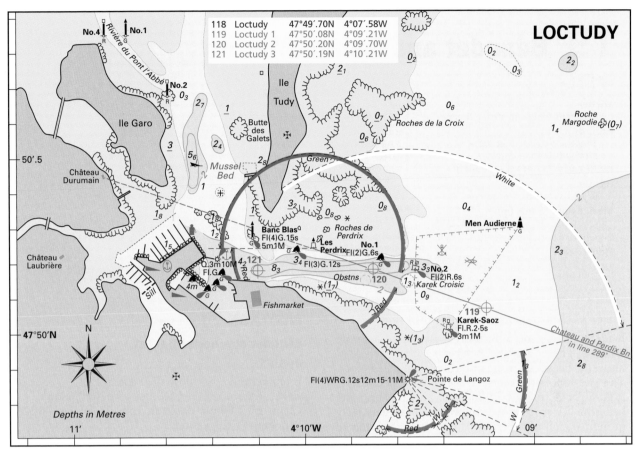

118	Loctudy	47°49´.70N	4°07´.58W
119	Loctudy 1	47°50´.08N	4°09´.21W
120	Loctudy 2	47°50´.20N	4°09´.70W
121	Loctudy 3	47°50´.19N	4°10´.21W

Plan 18

approach to the marina is not lit but there are three lit green buoys which lead into the fishing harbour. Note that Les Perdrix is no longer lit.

Loctudy from E

By GPS

From the Baie de la Forêt use
⊕126-Mousterlin, ⊕118-Loctudy,
⊕119-Loctudy 1, ⊕120-Loctudy 2,
⊕121-Loctudy 3.

From the SE use
⊕160-E Glénan, ⊕118-Loctudy,
⊕119-Loctudy 1, ⊕120-Loctudy 2,
⊕121-Loctudy 3.

By day

From the E and SE leave Ile aux Moutons to port and steer NW, leaving Les Poulains beacon and Men Dehou tower to port. To avoid the rock (depth 2.1m) NW of Men Dehou, keep Ile aux Moutons lighthouse midway between Les Poulains and Men Dehou. Continue to Bilien ECM and enter Loctudy as from the N and W.

By night

Leave Ile aux Moutons light to port and steer N to get into the white sector of Pointe de Langoz light. Stay in the white sector until Bilien ECM is abeam to port. Then proceed as above.

Rivière de Pont l'Abbé

The channel is reported to have silted and a visit to Pont l'Abbé is best made by dinghy.

BERTHS AND ANCHORAGES

Loctudy Marina

Visitors should berth on pontoon A, with larger boats using the inside of the wave breaker. There are some white visitors' buoys NE of the marina. The marina is well managed, modern and has all facilities. It would be a good place to leave a boat.

⚓ Ile Chevalier

Sheltered from all directions, there is a useful neap tide anchorage at the SE end of Ile Chevalier (north of Rivière du Port l'Abbé).

⚓ Ile Tudy

It may be possible to find space to anchor beyond the moorings W of Ile Tudy.

ASHORE IN LOCTUDY

Loctudy has a full range of shops, bars and restaurants plus a good vegetable market on Tuesdays and excellent fish shops at the fishing port.

Ile Tudy is a pretty holiday village. It has only basic facilities but it does have a magnificent beach and good walking.

19 Bénodet and Sainte Marine

Location
47°53′N 4°07′W

Shelter
Excellent except in strong S wind

Hazards
Shallow patches in approach
Strong tide in marinas

Night entry Lit but care required

HW time
Brest HW neaps, −¼ springs

Mean height of tide (m)

	HWS	HWN	LWN	LWS
Bénodet	5.2	4.1	2.1	0.9

Tidal stream
In the marinas, spring rates reach
2.5 knots

Berthing
Marinas and visitors' buoys

Fuel
Penfoul marina, base of E pontoon

Facilities
All facilities

Charts
BA 2820 (50), 3641 (20)
SHOM 7146 (50), 6679 (20)
Imray C37 (large scale)

Radio
Marinas VHF 9

Telephone
Penfoul Marina *t* 02 98 57 05 78
Ste Marine HM *t* 02 98 56 38 72

Major yachting centre in a beautiful river

Bénodet is one of S Brittany's principal yachting centres. There are two marinas, many visitors' buoys, a beautiful river and good facilities ashore. The location, in the centre of the Anse de Bénodet, is a good base for day sailing and there is also the beautiful River Odet to explore. Bénodet gets busy in high season but there is usually space to squeeze in somewhere.

Bénodet town occupies the E bank of the Odet. It is a busy holiday resort with beaches, hotels, shops, a casino and a large supermarket. Sainte Marine, on the W bank, is a quiet holiday village with a few shops and restaurants.

PILOTAGE

Bénodet approach from SW

By GPS

From Penmarc'h follow the route to ⊕116-Malvic or ⊕117-Bilien as described in Chapter 17 Pointe de Penmarc'h. Then use ⊕122-Bénodet, ⊕123-Bénodet 1.

By day

There are many hazards between Ile aux Moutons and the mainland but they are well marked and the approach is not difficult. The usual route, which relies on the buoys, passes between Boulanger SCM and Roche Hélou WCM, then between Chenal du Bénodet ECM and Bas Malvic WCM. If the buoys are hard to identify, Pyramide lighthouse at Bénodet (white tower with green top) in line with Pte de Combrit Light (white square tower, grey corners) bearing 001° leads safely in from the S. Once within

19.1 Bénodet, Sainte Marine and the river Odet looking NW. Sainte Marine is on the W bank and Bénodet on the E. Beyond the bridge the Odet turns to the N and continues for about 14M to Quimper. The long inlet on the W side of the river above the bridge is the anchorage of Anse de Combrit

a mile of Pte de Combrit, alter course to starboard for the entrance. The Pyramide/Pte de Combrit transit of 001° ultimately leads onto the shore, not into the river.

In good conditions and with sufficient tide there are several other routes through the shallow patches.

By night

Stay outside the lit buoys marking the hazards S of Pte de Penmarc'h. After passing Spinec buoy SCM, continue SE until Ile aux Moutons light turns from red to white. Keep within this white sector, until Pte de Combrit and Bénodet Pyramide lights come into line bearing 001°. Turn onto this transit and maintain it watching the Pte de Langoz light; it will change colour as one progresses N. When it changes from green to white bearing 257°, the way is clear to turn to starboard to bring the Bénodet leading lights in line on 346° and enter the river. Many other lights will also be seen.

Bénodet approach from S and SE

By GPS

From Glénan use
⊕128-Porceaux, ⊕122-Bénodet, ⊕123-Bénodet 1.
From the SE use ⊕126-Mousterlin, ⊕122-Bénodet, ⊕123-Bénodet 1.
From the Baie de la Forêt use
⊕143-SE Beg Meil, ⊕126-Mousterlin, ⊕122-Bénodet, ⊕123-Bénodet 1.
In good weather and with enough rise of tide use ⊕144-Laouen Pod, ⊕127-Men Vras, ⊕125-La Voleuse, ⊕122-Bénodet, ⊕123-Bénodet 1. This shortcut has a least depth of 2.2m but passes very close to several shallow patches that would be very dangerous at low water.

By day

The easiest entrance is N of Plateau de la Basse Jaune, leaving Les Porceaux, Ile aux Moutons, Les Poulains tower NCM and Men Dehou all to port. La Voleuse buoy SCM marks the limit of the dangers off Pte de Mousterlin and must be left to starboard. Once past Men Dehou it is safe to turn towards the harbour entrance leaving Le Taro tower WCM ½M to starboard.

By night

Approach within or just S of the intensified sector of Ile aux Moutons light, leaving Jaune de Glénan buoy to port. Continue in this sector until Pte de Langoz light is identified and Trévignon light has turned from white to green bearing more than 051°.

Steer to starboard to get into the white sector of Pte de Langoz light, bearing about 295° and keep within it until Pte de Combrit light opens white bearing 325°. Then steer for this light, crossing the green sector of Pte de Langoz light, and bring the Bénodet leading lights in transit on 346°. Many lights other than those described will be seen.

19.2 Rows of moored boats at Sainte Marine

Entrance to the river Odet

By day

During the season and particularly at weekends the entrance to Bénodet is so busy that speed is limited to 3kts above the Pte de Coq beacon. This rule is widely ignored.

The leading line is the tower of Pyramide light in transit with Le Coq light (346°). However, the dangers in the entrance are marked and it is not necessary to keep strictly to the transit. Pyramide light is conspicuous, but Le Coq is less easy to identify. It will be seen to the left of the conspicuous letters YCO on the grassy bank in front of the old yacht club.

When within 400m of Le Coq, alter to port and steer up the middle of the river.

By night

Entrance is straightforward, but the river is congested with moorings, and anchoring is prohibited in the channel until well beyond the bridge. The leading lights lead clear of all unlit buoys and beacons. When within 400m of Le Coq, turn to port to pass halfway between Le Coq and Pte du Toulgoët flashing red light. Fixed red and green lights will be seen on the bridge and the shore lights may give some guidance.

BERTHS AND ANCHORAGES

Ste Marine visitors' pontoon

Sainte Marine visitors' pontoon is on the W side of the river ¼M beyond Pte du Toulgoët. It is a long pontoon where yachts can lie alongside and raft if necessary. Time on the pontoon is normally limited to one night. After that, move into the marina or use a river mooring.

The tidal stream is roughly parallel to the pontoon so, unlike Bénodet marina, manoeuvring in a strong tide is feasible.

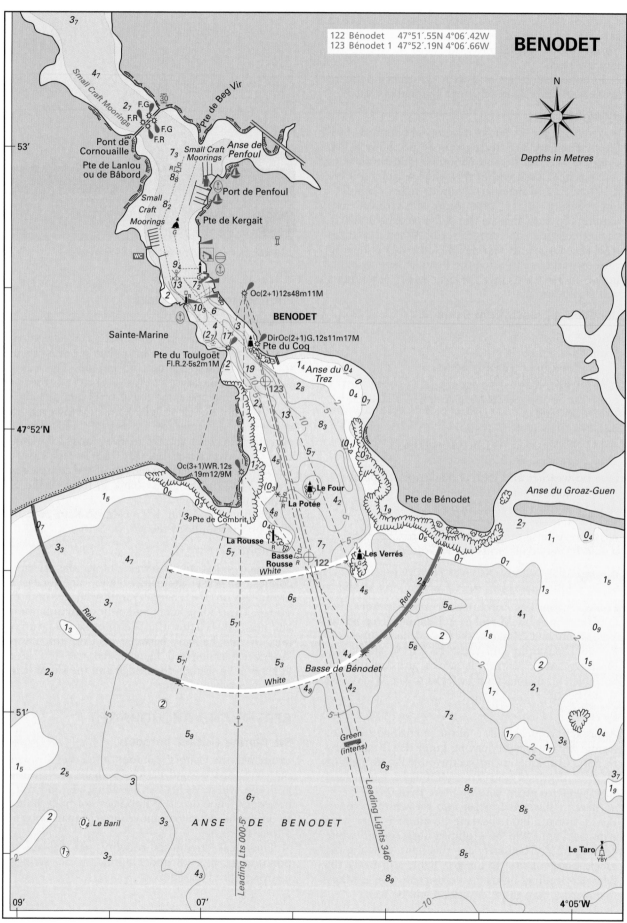

BENODET

N

Depths in Metres

Small Craft Moorings

F.G
F.R
F.G
F.R

Pont de Cornouaille

Pte de Beg Vir

Anse de Penfoul

Small Craft Moorings

Port de Penfoul

Pte de Lanlou ou de Bâbord

Small Craft Moorings

Pte de Kergait

WC

Sainte-Marine

Oc(2+1)12s48m11M

BENODET

DirOc(2+1)G.12s11m17M

Pte du Coq

Pte du Toulgoët
Fl.R.2·5s2m1M

Anse du Trez

Oc(3+1)WR.12s 19m12/9M

Le Four

La Potée

Pte de Bénodet

Anse du Groaz-Guen

Pte de Combrit

La Rousse

Basse Rousse
White

Les Verrés

122

Red

Basse de Bénodet

White

Red

Green (intens)

ANSE   DE   BENODET

Leading Lts 000·5°

Leading Lights 346°

Le Baril

Le Taro
YBY

09′

07′

4°05′W

53′

47°52′N

51′

19.3 Bénodet looking NW.
Sainte Marine is on the far bank of the river and the visitors' pontoon is just visible downstream of the marina. Bénodet Marina, on the near side, has two parts. Large boats use the downstream marina and visitors moor on the outer pontoon

Bénodet marina

Bénodet marina is on the E side of the river about ¼M beyond Ste Marine at the entrance to the Anse de Penfoul. There are long outer pontoons that may be used by visitors. They lie across the tide and manoeuvring is difficult except at slack water. The current can press a yacht against the pontoon so plenty of fenders are needed. Finger berths inside the marina are sometimes available from the harbourmaster. The current inside is less than on the outer pontoons but it is best to enter at slack water.

Short stays are free in the morning for shopping.

Visitors' moorings

Both Bénodet and Sainte Marine provide river moorings which are usually marked with a V. On the Sainte Marine side, the harbourmasters buzz around in dorys and will often direct visiting yachts to a free mooring. On the Bénodet side, the harbourmasters are less active and it is necessary to look around for available buoys.

⚓ Anse du Trez

Sheltered from W through N to E, Anse du Trez is an attractive sandy bay just inside the mouth of the Odet on the E side. During the day, the bay is a centre for Optimist and sailboard sailing but it is peaceful at night.

⚓ Plage du Treven

Sheltered from N and W, the long sandy beach W of Pointe de Combrit makes a pleasant lunchtime stop.

ASHORE IN BENODET AND STE MARINE

Facilities in Bénodet

Bénodet has all the facilities of a major yachting centre and holiday resort. Most repairs can be carried out either at Bénodet or Sainte Marine. Chandlery is available at Bénodet marina.

Fuel is available at the Anse de Penfoul marina, but the berth lies across the current so must be used with care.

There is a full range of shops and a good supermarket on the road to Quimper. Buses run to the RER rail station in Quimper so Bénodet is a convenient place to change crews.

Facilities in Sainte Marine

Sainte Marine is a pleasant holiday resort with a small supermarket, a few shops and delightful bars and restaurants.

There is a pleasant walk to Pointe de Combrit from where the energetic can continue along the magnificent three mile Plage du Treven to Ile Tudy.

20 River Odet

Location
47°53'N 4°07'W

Shelter Excellent

Depth restrictions
2.6m to Lanroz, 0.5 to Quimper

Night passage Not recommended

HW time
Brest HW+¼

Mean height of tide (m)

	HWS	HWN	LWN	LWS
Corniguel	4.9	3.8	1.6	0.3

Tidal stream
Spring rates can reach 2.5 knots

Berthing
Anchorages

Fuel
Penfoul marina, base of E pontoon

Charts
SHOM 6649 (15)
Imray C37 (large scale)

Beautiful river to Quimper

The Odet is a beautiful river with steep, tree-covered banks. Unfortunately there is a bridge (height 5.8m) about ½M from the town of Quimper so masted boats must anchor and use a dinghy for the last leg. Even without a visit to Quimper, the river is well worth exploring. As far as Lanroz there is plenty of water at all states of the tide and there are several attractive anchorages.

PILOTAGE

Bénodet to Quimper

Leave Bénodet and pass under the Pont de Cornouaille (height 30m). After about 1M the Anse du Combrit opens out on the W side. This is an attractive creek and a nice anchorage.

The river then narrows as it runs between steep wooded banks. After about 2M it narrows dramatically and makes a sharp turn to starboard. Port and starboard beacons mark this turn but care should be taken because the shallows extend beyond the starboard mark.

The next stretch is narrow, winding and very attractive. After about 2M there is a little fjord that forms the Anse de St-Cadou (see anchorages). About ½M beyond this, at Lanroz, the river opens out quite suddenly into a broad lake from where there is a good view of Quimper.

The route across the lake is well marked by beacons but the river shallows rapidly to a least depth of 0.5m. At the far end of the lake is a sharp turn to port at the commercial jetties of Corniguel.

Above Corniguel the river nearly dries and the beacons are further apart. A bridge prevents masted yachts from reaching Quimper, but boats that can take the ground may anchor or borrow a mooring below the bridge and visit Quimper by dinghy. Motor yachts can carry a depth of drying 1.5m up to the first quays in Quimper. The bottom here is hard and rather uneven for drying out.

There is also a regular ferry service from Bénodet to Quimper.

20.1 Frank Cowper's *Sailing Tours,* written in 1894, described Château Kérouzien as 'a comfortable-looking white house'

20.2 Château Keraudren was less favoured and was described as 'a new and rather stuck-up-looking château'

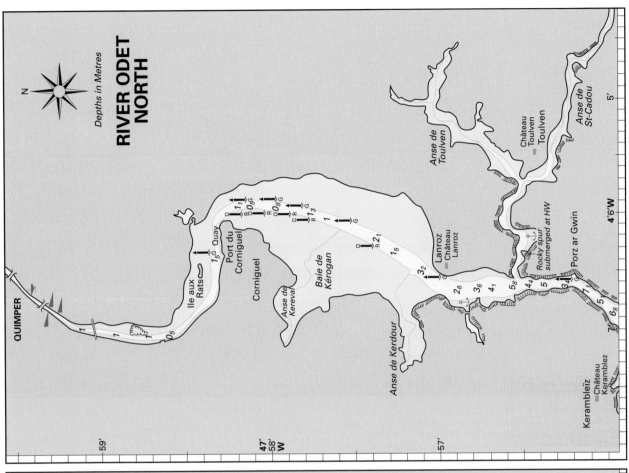

RIVER ODET NORTH

Depths in Metres

QUIMPER

Ile aux Rats

Port du Corniguel
Corniguel
1₅ G Quay

Anse de Kereval

Baie de Kérogan

Anse de Kerdour

Lanroz
Château Lanroz

Rocky spur submerged at HW

Porz ar Gwin

Anse de Toulven

Château Toulven
Toulven

Anse de St-Cadou

Kerambleïz
Château Kerambleiz

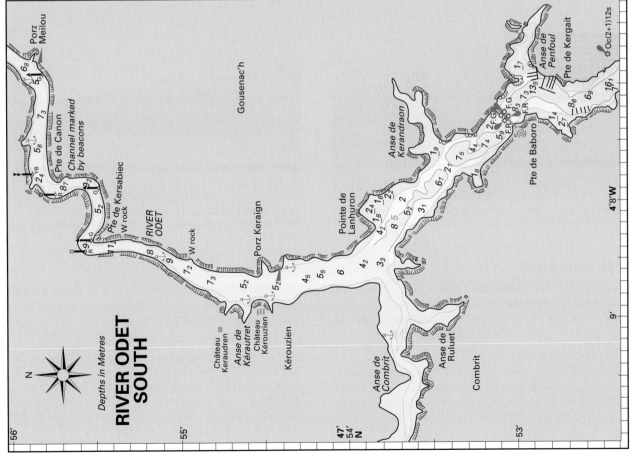

RIVER ODET SOUTH

Depths in Metres

Porz Meilou

Pte de Canon

Channel marked by beacons

Pte de Kersabiec
W rock

RIVER ODET

W rock

Porz Keraign

Château Keraudren
Anse de Kérautret
Château Kérouzien

Kérouzien

Pointe de Lanhuron

Gousenac'h

Anse de Kerandraon

Pte de Baboro

Anse de Penfoul
Pte de Kergait

Anse de Combrit

Anse de Ruluet

Combrit

☆ Ocl(2+1)12s

Plan 20

20.3 The River Odet looking S.
The two sharp bends downriver are in a very steep, wooded section called Les Vire-Court. The first bend is so sharp that the Spanish fleet, approaching to attack Quimper, did not dare to continue and turned back

20.4 The narrow entrance to Anse de St-Cadou. Keep to the far bank to avoid a rocky plateau on the starboard side

20.5 The first small pool in Anse de St-Cadou with just enough room for two boats to anchor. The second pool is a little larger

ANCHORAGES

Anchoring is forbidden near the Pont de Cornouaille, but elsewhere it is possible to anchor anywhere out of the stream. The bottom is rock in the main channel so the holding is poor.

⚓ Anse de Combrit

Sheltered except from the E, the Anse de Combrit is an inlet on the W side of the Odet about 1M above Pont de Cornouaille. It is possible to go in quite a long way with a large-scale chart.

⚓ Porz Keraign

Sheltered except from due N or due S, this is a small inlet on the E side of the Odet between the Châteaux of Kérouzien and Keraudren.

⚓ Porz Meilou

Sheltered from all directions, Porz Meilou is on the E side about 1½M above the sharp turn at Pointe de Kersabiec. There is not much of an inlet but there is a shallow area at the edge of the river, marked by a starboard beacon. Tuck in as far as possible to get out of the tide.

20.6 Kerogan Bay and Quimper looking N.
At Lanroz the river opens out into a broad lake. The route across the lake is marked by beacons and the deeper water is close to the port-hand side. At the far end is a sharp turn to port at the modern, commercial jetties of Corniguel.

⚓ Anse de St-Cadou

Sheltered from all directions, this delightful little fjord is on the E side of the Odet about ½M before the river widens out at Lanroz. It is hard to spot at first because the entrance is quite narrow. Once identified, keep close to the N bank to avoid the drying rocky plateau on the south side. In this pool a large area has 1m depth and 2m can be found in which to swing on short scope. At the end of the first pool there is a rock with 1m or less, on the inside corner of the sharp turn to the north.

⚓ Lanroz

Sheltered from all directions except N, there is a shallow bay on the E side of the river just S of Lanroz.

⚓ Port du Corniguel

It is reportedly possible to anchor above Corniguel and even to go alongside at Corniguel.

ASHORE IN QUIMPER

There are no facilities in the river beyond Bénodet but Quimper has everything. It is the regional capital of W Brittany and is an attractive city with many half-timbered buildings and a fine cathedral. At the heart of the city is an area known as the Quays where flower-decked footbridges criss-cross the Odet.

Quimper has three fine museums for those with time to spare. The Fine Arts Museum has one of the best collections of Breton 19th Century art. The Brittany Museum covers regional history and the Museum of the Faience has displays that explain the development of traditional painted pottery.

21 Iles de Glénan

Location
47°43′N 3°57′W

Shelter
Limited particularly at high water

Hazards
Many unmarked rocks
Difficult to leave anchorages at night

Depth restrictions
1m or more in most anchorages but much less in some channels

Night entry Not recommended

HW time
Brest HW neaps, −½ springs

Mean height of tide (m)

	HWS	HWN	LWN	LWS
Ile Penfret	5.0	3.9	1.9	0.8

Tidal stream N approach
Slack – Brest HW−6 to −4
E – Brest HW−4 to +1 (0.5kts)
Slack – Brest+1 to +3
W – Brest HW+3 to −6 (0.6kts)

Berthing
Anchorages

Facilities
Boat vendors in season, restaurant, small shop, no water

Charts
BA 2820 (50), 3640 (30)
SHOM 7146 (50), 6648 (20)
Imray C37 (77)

Radio
Glénans sailing school VHF 16

Beautiful archipelago with a famous sailing school (CNG)

The Iles de Glénan is a beautiful archipelago of small islands about 12M SSE of Bénodet. It has crystal clear water, white sandy beaches and in good weather is as close to the Caribbean as you can get in S Brittany.

PILOTAGE

Charts

A large-scale chart is strongly recommended. The plans in this book will suffice for the main channels but should not be used for exploration.

Iles de Glénan approaches

By GPS

From Penmarc'h use
⊕109-Spineg, ⊕129-La Pie. This route passes close to the N edge of the Iles de Glénan. Most of the rocks never cover but some outliers on the NW corner are dangerous.

From Loctudy or Bénodet pass W of Ile aux Moutons using
⊕115-Roustolou, ⊕129-La Pie.

Alternatively, from Bénodet pass E of Ile aux Moutons using
⊕128-Porceaux, ⊕129-La Pie.

From the Baie de la Forêt,
⊕129-La Pie or ⊕132-N Penfret can be approached directly.

From the S or SE,
⊕138-Brilimec or ⊕136-Ruolh can be approached directly. However, neither the Brilimec nor the Ruolh channels are recommended for a first visit.

By day

The main islands are easily distinguished by the conspicuous lighthouse on Ile de Penfret and by the stone fort on the SE side of Ile Cigogne which has a tall, partially black-topped concrete tower. The W edge is marked by Bluiniers tower, the S and E by buoys.

Other useful daymarks are a conspicuous disused factory chimney on Ile du Loc'h; some houses on the SE side of Ile de Drénec and the buildings on Ile de St Nicolas.

The easiest entrances are from the N and NE but take care to avoid Les Porceaux rocks in the N approaches.

Iles de Glénan entrances

In the descriptions of the entrances, the letters refer to the plan. Note that all routes go to La Chambre so appropriate changes must be made for the other anchorages.

By GPS

Warning The use of an incorrect GPS datum could make some of these routes dangerous. See page 8 for a note on GPS pilotage and datum correction.

The easiest route into La Chambre is from the N using
⊕129-La Pie, ⊕130-Bananec, ⊕131-Chambre. Once La Pie isolated danger beacon has been identified, the waypoints are hardly necessary.

The NE route is almost as easy using
⊕132-N Penfret, ⊕133-W Penfret, ⊕131-Chambre. The dangers are Tête de Mort and the two shallow patches S of Ile de Guiriden and the shallow patch between Ile Cigogne and Vieux Glénan.

The Brilimec channel from the S uses
⊕138-Brilimec, ⊕139-Brilimec 1, ⊕140-Brilimec 2, ⊕131-Chambre. This is an easy route using GPS and is worth knowing because replacing ⊕131-Chambre with ⊕132-N Penfret provides a short cut straight through the Iles de Glénan.

The SE entry uses
⊕135-Ruolh, ⊕136-Roulh 1, ⊕140-Brilimec 2,

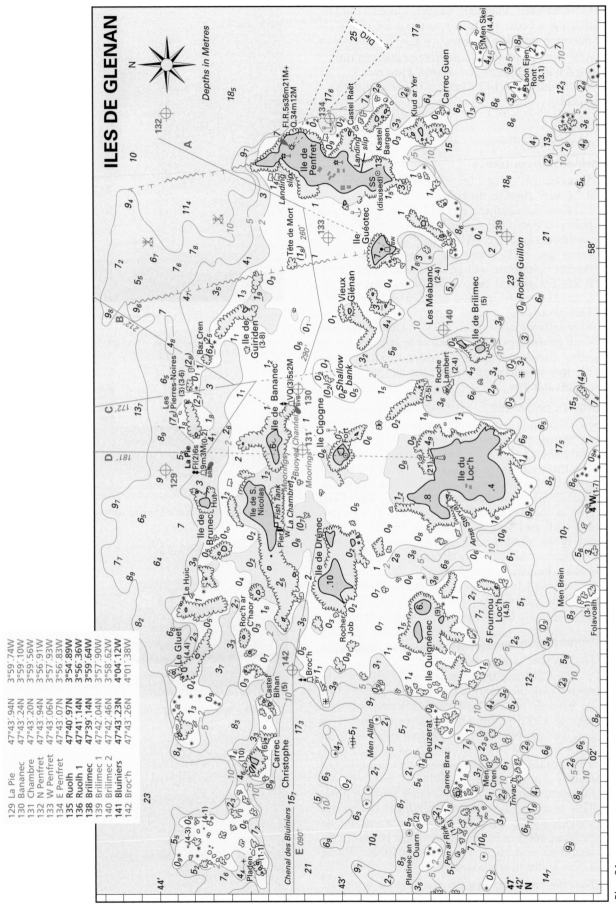

ILES DE GLENAN

Depths in Metres

129	La Pie	47°43′.94N	3°59′.74W
130	Bananec	47°43′.24N	3°59′.10W
131	Chambre	47°43′.20N	3°59′.56W
132	N Penfret	47°43′.94N	3°56′.91W
133	W Penfret	47°43′.06N	3°57′.93W
134	E Penfret	47°43′.07N	3°56′.83W
135	**Ruolh**	**47°40′.97N**	**3°54′.89W**
136	**Ruolh 1**	**47°41′.14N**	**3°56′.36W**
138	**Brilimec**	**47°39′.14N**	**3°59′.64W**
139	Brilimec 1	47°42′.04N	3°57′.90W
140	Brilimec 2	47°42′.46N	3°58′.62W
141	**Bluiniers**	**47°43′.23N**	**4°04′.12W**
142	Broc'h	47°43′.26N	4°01′.38W

Plan 21

⊕131-Chambre. There are dangers close to this route so it is better to start by using it for exit in conjunction with the transits.

The W entry requires visual pilotage and can only be used with sufficient rise of tide. However, ⊕141-Bluiniers, ⊕142-Bloc'h may assist with the approach.

By day

The letters A to E refer to plan 21.

Northeastern entrance

A This channel carries 1m with shallow patches of 0.7m very close to the route.

Leave the northern end of Le Penfret 300m to port and steer 205° toward the stone wall beacon on Ile de Guéotec. When Ile Cigogne concrete tower (see 21.2) bears 260° alter course to 260°. Penfret lighthouse will be dead astern (see 21.1). If the E Cardinal beacon SE of Bananec can be located, alter course for it when it bears 290°. This avoids the shallow patch E of Ile Cigogne. Alternatively alter onto 283°, steering for the wind generator on the W end of St Nicolas. Using either course, leave the E Cardinal beacon SE of Bananec to starboard to enter the buoyed channel of La Chambre.

Northern entrances

These three entrances should be regarded as carrying 1m although a little more water can be found with careful pilotage.

The three entrances are taken in order from east to west; the easiest being La Pie (D). The marks for B and C are four above-water rocks: Baz Cren (3.5m) in the E, two adjacent rocks of Les Pierres Noires (5.6 and 5m) and finally, in the W, a single Pierre Noire (4.6m) with others to its SW which seldom cover. All these rocks stand on rocky bases and must be distinguished from Ile de Guiriden to the SE, which has a considerable sandy expanse that covers near high water.

B The entrance leaves Baz Cren 50m to 100m to port steering on Fort Cigogne tower, bearing 212°. Once Baz Cren is passed it is possible to bear to port as convenient.

The CNG use the chimney on Ile du Loc'h in transit with the E cardinal beacon southeast of Ile de Bananec on 200° for this entrance. Although easy to identify, this transit leaves an outlier of Les Pierres Noires (dries 2.8m) only 60m to starboard.

C This entrance leaves the two adjacent heads of Les Pierres Noires 20m to 60m to port. Ile de Brilimec, bearing 172°, leads fairly into the pool. This is a popular entrance for local boats, but should not be used for a first visit, as Ile de Brilimec and Les Pierres Noires must be positively identified and there is a rocky plateau drying 2.7m, 100m to starboard.

D For this entrance, identify La Pie and bring the chimney on Ile du Loc'h just open to the right-hand side of the Cigogne tower, bearing 181°.

21.1 The lighthouse on the N end of the Ile de Penfret

21.2 The 'partially' black-topped fort on Ile Cigone

21.3 The small group of cottages on Ile de Bananec

21.4 The stone wall beacon on Ile de Guéotec is the mark for the NE approach

Steer this course until inside Les Pierres Noires leaving La Pie isolated danger light beacon abeam to starboard. Near low water the chimney dips behind the fort but it is good enough to leave La Pie 100m to starboard.

Except near high water there is no problem knowing when Les Pierres Noires are passed because a rock that seldom covers marks their SW extremity. Once La Pie beacon is passed and in transit with the N side of Ile de Brunec, steer into the pool towards the E cardinal beacon at the E end of Ile de Bananec.

Western entrance

E The Chenal des Bluiniers dries 0.5m, but it is safer to regard it as drying 0.8m. If this gives insufficient margin, skirt the N edge of the rocks and enter by La Pie. Visibility of three miles is needed for this channel except towards high water.

Start about 200m S of Les Bluiniers tower WCM. Coming from the NW be sure to give this tower at least 200m clearance. From this point, steer E for Le Broc'h tower NCM, keeping at least 100m S of a line joining all the dangers that show to the N and keeping Penfret lighthouse open to the N of Le Broc'h tower, bearing about 090°. Approaching Le Broc'h tower, leave it 100m to starboard and bring the semaphore, near the southern point of Ile de Penfret, open to the left of Fort Cigogne by the width of the fort (not the tower), bearing 100°. Steer so until the eastern part of Ile de Drénec is abeam to starboard; this island is in two clearly defined parts separated by a sandy strip which covers at HW. Now steer 035° on the summer cottages to the east of the shellfish tank to enter La Chambre. Near HW the detailed directions above can be disregarded; having passed Le Broc'h tower it is only necessary to sail 100m N of Ile de Drénec and then make straight for La Chambre or the pool as required.

For those already familiar with the islands the transits shown on BA chart 3640 may be used, but it is necessary to identify the semaphore mast on Penfret at a distance of 5M as well as the farm buildings on Drénec.

ANCHORAGES

⚓ E of Ile de Penfret

Sheltered from the W but exposed to the *vent solaire*, this anchorage is in the sandy bay south of the hill on which the lighthouse stands. Approach with the middle of the bay bearing 270°. There is a potentially dangerous rock 150m N of Castel Raët, which is the islet in the S of the bay.

There is a large metal mooring buoy on the N side of the bay. However, it is preferable to anchor closer to the beach on sand, taking care to avoid the patches of weed.

S of Castel Raët is another bay with a slip and some CNG moorings. This bay is unsuitable for anchoring.

⊕134-E Penfret (47°43'.07N 3°56'.83W)

⚓ SW of Ile de Penfret

Sheltered from the W by Guéotec and from the E by Penfret, there is a good anchorage in 2.5m outside the CNG moorings between Penfret and Guéotec. The tide runs fairly hard.

The easy approach is from the N. An approach from the S is possible but requires intricate pilotage and a large-scale chart.

⊕133-W Penfret (47°43'.06N 3°57'.93W)

⚓ E of Ile Cigogne

Anchor in 1m to 1.4m, N of the rocky ledge running SE from Ile Cigogne.

⊕131-Chambre (47°43'.20N 3°59'.56W)

⚓ La Chambre

This anchorage S of Ile de St Nicolas is the most popular one for visitors although there are now many moorings. The depths are up to 3m but avoid anchoring in the *vedette* channel, which is marked by small port and starboard buoys.

A rocky ledge extends 100m along the S shore of St Nicolas and Bananec. The shoal also extends E of Bananec and an E cardinal beacon marks its limit. Between the islands there is a sandy ridge with shallow sandy bays (drying 1m) to the N and S. These make excellent anchorages for yachts that can take the ground.

Enter La Chambre from a position 100m S of the beacon ECM SE of Ile de Bananec. If La Chambre is full of yachts, follow the marked channel until a suitable anchorage is found. If the shellfish tank is not obscured, keep it on 285° until Bananec is passed and then bear a little to port if wishing to proceed further into La Chambre. At low water depths of less than 1m may be encountered in La Chambre. The water is clear and it is necessary to look for a sandy patch on which to anchor, as there is much weed.

⊕131-Chambre (47°43'.20N 3°59'.56W)

21.5 Sailing dinghies from the Centre Nautique on the SW shore of Ile de Penfret

21.6 Ile de Penfret looking N.
Anchored boats can be seen on the E side of the island near the lighthouse. There is an alternative anchorage to the SW of the island

⚓ N of Ile de Bananec

Sheltered, except from N and E at high water, the bay NW of Bananec and E of St Nicolas is a popular fair-weather anchorage. The bay shoals from 2m and has a clean sandy bottom so choose a spot outside the moorings according to draught.

⊕129-La Pie (47°43′.94N 3°59′.74W)

⚓ N of Ile du Loc'h

Sheltered from the N by Ile Cigogne and from the S by Ile du Loc'h, there is a neap anchorage about 400m N of the Ile du Loc'h chimney.

ASHORE IN ILES DE GLENAN

Facilities

During the season enterprising vendors tour the anchorages each morning with bread, seafood and, occasionally, fresh vegetables.

There is a famous restaurant and a bar on Ile St Nicolas together with a small shop that occasionally stocks very limited provisions.

Fresh water is in short supply and visitors should not expect to obtain any.

There are islands that can be explored but the best activities are on the extraordinary clear water. The shallow areas between the islands are sometimes just a few inches deep depending on the tide. Viewed from a rowing dinghy, the underwater gardens just below the surface are quite unique.

21.7 The anchorage E of Ile de Penfret can be a convenient night stop when sailing along the S Brittany coast. It is protected from the W but exposed to the *vent solaire* which can blow from the NE during the night and early morning. The small boats in the picture are the Centre Nautique training boats

21.8 Ile du Loc'h in the foreground looking N.
The small island with the tower is Ile Cigogne. Beyond that, the long islands are Ile de St Nicolas which is connected to the smaller Ile de Bananec by a sandy isthmus that covers at HW

Centre Nautique de Glénan

The Iles de Glénan is home to the Centre Nautique de Glénan (CNG), the largest sailing school in Europe. The school's main base is on Ile Cigogne but their fleets of training boats are in evidence throughout the islands. They are very hospitable to visitors, but obviously that hospitality should not be abused.

21.9 The moorings and anchorages S of St Nicolas are the most popular for visitors. The ferry channel, marked with small port and starboard buoys, must be kept clear for the *vedettes* from Bénodet and Concarneau. Before anchoring check in the clear water for a sandy patch free from weed

22 Port-La-Forêt

Location
47°54′N 3°58′W

Shelter
Excellent in marina

Hazards
Rocks on SW corner and E side of Baie de la Forêt

Depth restrictions
0.6m bar at entrance of channel

Tidal restrictions
Depth restricts entry at LW±1½

Night entry Partially lit

HW time
Brest HW–¼ neaps, –½ springs

Mean height of tide (m)

	HWS	HWN	LWN	LWS
Concarneau	5.0	3.9	1.9	0.8

Tidal stream
Weak in the bay, strong in entrance

Berthing
Large modern marina

Fuel
Base of pontoon C

Facilities
All repair facilities and some marina shops. 1M walk to town

Charts
BA 2820 (50), 3641 (20)
SHOM 7146 (50), 6650 (15)
Imray C38 (large scale)

Radio
Marina VHF 9

Telephone
Marina t 02 98 56 98 45

Huge marina in sheltered bay

Port-La-Forêt is a large modern marina complex. The facilities are good and the staff helpful so it is a good place to leave a yacht.

Shopping is limited but there is a pleasant walk over the causeway to the town at La Forêt-Fouesnant.

PILOTAGE

Port-La-Forêt approach and entrance

By GPS

From Loctudy or Bénodet use ⊕126-Mousterlin, ⊕143-SE Beg-Meil, ⊕147-La-Forêt.

In good weather with enough rise of tide it is possible to use ⊕125-La Voleuse, ⊕127-Men Vras, ⊕144-Laouen Pod, ⊕147-La-Forêt. This route passes close to several unmarked

dangers and must be used with care.
From Concarneau use ⊕149-Concarneau, ⊕148-Vas Hir, ⊕147-La-Forêt.

From Glénan use ⊕129-La Pie, ⊕143-SE Beg-Meil, ⊕147-La-Forêt or ⊕132-N Penfret, ⊕143-SE Beg-Meil, ⊕147-La-Forêt.

By day

In the approach, there are marked dangers off Beg-Meil. There are also extensive unmarked dangers W of Concarneau. Many of these rocks never dry but they can be avoided by keeping the slender Le Score beacon SCM open E of the end of Cape Coz breakwater or, more simply, by keeping well off the E side of the bay.

The entrance to Port-La-Forêt lies to the E of the wooded promontory of Cap Coz. The channel to the

22.1 Port-La-Forêt looking S. There are three waiting buoys in the deeper water just off the entrance. The channel to the marina is marked by lateral buoys and beacons. Just before the marina there is a sharp turn to starboard round the rocky breakwater head (inset) and the visitors' pontoon is immediately ahead

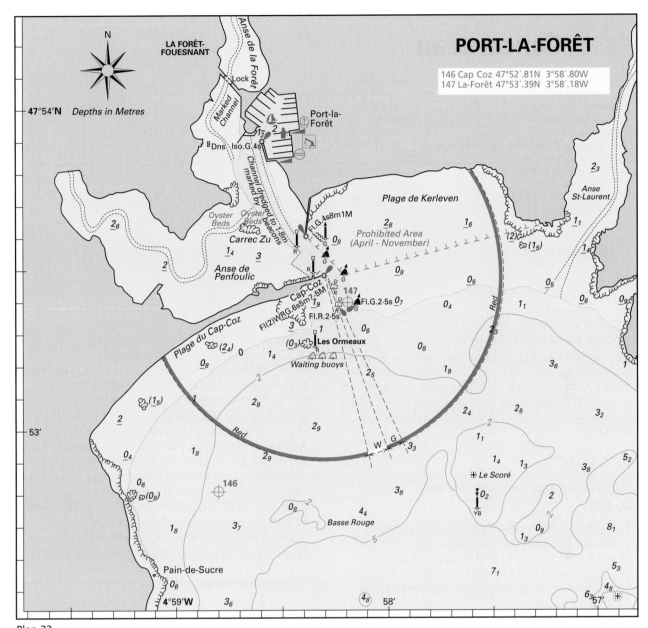

PORT-LA-FORÊT

146 Cap Coz 47°52'.81N 3°58'.80W
147 La-Forêt 47°53'.39N 3°58'.18W

Plan 22

marina is well marked.

By night

The white sector of Cap Coz light marks the deepest water. The green sector guards a 2.6m shallow patch in the mouth of the bay.

BERTHS AND ANCHORAGES

Port-La-Forêt marina

On entering the marina, the visitors' pontoon is immediately ahead. Secure here and visit the helpful harbour office to be allocated a berth.

⚓ Beg Meil

Sheltered from the W, Beg-Meil is a pretty holiday resort in the SW corner of Baie de la Forêt. Approach from the E to avoid the dangers off the point. Also avoid the Louen Jardin shallow patch (depth 0.8m) off Beg-Meil pier and the rocks close inshore. There are a lot of moorings along the coast but there is still plenty of room to anchor.

Night departure is difficult without GPS.

⊕ 145-Beg-Meil (47°51'.87N 3°58'.53W)

⚓ Plage de Cap Coz

Well sheltered from NW and W, the Plage du Cap-Coz is in the NW corner of Baie de la Forêt. The best spot is usually at the W end of the beach. There are several rocky patches but all close inshore. Night departure is difficult without GPS.

⊕ 146-Cap Coz (47°52'.81N 3°58'.80W)

ASHORE IN PORT LA-FORÊT

Port-la-Forêt has all the facilities of a large modern marina and yacht sales centre. There are pleasant beaches nearby.

The town of La Forêt-Fouesnant lies 1M upstream on the west side of the estuary. It can be reached by dinghy when the tide is up or there is a pleasant walk over the causeway. The lock marked on the charts is now permanently open. There are fairly frequent buses from the port to Quimper and Concarneau.

23 Concarneau

Location
47°52'N 3°55'W

Shelter
Good in marina

Hazards
Rocks on E side of Concarneau bay
Intricate entrance
Rocks by fuel berth wall

Depth restrictions
1m to 2.5m in marina

Night entry Well lit

HW time
Brest HW–¼ neaps, –½ springs

Mean height of tide (m)

	HWS	HWN	LWN	LWS
Concarneau	5.0	3.9	1.9	0.8

Tidal stream
Weak in bay but stronger in entrance

Berthing
Visitors' pontoon and inside floating breakwater

Fuel
S corner of marina

Facilities
All facilities

Charts
BA 2820 (50), 3641 (20)
SHOM 7146 (50), 6650 (15)
Imray C38 (large scale)

Radio
Marina VHF 9

Telephone
Marina *t* 02 98 97 57 96

Ancient fort and fishing port

The remarkable old town of Concarneau is on an island connected to the mainland by a drawbridge. Secure within massive defensive walls is a labyrinth of beautifully preserved little streets that are packed with tourist shops and restaurants and an excellent museum.

PILOTAGE

Concarneau approach and entrance

By GPS

The entrance to Concarneau requires careful visual pilotage. The following waypoints may assist: ⊕149-Concarneau, ⊕150-Concarneau 1, ⊕153-Concarneau 2, ⊕154-Concarneau 3.

The following suggested approaches terminate at ⊕149-Concarneau.

From Penmarc'h use ⊕115-Roustelou, ⊕124-Astrolabe, ⊕126-Mousterlin, ⊕143-SE Beg-Meil, ⊕149-Concarneau. This route passes close to several shallow patches between ⊕115-Roustelou and ⊕124-Astrolabe.

From Loctudy and Bénodet use ⊕126-Mousterlin, ⊕143-SE Beg-Meil, ⊕149-Concarneau. In good weather with enough rise of tide it is possible to use ⊕125-La Voleuse, ⊕127-Men Vras, ⊕143-SE Beg-Meil, ⊕149-Concarneau. This short cut passes close to several dangerous rocks, particularly off Beg-Meilpoint, so use it with care.

From Port-La-Forêt use ⊕147-La-Forêt, ⊕148-Vas Hir, ⊕149-Concarneau.

From E and SE use ⊕159-SW Trévignon, ⊕158-W Trévignon, ⊕157-An Houarnou, ⊕149-Concarneau.

23.1 The approach to Concarneau looking NW. The bay at the bottom of the picture is Anse de Kersos where it may be possible to find space to anchor. The Lanriec light is situated on the house-covered promontory to starboard as you approach Concarneau

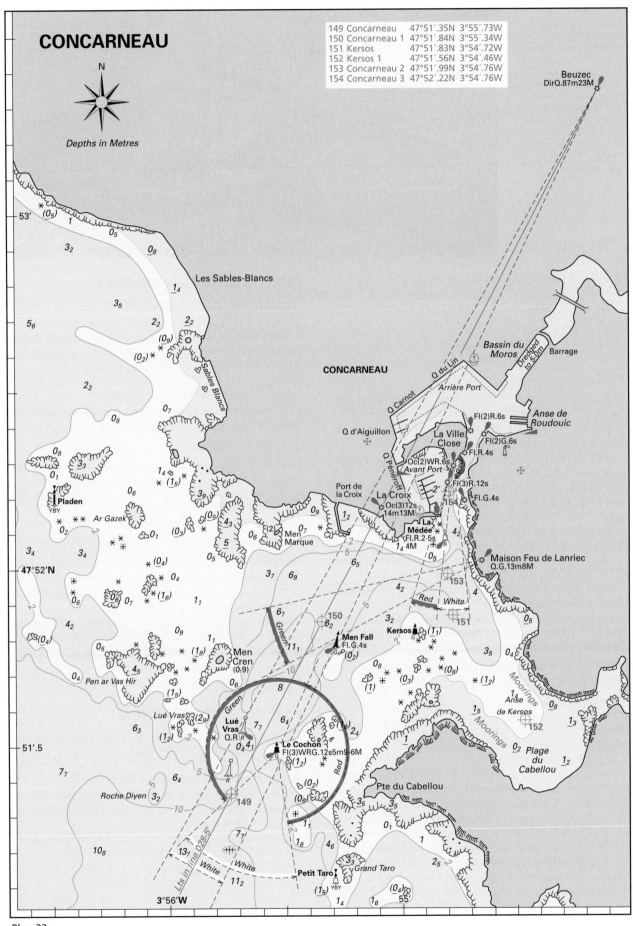

CONCARNEAU

N

Depths in Metres

149 Concarneau	47°51′.35N	3°55′.73W
150 Concarneau 1	47°51′.84N	3°55′.34W
151 Kersos	47°51′.83N	3°54′.72W
152 Kersos 1	47°51′.56N	3°54′.46W
153 Concarneau 2	47°51′.99N	3°54′.76W
154 Concarneau 3	47°52′.22N	3°54′.76W

Beuzec
DirQ.87m23M

Les Sables-Blancs

Sables Blancs

CONCARNEAU

Bassin du
Moros

Dredged
to 5.0m

Barrage

Anse de
Roudouic

Q du Lin

Q Carnot

Arrière Port

Fl(2)R.6s

La Ville
Close

Fl(2)G.6s

Q d'Aiguillon

Fl.R.4s

Q Pénéroff

Oc(2)WR.6s
Avant Port

Port de
la Croix

Fl(3)R.12s

La Croix
Oc(3)12s
14m13M

Fl.G.4s

Pladen
YBY

Ar Gazek

**La
Médée**
Fl.R.2·5s
1₄ 4M

Men
Marque

Maison Feu de Lanriec
Q.G.13m8M

47°52′N

153

Red | White

Green

150

Kersos

151

Men Fall
Fl.G.4s

Moorings

Men
Cren
(0·9)

Moorings

Anse
de Kersos

152

Pen ar Vas Hir

Lué Vras

**Lué
Vras**
Q.R

Le Cochon
Fl(3)WRG.12s5m9-6M

Green

Red

Plage
du
Cabellou

Roche Diyen

Pte du Cabellou

149

Lts in line 028·5

White | White

Petit Taro

Grand Taro

YBY

3°56′W

Plan 23

23.2 Concarneau looking NW. La Ville Close, the walled fort, splits the harbour into two sections. The outer part is for pleasure boats and has spaces for visitors on the wave breaker and on finger pontoons. The inner harbour is used by the fishing boats

From S of Belle Ile use ⊕160-E Glénan, ⊕158-W Trévignon, ⊕157-An Houarnou, ⊕149-Concarneau.

From Glénan use ⊕129-La Pie, ⊕149-Concarneau or ⊕132-N Penfret, ⊕149-Concarneau.

By day

From any direction, the buildings on the hill at the back of the town are unmistakable. Steer for a position about half a mile W of the promontory of Pointe de Cabellou.

The official leading line is Beuzec belfry, on the ridge a mile inland, in transit with La Croix lighthouse, on the seafront, bearing 028.5°. This works at night but is not clear by day. Le Cochon green beacon tower is more easily identified and it is sufficient to pass midway between it and the two red buoys on a course of about 030°.

Continue on this course for 600m towards Men Fall SHM. Round the buoy and steer 065° for Lanriec light. This is the end gable of a white house, among many, and is hard to spot. Binoculars may reveal a black window in the upper half and the name in green under the window. Fortunately, the channel is wide. Simply leave Kersos green beacon tower 200m to starboard and La Médée red beacon tower to port to enter the marina.

By night

Approach in the white sector of Le Cochon and bring Beuzec and La Croix lights in transit on 029°. Hold this course past Le Cochon and Basse du Chenal buoy towards Men Fall buoy. As Men Fall is passed, Lanriec Q.G light will open. Steer about 070° in the green sector until the Passage de Lanriec light on the Ville Close opens red. Continue to head for Lanriec until the red light turns white. Then alter to about 000° to keep in the white sector, leaving La Médée to port and No. 1 beacon to starboard.

The floodlights, illuminating La Ville Close, give plenty of background light to the marina area. The channel beyond the marina, past the Ville Close, is marked by further red and green lights.

BERTHS AND ANCHORAGES

Concarneau visitors' pontoons

Visitors' berth on the inner side of the floating wave breaker or on the visitors' pontoon, directly inside the marina entrance. The wave breaker is claimed to be less disturbed by the wash of passing fishing boats coming from the fishing harbour. Only ferries can use the outside of the wave breaker.

Beware of the shallow rocky patch by the fuel berth. It is a hazard near low water.

⚓ Anse de Kersos

Sheltered from the N through E to SW, but exposed to the W and NW, the Anse de Kersos is a large bay in the approach to Concarneau. Go in clear of the moorings as far as draught permits.

⊕152-Kersos 1 (47°51′.56N 3°54′.46W)

⚓ Baie de Pouldohan

Sheltered from the E, the Baie of Pouldohan is about 1½M S of Concarneau. It is surrounded by rocks and best visited in quiet weather at neaps. A large-scale chart is essential.

Start from a position about 1M S of Pointe de Cabellou and enter on 060° between Roche Tudy green beacon tower and Karek Steir red beacon. This route passes over a 2.3m shallow patch.

⊕156-Pouldohan 1 (47°50′.81N 3°54′.08W)

ASHORE IN CONCARNEAU

There are all the facilities of a sizeable town and busy fishing and leisure port. All repairs can be undertaken. Shops, including a large supermarket, banks, hotels and restaurants are close.

There is a delightful beach just over a mile NW of the port. The Ville Close and the Fishing Museum are interesting tourist attractions.

A bus service connects Concarneau to the railway at Quimper and Rosporden.

Belon River

III. Groix and the Rias

Port ... ce light, Port ... Groix

Etel

Locmaria, Ile de Groix

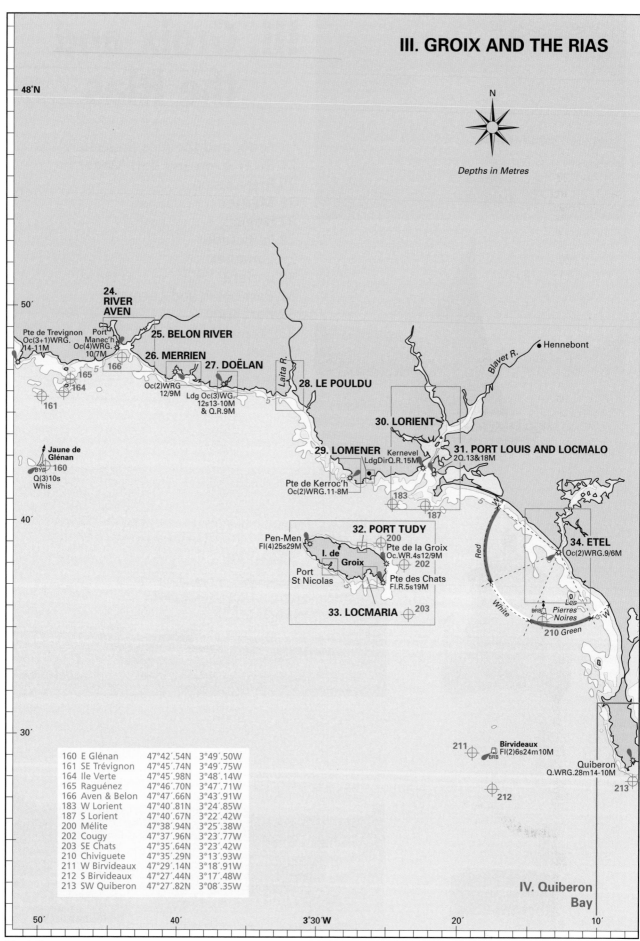

III. GROIX AND THE RIAS

N

Depths in Metres

48°N

50′

24.
RIVER
AVEN

Pte de Trevignon
Oc(3+1)WRG.
14-11M

Port
Manec'h
Oc(4)WRG.
10/7M

25. BELON RIVER

26. MERRIEN

27. DOËLAN

166

165

164

161

Laita R.

28. LE POULDU

Blavet R.

Hennebont

5

5

30. LORIENT

Jaune de
Glénan

BYB
160
Q(3)10s
Whis

29. LOMENER

Kernevel
LdgDirQ.R.15M

31. PORT LOUIS AND LOCMALO
2Q.13&18M

Pte de Kerroc'h
Oc(2)WRG.11-8M

183

187

5

Red

40′

Pen-Men
Fl(4)25s29M

32. PORT TUDY

200

Pte de la Groix
Oc.WR.4s12/9M

202

34. ETEL
Oc(2)WRG.9/6M

I. de
Groix

Les
Pierres
Noires

BRB

Port
St Nicolas

Pte des Chats
Fl.R.5s19M

White

33. LOCMARIA

203

210 Green

30′

211

Birvideaux
Fl(2)6s24m10M
BRB

Quiberon
Q.WRG.28m14-10M

213

212

160	E Glénan	47°42′.54N	3°49′.50W
161	SE Trévignon	47°45′.74N	3°49′.75W
164	Ile Verte	47°45′.98N	3°48′.14W
165	Raguénez	47°46′.70N	3°47′.71W
166	Aven & Belon	47°47′.66N	3°43′.91W
183	W Lorient	47°40′.81N	3°24′.85W
187	S Lorient	47°40′.67N	3°22′.42W
200	Mélite	47°38′.94N	3°25′.38W
202	Cougy	47°37′.96N	3°23′.77W
203	SE Chats	47°35′.64N	3°23′.42W
210	Chiviguete	47°35′.29N	3°13′.93W
211	W Birvideaux	47°29′.14N	3°18′.91W
212	S Birvideaux	47°27′.44N	3°17′.48W
213	SW Quiberon	47°27′.82N	3°08′.35W

IV. Quiberon
Bay

50′ 40′ 3°30′W 20′ 10′

Chart III

24 River Aven and Port Manec'h

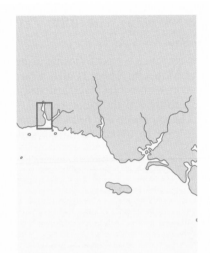

Location
48°47'N 3°44'W

Shelter
Reasonable from SW to NE

Hazards
Unmarked rocks in W approach

Depth restrictions
Bar dredged to 0.6m
River dries 1.5m

Night entry Well lit to Port Manec'h

HW time
Brest HW–¼ neaps, –½ springs

Mean height of tide (m)

	HWS	HWN	LWN	LWS
Concarneau	5.0	3.9	1.9	0.8

Tidal stream
Weak in bay, strong in the river
3 knots in Rosbraz narrows

Berthing
Visitors' moorings and anchorages, drying quays at Rosbraz and Pont Aven

Facilities
Water, a few shops, bars and restaurants

Charts
BA 2821 (50)
SHOM 7031 (50), 7138 (10)
Imray C38 (large scale)

Telephone
Yacht club *t* 02 98 06 84 30

Lovely river scenery to Pont Aven

The Aven is a popular and very pretty river. The holiday resort of Port Manec'h is at its mouth on the W bank. It is a further 7M inland to the picturesque artists' town of Pont Aven.

PILOTAGE

Approach to the River Aven

By GPS

From NW (see Chart II) use
⊕159-SW Trévignon, ⊕161-SE Trévignon,
⊕164-Ile Verte, ⊕166-Aven & Belon,
⊕167-Port Manec'h.

In good weather it is possible to use the short cut ⊕159-SW Trévignon, ⊕165-Raguenez, ⊕166-Aven & Belon. This route requires care because it passes close the unmarked Cochons de Rospico.

From Glénan use
⊕164-Ile Verte, ⊕166-Aven & Belon,
⊕167-Port Manec'h.

From S use
⊕166-Aven & Belon, ⊕167-Port Manec'h but take

24.1 The entrance to the River Aven and River Belon looking NE. The insets are (left) the Port Manec'h lighthouse and (right) the Amer at Pointe de Kerhermen

great care to avoid Le Cochon (dries 0.8m) almost ½M NW of Les Verrès IDM.

By day

The entrance is easy to locate using the lighthouse at Port Manec'h. There is also a large white masonry beacon with a black vertical stripe on the E side of the entrance to the Belon river

The approach can be made from any direction but take care to avoid the unmarked Les Cochons de

Rospico (dries 0.5m) to the W; and Le Cochon (dries 0.8m) NW of Les Verrès IDM to the E.

The ½M passage between Les Verrès and the land, has a least depth of 2.6m. The passage between Ile Raguenez and Ile Verte is deep but there is a 1m shallow patch S of the channel W of Ile Verte.

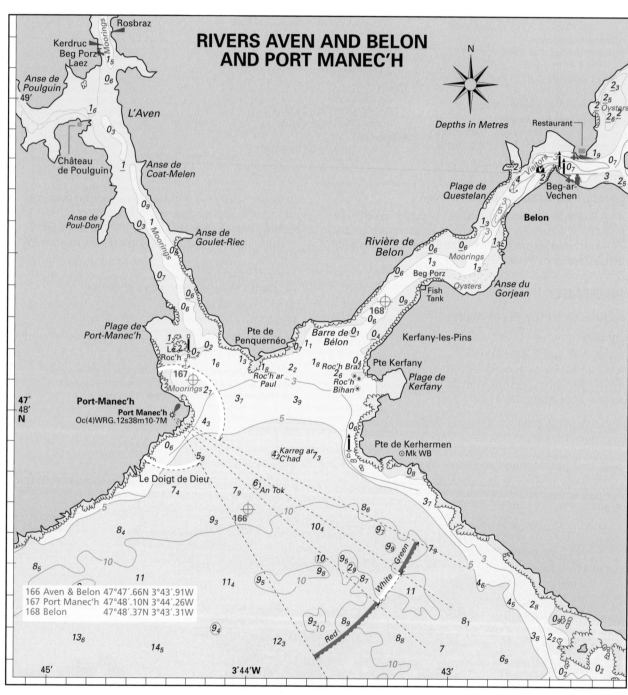

RIVERS AVEN AND BELON AND PORT MANEC'H

166 Aven & Belon 47°47'.66N 3°43'.91W
167 Port Manec'h 47°48'.10N 3°44'.26W
168 Belon 47°48'.37N 3°43'.31W

Plan 24

24.2 Port Manec'h looking W.
Port Manec'h is a small holiday village. There are a few white visitors' moorings and room to anchor outside the moorings. From here you can access the beautiful GR34 coastal footpath

By night

Use either of the white sectors of Port Manec'h light. The red sector covers the dangers of Les Verrès.

The River Aven to Pont Aven

The mouth of the river is shallow and the position of the bar changes periodically. Within ½M of the mouth it dries apart from a few pools.

Enter on a rising tide leaving the beacon well to port and proceed up the centre of the river. Half a mile up there is an inlet called Anse de Goulet-Riec on the E side. Here the river deepens and 2m or more may be found.

Further on the river shoals to dry 0.6m in places and there is a large drying creek branching off to the west with a château at its mouth. Then the river narrows between the quays and slips of Kerdruc on the W bank and Rosbraz on the E.

Above Rosbraz the river widens and shoals, but is navigable on the tide or by dinghy a further 2½M to Pont Aven. The channel is marked by buoys and easy to follow

BERTHS AND ANCHORAGES

Port Manec'h

The short Port Manec'h breakwater runs N from the point. Behind it is a small quay and slipway. To the E are a number of white visitors' mooring buoys with 2.5m or more. Upstream are some fore and aft moorings, in shallower water, for boats of less than 10m. During the season, all of these moorings are likely to be taken by early afternoon but there is room to anchor outside them.

Rosbraz

It is possible to dry out alongside the quays on mud at Kerdruc or shingle and mud at Rosbraz or to borrow a mooring.

The ebb runs at over 3kts and there is so little space between the moorings that it is difficult for a yacht of over 10m to turn.

Pont Aven

There are drying quays but these tend to be crowded.

ASHORE

Port Manec'h

There is water on the quay and modest shops and restaurants.

Pont Aven

All the facilities of a tourist town. Gauguin lived and worked here and it is still a magnet for artists and connoisseurs. Pont Aven Museum and Art Gallery is particularly worth visiting.

25 River Belon

Location
47°48′N 3°44′W

Shelter Good in river

Hazards
Unmarked rocks in W approach
Bar dangerous in strong SW wind

Depth restrictions
Bar dries 0.1m
Visitors' moorings have 3m or more

Night entry Not recommended

HW time
Brest HW–¼ neaps, –½ springs

Mean height of tide (m)

	HWS	HWN	LWN	LWS
Concarneau	5.0	3.9	1.9	0.8

Tidal stream
Weak in bay, moderate in the river

Berthing
Visitors' moorings

Facilities
Excellent seafood

Charts
BA 2821 (50)
SHOM 7031 (50), 7138 (10)
Imray C38 (large scale)

Telephone
Harbourmaster t 02 98 71 08 65

Oyster lovers' paradise

Belon, home of the Belon oyster, is a must for seafood enthusiasts. It is a pretty, sheltered river with convenient visitors' buoys. However, in bad southerly weather the bar is impassable.

PILOTAGE

(See Plan 14)

Approach to the River Belon

By GPS

From NW use
⊕159-SW Trévignon, ⊕161-SE Trévignon,
⊕164-Ile Verte, ⊕166-Aven & Belon,
⊕168-Belon.

In good weather it is possible to use the short cut ⊕159-SW Trévignon, ⊕165-Raguenez, ⊕166-Aven & Belon. This route requires care because it passes close to the unmarked Cochons de Rospico.

From Glénan, use
⊕164-Ile Verte, ⊕166-Aven & Belon, ⊕168-Belon.

From S use
⊕166-Aven & Belon, ⊕168-Belon but take great care to avoid Le Cochon (dries 0.8m) almost ½M NW of Les Verrès IDM.

25.1 The River Belon looking E.
The village consists of the attractive row of houses on the S bank. There are no shops, only a small fish market. The famous restaurant and fish shop, Chez Jacky, is the white building on the opposite bank.

By day

The outer entrance is easily identified by a large white day mark with a black vertical stripe on the E side of the entrance at Pointe de Kerhermen (see 24.1).

The approach can be made from any direction. Be sure to avoid Les Cochons de Rospico (dries 0.5m) to the W; and Le Cochon (dries 0.8m) NW of Les Verrès IDM to the E. Both are unmarked.

The passage between Les Verrès and the land has a least depth of 2.6m. The passage between Ile Raguenez and Ile Verte is deep but there is a 1m shallow patch S of the channel W of Ile Verte.

By night

Not recommended.

River Belon

(See Plan 24)

It is best to enter the river above half tide. Start from a position midway between the headland at Port Manec'h and Pointe de Kerhermen and enter the river from the SW. When Pointe Kerfany is abeam to starboard, steer down the middle of the dredged channel on 035°.

Just after Beg Porz, a bar extends from the N bank. The deepest water is on the S side, close to the stakes marking the oyster beds. Half a mile further, the river turns to starboard, and on the N side of the curve there are three large white metal head and stern visitors' buoys, suitable for rafting.

Beyond the visitors' moorings is a quay and there are a few more fore and aft visitors' moorings. The Belon River winds further inland through steep, wooded valleys. It may be possible to explore in a dinghy or else on foot. The GR34 coastal footpath leads for miles around the banks of both the Aven and the Belon rivers. The TOP25 map of Quimperlé *No 0620* is recommended for those with time to explore further.

ASHORE IN BELON

Belon village is on the S bank. There is water and fuel on the quay and a few bars but no shops. Fish can sometimes be bought from the fishermen at high water. The Plage de Kerfany is a pleasant walk and, in season, has a shop for the campsite.

Chez Jacky on the N bank is a famous seafood restaurant that also has a shop selling shellfish.

25.2 Early morning on the River Belon

25.3 Looking upriver, the three white head and stern visitors' buoys are vacant on the left

26 Merrien

Location
47°47′N 3°39′W

Shelter
Good in the river, but visitors' buoys are exposed.

Hazards
Marked rocks in entrance

Depth restrictions
1m in approach
Dries 0.6m except in channel

Night entry Possible but not recommended

HW time
Brest HW neaps, −½ springs

Mean height of tide (m)

	HWS	HWN	LWN	LWS
Port Tudy	5.1	4.0	2.0	0.9

Tidal stream
Weak in bay, stronger in harbour

Berthing
Anchorage and visitors' buoys

Facilities
Pleasant walking

Charts
BA 2821 (50)
SHOM 7031 (50), 7138 (10)
Imray C38 (large scale)

Telephone
Harbourmaster *t* 02 98 71 08 65

Attractive drying creek

Merrien is delightful, particularly for boats that can take the ground. There are three good weather visitors' buoys in the bay outside. Inside it dries apart from a dredged channel.

PILOTAGE

Merrien approach and entrance

By GPS

From the W use
169-W Brigneau, ⊕172-Merrien, ⊕173 Merrien 1.

From S and SE use
⊕172-Merrien, ⊕173 Merrien 1. There are unmarked rocks and shallow patches for 400m S of⊕173-Merrien 1.

By day

From the W, Merrien is easily identified ¾M beyond the ruined factory at Brigeau. From the E, the entrance will open after passing a headland topped by some white houses with grey roofs, 1¾M W of Doëlan.

There are marked dangers on both sides of the entrance. The official transit is the white lighthouse at the head of the pool with a large grey-roofed house with a gable on 005°. Unfortunately the lighthouse is almost obscured by the trees and it is adequate to line up the grey roof on 005°.

By night

Entry to the pool is possible, though not recommended without GPS, using the narrow red sector of the light on 005°.

BERTHS AND ANCHORAGES

Merrien visitors' buoys

The two visitors' buoys outside are the best place in calm conditions.

There are fore and aft moorings for visitors up to about 9m length in depths of about 1m.

26.1 Merrien looking N. The white light tower is visible just below the building at the top of the hill on the N bank. From the sea (below), the light tower is concealed by the trees

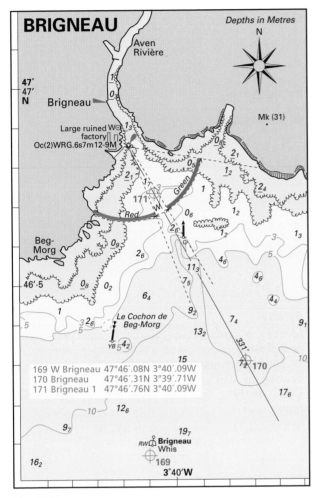

BRIGNEAU

Depths in Metres

Aven Rivière

47° 47' N

Brigneau

Large ruined factory
Oc(2)WRG.6s7m12-9M

Mk (31)

Green

171

Red

Beg-Morg

46'·5

Le Cochon de Beg-Morg

YB

331°

170

15

169 W Brigneau	47°46'.08N	3°40'.09W
170 Brigneau	47°46'.31N	3°39'.71W
171 Brigneau 1	47°46'.76N	3°40'.09W

RWC Brigneau Whis

169

3°40'W

Plan 26A

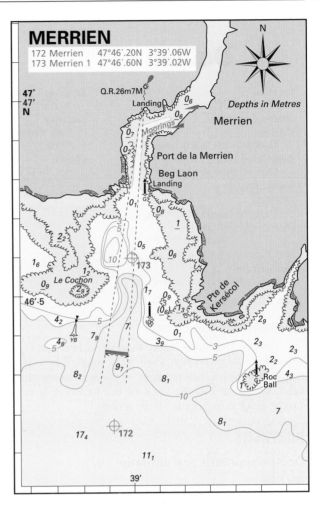

MERRIEN

172 Merrien	47°46'.20N	3°39'.06W
173 Merrien 1	47°46'.60N	3°39'.02W

N

47° 47' N

Q.R.26m7M

Landing

Depths in Metres

Merrien

Moorings

Port de la Merrien

Beg Laon
Landing

Le Cochon

173

Pte de Kersécol

46'·5

YB

Roc Ball

172

17₄

39'

Plan 26B

Merrien Pool

The 10m pool just inside the Merrien entrance is inviting but keep out of the channel and at least 50m offshore because the sides of the pool are rocky.

Brigneau

Brigneau is completely exposed to the SE so wind or swell from the S makes it untenable. It is ¾M W of Merrien and in good weather is an interesting place to visit. It was once a major sardine port but now has a small amount of fishing and a sailing school. The port dries but it is possible to anchor outside the harbour or borrow a mooring. Small boats may be able to use the fore and aft moorings just inside the harbour.

ASHORE IN MERRIEN

There is a stone jetty and steps on the starboard side of the entrance. The jetty is submerged at high water but is marked by a green beacon. Water is available on the quay.

There are some bars and a restaurant in the village, about ½M up the hill.

The GR34 footpath offers wonderful walking either along the coast path or inland on the banks of the river.

26.2 The ruined factory at Brigneau.
In good weather Brigneau is an interesting place to visit but it is completely exposed to the SE and untenable in swell

27 Doëlan

Location
47°46'N 3°36'W

Shelter Exposed to S

Hazards
Marked rocks in entrance.

Depth restrictions
Channel dredged 2.0m

Night entry Lit

HW time
Brest HW neaps, −½ springs

Mean height of tide (m)

	HWS	HWN	LWN	LWS
Port Tudy	5.1	4.0	2.0	0.9

Tidal stream
Little stream in bay or harbour

Berthing
Visitors' moorings and drying quay

Facilities
Bars, restaurants, fish market but no shops

Charts
BA 2821 (50)
SHOM 7031 (50), 7138 (10)
Imray C38 (large scale)

Radio VHF 16, 69

Telephone
Harbourmaster *t* 02 98 71 53 98

Small friendly fishing port

The port of Doëlan is larger than the other ports on this stretch of coast but is still very small. There is a small but active fishing fleet and some boats that take the ground at the back of the harbour. It is a pretty place and popular with artists.

PILOTAGE

Doëlan approach and entrance

By GPS

Use ⊕174-Doëlan, ⊕175-Doëlan 1.

By day

Identify a pink house on the E headland and a conspicuous factory with a tall, slender chimney.

Two lighthouses provide the entry transit on a bearing of 014°. This transit passes a red beacon PHM marking Basse le Croix and Le Four SHM buoy.

27.1 Doëlan looking N.
A large white metal mooring buoy is visible just inside the breakwater. Not shown in the picture is another similar mooring buoy just outside the breakwater

By night

Approach and enter with the leading lights in line on 014°. Coming from the direction of Lorient, a vessel can avoid the rocks SE of Le Pouldu (Les Grand et Petit Cochons) by keeping out of the green sector of the front light, which covers them.

BERTHS

Doëlan visitors' buoys

Visitors raft to a large white metal buoy with a rail round its edge. There is one of these just outside and another inside the breakwater on the W side of the entrance. There are also fore and aft visitors' buoys in the dredged channel.

The fishermen are friendly, and it may be possible to borrow one of their moorings. A boat that can take the ground may be able to borrow a mooring up-harbour.

Doëlan quays

It is possible to dry out at one of the quays. Near the entrance to the harbour there is a landing slip and quay on the W side, a pair of slips forming a V on the E side. Other quays lie further up. Local advice should be obtained before drying out. The inner quay on the W is not suitable as the bottom slopes outwards. The first two quays on the E dry about 1.5m and should be suitable.

ASHORE IN DOËLAN

Water and electricity are available on the quays and there is a fish market on the outer port-side quay, Quay Neuf.

There are bars and restaurants on both sides of the river and a good chandlery but apart from that, the nearest shops are at Clohars Carnoet, 3km inland.

The GR34 footpath is easy to access and can be followed along the rocky coast or inland beside the banks of the river.

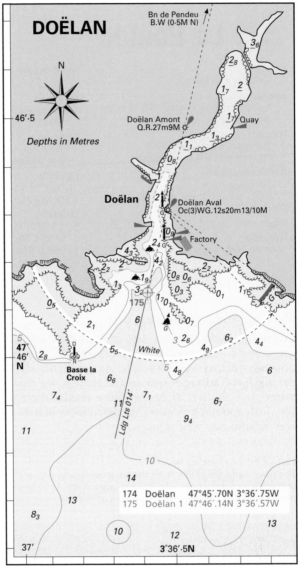

| 174 | Doëlan | 47°45'.70N 3°36'.75W |
| 175 | Doëlan 1 | 47°46'.14N 3°36'.57W |

Plan 27

27.2 The approach to Doëlan with the leading lighthouses almost in transit. The slender chimney associated with the factory is further up the hill

28 Le Pouldu

Location
47°46′N 3°32′W

Shelter
Good in river, exposed to S in outer anchorage

Hazards
Dangerous bar in entrance
Possible to be trapped inside

Depth restrictions
Bar dries 2.2m
2.0m in marina and parts of the river

Night entry Not lit

HW time
Brest HW neaps, −½ springs

Mean height of tide (m)

	HWS	HWN	LWN	LWS
Port Tudy	5.1	4.0	2.0	0.9

Tidal stream
Weak in bay, up to 6kts in river

Berthing
Tiny marina, visitors' buoy and anchorages

Facilities
Bars, restaurants and supermarket
Other shops 1M away

Charts
BA 2821 (50)
SHOM 7031 (50), 7138 (10)
Imray C38 (large scale)

Telephone
Yacht club *t* 02 98 96 92 98

Shifting sands and searing tide

Le Pouldu is challenging. The entry is difficult and can only be attempted an hour before HW in calm offshore weather with no swell. The sandbanks shift, the tide is too strong at springs and there is not much water over the bar at neaps. Once inside, there is very little room for visitors, but the harbourmaster is very helpful and welcoming.

28.1 Le Pouldu looking NE.
The River Laita flows 9M from the town of Quimperlé and in the 19th century ships of 150 tons used to go up at high tide. Notice the tide race at the mouth of the river

PILOTAGE

Approach and entrance to Le Pouldu

Warning

The stream in the river runs like a millrace and except near slack water a yacht going aground will be slewed round uncontrollably and possibly dangerously.

By GPS

The entrance requires careful visual pilotage. The following may be helpful in the approach.
⊕176-Pouldu, ⊕177-Pouldu 1.

By day

The harbour entrance can be identified by the former pilot's house, white with a round tower, situated on the W headland. The final approach is made with the pilot's house bearing 010°.

Entry should only be attempted in calm conditions about an hour before HW. This means there will be no indication of where the channel lies.

It is not possible to give precise directions since the channel moves. However, the main channel usually follows the W bank. It is marked by the red beacon tower at the entrance and by a port-hand beacon pole. The channel then curves to starboard where a second port-hand beacon pole marks the end of a small rocky spit. Except for the stream from the river, this channel dries at LW.

Sometimes, the strong streams cut through the spit, so the channel moves E to follow the dotted lines shown on the plan. When this happens, a sandy island may build up and almost block the under-cliff channel.

To take the main channel, leave the second beacon pole 40m to port and keep this distance off to avoid a rocky shelf. The river opens out, with a wide shallow bay to starboard, and the protecting breakwater of the marina will be seen ahead on the E bank.

The river is navigable by dinghies at HW up to Quimperlé, but a bridge with 10m clearance two miles from the entrance prevents the passage of masted vessels.

By night

Night entry should not be attempted.

BERTHS AND ANCHORAGE

Le Pouldu visitors' buoys

There are red mooring buoys for visitors off the marina. Another option is to continue upriver to find 2m or more for anchoring. There is an anchorage on the W bank at the entrance to a shallow creek, above a line of moorings. The holding appears to be good in spite of the stream and some weed.

There is a drying sandbank in the middle of the river and there are many small-craft drying moorings on the E side and in the bay downstream.

The marina is small, mainly for boats under 9m. There is not much space for visitors.

⚓ Outside Le Pouldu

In settled offshore weather an anchorage can be found outside the bar. The best spot seems to be with the marina bearing 000° as far in as draught permits. The bottom is hard sand.

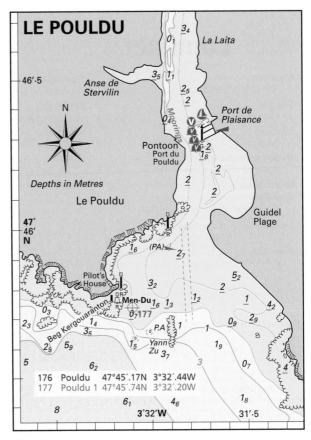

Plan 28

ASHORE IN LE POULDU

The pontoon on the W bank is for fishermen but there is space to leave a dinghy. There are two hotels close by and the shops of Le Pouldu are 1M along the road.

On the E bank, by the marina, there are restaurants catering for a camping site and there is a large supermarket a few minutes' walk round the bay towards the entrance.

28.2 The former pilot's house with a round tower above Men-Du beacon tower.

29 Loméner

Location
47°42'N 3°26'W

Shelter
Good from NW to NE.

Hazards
Marked and unmarked rocks

Depth restrictions
3.0m at breakwater

Night entry Lit

HW time
Brest HW neaps, −½ springs

Mean height of tide (m)

	HWS	HWN	LWN	LWS
Port Tudy	5.1	4.0	2.0	0.9

Tidal stream
Weak in approach and anchorage

Berthing
Anchorages

Facilities
As of a beach resort

Charts
BA 2821 (50)
SHOM 7031 (50), 7139 (20)
Imray C38 (78)

Pleasant seaside resort

The port of Loméner and the adjacent Anse de Stole, form a small harbour on the mainland opposite Ile de Groix.

It is open to the S but sheltered from the N and the *vent solaire*. In settled weather, it can be a better option than Port Tudy.

Loméner has good beaches and all facilities of a small seaside resort.

PILOTAGE

Approach and entrance to Loméner

By GPS

Use ⊕181-Loméner, ⊕182-Loméner 1.

By day

The harbour is easy to identify by a prominent block of flats behind the breakwater.

Enter by keeping the white tower with a red top in transit with Ploemeur church spire on 357°. Plomeur church is not easy to see but the dangers on the W side are well marked so following the exact transit is not critical. The dangers on the E are less well marked and in particular Grasu SCM should be given a good berth because rocks extend W of it.

By night

Enter using the white sector of Anse de Stole light. Beware of the many unlit fishing floats and moorings.

BERTHS AND ANCHORAGES

⚓ Anse de Stole

Anchor in the Anse de Stole where space and depth permit or borrow a mooring. The beaches behind the breakwater and in the Anse de Stole are excellent for drying out. There is a landing slip on the spur inside the harbour. Avoid the breakwater wall, as there are vicious rocks at its foot.

⚓ Kerroc'h

Sheltered from all directions except W and NW, this small harbour is about 4M W of Lorient. Approach from due S steering to pass about 150m W of the WCM marking Les Deux Têtes. This is necessary to avoid the unmarked Les Soeurs rocks on the W side of the entrance. Once past the WCM, turn to starboard to enter the harbour. Anchor where depth permits or borrow a mooring.

⊕179-Kerroc'h 1 (47°42'.18N 3°28'.09W)

29.1 Le Pérello looking E.
This stretch of rocky coast has several small, sandy bays which make useful anchorages. The first bay in the picture is Le Pérello. Further E, beyond the long breakwater is Loméner and the large curved bay is Anse de Stole. In the distance is the entrance to Lorient harbour

⚓ Le Pérello

Exposed to wind or swell from the S, Le Pérello is about 1M E of Kerroc'h. Approach from the SSE. The drying rocks on either side of the entrance can be avoided by aligning the elbow of the small slipway on the NE side of the bay with the seaward-facing gable end of the house behind it on 353°. The house is the one closest to the beach and distinctively painted half grey and half white.

There are some moorings but there is also room to anchor.

⊕180-Pérello (47°41′.69N 3°26′.40W)

ASHORE IN LOMENER

There is water at the root of the quay and shops, bars and restaurants. There is also a large supermarket close to the quay. Shellfish can often be bought direct from local fishermen.

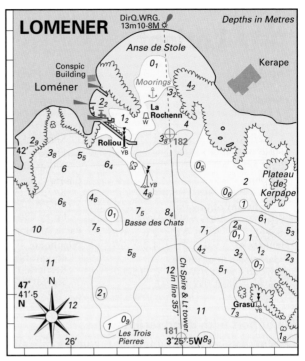

Plan 29A

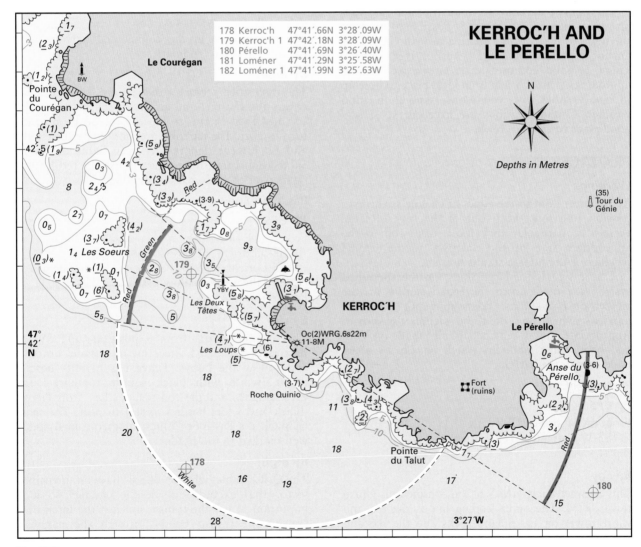

178 Kerroc'h	47°41′.66N	3°28′.09W
179 Kerroc'h 1	47°42′.18N	3°28′.09W
180 Pérello	47°41′.69N	3°26′.40W
181 Loméner	47°41′.29N	3°25′.58W
182 Loméner 1	47°41′.99N	3°25′.63W

Plan 29B

30 Lorient

Location
47°42′N 3°22′W

Shelter
Excellent in marinas

Hazards
Marked rocks in entrance

Depth restrictions None

Night entry Well lit

HW time
Brest HW neaps, −¼ springs

Mean height of tide (m)

	HWS	HWN	LWN	LWS
Lorient	5.1	4.0	2.0	0.8
Hennebont	5.0	3.9	1.8	0.7

Tidal stream in entrance:
Flood – Brest HW–5 to –2 (3.5kts)
Slack – Brest HW–2 to +2

Ebb – Brest HW+2 to +5 (4.0kts)
Slack – Brest HW+5 to –5

Berthing
Several marinas

Fuel
Kernéval S basin

Facilities
All facilities

Charts
BA 2821 (50), 304 (10)
SHOM 7031 (50), 7140 (20)
Imray C38 (large scale)

Radio All marinas VHF 9

Telephone:
Lorient Marina *t* 02 97 21 10 14
Kerneval *t* 02 97 65 48 25
Ste Catherine *t* 02 97 33 59 51

Major port with good facilities

Lorient was once an important commercial and naval port. Today it has the largest fishing fleet in Brittany and six marinas.

Parts of the harbour are industrial and not very attractive but against that, it is possible to moor in the heart of the city, in a marina near the beach, or anchor in perfect peace in a beautiful river. Also the sailing is good because Ile de Groix protects the approaches. Thus Lorient is an ideal place to hole up in bad weather but well worth visiting in good weather. Communications are excellent so it is a good place to change crews.

PILOTAGE

Warnings

Yachts must keep to the edges of channels wherever possible and must keep out of the way of large vessels. In particular they must keep well to the appropriate side of the narrows at the citadel whether or not a large ship is present.

Traffic signals for large ships, on the simplified system, are made from the signal station on the citadel of Port Louis. Boats may not enter the narrows when one of these signals is shown. Appropriate announcements are also made on VHF and boats must maintain watch on Ch 16 when underway in the harbour.

Passe de l'Ouest

By GPS

From the W or Port Tudy use
⊕183-W Lorient, ⊕184-Lorient,
⊕191-Cochon.

By day

This channel starts ¾M S of the conspicuous Grasu tower SCM. The outer leading line is the red and white tower on Les Soeurs rocks and the red and white banded day mark above the citadel walls (right of a conspicuous church spire) on 057°. The channel is well buoyed.

Soon after passing Les Trois Pierres beacon tower (BW horizontal bands), the narrows will open. The transit is two white towers with green tops on the W side of Ile Saint-Michel on 016°. However, the huge white grain silo in the commercial harbour also provides a useful landmark.

By night

The intensified sector of the leading lights on 057° covers the channel and all the lateral buoys are lit. Use Les Trois Pierres to identify the position of the turn to port. The narrows are marked by the citadel and La Jument. Ignore the green lights of the Ile Saint-Michel transit and instead use the red leading lights over the fish market on 008.5°.

Passe du Sud

By GPS

From the E or SE use
⊕187-S Lorient, ⊕188-Goeland,
⊕185-Lorient 1, ⊕191-Cochon. This route passes close to the 1.4m shallow patch near Basse de la Paix SHM.

By day

This channel starts from a position ¼M SW of Bastresses Sud SHM. Steer for the citadel on 010° and follow the buoys. Leave Les Errants beacon tower (white with black square topmark), Les Errants PHM and the conspicuous Les Trois Pierres (black and white beacon tower) to port. The main channel, the Passe de l'Ouest, is then joined and is well marked to the citadel.

By night

The Q.R leading lights on 008.5° have an intensified sector that extends outside the channel so it is important to use the transit, not just the intensified sector. The transit passes through the narrows, where La Jument and the citadel mark the port and starboard sides.

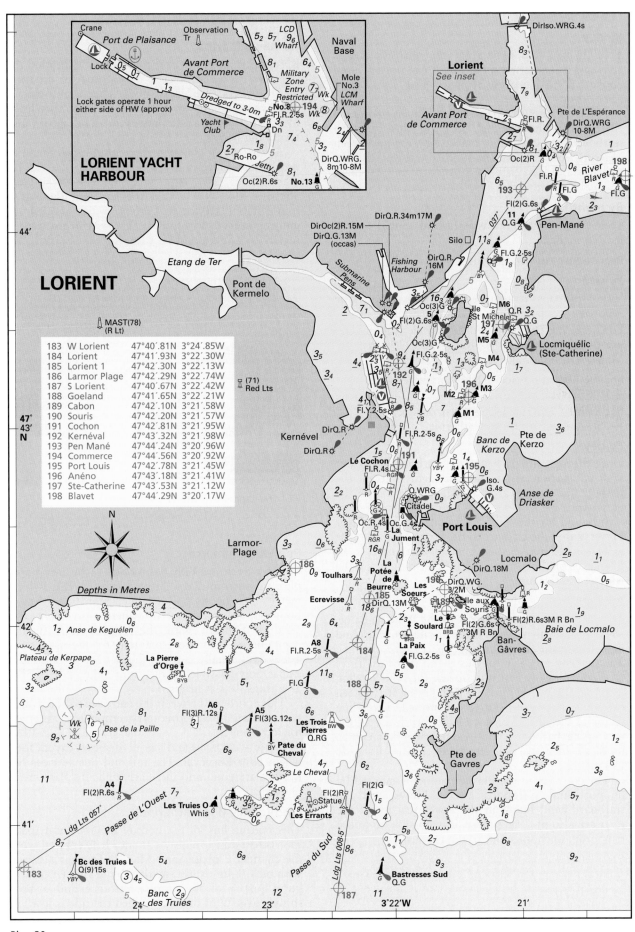

LORIENT YACHT HARBOUR

Lock gates operate 1 hour either side of HW (approx)

183	W Lorient	47°40´.81N 3°24´.85W
184	Lorient	47°41´.93N 3°22´.30W
185	Lorient 1	47°42´.30N 3°22´.13W
186	Larmor Plage	47°42´.29N 3°22´.74W
187	S Lorient	47°40´.67N 3°22´.42W
188	Goeland	47°41´.65N 3°22´.21W
189	Cabon	47°42´.10N 3°21´.58W
190	Souris	47°42´.20N 3°21´.57W
191	Cochon	47°42´.81N 3°21´.95W
192	Kernéval	47°43´.32N 3°21´.98W
193	Pen Mané	47°44´.24N 3°20´.96W
194	Commerce	47°44´.56N 3°20´.92W
195	Port Louis	47°42´.78N 3°21´.45W
196	Anéno	47°43´.18N 3°21´.41W
197	Ste-Catherine	47°43´.53N 3°21´.12W
198	Blavet	47°44´.29N 3°20´.17W

LORIENT

Etang de Ter

Pont de Kermelo

MAST(78) (R Lt)

Depths in Metres

Plan 30

Chenal Secondaire

By day

This channel is a bypass for the narrows and is convenient for Kernével marina. It can only be used above half tide because it passes over Le Cochon (dries 1m).

A RGR can buoy, WSW of La Jument marks the entrance to the channel. Leaving this buoy to starboard, the channel is marked by red and green beacons up to Le Cochon beacon tower (RGR), which should be left to starboard as the main channel is re-entered.

By night

The Chenal Secondaire is unlit and should not be used at night.

Proceeding up the Harbour

By GPS

Visual pilotage is required in the harbour. The following waypoints may provide assistance.

For Kernéval, Pen Mané or the Port de Commerce use ⊕191-Cochon, ⊕192-Kernéval, ⊕193-Pen Mané, ⊕194 Commerce.

For the Blavet, replace ⊕194-Commerce with ⊕198-Blavet.

For Sainte-Catherine use ⊕191-Cochon, ⊕196-Anéno, ⊕197-Ste Catherine.

By day

Once through the narrows, the harbour opens out and navigation is straightforward. Within the harbour, the dangers are marked, and the chart is the best guide.

If bound for the Port de Commerce or the River Blavet, either the channel to the E or to the W of Ile Saint-Michel may be used. Note that there is an unmarked shallow patch, with 0.5m over it, on the edge of the E channel.

By night

The usual route up harbour is to the W of Ile Saint-Michel although there is often enough background light to see the unlit buoys in the eastern channel. The shallow area SSW of this island (Banc du Turc) is a hazard below half tide, so use the 350° leading lights until Banc de Turc SHM, marking its western extremity, has been positively identified. The white sector of Pte de L'Espérance light then leads all the way up the harbour. The RoRo terminal light can be used to identify the entrance to the Port de Commerce.

The entrance to the Blavet channel is marked by lit port and starboard lateral buoys and the starboard-hand buoys in the lower reaches of the river are also lit. Using these, it is possible to find a temporary anchorage out of the channel.

BERTHS AND ANCHORAGES

Kernéval Marina

Kernéval is on the W of the harbour ½M beyond the narrows. It is protected by a line of floating wavebreakers secured to piles. The N entrance is used when looking for a berth. The S entrance leads to the fuel pontoon, a slipway for hauling out and scrubbing berths.

Apart from a chandler there are limited facilities nearby but bicycles are available from the helpful marina staff. Two large supermarkets are situated about a mile NW round the bay and there is a frequent bus service to Lorient, where workshops and engineers can be found. There is also a waterbus service to Lorient and Port Louis.

30.1 The capitainerie at Kernéval Marina

Port de Commerce

The wet dock is a fully pontooned yacht harbour in pleasant surroundings. At busy times yachts will be met by marina staff in a launch and directed to a pontoon; otherwise tie up where convenient and arrange a berth with the helpful staff in the capitainerie. Only those planning to stay more than a few days usually berth in the wet basin. Entry and exit is only possible for one hour either side of HW at springs, less at neaps.

The pontoons between the entrance to the avant-port and the Ile de Groix ferry terminal are reserved for local boats.

It is a lively place and has all facilities, except fuel, which is at Kernéval. The rail and bus services for Lorient are good and there are flights to Paris from Quimper.

Locmiquélic (Ste-Catherine)

This marina has all the normal facilities and space for visitors can usually be found. It is entered from the channel E of Ile Saint-Michel. There is a wreck with only 0.4m over it, marked by M5 green conical buoy, just S of the marina entrance and a boat should pass W of this buoy when the tide is low.

30.2 Port de Commerce in Lorient looking NW.
The Wet Basin at the top of the harbour is only open for one hour either side of HW at springs and less at neaps. Visitors usually stay in the Avant Port near the capitainerie

30.3 Locmiquélic (Ste-Catherine) looking N.
In the foreground is Locmiquélic Marina while Pen-Mané, at the mouth of the River Blavet can be seen on the next headland

Enter between the floating breakwater to the S and the red buoy to the N and secure temporarily before being allocated a berth. Access is possible at night as both the breakwater and red buoy have lights but, as the channel is unlit, it is easiest for the stranger to approach from N of Ile Saint-Michel.

There are shops and the usual facilities of a small town about 500m from the marina.

Pen-Mané marina

This modern marina at the mouth of the Blavet is attractive and peaceful. It is a long way from any facilities but there is a waterbus to Lorient.

According to a notice in the marina, visitors' berths are available on request to Ste-Catherine marina.

⚓ The River Blavet and Hennebont

The upper reaches of this little-visited river are most attractive, with an abundance of bird-life. At half tide it is possible to find plenty of water all the way to Hennebont. The two shallowest patches lie just after the first and second road bridges where only 1.5m could be found at LW neaps.

Three bridges cross the river between the entrance and Hennebont. The first two have 22m clearance and the last 21m. Power cables cross the river above the second bridge. Their height is unknown but they appear to be higher than the bridges.

The channel is marked by buoys or beacons to the second road bridge. Above the first bridge at Bonhomme the river narrows and winds a further four miles to Hennebont.

A concrete obstruction, which dries, is reported to lie under the second road bridge, approximately one third of the way out from the left supporting column (heading upriver). When passing under the bridge keep to the centre, or to starboard if proceeding upriver.

There are many possible anchorages on the way to Hennebont, where there is a small, short-stay pontoon. The bottom is very soft mud so an overnight stay may be possible. There are head and stern visitors' moorings for yachts less than 10m.

Hennebont is a pleasant walled market town with a market in the square on Thursday mornings. There are shops, including a large supermarket, banks and restaurants. Fuel can be obtained from a garage close to the bridge and there is a water tap close to the pontoon. It has good rail connections.

30.4 A boat graveyard on the River Blavet

31 Port Louis and Locmalo

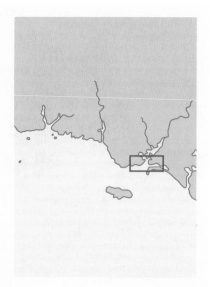

Location
47°42'N 3°22'W

Shelter
Excellent in marina

Hazards
Intricate entry to Locmalo

Depth restrictions
1.1m in approach to Port Louis
0.2m in approach to Locmalo

Night entry
Partially lit but not recommended

HW time
Brest HW neaps, −¼ springs

Mean height of tide (m)

	HWS	HWN	LWN	LWS
Port Louis	5.1	4.0	2.0	0.9

Tidal streams
Approach as Lorient
4 knots in entrance to Locmalo

Berthing
Marina and moorings at Port Louis;
anchorage at Locmalo

Facilities
All facilities; interesting historic
town

Charts:
BA 2821 (50), 304 (10)
SHOM 7031 (50), 7140 (20)
Imray C38 (large scale)

Radio VHF 9

Telephone
Port Louis Marina *t* 02 97 82 59 55

The other side of Lorient

Port Louis is no distance from Lorient by water but a world away in charm and character. It is a small tuna port and seaside resort with a magnificent 16th century citadel that contains several interesting museums with a nautical theme.

There is a marina on the N side of the town. To the S, completely protected by the Gâvres peninsula, is the delightful bay of Locmalo.

PILOTAGE (see Plan 30)

Port Louis entrance

By GPS

Use the instructions for the Passe de l'Ouest or Passe du Sud to ⊕191-Cochon and continue to ⊕195-Port Louis.

By day

Leave the main channel N of the citadel near Le Cochon RGR beacon and steer about 100° leaving two SHMs to starboard. Just beyond the second SHM is a beacon SHM marking the beginning of the channel to the marina. Keep close to the starboard side of the channel because the bay shoals quickly and there are some wrecks.

By night

Not recommended.

Locmalo NW entrance

Warning

A large-scale chart is essential.

By GPS

This entrance requires careful visual pilotage. ⊕185-Lorient 1, ⊕190-Souris may provide some assistance.

31.1 Port Louis and Locmalo looking S. The marina at Port Louis is in the foreground. Beyond is the bay of Locmalo and the new marina at Ban-Gâvres. The small town of Port Louis is good for strolling and the citadel (not shown in the picture) has several nautical museums

By day

Pass N of La Potée de Beurre with the N side of Ile aux Souris in transit with the end of the ferry slip on the S side of the entrance to the Baie de Locmalo, bearing 112°. Alternatively use La Potée de Beurre in line with Larmor church on a back bearing of 278°. On approaching Ile aux Souris, with a green light tripod on its western side, alter course to leave the islet to starboard and steer on the N side of the channel. Leave a green buoy to starboard and pass between the red and green beacon towers. The channel then curves NE towards the jetty at Locmalo.

By night

Not recommended.

Locmalo SW entrance

Warning A large-scale chart is essential.

By GPS

This entrance requires careful visual pilotage. ⊕188-Goeland, ⊕189-Cabon, ⊕190-Souris may provide some assistance.

By day

Start at the green conical buoy ½M SW of Ile aux Souris and head for Ile aux Souris, on a heading of 045°. Once past Le Soulard IDM beacon alter course to about 000° to pass between Le Cabon reef and Ile aux Souris. Neither the beacon on Le Cabon, nor the light beacon on Ile aux Souris mark the extremities of the dangers. Le Pesquerez green pole beacon astern should be kept open W of Le Soulard. After Ile-aux-Souris has been passed the channel described above is joined.

By night

Partially lit but not recommended.

BERTHS AND ANCHORAGES

Port Louis

Port Louis welcomes visitors and has a 50m visitors' pontoon. Other berths in the marina may be available. There are also some moorings in the shoaling bay to the E of the citadel, which may be available on application to the yacht club.

The nearest fuel and repair facilities are at Kernéval.

Locmalo

There are many moorings off Pen-er-Run and it may be possible to borrow one. The pool E of the Grand and Petit Belorc'h beacons is clear of moorings and offers good anchorage in up to 4m.

Facilities at Locmalo

There are shops, banks and restaurants at Port Louis. The best dinghy landing is at Locmalo jetty.

Ban-Gâvres

There is a new marina at Ban-Gâvres, opposite Locmalo. It is reported to have a few berths for visitors but with difficult manoeuvring.

There are also moorings off Ban-Grâves and it is possible to take the ground at Ban-Grâves jetty.

⚓ Larmor-Plage

Protected from W and N there is a rather open anchorage opposite Port Louis in the approaches to Lorient. Leave the main channel near Toulhars PHM and head towards the two red beacons near Larmor breakwater. It is possible to anchor near the N red beacon. At neaps anchor beyond the beacons towards the Plage de Toulhars. Keep clear of the two cardinals that mark a wreck. A large-scale chart is essential.

⊕186-Larmor Plage (47°42′.29N 3°22′.74W)

⚓ Anse de Goërem

Sheltered from the E there is a useful bay at the W end of the Gâvres peninsula. Anchor S of La Pesquerez beacon. It is rather exposed for a night anchorage but it possible to leave at night using the lit SHM S of La Paix.

⊕188-Goeland (47°41′.65N 3°22′.21W)

ASHORE IN PORT LOUIS

There are plenty of shops, bars and restaurants. Port Louis itself is a pleasant and interesting 18th century walled town. The citadel contains an excellent museum and there are good views of Lorient and Groix from the ramparts.

31.2 The visitors' pontoon at Port Louis marina

31.3 Locmalo Bay look S towards Ban-Gâvres. The red and green beacon towers mark the entrance to Locmalo Bay

32 Port Tudy

Location
  47°38'N 3°28'W

Shelter
  Good except from N or NE.

Hazards
  Unmarked rocks near leading line
  Ferries manoeuvring in harbour

Depth restrictions
  2.0m on visitors' moorings

Lock to inner harbour HW ±2

Night entry Lit

HW time
  Brest HW neaps, −½ springs

Mean height of tide (m)

	HWS	HWN	LWN	LWS
Port Tudy	5.1	4.0	2.0	0.9

Tidal stream in approaches
  E – Brest HW–4 to HW (0.4kts)
  Slack – Brest HW to +3
  W – Brest HW +3 to +6 (0.4kts)
  Slack – Brest HW+6 to –4

Berthing
  Visitors' buoys and marina

Fuel
  Base of inner harbour (cans)

Facilities As of a small port

Charts
  BA 2821 (50)
  SHOM 7031 (50), 7139 (20/5)
  Imray C38 (large scale)

Radio VHF 9

Telephone
  Harbourmaster *t* 02 97 86 54 62

Attractive busy harbour

Port Tudy is an attractive 19th-century tuna port that is now almost entirely devoted to tourism. The outer harbour is rather exposed to the N and NE, which makes it uncomfortable if the *vent solaire* blows in the early hours of the morning.

It is the only real port on Ile de Groix (plan 33C) and gets very crowded, particularly at weekends. The large numbers of tourists and the noisy ferries make Port Tudy lively but rarely peaceful.

32.1 Port Tudy looking S.
All three harbours may be used by visitors if there is space. Boats can moor fore and aft between buoys in the outer harbour. There are pontoon berths in the inner harbour or boats raft to the pontoons in the wet dock

PILOTAGE

Port Tudy approach and entrance

By GPS

From Lorient or the NW use
⊕199-Port Tudy.
From Etel use ⊕200-Mélite, ⊕199-Port Tudy.
From the SE use ⊕202-Cougy, ⊕200-Mélite, ⊕199-Port Tudy.

By day

The harbour is easily identified and the approach from the W and N is straightforward; there are some mooring buoys and a fish farm off Port Lay, but no other dangers.

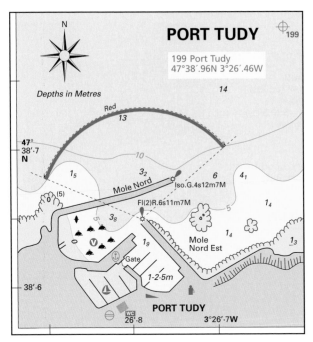

PORT TUDY

199 Port Tudy
47°38'.96N 3°26'.46W

Depths in Metres

Plan 32

From the E and SE there are some unmarked dangers. The safe transit uses the harbour lighthouses in line on 217°. This leaves a rock (depth 0.8m) 200m to port. A red beacon marks some other dangers closer inshore.

Enter the port midway between the breakwater heads, and then steer parallel to the N breakwater to avoid the rocks at the end of the E breakwater. If a ferry is manoeuvring, stand off because it needs all the room there is.

By night

The buoys in the approaches are unlit. The E breakwater light is obscured over the dangers to the E of the harbour. It is therefore safe to keep this light showing and just open to the left of the N breakwater light. If they are exactly in transit, the rear light is obscured.

BERTHS AND ANCHORAGES

Port Tudy outer harbour

In the season yachts entering may be met by a high-speed harbour launch and directed to a berth. In the outer harbour yachts moor between the large white mooring buoys, ensuring that there is room for the ferry to manoeuvre. Long warps are necessary and springs are advisable to ensure that spreaders will not foul if the swell gets up. The landing slip is reserved for ferries.

Port Tudy inner harbour

The inner harbour shoals inwards, but there is plenty of water for most yachts. There are pontoon berths and yachts lie rafted together.

Port Tudy wet dock

Entry to the wet dock is possible during the day for two hours either side of HW. If waiting for the gates to open, it is best to tie up on a pontoon rather than the inner landing slip. A stone shelf protrudes below the top end of the slip near the gates.

Visitors will be directed to a berth in 2m to 3m. The wet basin is the most crowded part of the harbour; yachts are rafted to the pontoons and it is only really useful for a long stay.

⚓ Port Tudy anchorage

The harbour has no room to anchor and the bottom is foul. In settled weather it is possible to anchor outside providing the ferries are not obstructed. However, their wash makes the anchorage rather uncomfortable.

⚓ Port-Melin and Beg-er-Vir

Open to the N but protected from the S, Port Melin is a small cove 1M W of Port Tudy, Beg-er-Vir is the larger bay W of Port Melin. Approach from the N at low water taking care to avoid the rock ledges. Anchor in 2m on sand. A large-scale chart is essential.

Port-Lay

Open to the N, this very pretty harbour is believed to be one of the tiniest in Brittany. It is about ½M W of Port Tudy and anchoring is forbidden but the local sailing school has some mooring buoys that can sometimes be borrowed.

⚓ Pointe de la Croix

Protected from the SW but otherwise rather exposed, there are a number of possible anchorages off the beach near Pointe de la Croix.

⊕201-Pte de la Croix 47°38'.14N 3°24'.87W

ASHORE IN PORT TUDY

Fuel is available in cans from the depot at the SE corner of the inner harbour. There is a marine engineer, a hauling-out slip, some chandlery and a launderette on the quay. There are cafés around the harbour and bread may be obtained nearby. All other shops, including a supermarket, are available up the hill in town.

Bicycles may be hired to explore this picturesque island and there are frequent ferries to Lorient.

32.2 Port Tudy entrance

33 Locmaria

Location
47°37′N 3°26′W

Shelter
Locmaria – open to S

Hazards
Many unmarked rocks

Depth restrictions
1.0m in Loc Maria anchorage

Night entry Not recommended

HW time
Brest HW neaps, –½ springs

Mean height of tide (m)

	HWS	HWN	LWN	LWS
Port Tudy	5.1	4.0	2.0	0.9

Tidal stream Pte des Chats
NE – Brest HW–6 to –2 (0.5kts)
Slack – Brest HW–2 to +1
SW – Brest HW+1 to +5 (0.5kts)
Slack – Brest HW+5 to –6

Berthing Anchorages

Facilities
A few shops and bars, good beach, nice 1½M walk to Port Tudy

Charts
BA 2821 (50)
SHOM 7031 (50), 7139 (20)
Imray C38 (large scale)

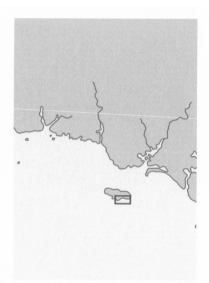

Charming unspoilt harbour

This charming unspoilt little harbour is situated on the S of Ile de Groix, ¾M W of Pointe des Chats (plan 33C). It is well worth a visit under the right conditions.

The approach is open to the Atlantic, and the anchorage is dangerously exposed to swell or wind with any S in it. However, it is well sheltered from the W through N to E. The harbour dries but outside there is space to anchor in depths of 1m or more.

PILOTAGE

Locmaria approach and entrance

By GPS

From Port Tudy use
⊕199-Port Tudy, ⊕200-Mélite, ⊕202-Cougy, ⊕203-SE Chats, ⊕204-Les Chats, ⊕205-Locmaria, ⊕206-Locmaria 1.

In good weather with enough rise of tide, ⊕203-SE Chats (plan 33C) can be omitted but the resulting route must be used with care because it passes close to the unmarked dangers of Les Chats.

From Lorient, join the above route at ⊕202-Cougy; from Etel join at ⊕203-SE Chats (plan 33C).

By day

Coming from the N, E or SE it will be necessary to make a detour round Les Chats (see plan 33C).

From an initial position S of Les Chats, Locmaria will be seen on the E side of the bay, together with Er Brazelleg green beacon tower and a white masonry beacon on the land. There is another village on the W side. Between the villages, on the NW side of the bay, is a small group of cottages with a small white masonry beacon in front of them. These form the leading line.

Approach Er Brazelleg on 005° until the cottages and beacon have been identified. The transit for the entrance is the masonry beacon in line with the centre window of a white cottage on 350°. There are several cottages in the area but the correct one is the right-hand, lowest one of a group of three. The group of cottages is distinctive because the left-hand one shows its gable end.

33.1 Locmaria harbour looking E.
The harbour itself is full of moorings but it is possible to anchor outside the harbour in good holding. The inset shows the leading line

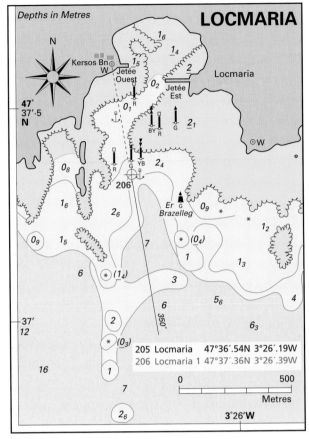

Plan 33A

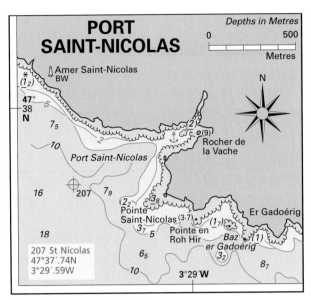

Plan 33B

Follow the transit between the first port and starboard beacons. The line to the second port beacon passes close to the rocks so keep on the transit until the pier head bears about 055°. Then bear to starboard for the pier head, keeping rather closer to the inner port-hand beacon.

By night

There are no lights and a night entry should not be attempted.

BERTHS AND ANCHORAGES

⚓ Locmaria

The harbour is choked with small-boat moorings and there is no room to anchor and remain afloat. Anchor outside the harbour in good holding just W of the leading line or, at neaps, between the second red beacon and the pier head. There is also a good anchorage just outside the reef, S of the beacon SCM, in about 2m. It is not possible to lie alongside the jetty because it may be used for landing.

Locmaria is an attractive white painted village that feels like somewhere much further S. There are shops, a bar and a crêperie and good beaches. It is a pleasant walk of 1½M to Port Tudy and there are lots of other walks in the area.

⚓ Port Saint-Nicolas

Protected from NW to E and from the *vent solaire* but wide open to the SW, this magical crack in the cliffs is about 1M E of Pen Men. It can be identified by the black and white day mark 900m to the west of the cove.

Approach from the SW and, leaving Pointe Saint-Nicolas to starboard, steer for the centre of the cove. The bottom is sand with a lot of rock and weed so it is best to buoy the anchor. Since there is not much swinging room, it may be necessary to use two anchors.

⊕207-St-Nicolas (47°37′.74N 3°29′.59W)

33.2 Port Saint-Nicolas looking NE.
This magical and challenging crack in the cliffs has very little swinging room

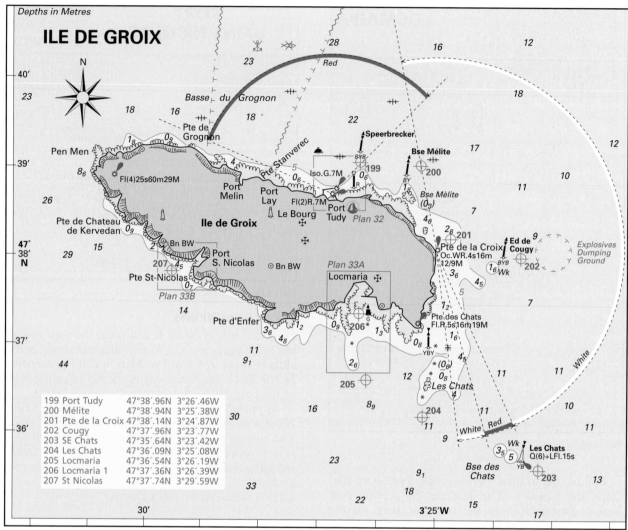

Depths in Metres

ILE DE GROIX

199 Port Tudy	47°38′.96N	3°26′.46W
200 Mélite	47°38′.94N	3°25′.38W
201 Pte de la Croix	47°38′.14N	3°24′.87W
202 Cougy	47°37′.96N	3°23′.77W
203 SE Chats	47°35′.64N	3°23′.42W
204 Les Chats	47°36′.09N	3°25′.08W
205 Locmaria	47°36′.54N	3°26′.19W
206 Locmaria 1	47°37′.36N	3°26′.39W
207 St Nicolas	47°37′.74N	3°29′.59W

Plan 33C

34 Etel

Location
47°39'N 3°13'W

Shelter
Excelent in marina

Hazards
Dangerous shifting bar at entrance

Depth restrictions
0.6m, sometimes much less, on bar
1.5m in marina

Other restrictions
Must call pilot for entry instructions

Night entry Forbidden

HW time
Brest HW+¼ neaps, −¼ springs

Mean height of tide (m)

	HWS	HWN	LWN	LWS
Etel	4.9	4.1	2.2	1.5

Tidal stream in river
Slack – Brest HW–5 to –4
Flood – Brest HW–4 to +2 (1.5kts)
Ebb – Brest HW+2 to –5 (1.3kts)

Berthing
Marina and anchorages

Facilities
All facilities

Charts
BA 2821 (50), 304 (10)
SHOM 7031 (50), 7138 (10)
Imray C38 (large scale)

Radio Semaphore d'Etel VHF 13

Telephone
Marina *t* 02 9755 46 62
Semaphore *t* 02 97 55 35 35

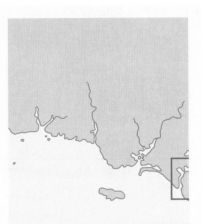

Delightful river with fierce tides

Etel bar has a bad reputation and should be avoided in strong S wind or swell. In settled weather it is not a problem.

The bar can shift from day to day so it is necessary to follow VHF directions in French from the pilot, Mme Josiane Pene. Since she speaks in clear simple French, even this is not much of a challenge.

Once inside, Etel is a delightful place. It has clean blue water, a friendly marina, a pleasant town, spectacular beaches and an inland sea almost as big as the Morbihan.

PILOTAGE

Etel Bar and the semaphore

During the approach it is essential to make contact with the semaphore station and until then to keep at least ½M off. The following visual signals are displayed:

- Arrow horizontal: no entry for any vessels.
- Black ball: no entry for undecked vessels under 8m length.
- Red flag: Not enough water or pilot not on duty.

Once VHF contact has been established, Madame Josiane Pene, the only woman pilot in France, will give instructions in clear, simple French.

The semaphore is hardly ever used but if necessary it is easy to understand. Mme Pene simply points the arrow right or left depending on the direction she wants the boat to turn.

The harbourmaster recommends crossing the bar between Port Tudy HW–2 and –1 (roughly Brest HW–2½ to –1½). Note that the flood stream will still be running strongly.

34.1 The semaphore station at Etel with the semaphore arrow in the vertical position. If it is horizontal it means that there is no entry for vessels. If the red flag is flying then either there is not enough water or the pilot is not on duty

ETEL APPROACH AND ENTRANCE

(See Plan 34)

By GPS

From the W or S use
⊕208-Etel; from the S use ⊕210-Chivguete,
⊕208-Etel.

The continuation into the river will depend on instructions from the pilot but will end up at ⊕209-Etel 1.

By day

The position of the deepest water across the bar varies considerably and can change overnight. However, it is usually best to approach with the distinctive 76m red and white radio mast at the back of the town on 020°.

The stream is weak outside the bar, but may reach six knots as the port-hand beacon is passed. Shortly after entering the river continue along the W side,

34.2 The marina at Etel looking E.
The pontoons are quite small and larger boats tie up at the hammerheads. The long jetty is very popular with summer residents for an early evening promenade.

leaving an unlit red beacon to port, a green buoy and beacon to starboard and a final red buoy to port. From there, keep in the centre of the channel where the water is deep.

By night
Visitors must not attempt to enter at night.

BERTHS AND ANCHORAGES

Etel marina
The marina has a depth of 2.5m. Larger boats secure to the hammerheads, smaller boats use a finger berth.

Do not secure to the main jetty because it is reserved for the fishing fleet, and keep clear of the ferry berth on the innermost pontoon.

⚓ Etel
Moorings occupy the best places and it is difficult to find an anchorage out of the stream.

Just above Etel the holding is good on both sides of the river, but springs run at 6kts and there are oyster beds in the shallows.

⚓ Pont Lorois
It is possible to anchor just into the northern side of the bay on the E bank below Pont Lorois. The southern part of this bay is foul.

⚓ Vieux passage
There is an anchorage just above Vieux Passage, but do not go far into the bay as the bottom is foul.

ASHORE IN ETEL

Facilities
There are limited repair facilities and fuel is only available in cans.

Etel is a thriving holiday resort with plenty of shops, bars and restaurants. There is a good supermarket, several fish shops and a street market on Tuesdays.

The beaches on either side of the river mouth are interesting. They have a particularly rich sand dune flora and are also very popular with male nudists.

The tuna festival is on the second Sunday in August when the town gives itself over to fun and feasting.

La Mer d'Etel
The Mer d'Etel is a like a small version of the Morbihan. It is not navigable by masted yachts because the road bridge only has 9m clearance and the tide runs very fast. However, it is well worth seeing it from the tourist boat that runs several times a day in season.

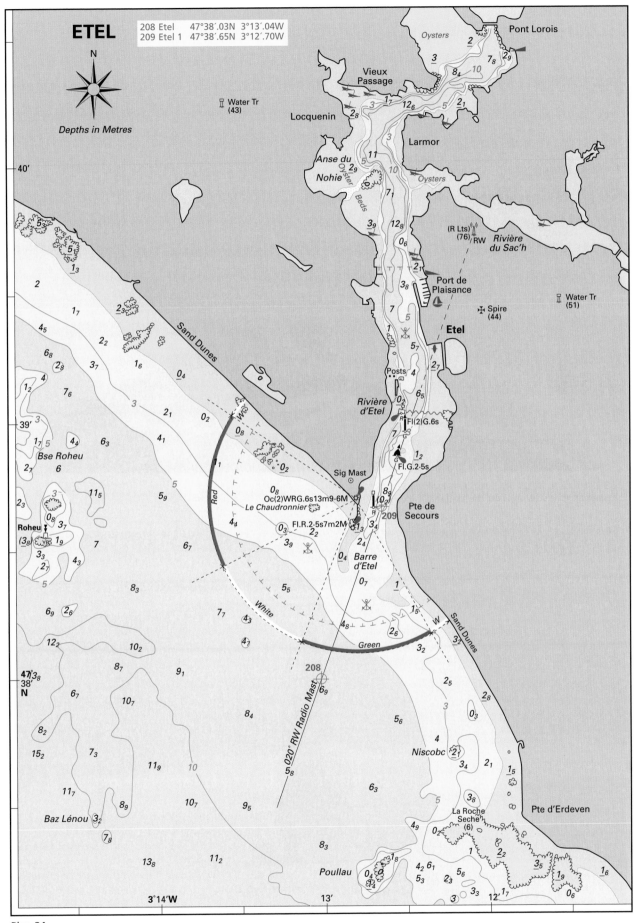

ETEL

208 Etel	47°38′.03N	3°13′.04W
209 Etel 1	47°38′.65N	3°12′.70W

N

Depths in Metres

Water Tr (43)

Locquenin

Pont Lorois

Oysters

Vieux Passage

Larmor

Anse du Nohie

Oyster Beds

Oysters

Rivière du Sac'h

(R Lts) (76)/RW

Port de Plaisance

Water Tr (51)

Spire (44)

Etel

Sand Dunes

Bse Roheu

Posts

Rivière d'Etel

Roheu

Sig Mast

Oc(2)WRG.6s13m9-6M
Le Chaudronnier

Fl(2)G.6s

Fl.R.2·5s7m2M

Fl.G.2·5s

209

Pte de Secours

Red

White

Green

W

Barre d'Etel

Sand Dunes

W

208

0·20° RW Radio Mast

Niscobc

Pte d'Erdeven

Baz Lénou

La Roche Seche (6)

Poullau

3°14′W

13′

34.3 The mouth of the Rivière d'Etel looking SE.
The semaphore station is on the W bank

34.4 Etel bar

Goulphar lighthouse, Belle-Ile

IV. Quiberon Bay

Morbihan

Ile Houat

Sauzon, Belle-Ile

Le Palais, Belle-Ile

Pointe de Port Navalo

Stêr-Wenn

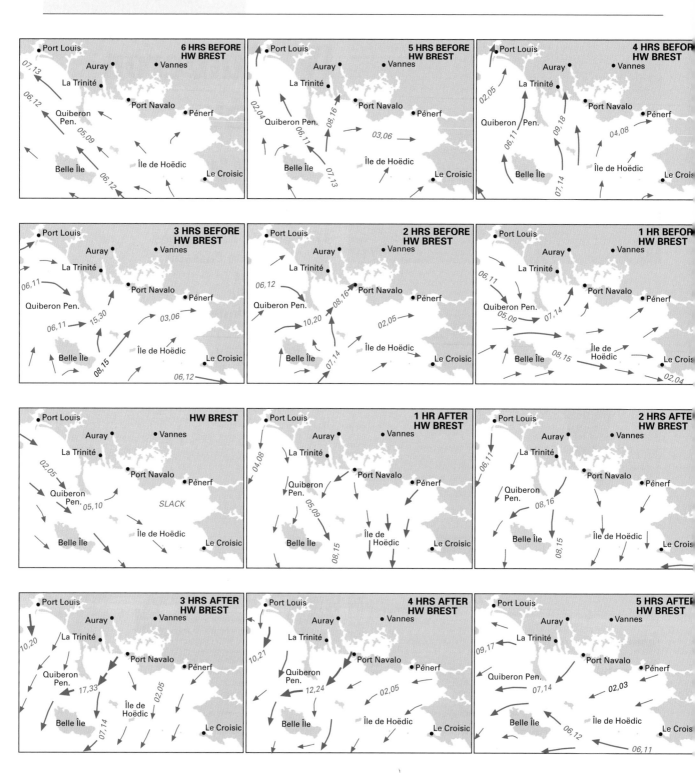
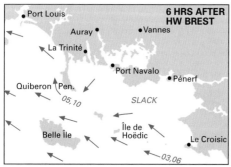

QUIBERON BAY TIDAL STREAMS

Chart IVA

210	Chiviguete	47°35′.29N 3°13′.93W
211	W Birvideaux	47°29′.14N 3°18′.91W
212	S Birvideaux	47°27′.44N 3°17′.48W
213	SW Quiberon	47°27′.82N 3°08′.35W
216	Poulains	47°23′.94N 3°14′.88W
217	Sauzon	47°22′.80N 3°12′.81W
220	Taillefer	47°22′.03N 3°09′.28W
233	S Goué Vas	47°25′.44N 3°04′.87W
234	E Goué Vas	47°26′.28N 3°03′.98W
235	Teignouse	47°27′.54N 3°02′.30W
236	E Teignouse	47°27′.02N 3°01′.26W
237	S Beniguet	47°23′.67N 3°00′.70W
240	N Béniguet	47°24′.55N 2°59′.97W

IV. QUIBERON BAY

N

Depths in Metres

III. Groix and the Rias

50′

40′

34. ETEL
Oc(2)WRG.9/6M

Red

White

210

Green

W

V. SE Brittany

Auray

43. RIVER AURAY

44. VANNES

42. LA TRINITÉ

Rivière de Crac'h
Ldg.Q.WRG.
10-7M Q.15M

278

Presqu'île de Quiberon

Port Navalo
Ldg.DirQ.19M

46. PORT DU CROUESTY

281

282

Golfe de Morbihan

45. GOLFE DE MORBIHAN

Penerf

47°30′N

White

Green

211
Birvideaux
Fl(2)6s10M

Port Maria
-Q.WRG.
14-10M

212

213

41. PORT HALIGUEN
Oc(2)WR.6s10m11/8M

235

La Teignouse
Fl.WR.4s15/11M

236

Baie de

291

293

Quiberon

38. PASSAGE DE TEIGNOUSE

234

233

White

Red

Green

du Béniguet

240

237

Recherche
Q(9)15s
YBY

292

Plateau de la Recherche

I. Dumet
Fl(3)WRG.
12s14m7-4M

37. BELLE-ILE ANCHORAGES

216

Pte des Poulains
Fl.5s23M

Ster Wenn

217

220

35. SAUZON

36. LE PALAIS

Belle Ile

Port Guen

Goulphar
Fl(2)10s27M

Port Kérel

Port Helin

Port Goulphar

Port Pouldon

Port Maria

Pte de Kerdonis
Fl(3)R.15s15M

Passage

39. I. HOUAT

253

259

258

40. I. HOËDIC

Les Gd Cardineaux
Fl(4)15s13M

270

267

Binner du Four
Q.Whis
BY

Le Four
Fl.5s18M

Plateau de Four

O. Bse Capella
Q.(9)15s
Whis
YBY

Groue-Vas-du Four
Q(6)+LFl
YB

20′

253	Chevaux	47°21′.65N 2°58′.23W
258	S Soeurs	47°20′.15N 2°55′.36W
259	N Soeurs	47°21′.22N 2°54′.82W
267	SE Hoedic	47°18′.74N 2°50′.34W
270	S Hoedic	47°18′.80N 2°53′.06W
278	E Trinité	47°32′.59N 2°59′.86W
281	Meaban	47°31′.20N 2°57′.86W
282	SW Crouesty	47°30′.68N 2°55′.32W
291	Chimère	47°28′.76N 2°54′.08W
292	Recherche	47°25′.73N 2°47′.58W
293	St Jacques	47°28′.09N 2°47′.38W

10′

10′

3°W

50′

40′

Chart IVB

35 Sauzon

Location
47°22'N 3°13'W

Shelter
Reasonable from S to W but exposed to N and *vent solaire*

Depth restrictions
2.5m on visitors' moorings
1.0m in outer harbour
Inner harbour dries 1.8m

Night entry Lit

HW time
Brest HW neaps, −½ springs

Mean height of tide (m)

	HWS	HWN	LWN	LWS
Le Palais	5.1	4.0	1.9	0.7

Tidal stream Sauzon approaches
SE – Brest HW–5½ to –1½ (0.8kts)
Slack – Brest HW–1½ to +½
NW – Brest HW+½ to +5½ (0.9kts)
Slack – Brest HW+5½ to –5½

Berthing
Visitors' buoys and drying harbour
Anchoring outside possible

Facilities
Cafés, restaurants, a few shops and bike hire

Charts
BA 2822 (50)
SHOM 7032 (50), 7142 (25)
Imray C38 (78)

Radio VHF 9

The jewel of Belle-Ile

Sauzon is an attractive little harbour on the N coast of Belle-Ile. It is well placed for exploring the magnificent NW coast and not far from Le Palais by bicycle.

The inner harbour dries but it is well set up for visitors and offers a secure haven for vessels that can take the ground. The outer harbour has a number of visitors' buoys. These are well sheltered from the S and W but exposed to the N and E and the *vent solaire*.

PILOTAGE

Sauzon approach and entrance

By GPS

From Penmarc'h use ⊕137-S Glénan, ⊕216-Poulins, ⊕217-Sauzon, ⊕218-Sauzon 1.

From Lorient or Groix use ⊕211-W Birvideaux, ⊕217-Sauzon, ⊕218-Sauzon 1.

Otherwise, from NW through E, ⊕217-Sauzon can be approached directly.

From the SW and Le Palais use ⊕220-Taillefer, ⊕217-Sauzon, ⊕218-Sauzon 1.

By day

The harbour is easy to identify. The Gareau SHM beacon tower off the Pointe du Cardinal N of the entrance is distinctive. Low white lighthouses, with red and green tops, mark the ends of the two outer breakwaters. In addition, the taller main lighthouse, also with a green top, can be seen behind the breakwater lights.

The official transit aligns the two green-topped lighthouses on 205°. However, this need not be followed closely.

35.1 Sauzon Harbour looking SW.
The inner harbour visitors' buoys are the two rows of bow and stern moorings on the W side near the ferry berth. The drying harbour, through the gap in the breakwater, has space available for boats that can take the ground

35.2 The entrance to Sauzon harbour

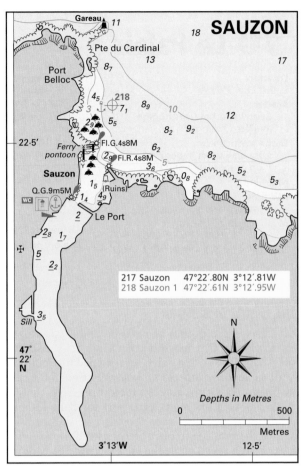

Plan 35

SAUZON map labels: Gareau 11, Pte du Cardinal 13, 17, 18, Port Belloc, Ferry pontoon, Fl.G.4s8M, Fl.R.4s8M, Sauzon, Q.G.9m5M, WC, Le Port, (Ruins), Sill

217 Sauzon   47°22′.80N 3°12′.81W
218 Sauzon 1 47°22′.61N 3°12′.95W

Depths in Metres   0 ... 500 Metres

By night

The approach uses the day transit of the pier head and main green light in line on 205°. Note that these lights are obscured by the Pointe du Cardinal when approaching from the NW so keep well N until they are positively identified.

There is very little light from the shore so a powerful spotlight will be necessary to find and pick up a buoy.

BERTHS AND ANCHORAGES

Outer visitors' buoys

There are visitors' buoys outside the outer N mole. Anchoring on the E side of the entrance is permitted when the mooring buoys are full.

Inner visitors' buoys

Between the outer and inner moles on the E side there are some white buoys that are reserved for fishermen. On the W side are two rows of bow and stern moorings. When the harbour is crowded, up to eight yachts may be rafted between each pair of buoys.

Inner harbour

The inner harbour dries to a firm sandy bottom. Boats able to take the ground may moor, secured bow and stern in the lines of red buoys inside the entrance, or anchor further up the harbour. It may also be possible to lie against a wall after consulting the harbourmaster.

The creek is over 500m long and if there is a crowd near the entrance there is plenty of room higher up for those prepared to dry out for longer each tide.

ASHORE IN SAUZON

There is a tap at the root of the inner W jetty. Showers and toilets are on the west wall of the inner harbour, near the harbourmaster's office. There are hotels, restaurants, bars and a few shops. Bicycles and scooters can be hired from a van in the carpark but walkers may prefer to explore the spectacular coast path.

35.3 Sauzon inner harbour

35.4 Visitors' mooring outside the harbour

36 Le Palais

Location
47°21′N 3°09′W

Shelter
Good in harbour, anchorage sheltered from SW

Depth restrictions
3.0m on visitors' moorings
1.7m or more in wet basin

Night entry Lit

HW time
Brest HW neaps, −½ springs

Mean height of tide (m)

	HWS	HWN	LWN	LWS
Le Palais	5.1	4.0	1.9	0.7

Tidal stream Pte de Taillefer
SE – Brest HW−5½ to +½ (1.1kts)
Slack – Brest HW+½ to +1½
NW – Brest HW+1½ to −5½ (1.2kts)

Berthing
Visitors' buoys and wet harbour
Anchorage outside harbour

Facilities
As of a busy tourist port

Charts
BA 2822 (50)
SHOM 7032 (50), 7142 (25)
Imray C38 (large scale)

Radio VHF 9

The capital of Belle-Ile

Le Palais is the capital of Belle-Ile and a good base for exploring this magnificent island. It is also the site of the citadel, a massive, star-shaped fort built by Vauban in the 18th century. It was thought to be invulnerable but the English took it in 1761.

Le Palais is the main ferry port for Belle-Ile and unfortunately it gets very crowded in summer. To add to the fun, the frequent ferries need to maintain quite a high speed while they manoeuvre. They don't have much room, so it is vital for other craft to keep out of their way.

PILOTAGE

Le Palais approach and entrance

By GPS

From Penmarc'h use
⊕137-S Glénan, ⊕216-Poulains, ⊕220-Taillefer, ⊕221-Le Palais.

From Lorient use ⊕220-Taillefer, ⊕221-Le Palais
From Etel use ⊕210-Chiviguete, ⊕220-Taillefer, ⊕221-Le Palais.
From the Teignouse, Beniguet or Sœurs passage, ⊕221-Le Palais can be approached directly.
From the SE use ⊕270-S Hoedic, ⊕221-Le Palais.

By day

The citadel is easy to identify and there are no dangers in the approach. Steer for the lighthouse with the green top on the end of the N jetty and keep a sharp lookout for the ferries. They enter and leave at speed and take up most of the channel. In the entrance, keep in the middle of the channel because there are dangers off both pier heads.

By night

Steer for the lighthouse, flashing (2+1) green 12s. and keep a sharp lookout for the unlit buoys near the entrance.

36.1 Le Palais looking E. The harbour is in three parts: the outer harbour which contains the busy ferry terminal and a few moorings, the inner harbour which dries, and the wet basin and La Saline marina that extend past the citadel like a canal

36.2 From a distance the Vauban citadel dominates the harbour

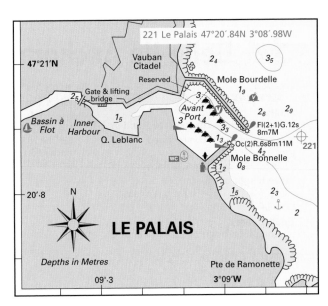

Plan 36

BERTHS AND ANCHORAGES

Outer harbour

The outer harbour is well sheltered from the S and W. However, strong NE winds cause seas to break over the breakwater and strong winds from any N or E direction can cause some swell to enter the harbour.

Yachts raft between bow and stern mooring buoys or between buoys and chains suspended from the breakwater wall. Either way, a dinghy is needed to get ashore. The moorings are subject to ferry wash so it is necessary to check that spreaders are clear of adjacent yachts.

Inner harbour

It is possible to dry out in the inner harbour. Either moor bow to the N wall on either side of the grid, or alongside the quay if a space can be found. The bottom is foul in places so consult the harbourmaster. Note that the white stripes on the harbour walls reserve spaces for fishing boats and that anchoring is forbidden in the harbour.

The wet basin and La Saline marina

The gate and lifting bridge to the wet dock opens local HW ±1 between 0600 and 2200. The opening times vary between springs and neaps so consult the harbourmaster for exact times. In the wet dock, yachts raft either side of a pontoon in 2.5m.

Beyond the wet dock, a lifting bridge, that opens 0700 daily, gives access to La Saline marina. This offers perfect shelter on finger pontoons with electricity and water.

⚓ Anchorage outside

Outside the harbour, anchor to the E of the N jetty in 3m, keeping well clear of the fairway. In offshore winds, this is safe and has good holding. Two large mooring buoys have been placed here for visitors' use but they are usually occupied by local *vedettes* between 1000 and 1830.

Anchoring is prohibited between the citadel at Le Palais and the approaches to Sauzon because of cables.

ASHORE IN LE PALAIS

Water, showers and toilets are available by the harbourmaster's office and also in the wet basin. Fuel, by long hose, is purchased from the root of the S breakwater. There are haul-out facilities, marine and electrical engineers, and chandlery.

Le Palais is a bustling tourist resort with a wide range of restaurants, bars and shops. It is possible to hire bicycles and cars to explore the island.

The Vauban citadel is a museum and also has fine views from the belvedere that runs round the central fortifications.

36.3 The busy entrance to Le Palais

37 Belle-Ile Anchorages

Location
47°23'N 3°15'W

Shelter
All anchorages exposed to S and W

Night entry Not recommended

HW time
Brest HW neaps, −½ springs

Mean height of tide (m)

	HWS	HWN	LWN	LWS
Le Palais	5.1	4.0	1.9	0.7

Tidal streams
Complex, strong at E and W ends of Belle Isle

Berthing Anchorages
Facilities Limited.
Charts
    BA 2822 (50)
    SHOM 7032 (50), 7142 (25)
    Imray C38 (78)

Beautiful Island

(See Plan 37B)

Belle-Ile is 10M long and up to 5M wide, which makes it the largest island off the Brittany coast. There are many attractive anchorages that can be used as day anchorages or overnight in good weather. The N coast anchorages are well protected from the SW but mostly open to the N and the *vent solaire*. The S coast is rugged, deeply indented and has a profusion of rocks. There are a number of anchorages that can be used in settled weather but it is no place to be in bad weather or if there is any swell from the S or W.

37.2 The inlet and anchorage of Stêr-Wenn looking S. Stêr-Vraz, the main inlet, can also be used as a day anchorage in very calm weather

37.1 The Port du Vieux Château looking SE. The port is divided into two parts: the main inlet Stêr-Vraz, and a smaller inlet, Stêr-Wenn

STER-WENN (PORT DU VIEUX CHÂTEAU)

The most beautiful harbour in France

Stêr-Wenn is a beautiful fjord on the NW coast of Belle-Ile, about a mile S of Pointe des Poulains. The anchorage itself is perfectly sheltered except in strong onshore winds but the entrance (or exit) becomes a death trap in bad weather or heavy swell.

It has been likened to a lobster pot: easy to get in but hard to get out. However, the French rate it as the most beautiful harbour in France so it is usually crowded. Needless to say, at the first hint of bad weather or swell, it is essential to get out.

The directions and plan should be used with caution because the largest-scale published chart is too small a scale to show much detail. The names Pointe Dangéreuse and Pointe Verticale are unofficial but they are appropriate.

PILOTAGE

Stêr-Wenn approach and entrance

By GPS

Stêr-Wenn requires very careful visual pilotage. The following waypoint may be helpful:
⊕232-Stêr-Wenn 1 (47°22'.40N 3°15'.15W).

37.3 Stêr-Wenn on a busy summer day

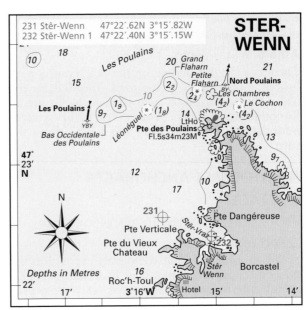

Plan 37A

By day

Coming from the N the dangers off the Pointe des Poulains must be avoided. The completely safe route goes outside Basse Occidentale des Poulains buoy. The Port du Vieux Château is divided into two parts: the main inlet, Stêr-Vraz, and a smaller inlet, Stêr-Wenn. The latter opens from the S side of the former. Stêr-Vraz is 400m wide and 900m long; Stêr-Wenn is only 50m wide and 500m long.

The entrance to Stêr-Vraz is quite hard to locate because there are several inlets that look similar from seaward but closer to it is quite distinctive. The N side is encumbered with rocks as much as 300m offshore and should not be approached too closely. However, the S side, shown on the plan as Pointe Verticale, is steep to and forms a cliff that makes identification easy. Also, there is a conspicuous hotel on the skyline about ¾M S of Pointe Verticale.

Do not cut the corner on the N side of Stêr-Vraz but start from a position at least ½M offshore and approach on about 120°. Both the tidal stream and the swell will weaken as Stêr-Vraz is entered.

Coming from the S, the cliffs along the southern shore of Stêr-Vraz are steep to. However, unless another yacht is entering or leaving, Stêr-Vraz will not be seen until it opens up, quite dramatically, to starboard. When it is fully open, alter course sharply to starboard and enter.

ANCHORAGES

⚓ Stêr-Wenn

Stêr-Wenn is deep near the entrance and shoals gradually up to a sandy beach after a small fork. A cable is slung across the inlet at the fork to provide moorings for small fishing boats. On both sides iron rings are set into the rock above the high-water line. Drop anchor in the middle of the inlet (1.5m or more) and take a stern line ashore to one of the rings. The holding is good, but make sure that the anchor is well dug in before going ashore. Do not allow other yachts to raft to you with slack cables and shore lines if you are to survive a *vent solaire* during the night. Also, in the event of a *vent solaire*, check that the anchor is not dragging.

The water is smooth in all winds except NW. But surge does enter when there is a heavy onshore wind, and the anchorage becomes dangerous.

⚓ Stêr-Vraz day anchorage

If Stêr-Wenn is overcrowded, there is a day anchorage further up Stêr-Vraz but for use in calm weather only. Keep to starboard and look out for

37.4 Stêr-Vraz day anchorage

rocks as the beach is approached. Most of the rocks occupy the northern half of the inlet.

Ashore in Stêr-Wenn

There is a dinghy landing on the beach and a path leading up the valley to the road. Turn left for the 3M walk to Sauzon or right to visit the Grotte de l'Apothicairerie (¾M). There is a nature reserve information centre, an hotel and a café above the cave.

NORTH COAST ANCHORAGES
PILOTAGE

These anchorages all require a large-scale chart.

⚓ Port Jean

Sheltered from the S but completely exposed to the NE, Port Jean is about a mile E of Sauzon and a useful alternative if Sauzon is very crowded. Approach from the NNE and anchor off the beach. It is relatively easy to leave at night.
⊕219-Port Jean (47°21´.94N 3°11´.29W)

37.5 Port Jean anchorage on the N coast

37.6 Ancient Fort Larron at Port Salio

⚓ Port Guen and Port Salio

Protected from the S and W but exposed to the NE, this bay is 1M E of Le Palais. There are no dangers in the approach but it is necessary to tuck in well to minimise the swell and ferry wash.
⊕222-Salio (47°19´.84N 3°08´.19W)

37.7 Anchorage at Port Yorc'h

⚓ Port Yorc'h

Protected from the W through S to SE but exposed to the NE, this bay is 1½M E of Le Palais. There are a number of local moorings but it is possible to anchor outside them to the W or off the beach.
⊕223-Yorc'h (47°19´.65N 3°07´.23W)

SOUTH COAST ANCHORAGES
PILOTAGE

These anchorages all require a large-scale chart.

⚓ Port Goulphar

Sheltered from the N but completely open to the S, Port Goulphar is a mini-fjord close to Goulphar lighthouse. There are a lot of rocks in the entrance and it is necessary to start from a position close to ⊕228-Goulphar. Approach the bay with Goulphar lighthouse on 015°, which will put it a bit to the right of the hotel on the cliff top. Hold this course through the outer rocks and bear to starboard into the bay. Anchor outside the local moorings. A French cruising guide classifies Port Goulphar as a *mouillage gastronomique* because of the excellent restaurant in the hotel.
⊕230-Goulphar 2 (47°18´.11N 3°13´.72W)

⚓ Port Kérel

Sheltered from the N but completely open to the S, Port Kérel is a very attractive little bay about 1M E of Port Goulphar. Approach from due S starting from a position W of La Truie IDM. Locals anchor in the fjords but the easiest spot is off the beach in the NE part of the bay.
⊕227-Kerel (47°17´.79N 3°12´.22W)

⚓ Port Herlin

Sheltered from NW to NE but completely open to the S, Port Herlin is a fairly wide bay about 1½M E of Port Kérel. Approach from due S to avoid the

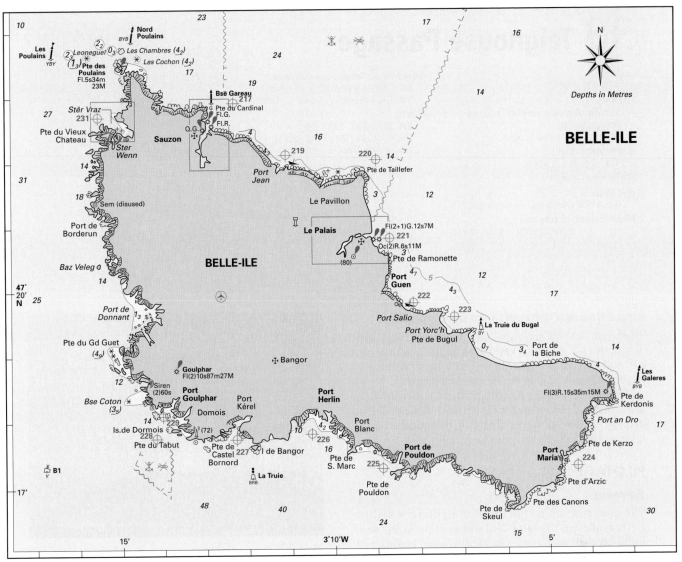

Plan 37B

rocks on either side of the bay. Anchor almost ¼M from the shore because of the rocky foreshore.

⊕226-Herlin (47°17'.94N 3°10'.39W)

⚓ Port de Pouldon

Sheltered from N through E, Port de Pouldon is 2M W of Pointe du Skeul. Approach from the WSW and anchor close to the N side of the headland. There are drying rocks just off the N side of the bay.

⊕225-Pouldon (47°17'.29N 3°08'.58W)

⚓ Port Maria

Protected from W to N, Port Maria is an attractive little creek between Point de Kerdonis and Pointe du Skeul. The tide can be strong along the ends of Belle-Ile so approach with caution from the SE. Port Maria is quite narrow and it is best to keep in the middle steering 315°. It is possible to leave at night but not to enter.

⊕224-Port Maria BI (47°17'.56N 3°04'.38W)

38 Teignouse Passage

Location
47°26'N 3°06'W

Hazards
Strong tide over uneven seabed
Rough water
Many well marked rocks

Depth restrictions
The channel is deep

Night entry Well lit

HW time
Brest HW+¼ neaps, −½ springs

Mean height of tide (m)

	HWS	HWN	LWN	LWS
Le Palais	5.3	4.1	2.1	0.9

Tidal stream Teignouse passage
NE – Brest HW−6 to +½ (1.8kts)
SW – Brest HW+½ to +6 (2.1kts)

Charts
BA 2823 (50), 2357 (20)
SHOM 7033 (50), 7141 (20)
Imray C38 (78)

Route through the reefs into Quiberon Bay

There are several passages into Quiberon Bay. The Teignouse is a well-marked big ship passage that can be used by day or night. It is ¼M wide and there is deep water either side of the marked channel.

The other passages through the Quiberon reefs are described below under Houat and Hoëdic. There are also many shortcuts that can be found using a large-scale chart.

PILOTAGE

Warning

The tides run strongly in the channel and the seabed is very uneven. As a result, surprisingly steep seas build up even with only a moderate wind against the tide. If possible take it at slack water and treat it with great respect if there is any swell running.

Teignouse passage from SW

By GPS

The big ship route is
⊕233-S Goué Vas, ⊕234-E Goué Vas, ⊕236-E Teignouse.

With good weather and sufficient rise of tide, ⊕236-E Teignouse can be replaced with ⊕235-Teignouse. This shortcut passes close to a 1m shallow patch and the rocks near the Teignouse light.

By day

Bring the white lighthouse on La Teignouse to bear 036°. This line leads S of Goué Vaz Sud SCM, which must not be confused with Goué Vaz Nord NCM, situated ½M to the NW. Steer 036°, leaving Goué Vaz Sud SCM to port, Basse du Milieu green buoy to starboard and Goué Vas Est PHM to port.

When this last buoy is abeam alter course to 068°. The official line is St-Gildas, 10M away, on 068°, but it is only necessary to leave Basse Nouvelle PHM to port and NE Teignouse SHM to starboard.

38.1 The Teignouse lighthouse looking W

By night

Enter the white sector (033°-039°) of La Teignouse light before Port Maria main light turns from white to green. Steer in this sector between the buoys. When between Basse du Milieu SHM and Goué Vaz Est PHM alter course to 068° to pass between the Basse Nouvelle PHM and NE Teignouse SHM.

Teignouse passage from E or N

By GPS and By day

Reverse the above course.

By night

Use the white sector of Port Haliguen light to keep off the dangers between Haliguen and La Teignouse light. Then enter the Teignouse Passage between the Basse Nouvelle PHM and NE Teignouse SHM. Steer 248° to pass between Basse du Milieu SHM and Goué Vaz PHM. Steer out on 216° using the white sector of La Teignouse light. When Port Maria main light turns from green to white all dangers are passed.

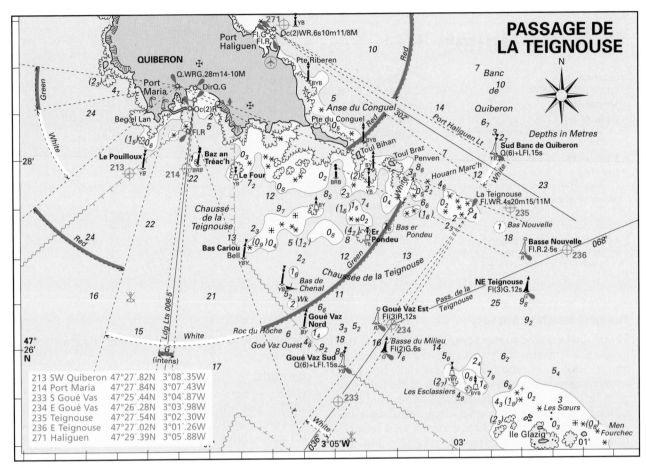

PASSAGE DE LA TEIGNOUSE

Depths in Metres

213 SW Quiberon	47°27′.82N	3°08′.35W
214 Port Maria	47°27′.84N	3°07′.43W
233 S Goué Vas	47°25′.44N	3°04′.87W
234 E Goué Vas	47°26′.28N	3°03′.98W
235 Teignouse	47°27′.54N	3°02′.30W
236 E Teignouse	47°27′.02N	3°01′.26W
271 Haliguen	47°29′.39N	3°05′.88W

Plan 38

38.2 Port Maria and the Teignouse Passage looking SE. The passage opens the way to the Morbihan and the Vilaine estuary. It is bordered on either side by many reefs and the tides run strongly

39 Ile Houat

Location
47°02′N 2°58′W

Shelter Poor

Hazards
Strong tides and unmarked rocks
Difficult to leave at night

Night entry Only lit to Port St Gildas

HW time
Brest HW+½ neaps, −½ springs

Mean height of tide (m)

	HWS	HWN	LWN	LWS
Ile de Houat	5.2	4.1	2.0	0.8

Tidal stream Beniguet channel
NE – Brest HW−5½ to −½ (1.5kts)
Slack – Brest HW −½ to +½

SW – Brest HW +½ to +5½ (1.3kts)
Slack – Brest HW+5½ to −5½

Berthing
Anchorages

Facilities
Very limited but good beaches,
walking and wild flowers

Charts
BA 2823 (50), 2835 (20)
SHOM 7032 (50), 7143 (25)
Imray C38 (78)

The best beach in Brittany

Houat, pronounced to rhyme with *that*, is one of the gems of S Brittany. This strangely shaped island is about 2M long and has spectacular beaches, wonderful walking, a profusion of wild flowers and very little else. The small harbour of St Gildas is generally full of fishing boats and the anchorages are exposed either to the sea breeze or the *vent solaire*. Despite this, Houat is extremely popular and the anchorage off the best beach, Tréac'h-er-Gourhed, can be uncomfortably crowded. However, don't be put off. A visit to Houat in good weather is likely to be the high point of a South Brittany holiday.

PILOTAGE

Port St-Gildas approach

By GPS

From NW to NE
⊕244-St-Gildas can be approached directly. Take care to avoid the well-marked mussel beds NNE of St-Gildas

From the E use
⊕245-Er Jeneteu, ⊕244-St-Gildas.

By day

The easiest approach is from the N and E. If possible come down with the ebb stream but, if planning to enter the harbour, do not arrive too near low water because manoeuvring room is much reduced.

From the N steer towards the E end of the island. Nearly one mile N is a conspicuous rock, La Vieille (14m high), and NNE of it is a mussel bed marked by buoys. Once La Vieille is identified it is easy to locate the harbour, which bears 200°, ¾M from it. Pass either side of the mussel bed. La Vieille is clean to the N and E but to the S the shoals extend about 200m.

From the E, the outer NE rock, Er Jenetëu (16m high), is distinctive. It can be passed at a distance of 100m but there are rocks in the direct line to the

harbour so keep well out before turning for St Gildas.

By night

Green sectors of the breakwater light cover La Vieille and the dangers to the E and W of the harbour. Approach in either white sector and anchor off the harbour. The mussel bed is in the green sector of the breakwater light, and the buoys on its N side are lit.

The Béniguet Passage

By GPS

From the S use
⊕237-S Béniguet, ⊕240-N Béniguet. Avoid the 1.5m shallow patch E of
Le Grand Coin.

By day

This is an easy daylight passage, immediately to the NW of Houat. It is the shortest route between Belle-Ile and Houat or the Vilaine. The strong tide and uneven seabed can cause steep seas in wind against tide conditions so take it close to slack water.

Coming from the SW, leave Le Rouleau tower WCM 600m to starboard and make good 030° to pass between Le Grand Coin tower ECM and Bonnenn Braz tower WCM. Keep closer to Le Grand Coin tower and well clear of Bonnenn Braz and the shoals (depth 1.5m) that extend 600m NNE. Le Grand Coin tower in transit with Le Palais citadel on 240° clears these shoals.

Use the 240° transit when leaving Quiberon Bay and alter to 210° when about 400m from Le Grand Coin.

The Chevaux Passage

By GPS

From the S use
⊕253-Chevaux, ⊕251-Beg Pell,
⊕250-Houteliguet, ⊕247-Er Yoc'h,
⊕246-En Tal.

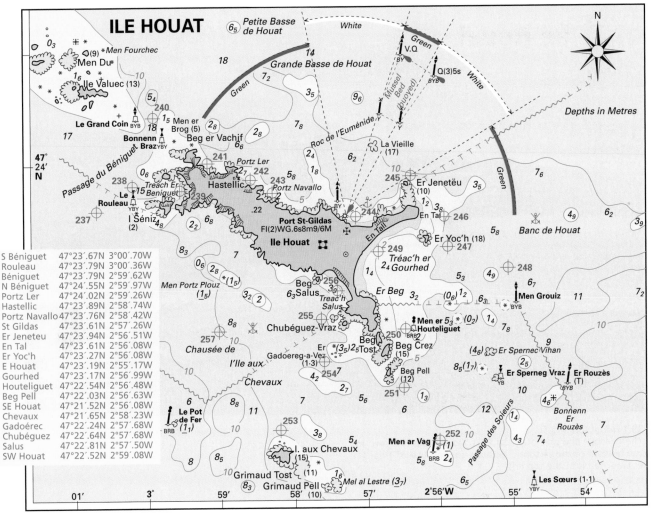

Plan 39

Continue to ⊕245-Er Jeneteu for St-Gildas and the N coast of Houat. This route should not be attempted in poor visibility or at night. In good visibility the waypoints are hardly necessary because they are all close to conspicuous marks.

By day

This is a fine-weather route from Le Palais to Hoëdic, and an attractive alternative to Le Beniguet for Houat.

Steer for a position ¼M N of Ile aux Chevaux, watching out for Pot de Fer IDM and the rocks on the N side of Ile aux Chevaux.

Bound for Houat, steer to leave Beg Pell (12m high) 200m to port. Don't go too much further out because there is a rock (depth 0.6m) about ½M to the SE of Beg Pell. Then leave the Men er Houteliguet 100m to starboard. A detour to visit the spectacular Tréac'h er Gourhed beach may be in order.

Proceeding to Port St-Gildas, cross the bay and leave the rock Er Yoc'h (18m high) 100m to port and the beach on point En Tal well to port. Round Er Jenetëu (10m high), leaving it 100m to port and enter Port St-Gildas.

Instructions for getting to Hoëdic via the Chevaux Passage are given under Hoëdic.

BERTHS AND ANCHORAGES

Port Saint-Gildas

Port St-Gildas is so small that a yacht over 10m is unlikely to find a berth. The breakwater is reserved for fishing boats but there is a row of head and stern moorings for yachts parallel to the breakwater. Do not obstruct the access for the ferry. If the harbour is full, anchor in the bay to the E where there are also some visitors' buoys. This anchorage and the visitors' buoys are open to the *vent solaire* and suffer from ferry wash.

⚓ Tréac'h er Béniguet

Sheltered from the E but exposed to S and W, this attractive bay is on the W end of Houat. Approach from a position N of Le Rouleau WCM. Steer E into the middle of the bay and anchor off the beach. It is difficult to leave at night without GPS.

⊕239-Béniguet (47°23'.79N 2°59'.62W)

⚓ Portz Ler

Sheltered from the S but open to N and E, this bay is at the W end of the N coast. The approach from the N is straightforward. There are two distinct bays and it is important to anchor in one of them and not

39.1 Houat looking SE.
The harbour and anchorage of Port Saint-Gildas is shown in the bottom of the picture. The wide curving bay of Tréac'h er Gourhed is at the top left

on the rocks between them. It is easy to leave at night.

⊕241-Portz Ler (47°24′.02N 2°59′.26W)

⚓ Hastellic

This bay, sheltered from S and W but open to the N and E, is between Beg Run er Vilin and Er Hastellic. The approach is straightforward from the NE and it is easy to leave at night.

⊕242-Hastellic (47°23′.89N 2°58′.74W)

⚓ Portz Navallo

Sheltered from S and W but open to the N and E, this bay is just E of Er Hastellic. The approach is simple from the NE and it is easy to leave at night.

⊕243-Portz Navallo (47°23′.76N 2°58′.42W)

⚓ Tréach er Gourhed

Sheltered for the W but horribly exposed to the *vent solaire*, this bay on the W end of Houat offers one of the finest beaches in S Brittany. It can be approached from the N or E by keeping clear of Er Jenetëu, En Tal and Er Yoc'h or from the SW using the Chevaux passage. Anchor wherever there is a space. It is important to plan for a night departure because the anchorage is famous for its *vent solaire* pyjama parties, with yachts rolling from beam to beam and dragging all over the place. The waypoint ⊕248-E Houat may provide an escape route but note that it is not safe to move round to Tréach Salus after dark.

⊕249-Goured (47°23′.17N 2°56′.99W)

⚓ Tréach Salus

Protected from the N and E and the *vent solaire* but exposed to the S and W, this magnificent beach is the other side of the headland from Tréach er Gourhed. It can be approached directly from the SW but from the N or Tréach er Gourhed it is necessary to round the many dangers off SE Houat. Anchor as close to the beach as draught permits. Shelter is often a little better at the W end but there is a wreck with a doubtful position marked on the chart.

Tréach Salus is exposed to the sea breeze and is often less crowded than Tréach er Gourhed. It is better protected from the *vent solaire* so is often a better place to spend the night. It is possible to escape to the SW at night, using waypoint ⊕257-SW Houat.

⊕256-Salus (47°22′.81N 2°57′.50W)

ASHORE IN HOUAT

There is water from the public tap in the centre of the pretty village of Saint-Gildas or at the toilets on the pier. The shops can supply simple needs, but they are limited. There are some bars, a medical centre, and a post office. The island is noted for its succession of wild flowers: roses in May, carnations in June, yellow immortelles in July and sand lilies in August. There are wonderful beaches on the north side of En Tal, at Tréac'h er Gourhed in the E, Tréac'h Salus in the SE and Tréac'h er Beniguet in the W.

40 Ile Hoëdic

Location
47°02'N 2°52'W

Shelter
Generally poor

Hazards
Strong tides and unmarked rocks
Difficult to leave at night

Night entry
Only lit to L'Argol

HW time
Brest HW+¼ neaps, −½springs

Mean height of tide (m):

	HWS	HWN	LWN	LWS
Hoëdic	5.1	4.0	1.9	0.7

Tidal stream Sœurs channel
NE – Brest HW–5½ to –½ (1.4kts)
Slack – Brest HW–½ to +½
SW – Brest HW+½ to +5½ (1.3kts)
Slack – Brest HW+5½ to –5½

Berthing
Anchorages

Facilities
Very limited

Charts
BA 2823 (50), 2835 (20)
SHOM 7032 (50), 7143 (25)
Imray C38 (78)

Picture postcard island

Hoëdic is 1M long and ½M wide and lies 4M SE of Houat. Argol, the main harbour, is on the N side. It is very small and yachts may prefer to lie outside. Port de la Croix in the S dries but in fine weather it is an attractive anchorage.

PILOTAGE

Argol approach from N and E

By GPS

From the Morbihan or Lorient approach ⊕261-Argol directly.

From the NE use ⊕262-N Hoëdic, ⊕261-Argol

From the E use ⊕263-NE Hoëdic, ⊕262-N Hoëdic, ⊕261-Argol.

From Houat use ⊕248-E Houat, ⊕261-Argol

By day

From the N make directly for the island passing either side of La Chèvre IDM. From Houat, be sure to leave Men Groise ECM and Er Rouzèz ECM to starboard. From the E give Beg Lagad a clearance of at least 400m.

By night

Approach in one of the white sectors of the harbour light. Green sectors cover La Chèvre and the dangers E and W of the approach.

Argol via the Soeurs Passage

By GPS

From the S use
⊕258-S Soeurs, ⊕259-N Soeurs, ⊕260-NW Hoëdic. Continuing to Argol, add ⊕261-Argol.

By day

Start from a position about ¼M W of Er Palaire WCM. Steer about 020° to leave Les Soeurs tower WCM 100m to starboard. Avoid Men er Guer and

Bonen Bras shoals by keeping Er Spernec Bras S beacon tower open to the left of Men Groise N beacon tower.

Bound for Hoëdic, do not let Les Soeurs tower bear more than 255° until Pointe du Vieux Château, bearing 175°, hides the W side of Hoëdic. This is necessary to avoid the shoals N and W of Point du Vieux-Château.

Bound N, leave Er Rouzèz ECM at least 200m to port.

Argol via the Chevaux Passage

By GPS

From the SW use
⊕253-Chevaux, ⊕252-SE Houat, ⊕260-NW Hoëdic, ⊕261-Argol. Take care to avoid the unmarked rocks and shallow patch between Les Soeurs WCM and the NW headland of Hoëdic.

By day

Start from a position about ¼M N of Ile aux Châteaux. Steer due E to leave Men er Vag IDM well to starboard. Continue on the same course, keeping well N of Les Soeurs until the Pointe du Vieux Château, bearing 175°, hides the W side of Hoëdic. It is then safe to steer for Argol.

Port de la Croix approaches

A large-scale chart is required.

By GPS

From the SE use
⊕267-SE Hoëdic, ⊕268-Madavoar, ⊕269-La Croix.

From the N, with enough rise of tide, use
⊕263-NE Hoëdic, ⊕265-Lanegui, ⊕268-Madavoar, ⊕269-La Croix. This shortcut passes close between unmarked drying rocks E of Madavoar tower.

40.1 Argol harbour looking S.

By day

From the N pass outside the Plateau des Cardinaux and then steer SW until the Madavoar tower SCM is in line with the right-hand edge of the fort on 320°. Approach Port de la Croix on this transit until close to Madavoar. Then make for a point just S of Men Cren beacon SCM. A slight curve to the N is needed to avoid the rocks SE of Men Cren.

With enough rise of tide it is possible to pass inside the Plateau des Cardinaux. This hazard is a chain of unmarked drying rocks E of Madavoar. Those closest to the beacon dry 0.8m but those further out dry 2.3m. If there is enough water to pass safely over the inner rocks, the outer ones can be avoided by staying within 400m of the beacon.

BERTHS AND ANCHORAGES

Port de l'Argol

Argol harbour has room for 20 to 30 visiting boats in settled weather. There are rocks in the approach; to avoid them keep the bearing to the E pier head less than 180°.

In the harbour, there are some visitors' buoys in rather shallow water, where yachts can raft. Alternatively, anchor just inside the entrance to port.

It is usually preferable to anchor outside the harbour but be sure to keep the bearing to the E pier head less than 180°. There is another anchorage further to the W, off the beach near the old lifeboat slip.

⚓ Port de la Croix

The harbour dries 2.8m and is often crowded so it is usually necessary to anchor outside. The shelter is good from the NW to NE but the anchorage is very exposed to any wind or swell from the S.

Anchor S of Men Cren tower or further in at neaps. Do not go in too close to the shore because there are some short posts set in concrete.

⚓ Beg er Lannegui

Sheltered from NW to W, there is a secluded anchorage on the E side of Hoëdic just S of Beg er Lannegui. Approach from about ½M offshore and anchor on sand, avoiding any patches of weed. It is only possible to stay overnight in perfect conditions.

⊕ 266-Lanegui 1 (47°20'.35N 2°51'.67W)

Other anchorages

Other anchorages around the island can be found. The water is so clear that in calm weather many of the submerged hazards can be seen and avoided.

ASHORE ON HOËDIC

Hoëdic has even fewer facilities than Houat but there is a small hotel, a food shop and some bars and créperies. There is also a shower and toilet block with a fresh-water tap near the harbour.

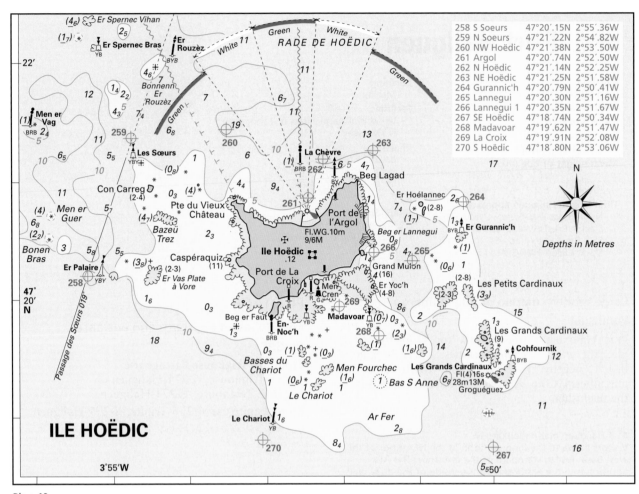

Plan 40

258 S Soeurs	47°20′.15N	2°55′.36W
259 N Soeurs	47°21′.22N	2°54′.82W
260 NW Hoëdic	47°21′.38N	2°53′.50W
261 Argol	47°20′.74N	2°52′.50W
262 N Hoëdic	47°21′.14N	2°52′.25W
263 NE Hoëdic	47°21′.25N	2°51′.58W
264 Gurannic'h	47°20′.79N	2°50′.41W
265 Lannegui	47°20′.30N	2°51′.16W
266 Lannegui 1	47°20′.35N	2°51′.67W
267 SE Hoëdic	47°18′.74N	2°50′.34W
268 Madavoar	47°19′.62N	2°51′.47W
269 La Croix	47°19′.91N	2°52′.08W
270 S Hoëdic	47°18′.80N	2°53′.06W

40.2 More than 40 visiting boats rafted to the visitors' buoys in Argol harbour

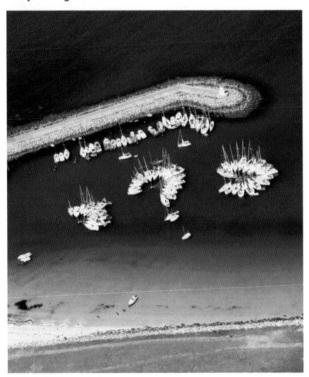

40.3 Looking NW to the anchorage at Pointe du Vieux Château

41 Port Haliguen

Location
47°29'N 3°06'W

Shelter Excellent

Night entry: Lit

HW time
Brest HW+¼ neaps, –¼ springs

Mean height of tide (m)

	HWS	HWN	LWN	LWS
Haliguen	5.2	4.1	2.0	0.7

Tidal stream Haliguen approaches
NW – Brest HW–5½ to –2½ (0.5kts)
Slack – Brest HW–2½ to +½
SE – Brest HW+½ to +5½ (0.6kts)
Slack – Brest HW+5½ to –5½

Berthing
Marina

Facilities
Good marina facilities but shopping is 1M away

Charts
BA 2823 (50), 2357 (20)
SHOM 7032 (50), 7141 (20)
Imray C39 (large scale)

Radio VHF 9

Telephone
Marina *t* 02 97 50 20 56
Yacht club *t* 02 97 30 49 51

Large modern marina on the Quiberon Peninsula

Port Haliguen is the marina for Quiberon. It is pleasant with excellent facilities. There is a good beach nearby but Quiberon town and the magnificent Côte Sauvage are on the other side of the peninsula.

PILOTAGE

Port Haliguen approach and entrance

By GPS

From the Teignouse Passage use
⊕235-Teignouse, ⊕271-Haliguen or
⊕236-E Teignouse, ⊕271-Haliguen.
From Trinité use ⊕276-Trinité, ⊕271-Haliguen.

41.1 Haliguen marina looking N.
Visitors tie up to the long pontoon in the NE corner of the west basin just to starboard of the entrance. The fuel pontoon is in the east basin on the inside of the quay wall

From the Morbihan use ⊕285-Kerpenhir, ⊕282-SW Crouesty, ⊕271-Haliguen, or with care and enough tide, ⊕285-Kerpenhir, ⊕281-Meaban, ⊕271-Haliguen provides a useful shortcut.

By day

The approach from the S is easy. Pass midway between La Teignouse lighthouse and the S cardinal buoy Sud Banc de Quiberon on a course of 305°, leaving Port Haliguen SCM to starboard.

Enter between the breakwaters and turn to starboard. The visitors' pontoon runs along the inside of the breakwater.

By night

Approach in the white 246°-252° sector of Port Maria light, or in one of the white sectors of Port Haliguen Marina light. Keep a lookout for unlit buoys and avoid the protective spur off the E breakwater head on entering.

BERTHS AND ANCHORAGES

Port Haliguen marina

Anchoring is not permitted in the harbour. Visitors moor in the West basin where there is a long visitors' pontoon just to starboard of the entrance. Floating pontoons for very large yachts may be available in the West basin. If the visitors' berths are full, go to the reception pontoon. It is beside the fuel pontoon, on the inside quay wall of the East basin.

⚓ Port d'Orange

Sheltered from the W but open to the E and the *vent solaire*, Port d'Orange is a small drying harbour 2¼M N of Port Haliguen. Approaching from the S, keep well offshore to avoid the dangers along the E coast of Quiberon. Approach from the SW and anchor off the pier.

⊕272-Orange (47°31′.32N 3°07′.37W)

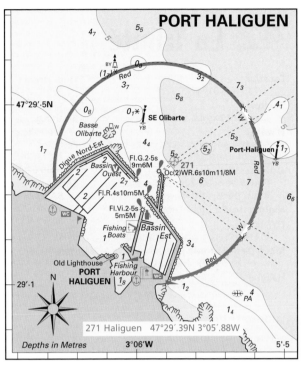

Plan 41

ASHORE IN PORT HALIGUEN

Port Haliguen has all the facilities of a major marina. There is a fuel pontoon, slip, crane, travel-lift, engineers, and a yacht club. Bread and limited shopping is available in the port. A 15-minute walk along the road to Quiberon finds a large supermarket with fish and oysters on sale outside. Quiberon town is about 1M away. It has all the facilities of a sizeable market town including a good market on Saturday. Market day at Port Haliguen is Wednesday. There are connections by bus, train and plane to all parts.

41.2 Quiberon town and Port Maria looking SW.
Port Maria is only open to fishermen and ferries and is not covered in this edition.
The town has good shops and a beach. It is possible to walk to the headland and explore the magnificent Côte Sauvage on the W of Quiberon peninsula

42 La Trinité

Location
47°35'N 3°01'W

Shelter
Excellent except at HW

Hazards
Marked and unmarked rocks on E side of approach

Other restrictions
Power vessels >20m and oyster boats have right of way

Night entry Lit but intricate

HW time
Brest HW+¼ neaps, –¼ springs

Mean height of tide (m)

	HWS	HWN	LWN	LWS
Haliguen	5.4	4.3	2.1	0.8

Tidal stream
Fairly weak and complex in the bay; up to 3 knots in the river

Berthing
Marina

Facilities
All facilities of a major yachting centre and busy town

Charts
BA 2823 (50), 2357 (20)
SHOM 7032 (50), 7141 (20)
Imray C39 (large scale)

Radio VHF 9

Telephone
Marina t 02 97 55 71 49

Major yachting centre

La Trinité is a flourishing oyster river and one of the most important sailing centres in the Bay of Biscay. It is a pleasant place and a perfect base for cruising or racing.

The town has excellent sailing facilities, plenty of bars, restaurants and shops and good connections to the rest of the World.

PILOTAGE

La Trinité approach and entrance

There is an official speed limit of 5kts. Power vessels over 20m, barges and oyster-culture vessels under tow have priority.

By GPS

From the S or W use
⊕276-Trinité, ⊕277-Trinité 1.

From the SE use
⊕278-E Trinité, ⊕276-Trinité, ⊕277-Trinité 1.

From the Morbihan use
⊕285-Kerpenhir, ⊕282-SW Crouesty, ⊕281-Meaban, ⊕278-E Trinité, ⊕276-Trinité, ⊕277-Trinité 1. With sufficient rise of tide it is possible to omit ⊕282-SW Crouesty but this shortcut has a least depth of 0.5m and passes close to unmarked rocks.

42.1 Looking downriver to the Bay of Quiberon from La Trinité Marina

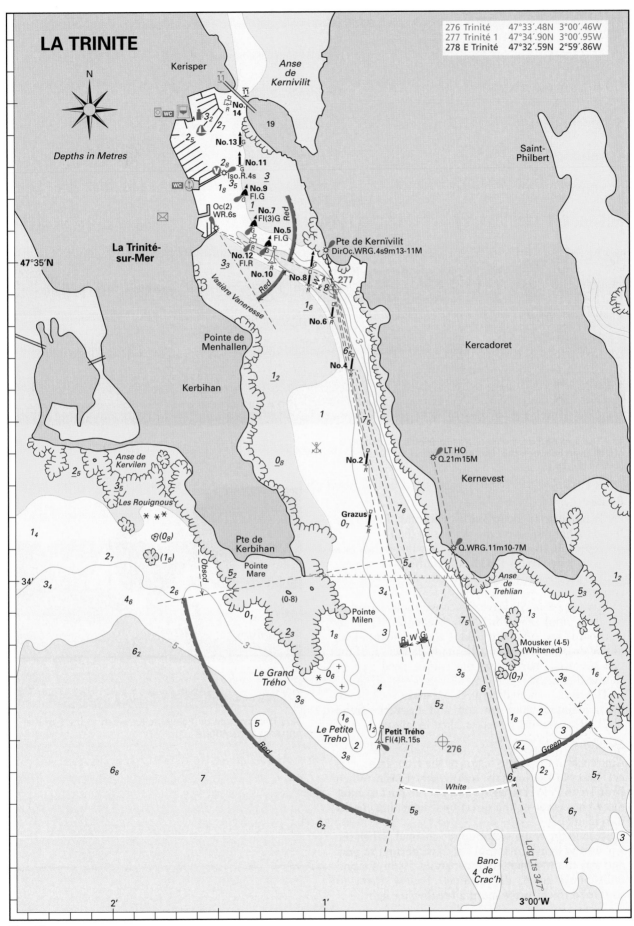

LA TRINITE

N

Depths in Metres

47°35'N

276 Trinité	47°33'.48N	3°00'.46W
277 Trinité 1	47°34'.90N	3°00'.95W
278 E Trinité	47°32'.59N	2°59'.86W

Kerisper

Anse de Kernivilit

Saint-Philbert

No.14

No.13 G

No.11
Iso.R.4s

No.9
Fl.G

No.7
Fl(3)G

Oc(2)
WR.6s

No.5
Fl.G

Pte de Kernivilit
DirOc.WRG.4s9m13-11M

No.12
Fl.R

No.10

No.8

277

La Trinité-sur-Mer

Red

Vasière Vaneresse

Red

No.6

Pointe de Menhallen

Kercadoret

Kerbihan

No.4

No.2

LT HO
Q.21m15M

Kernevest

Anse de Kervilen

Les Rouignous

(0.8)

(1.5)

Grazus
0.7

7.6

Obscd

Pte de Kerbihan

Pointe Mare

Pointe Milen

Anse de Trehlian

Q.WRG.11m10-7M

Mousker (4.5)
(Whitened)

(0.7)

Le Grand Trého

R W G

Le Petite Treho

Petit Trého
Fl(4)R.15s

276

Red

Green

White

Banc de Crac'h

Ldg Lts 347°

3°00'W

42.2 The approach to the marina at La Trinité. Anchoring is not allowed between the river entrance and the bridge (clearance 11m)

By day

La Trinité can be identified by a wooded hill to the W and a lighthouse on the skyline to the E.

Approach from the S, steer for the lighthouse until Le Petit Trého PHM is identified. This buoy marks the outer dangers on the W side of the entrance.

From the S or SE leave the conspicuous island of Méaban and Buissons de Méaban SCM to starboard. The official transit is the two lighthouses in line on 347°. However, the many dangers E of the line are well marked so the transit need not be followed exactly.

The river is entered between Mousker rock (4.5m high), painted white on top and Le Petit Trého PHM. The channel is well marked by buoys.

By night

Approach in the white sector of the front light, it is not necessary to exactly follow the transit. When Petit Trého PHM comes abeam, steer to port to enter the white sector of the directional light that marks the channel.

Keep in the white sector up the channel. When the S pier-head light turns from red to white alter to port and stay in the white sector for about 500m. Lit and unlit buoys mark the channel. Follow them to starboard towards the marina breakwater light.

42.3 The low light on Pointe de Kerbihan to the E of the entrance to La Trinité

42.4 La Trinité looking S

BERTHS AND ANCHORAGES

La Trinité Marina

The visitors' berths are on the first pontoon above the breakwater. A marina launch will normally meet visitors and direct them to a berth. In the marina the shelter is excellent from all except strong S and SE winds, which send in a sea near high water.

Anchoring is prohibited between the river entrance and the bridge (clearance 11m).

⚓ Pointe Saint-Colomban

Moderately sheltered from the N and NE, there is a pleasant neap anchorage near Saint-Colomban in the NW corner of Quiberon Bay. The approach is straightforward. Anchor close W of the Pointe St-Colomban.

⊕273-Colomban (47°33′.79N 3°05′.93W)

⚓ Carnac

Sheltered from the N but exposed to the SE, the dinghy sailing centre and holiday town of Carnac has two distinct bays. A rocky spur, marked by a beacon SCM, separates them. Approach from the S and watch the depth carefully because the bays shoal quickly. Anchor where depth permits.

⊕275-E Carnac (47°33′.92N 3°03′.32W)

⚓ Saint-Philbert River

Sheltered from all directions except S, this unspoilt river just E of Trinité offers a quiet neap anchorage. Start from a position about ¼M E of Er Gazeg beacon SCM and steer N to leave Le Grand Pellignon beacon PHM to port. Beyond that point there are only a few withies and some moorings to indicate the deepest water. The best spot is on the W side about ½M N of Le Grand Pellignon.

⊕280-Philbert 1 (47°33′.76N 2°58′.90W)

ASHORE IN LA TRINITÉ

Facilities

La Trinité has all the facilities that would be expected of a major yachting centre and small holiday town.

The Carnac Alignments

The Quiberon district is famous for a large number of carved menhirs, long mounds, stone circles, passage graves and alignments. This ritual landscape, created between 4000 and 2700 BC, was built by an energetic society that must have been living well above subsistence level. But nobody knows why they were such active builders. The monuments may have been religious, or astronomical or they may simply have been a means of expression.

A visit to the most extensive Alignments at Le Ménec, near Carnac, is highly recommended. The alignments are 1 kilometre long with stones in 12 rows laid out between two enclosures.

There is a bus service to Carnac, from which the Alignments can be reached on foot. It is also possible to hire bicycles in La Trinité.

43 River Auray

Location
47°35'N 2°57'W
Shelter
Reasonable
Depth restrictions
Deep to Le Rocher, 1.0m beyond
Height restriction
14m under bridge at Auray
HW time Port Navalo
Brest HW+½ neaps, HW springs
HW time Auray:
Brest HW+1 neaps, HW springs
Mean height of tide (m)

	HWS	HWN	LWN	LWS
Auray	4.9	4.0	1.8	0.8

Tidal stream Auray River
Flood – Brest HW–5 to +½ (3½kts)
Ebb – Brest HW +½ to –5 (3½kts)
Berthing
Visitors' moorings and anchorages
Facilities
Boatyard at Port du Parun, shops,
cafés and restaurants at several
locations
Charts
BA 2358 (25)
SHOM 7034 (25)
Imray C39 (78)
Telephone
Auray HM *t* 02 97 56 29 08
Le Bono HM *t* 02 97 57 88 98
Port du Parun *t* 02 97 57 88 98

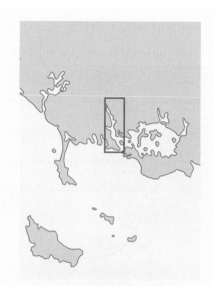

Attractive oyster river

Auray is a historic town in the NW corner of the Morbihan. It is approached by an oyster river that is somewhat less crowded than the rest of the Morbihan.

PILOTAGE

(See Plan 46)
Approach to the Morbihan

Tidal strategy

The tides in the Morbihan entrance are very strong and the final approaches can be rough in wind against tide conditions. Ideally, pass through the narrows a bit before local HW. The tide to Auray will still be flooding or slack for a couple more hours.

At Auray, the tide stands for quite a long time and then drops very quickly at about half tide. This causes strong currents in the narrows by Le Grand Huernic.

By GPS

From the S use
⊕282-SW Crouesty, ⊕285-Kerpenhir
⊕286-Grégan.

From the SE with sufficient rise of tide use
⊕281-Méaban, ⊕285-Kerpenhir,
⊕286-Grégan. This shortcut has a least depth of 0.5m and passes within ¼M of unmarked rocks.

By day

From the S, the outer approaches to the Morbihan present no difficulties. Méaban island to the W and the hill of Petit Mont, SW of Crouesty to the E are both distinctive. Approach leaving Méaban SCM and Bagen Hir ECM to starboard.

The entrance transit is Petit Vezid white pyramid in line with Baden Church on 001°. In reasonable visibility, these marks are easy to identify, although Petit Vezid can be confused with a white sail. The channel is deep so the transit need not be followed precisely. Watch out for the tide because the flood past Port Navalo sweeps first W towards Kerpenhir and then E towards Grégan.

Just inside the entrance, a shallow patch (0.9m depth) extends E of Goëmorent beacon. This is very close to the Petit Vezid transit so, at low water, it is better to use Grégan SCM in line with Baden Church

43.1 Gregan SCM (right) marks the turning point for the River Auray. Petit Vezid (left,) a white pyramid that can easily be confused with a white sail, is the front mark of the transit with Baden Church

on 359° for the final approach. Don't go E of this transit because the tide sets very strongly onto the Grand and Petit Moutons.

By night

The river is unlit beyond Grégan tower and night passage is not recommended.

THE RIVER AURAY TO AURAY

Pilotage in the Morbihan

The strong tides and confusingly large number of islands can make pilotage quite difficult. It is a good idea to mark all courses and their compass bearings on a large-scale chart and to tick off the marks as they are passed.

Auray bridge

The height of the bridge just below Auray is 14m above MHWS but with care and nerves of steel it is

43.2 The tide gauge below the bridge at Auray

43.3 The motorway bridge at Auray has a height of 14m above MHWS.

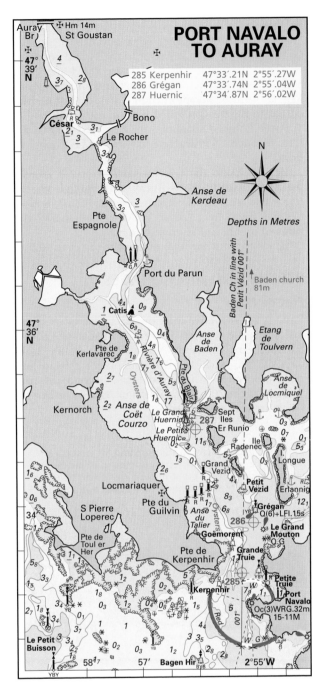

Plan 43

possible to get under it with more than 14m of air draught.

The distance from the riverbed to the bridge is 19.3m and there are height gauges on either side of the bridge. Thus by careful calculation, and use of the height gauges, it may be possible to find a combination of depth and height that works. For example at half tide there should be about 3m of water and about 16m of height.

By GPS

The River Auray requires careful visual pilotage. The following waypoints may be helpful in the first stretch. ⊕286-Grégan, ⊕287-Huernic.

By day

When ¼M S of Grégan, steer about 330° for Le Grand Huernic island. Pass it to the N and continue on the same course past Kerlavarec PHM and Catis SHM. From Catis SHM, steer due N for Point Espagnole and, except at high water, do not cut the corner to the beacon PHM beyond the point.

After Pointe Espagnole, it is easy to follow the river through the attractive narrows at Le Rocher to Bono.

Beyond Bono the river is shallow and it is only possible to continue to Auray with enough rise of tide. The shallowest patch (depth 0.2m) is just beyond Bono near César PHM, which marks the ruins of an ancient Roman bridge.

Beacons mark the remainder of the river to Auray.

BERTHS AND ANCHORAGES

Port de Bono

Bono is an attractive inlet on the E side of the river just above Le Rocher. There is no room to anchor, but there are 12 visitors' buoys in the Auray River opposite the inlet. In addition there are head and stern moorings, in the creek, just beyond the first bridge (height 20m). The tide runs hard so be careful when arriving or departing.

Bono is a pleasant village with a few shops, bars and restaurants. Also the hamlet and chapel of St Avoye, beyond the second bridge, can be visited by dinghy.

St Goustan (Auray)

There are moorings in the middle of the river opposite the quays and for high-masted yachts there are visitors' bow and stern moorings below the bridge. Both have enough water at most tides.

As the old bridge in the town is approached, the water shoals rapidly. At springs, the ebb pours violently through this bridge and eddies make the upper end of the mid-stream moorings uncomfortable. The quay should only be used as a temporary berth at high water.

ASHORE IN AURAY

At St Goustan, there are a few shops and restaurants and a fish market in the square. The harbour office has showers and a dinghy pontoon. Auray has all the facilities of a substantial town, including a marine engineer. Market day is Monday.

The train service is good, though the station is some way from St Goustan. There are buses to all parts, including La Baule for the airport and Carnac for the megaliths.

43.4 Bono and the deep-water fore and aft visitors' moorings. In summer the ferries use the quay just by the old suspension bridge but it may be possible to tie up to the little quay to starboard of the harbour entrance

43.5 St Goustan, the old bridge and beyond to the town of Auray. In the river, just below the bridge, are the visitors' fore and aft moorings

43.6 The old bridge at St Goustan was first built in 1295 but was not able to withstand the tidal stream. It was rebuilt several times and the existing successful bridge was built in the 14th century. Originally, Auray was a whaling port but by the 16th and 17th centuries it dealt in grain and wine and was one of the largest ports in Brittany

44 Vannes

Location
47°38′N 2°46′W

Shelter
Excellent in Vannes marina

Depth restrictions
Least depth 0.7m

Vannes lock
Opens Vannes HW ±2½

HW time Port Navalo
Brest HW+½ neaps, +0 springs

HW time Vannes
Brest HW+2¼ neaps, +2 springs

Mean height of tide (m)

	HWS	HWN	LWN	LWS
Port Navalo	4.9	3.9	1.8	0.7
Vannes	3.3	2.7	1.0	0.5

Tidal stream Grand Mouton
Flood – Brest HW–4½ to +1½ (8kts)
Ebb – Brest HW +1½ to –4½ (9kts)
Times may be ½hr later at neaps

Berthing
Marina

Facilities
Limited repairs but plenty of cafés, restaurants and shops

Charts
BA 2358 (25)
SHOM 7034 (25)
Imray C39 (78)

Radio Vannes HM VHF 9

Telephone
Vannes HM *t* 02 97 54 16 08

The heart of the Morbihan

Vannes has been the capital of the Morbihan since pre-Roman times. It has an old town with narrow streets and plenty of attractive old buildings but it is also a vibrant modern city with smart shops and excellent transport.

The marina is in a locked basin alongside the old town. It gets rather crowded but as it is completely sheltered the tight packing does not really matter.

PILOTAGE

(See Plan 46)

Morbihan approach

See Chapter 43 River Auray

The Vannes channel to Vannes

Tidal strategy

High water at Vannes is 2 hours after high water Port Navalo. Go through the Morbihan entrance at least half an hour before HW Port Navalo to carry the flood all the way to Vannes.

The lock and swing bridge at Vannes

The lock is open between Vannes HW ±2½ between the hours of 0800–2200 local time.

The swing bridge is ¼M to seaward of the lock and opens on demand in the first and last ½ hour and every even hour that the lock is open. Between 15 June and 15 September, it also opens on even ½ hours when the lock is open.

The traffic signals at the bridge are:

2 fixed red lights – no passage
2 flashing red lights – prepare to move
2 fixed green lights – passage permitted
2 flashing green lights – proceed if already underway and the passage is clear.

There are waiting pontoons on both sides of the bridge.

44.1 The swing bridge and the canal leading to the marina in the centre of Vannes. There are waiting pontoons either side of the bridge

In recent years, there was serious silting in the vicinity of the bridge but major dredging in 2003 should have cleared this.

Pilotage in the Morbihan

Strong tides and a large number of islands can make pilotage confusing. It is a good idea to mark courses and compass bearings on a large-scale chart and tick off the marks as they are passed.

By GPS

The Vannes channel requires careful visual pilotage. ⊕286-Grégan, ⊕288-Creizig may be useful in the first stretch.

By day

In the entrance, the Grand and Petit Moutons are dangerous because the tide sets directly onto them at up to 8 knots. To avoid them, hold the transit until close to Grégan. Then turn sharply to starboard.

The channel passes S of Iles Longue, Gavrinis and Berder before entering a larger area of water W of Ile aux Moines. Hold more or less the same course until N of Ile Crëizig.

After passing Ile Crëizig, turn N to pass through the narrows between Point de Toulingdag on Ile aux Moines and the mainland. Keep towards the E side of the channel to avoid the Banc de Kergonan. Beacons mark the narrows but take care because the stream runs very strongly.

Once through the narrows, pass between the N tip of Ile aux Moines and Pointe d'Arradon. Follow the mainland shore N of Iles Logoden and Roguédas beacon. The channel then turns N past a very distinctive pink house. It is important not to cut the corner because there are rocks and a shallow patch between Roguédas and the pink house.

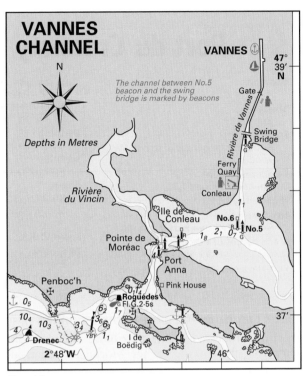

Plan 44

44.2 The distinctive pink house

Follow the channel past Port Anna to beacon No 6, which is the start of the canalised section to Vannes. The channel silts but was reported to have been dredged to 2.1m in 2003.

The swing bridge is a short distance past the *vedette* quay. It is operated from the capitainerie at Vannes, using closed-circuit TV cameras. If the bridge is not open, secure to the waiting pontoon on the starboard side until the bridge opens.

In season, a marina launch may meet visiting boats and direct them to a berth. Otherwise, secure to the visitors' pontoons that are either side of the marina just before the footbridge.

ASHORE IN VANNES

Vannes has limited sailing facilities but excels in most other respects. The marina is adjacent to the medieval old town with its lovely buildings, narrow streets and masses of little shops, bars and restaurants. On Wednesdays, Saturdays and Sundays there is a colourful street market where entertainers often perform. History buffs will enjoy the fine cathedral and museum and will no doubt walk along the ramparts. The modern shopping area is just beyond the old town.

Vannes is a main rail centre and communications by rail and bus (including a direct bus to Roscoff) are excellent. Buses from Conleau and Vannes marina pass the railway station. There is an airfield north of the city and a regular ferry service from the swing bridge to Conleau, Ile aux Moines, Port Navalo, Auray and other points in the Morbihan.

44.3 The marina at Vannes

45 Port du Crouesty

Location
47°32'N 2°55'W

Shelter
Excellent

Hazards
Entrance dangerous in strong SW wind

Depth restrictions
Channel dredged 1.8m

Night entry Lit

HW time
Brest HW+½ neaps, HW springs

Mean height of tide (m)

	HWS	HWN	LWN	LWS
Port Navalo	4.9	3.9	1.8	0.7

Tidal stream – Crouesty approaches
Slack – Brest HW–4½ to –3½
NW – Brest HW–3½ to +1½ (0.9kts)
SE – Brest HW+1½ to –4½ (1.4kts)

Berthing
Huge marina

Facilities
All facilities

Charts
BA 2823 (50), 2357 (20)
SHOM 7032 (50), 7141 (20)
Imray C39 (large scale)

Radio VHF 9

Telephone
Marina *t* 02 97 53 73 33

Huge marina on the edge of the Morbihan

Port du Crouesty is a huge, six basin marina about 2M from the entrance to the Morbihan. It has all facilities, plenty of visitors' berths, a good range of marina shops, restaurants and an excellent supermarket. It is an ideal place to stock up before a visit to the Morbihan. There is a good beach but few other tourist attractions.

PILOTAGE

Crouesty approach and entrance

By GPS

From S or W use
⊕282-SW Crouesty, ⊕283-Crouesty.

From the Vilaine use
⊕293-St Jacques, ⊕291-Chimère,
⊕282-SW Crouesty, ⊕283-Crouesty.

45.1 Port du Crouesty looking NE.
The second basin on the right is for visitors. The harbourmaster, shops and cafés are also on the right-hand side. The large grey roof on the left is the supermarket

45.2 Entrance channel and leading marks to Port du Crouesty

By day

From the S, Crouesty can be identified by the hill of Petit Mont and Crouesty lighthouse to the E of Méaban island. Leave Méaban SCM to port.

Use the Morbihan entrance transit of Petit Vezid white pyramid in line with Baden Church on 001° until, just past Petit Mont, the Crouesty channel buoys are seen to starboard. The leading marks are the lighthouse in line with a red panel with a vertical white stripe on 058°.

By night

Approach in the white sector of Port Navalo light on about 010°. When Crouesty leading lights come in transit on 058°, turn to starboard and follow the transit into the marina.

BERTHS AND ANCHORAGES

Port du Crouesty

In season, boats are normally met by a launch and directed to a vacant berth. Otherwise use the visitors' berths in the second basin on the S side.

⚓ Port Navalo

The bay is full of moorings and it may be possible to borrow one. Otherwise there is a tolerable anchorage in 1.5m off the end of the pier, among the moorings. This spot is exposed to the S and W and disturbed by the wash from ferries.

⚓ La Plage de Fogeo

Sheltered from N and E but wide open to wind or swell from the S, this sandy bay is the other side of Petit Mont from Crouesty. Approach from the S to avoid the rocks just E of Petit Mont. Anchor where depth permits. It is easy to move to Crouesty at night but be sure to clear the rocks E and S of Petit Mont.

⊕289-Fogeo (47°32'.04N 2°53'.26W)

⚓ Anse de Cornault

Sheltered from N and E but open to wind and swell from the SW, this bay is 2M SE of Petit Mont. Approach from the SW and anchor where depth permits. It is easy to leave at night but get well offshore before turning for Crouesty as there are several dangers close to the shore. The easiest escape route is to aim for ⊕282-SW Crouesty.

⊕290-Cornault (47°30'.86N 2°51'.37W)

ASHORE IN CROUESTY

Facilities

The marina has all boating facilities including chandlers, engineers, crane, scrubbing berth, fuel berth, 45-tonne travel-lift and all repairs. Around the marina are bars, restaurants and a number of shops including a launderette. There is an excellent supermarket and fish market just NW of the marina. The village of Arzon, ½M to the N has more extensive shops.

History

St-Gildas de Rhuys, a 6th-century British missionary, established a monastery near the entrance to the Morbihan. When St-Gildas died in 570 he was visiting Houat. His body, as he had wished, was placed in a boat and pushed out to sea. Two months later it came ashore at what is now the entrance to Crouesty Marina. A chapel was built at the spot, and it can be seen on the south side of the marina entrance.

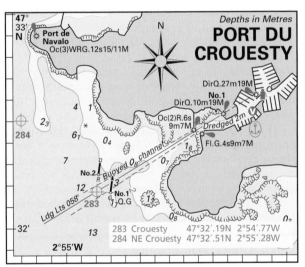

Plan 45

45.3 St-Gildas chapel to S of the Crouesty entrance

46 Morbihan Anchorages

Location
47°35'N 2°36'W

Shelter
Reasonable

HW time Arradon and Le Logeo
Brest HW+2 neaps, +1¾ springs

Mean height of tide (m)

	HWS	HWN	LWN	LWS
Arradon	3.2	2.7	1.0	0.5
Le Logeo	3.2	2.7	1.0	0.5

Tidal stream Arradon
Slack – Brest HW–4½ to –3½
Flood – Brest HW–3½ to +½ (0.5kts)
Slack – Brest HW+½ to +2½
Ebb – Brest HW+2½ to –4½ (0.7kts)

Berthing
Buoys and anchorages

Facilities
Limited cafés, restaurants and shopping

Charts
BA 2358 (25)
SHOM 7034 (25)
Imray C39 (78)

Telephone
Larmor Baden HM t 02 97 57 20 86
Port Blanc HM t 02 97 26 30 57
Ile Aux Moines HM t 02 97 26 30 57

Sixty islands in an inland sea

The Morbihan (see Plan 46) contains about 50 square miles of sheltered water and 60 islands (counting above-water rocks). All but Ile aux Moines and Ile d'Arz are privately owned and most are uninhabited.

Navigation is not difficult as the islands are easy to identify. There is deep water in the main channels and beacons and buoys mark most of the dangers.

Tidal streams are a major factor. They are fast enough for their direction to be seen on the surface and, except in the entrance, tend to follow the channels. There are plenty of counter-currents so it is often possible to make good progress against a foul tide. Nevertheless, the best time for cruising is neaps.

Moorings now fill most of the traditional anchorages so it is often necessary to borrow a buoy rather than anchor. When anchoring, it is important to tuck well in out of the stream and to avoid obstructing the many *vedettes*.

Only the popular places have been described here. Many other anchorages can be found using a large-scale chart.

RIVER AURAY ANCHORAGES
(See Plan 43)

⚓ Locmariaquer

This village is on the west side of the river near the entrance. There is a channel to it, with about 1m, marked by port-hand beacons, but it is narrow and used by the ferries. The quay dries 1.5m. Boats can take the ground between the village quay and the *vedette* jetty. Deep-keeled yachts may be able to dry out against the outer side of the jetty. It is possible to anchor off the entrance but it is a long way from the shore.

⚓ Larmor Baden

This village is usually approached from the Vannes channel but it can be approached from the Auray River between Grand Vezid and Er Runio. Leave Ile

46.1 Locmariaquer. It is possible to anchor off the entrance but it is a long way from shore

Radenec to starboard and keep in the N half of the channel because there is a rock and shallow patch NE of Radenec. Anchor near Pointe de Berchis or borrow a mooring closer to the pier.

⚓ Le Rocher

This is an attractive and popular spot. There is no room to anchor but it may be possible to borrow a mooring.

CENTRAL MORBIHAN ANCHORAGES
(See Plan 46)

⚓ Larmor Baden

This village is most easily approached from the Vannes channel between Gavrinis and Ile Berder. Anchor near Pointe de Berchis or borrow a mooring closer to the pier.

⚓ Ile Longue

There is a NE-facing bay on the SE end of this island which is more protected from the tide than would be expected from the chart. The bottom shelves rapidly, but there is room to anchor outside the moorings. The island is private and landing not allowed.

⚓ Ile de la Jument

There is a little bay on the E side. Go in as far as depth allows. Access from the N is easy; access from the S is possible with a large-scale chart.

⚓ Ile Berder

There is a little E-facing bay on the NE side of Ile Berder. Alternatively, anchor further N towards the Anse de Kerdelan. Moorings occupy the best spots.

⚓ Locmiquel

Ile aux Moines has a small marina on the NW corner at Locmiquel. There are a few pontoon berths for visitors and some visitors' moorings. It is difficult to find a comfortable anchorage outside the moorings. There are some shops, bars and restaurants.

⚓ Anse de Moustran

This is the bay just N of Port Blanc, opposite Locmiquel. The best spots are occupied by moorings and it is difficult to find a comfortable anchorage.

⚓ Pen er Men

N of Ile d'Irus there is room to anchor off the mainland shore, clear of the moorings.

⚓ Arradon

Rather exposed to the SW at high water, this popular yachting centre has moorings for visitors but little room to anchor.

46.2 The famous restaurant close to the moorings at Arradon

⚓ Ile de Boëdig

There is a pleasant, secluded anchorage off the NE end of the island. The island is private and landing is not allowed.

⚓ Pointe de Beluré

On the N tip of Ile d'Arz, there is an anchorage E of the green beacon which marks the end of the ferry slip.

⚓ Conleau

The inlet to the SW of the peninsula is full of moorings. The best anchorage is in the bight on the port side just before the far end of the narrows. There is a good restaurant.

46.3 Ile Drenec seen from Arradon. Moorings fill most of the traditional anchorages so it is often better to ring the local harbourmaster to see if there is a vacant mooring

S AND E MORBIHAN ANCHORAGES

The S and E parts of the Morbihan are slightly less crowded and more peaceful than the Vannes channel.

⚓ Anse de Kerners

SW of Ile aux Moines there is a large drying bay. Anchor outside the local boats. Water, showers and provisions are available at the campsite in season.

⚓ Anse de Pen Castel

Opposite the S tip of Ile aux Moines, it is possible to anchor outside the moorings.

⚓ Anse de Penhap

This is a nice spot in the SE corner of the Ile aux Moines. There is plenty of space to anchor but tuck in well to get out of the stream.

⚓ Ile Pirenn

There is a quiet anchorage SW of Ile Pirenn but watch out for the oyster beds. It is possible to land at Pointe de Brouel on Ile aux Moines.

⚓ Ile d'Arz

There is an anchorage in the bay on the E side. Anchor outside the moorings and do not go in too far because it shoals quickly. Land at the slipway, marked by a red beacon to visit Le Bourg where there are modest shops.

⚓ Le Passage

This is in the extreme E of the Morbihan. It can be difficult to identify and the secret is to first identify Grand Rohu red beacon tower.

In the final approach, do not pass too close to the red beacon on the northern shore. It marks the end of a slipway and not the southern extremity of the dangers.

Anchor midstream in the narrows to the N of the island if space can be found among the moorings. Alternatively, in settled weather, anchor E of the narrows. The tide is strong and there may be some silting so check the depth carefully.

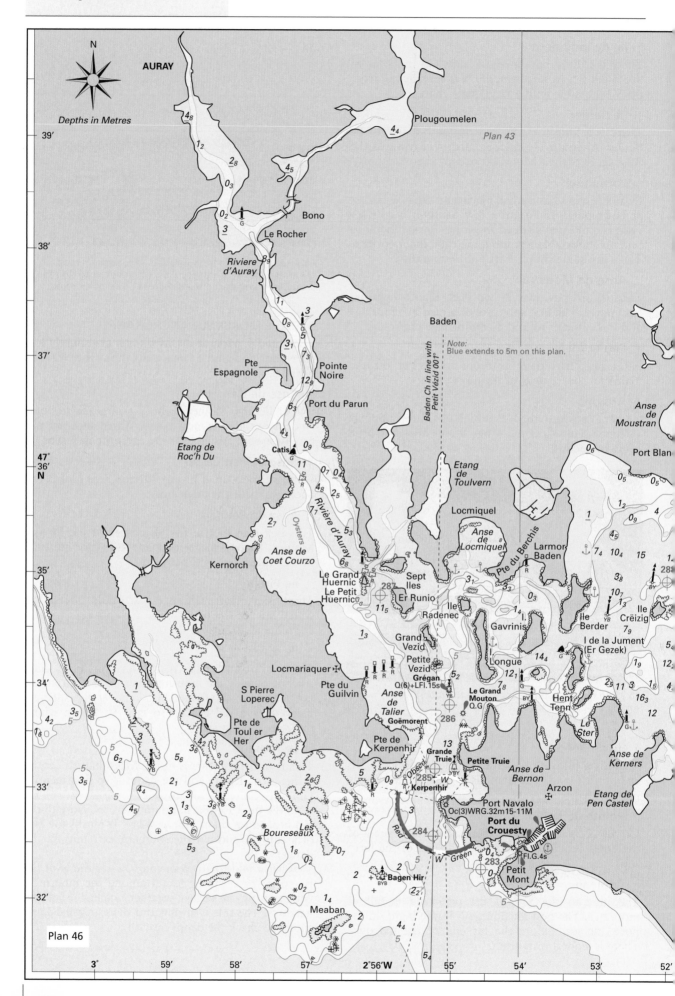

N

AURAY

Depths in Metres

Plougoumelen

Plan 43

Bono

Le Rocher

Riviere d'Auray

Baden

Note:
Blue extends to 5m on this plan.

Pte
Espagnole

Pointe
Noire

Port du Parun

*Anse
de
Moustran*

Port Blan

*Etang de
Roc'h Du*

Catis

*Etang
de
Toulvern*

Locmiquel

*Anse
de
Locmiquel*

Pte du Berchis

Larmor
Baden

Kernorch

*Anse de
Coet Courzo*

Le Grand
Huernic
Le Petit
Huernic

Sept
Iles

Er Runio

Ile
Radenec

Gavrinis

Ile
Berder

I de la Jument
(Er Gezek)

Ile
Crëizig

Hent
Tenn

Locmariaquer

Grand
Vezid

Petite
Vezid

Grégan
Q(6)+LFl.15s

I.
Longue

Le Grand
Mouton
Q.G

Le
Ster

Anse de
Kerners

S Pierre
Loperec

Pte du
Guilvin

*Anse
de
Talier*

Goëmorent

286

Pte de
Toul er
Her

Pte de
Kerpenhir

Grande
Truie

Petite Truie

*Anse de
Bernon*

Arzon

*Etang de
Pen Castel*

285

Kerpenhir

Port Navalo
Oc(3)WRG.32m15-11M

**Port du
Crouesty**

*Les
Boureseaux*

Red

284

W

Green

283

Fl.G.4s

Petit
Mont

Bagen Hir

Meaban

283	Crouesty	47°32´.19N	2°54´.77W
284	NE Crouesty	47°32 51N	2°55´.28W
285	Kerpenhir	47°33´.21N	2°55´.27W
286	Grégan	47°33´.74N	2°55´.04W
287	Huernic	47°34´.87N	2°56´.02W
288	Creizig	47°34´.92N	2°52´.01W

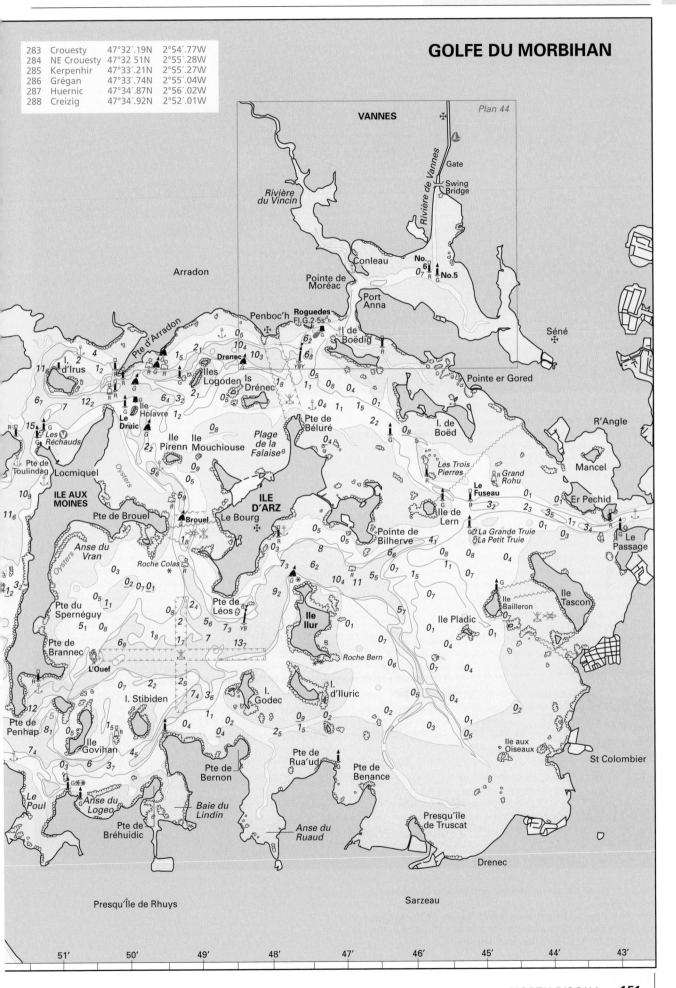

GOLFE DU MORBIHAN

46.4 Crouesty marina looking NE.
Beyond Crouesty are a few of the many small islands in the
Morbihan. Fogeo beach stretches away to the right of the
picture. The tumulus called Petit Mont is on the headland S
of Crouesty

46.5 Pointe de Kerpenhir and the entrance to the Morbihan
looking NE
On the E side of the entrance is Port Navalo which has been
used as a harbour since before the Romans and is now the
ferry port for the Morbihan and Belle-Ile

46.6 Pointe de Kerpenhir looking NE.
Petit Vezid, the white beacon on the small island, and the
aptly named Ile Longue, are kept due N when going to
Vannes. Lamor Baden is the village beyond Ile Longue.
Gavrinis, an island just S of the village, has a 5,000-year-old
cairn with many engraved pillars. It can only be visited by
ferry

46.7 Pointe de Saint-Nicolas looking N to Ile aux Moines.
Anse de Kerners to the W of the point and Anse de Pen
Castel to the E have moorings and an anchorage. Anse de
Penhap is an alternative anchorage in the SE corner of Ile
au Moines

46.8 Port Blanc looking E.
Across the water is Locmiquel on the NW corner of Ile aux
Moines (Monks' Island). There are a few pontoon berths for
visitors and some visitors' moorings but it is difficult to find
a comfortable anchorage outside the moorings. Ile aux
Moines is one of the largest islands and a delightful place
for walkers

46.9 Port Anna looking N to Conleau and the outskirts of
Vannes.
The best anchorage is in the bight on the W, opposite
Port Anna. Ferries go from Conleau to Ile d'Arz. This
island was home to the sea captains when Auray, Vannes
and Port Navalo were all large, busy ports. There is an
anchorage at Ile d'Arz on the E side of the island

Pornic

V. Southeast Brittany

Redon

Piriac

Vilaine

Piriac

Pornic

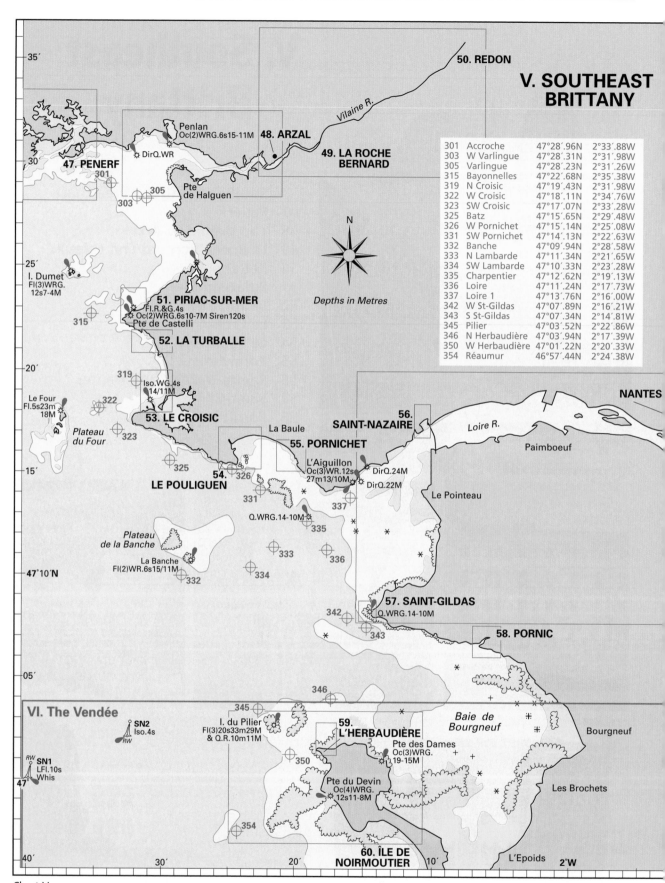

V. SOUTHEAST BRITTANY

50. REDON

48. ARZAL

49. LA ROCHE BERNARD

47. PENERF

Penlan
Oc(2)WRG.6s15-11M

DirQ.WR

301

305

303

Pte
de Halguen

301	Accroche	47°28′.96N	2°33′.88W
303	W Varlingue	47°28′.31N	2°31′.98W
305	Varlingue	47°28′.23N	2°31′.26W
315	Bayonnelles	47°22′.68N	2°35′.38W
319	N Croisic	47°19′.43N	2°31′.98W
322	W Croisic	47°18′.11N	2°34′.76W
323	SW Croisic	47°17′.07N	2°33′.28W
325	Batz	47°15′.65N	2°29′.48W
326	W Pornichet	47°15′.14N	2°25′.08W
331	SW Pornichet	47°14′.13N	2°22′.63W
332	Banche	47°09′.94N	2°28′.58W
333	N Lambarde	47°11′.34N	2°21′.65W
334	SW Lambarde	47°10′.33N	2°23′.28W
335	Charpentier	47°12′.62N	2°19′.13W
336	Loire	47°11′.24N	2°17′.73W
337	Loire 1	47°13′.76N	2°16′.00W
342	W St-Gildas	47°07′.89N	2°16′.21W
343	S St-Gildas	47°07′.34N	2°14′.81W
345	Pilier	47°03′.52N	2°22′.86W
346	N Herbaudière	47°03′.94N	2°17′.39W
350	W Herbaudière	47°01′.22N	2°20′.33W
354	Réaumur	46°57′.44N	2°24′.38W

I. Dumet
Fl(3)WRG.
12s7-4M

315

51. PIRIAC-SUR-MER
Fl.R.&G.4s
Oc(2)WRG.6s10-7M Siren120s
Pte de Castelli

52. LA TURBALLE

319

Iso.WG.4s
14/11M

53. LE CROISIC

Le Four
Fl.5s23m
18M

322

Plateau
du Four

323

325

La Baule

55. PORNICHET

56. SAINT-NAZAIRE

NANTES

Loire R.

Paimboeuf

L'Aiguillon
Oc(3)WR.12s
27m13/10M

DirQ.24M

DirQ.22M

Le Pointeau

54.
326

LE POULIGUEN

331

Q.WRG.14-10M

335

337

Plateau
de la Banche

333

336

La Banche
Fl(2)WR.6s15/11M

334

47°10′N

332

57. SAINT-GILDAS

342

Q.WRG.14-10M

343

58. PORNIC

05′

Baie de
Bourgneuf

Bourgneuf

VI. The Vendée

SN2
Iso.4s

346

RW

345

I. du Pilier
Fl(3)20s33m29M
& Q.R.10m11M

59.
L'HERBAUDIÈRE

Pte des Dames
Oc(3)WRG.
19-15M

SN1
LFl.10s
Whis

RW

47

350

Pte du Devin
Oc(4)WRG.
12s11-8M

Les Brochets

354

**60. ÎLE DE
NOIRMOUTIER**

L'Epoids

2°W

N

Depths in Metres

Chart V

156   NORTH BISCAY

47 Pénerf

Location
47°30'N 2°39'W

Shelter
Good except in strong W wind

Hazards
Intricate approach

Depth restrictions
0.5m in Central passage
4.5m in E passage
Deep inside

Night entry Lit but not recommended

HW time
Brest HW+¼ neaps, −½ springs

Mean height of tide (m)

	HWS	HWN	LWN	LWS
Pénerf	5.4	4.3	2.0	0.7

Tidal stream in passages
3kts when rocks are uncovered, 2kts when rocks are covered

Berthing
Visitors' buoys and anchorage

Facilities
Bar, restaurant and a few shops

Charts
BA 2823 (50)
SHOM 7033 (50), 7135 (15)
Imray C39 (78)

Quiet unspoilt river

The Pénerf is an unspoilt oyster river about 6M W of the Vilaine. There are many rocky ledges at the entrance that provide good protection but also make the entrance a bit tricky. A first visit should be in good weather close to high water.

The villages of Pénerf and Cadenic are both small, quiet and attractive. They offer excellent oysters but not a great deal else.

PILOTAGE

Pénerf W passage

Local fishing boats use this entrance in strong W winds. It can only be used safely with local knowledge.

Pénerf Central passage

This passage is the easiest of the three. It can only be used above half tide when Pénerf presents a daunting expanse of water with only Le Pignon for guidance.

47.1 Le Pignon and the steeple showing just above the trees to the right of the white house with the gable

By GPS

Careful visual pilotage is required. The following waypoints may help in the approach
⊕297-Pénerf, ⊕298-Pénerf 1.

By day

Start from a position close to ⊕297-Pénerf but watch out for extensive fishing nets. The distinctive white Tour des Anglais will be roughly in line with Pénerf church on 030° and Le Pignon red beacon tower will be due N.

The entry transit is Le Pignon in line with the steeple of Le Tour du Parc on 001°. If trees obscure the steeple, use Le Pignon in line with the prominent white house on 359°. The house has a single gable and is just right of the water tower (see 47.1). Borenis SHM and La Traverse SHM mark the dangers to starboard.

On close approach, turn to starboard leaving Le Pignon 40m to port. Then steer to leave Bayonnelle beacon to starboard and follow one more starboard beacon into the river. At the last beacon, turn onto about 060° and head for the moorings off Pénerf village. On the way there is a red beacon. Do not go too close as it is in very shallow water.

By night

Le Pignon is lit but otherwise the river is unlit and night entry is not recommended.

Pénerf E passage

This passage is deep but very narrow and there are rocky shoals close E of it. Also, the front mark is not easy to see from a distance and trees may hide the back mark. It should not be used in poor visibility.

By GPS

Careful visual pilotage is required. The following waypoints may help in the approach
⊕299-E Penerf, ⊕300-E Penerf 1.

By day

Start from a position near Borénis SHM. The transit is a PHM post (SE of Le Pignon) in line with Le Tour

47.2 The River Pénerf looking NE.
The Port of Pénerf is on the E side of the river near the jetty. The anchorage at Cadenic is ½M further on the N side. The River Pénerf is mostly devoted to oyster farming

du Parc steeple on 354°. Both marks may be hard to see. Above half-tide it is safe to go in cautiously towards Le Pignon. However, do not attempt the passage unless the PHM post can be positively identified, particularly if the tide is running strongly.

Leave the PHM post fairly close to port. Then steer to leave Le Pignon to port and join the central passage described above.

BERTHS AND ANCHORAGES

Pénerf

There are visitors' buoys near Penerf quay and it may be possible to anchor outside the moorings. This anchorage is quite choppy when wind and tide are opposed.

Cadenic

Cadenic is on the N bank less than ½M beyond Pénerf. Leave the IDM, just N of Pénerf, to port and aim for the beacon PHM and SHM buoy just off Cadenic. There are some fishing boat moorings off the pier and a quiet neap anchorage upstream of the moorings. There is not much room at springs and the holding in deeper water is reported to be poor.

⚓ Pointe de St-Jacques

Sheltered from NW to NE, there is a small harbour off the S tip of the Presqu'île de Rhuys. Approach from St-Jacques SCM and anchor off the pier. A night departure is possible using the pierhead light.

⊕294-St-Jacques 1 (47°28'.97N 2°47'.08W)

⚓ Anse de Succino

Well protected from the N and NW but completely open to the S, this wide shallow bay is 3M E of Pénerf entrance. Approach from due S and anchor where depth permits. A night departure without GPS would be unsafe. The ruins of the Château de Sucinco are visible from the anchorage and can be visited.

⊕296-Succino 1 (47°29'.94N 2°43'.38W)

47.3 The Port du Pénerf moorings

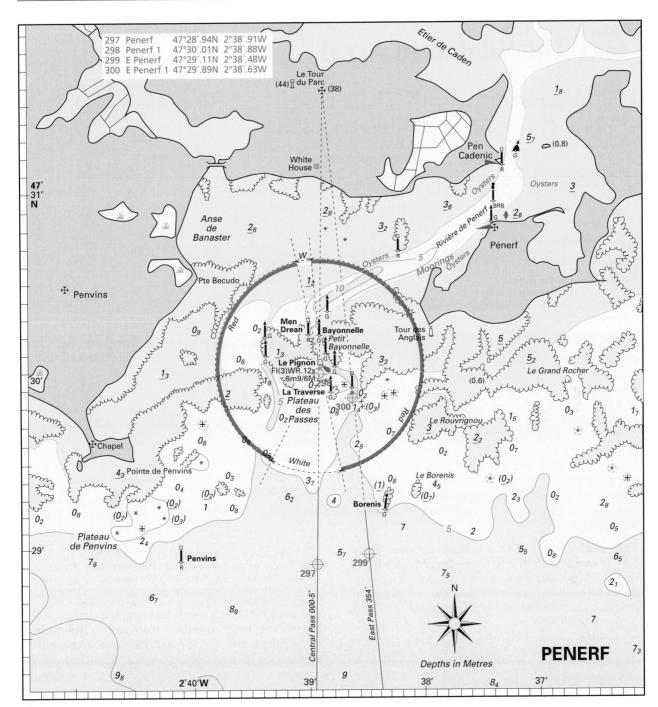

297	Penerf	47°28′.94N	2°38′.91W
298	Penerf 1	47°30′.01N	2°38′.88W
299	E Penerf	47°29′.11N	2°38′.48W
300	E Penerf 1	47°29′.89N	2°38′.63W

Plan 47

ASHORE IN PÉNERF AND CADENIC

Pénerf has shops, bars and a restaurant. It also has a nice chapel with a couple of traditional model fishing boats as votive offerings.

Cadenic has almost no facilities but, like Pénerf, it is often possible to buy seafood from the fishermen.

47.4 The Bureau du Port at Pénerf

48 The Vilaine to Arzal

Location
47°30'N 2°28'W

Shelter
Excellent

Depth restrictions
0.8m over the bar

Night entry
Partially lit

Arzal lock Opens on most hours

HW time
Brest HW+½ neaps, −¼ springs

Mean height of tide (m)

	HWS	HWN	LWN	LWS
Tréhiguier	5.5	4.4	2.1	0.7

Tidal stream in the river
Flood 2kts, ebb 3kts in river but much influenced by inland rain

Berthing
Two marinas

Fuel
N side of marina near lock

Facilities
Good marina facilities

Charts
BA 2823 (50)
SHOM 7033 (50), 5418 (15)
Imray C39 (78)

Radio
Lock VHF 18
Marina VHF 9

Telephone
Lock *t* 02 97 41 28 39
Marina *t* 02 97 45 02 98
Call marina for lock opening times

Gateway to the Vilaine

(See Plan 48B)

The Vilaine has a large lock at Arzal that protects it from the sea and keeps the water level permanently at 3.0m or more. This has created a beautiful, long boating lake with flat water and almost no commercial traffic. Once through the lock, you may never want to leave.

There is a large marina just beyond the lock. It is useful for fuel or repairs and would be a good place to leave a boat but it has little to offer the tourist.

PILOTAGE

The mouth of the Vilaine is shallow and open to the SW. It can be rough and even dangerous when a strong SW wind blows against the ebb. The three passes have a bit more depth than the rest of the bay but in good weather, above half tide on the flood,

they need not be followed. The Varlingue rock (dries 0.3m) on the E side is dangerous below half tide or in rough weather.

The Grande Accroche Passage

This is the most convenient passage to or from the Morbihan but the seas break heavily in strong W and SW winds.

By GPS

Use ⊕301-Accroche, ⊕302-Accroche 1, ⊕307-Vilaine.

48.1 The approaches to the Vilaine looking NE.
The whole of the bay is shallow and the mouth of the Vilaine can be rough if a strong SW wind blows against the ebb. There are three passages with more depth than the rest. In good weather, above half tide, they need not be followed and this is a wonderful sailing bay

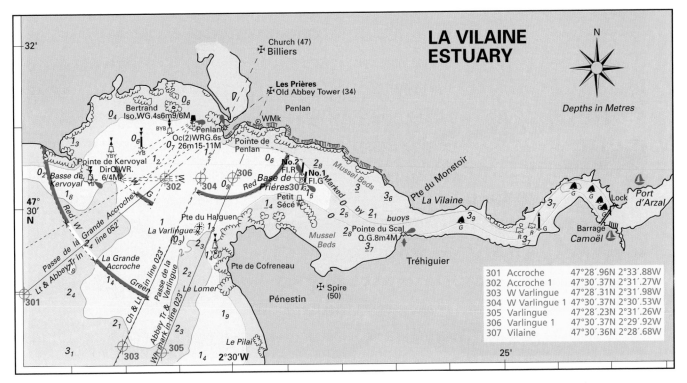

Plan 48A

By day

Start from a position ½M SE of Les Mats SCM. The transit is Penlan lighthouse in line with the Abbaye de Prières on 052°. Both marks are fairly easy to see but in practice it is good enough to steer for Penlan lighthouse, keeping a reasonable distance from Kervoyal tower.

Once Kervoyal tower is due W, steer due E to enter the river between the buoys. A useful transit is Kervoyal tower in line with Tour des Anglais (at Pénerf) on 267°.

By night

The Grande Accroche is lit by the white sector of Penlan and the narrow white sector of Kervoyal. However, the river is not lit beyond Tréhiguier so night entry is not recommended.

The W Varlingue passage

By GPS

Use ⊕303-W Varlingue, ⊕304-W Varlingue 1, ⊕307-Vilaine. This route passes close W of La Varlingue (dries 0.3m).

By day

Start towards the E side of the bay with Penlan lighthouse bearing about 025°. The transit is Biliers church in line with Penlan lighthouse on 026°. At low water, it is important to hold it accurately because it passes close to La Varlingue rock (dries 0.3m).

Once Kervoyal tower is due W, steer due E to enter the river between the buoys.

The Varlingue passage

This is the most convenient passage from the S. It is

also the deepest and the most protected in bad W and SW weather.

By GPS

Use ⊕305-Varlingue, ⊕306-Varlingue 1, ⊕307-Vilaine. This route passes close E of La Varlingue (dries 0.3m).

By day

The official transit is the Abbaye de Prières in line with a small white daymark on 023°. The front mark will be invisible to a stranger. Fortunately a beacon WCM on the shore indicates the approximate position of La Varlingue (dries 0.3m).

Once Kervoyal tower is due W, or Petit Sécé tower bears 105° steer due E to enter the river between the buoys.

The Vilaine entrance to the Arzal lock

By day

The channel is well buoyed to Tréhiguer. There will be as little as 0.8m or even less in places so take the curves wide and if possible go in or out at high water.

Beyond Tréhiguier there are fewer marks, but the channel is still easy to follow with red and green buoys and the occasional beacon. The approach to the lock is marked with starboard-hand buoys.

The Arzal lock

The lock is on the N side of the river, adjacent to the conspicuous control tower. The lower gates are normally left open so yachts arriving from sea can wait in the lock. There are some mooring buoys below the dam and room to anchor. The danger area around the dam spillway is marked off by yellow buoys.

48.2 The Arzal Barrier looking upriver to the E.
The lock is on the far left by the control tower. The marina
on the left is Arzal marina which has all facilities. On the
right is the related Camoel marina which is more peaceful
but does not have the same facilities. It is possible to
anchor on the far bank beyond the moorings

The lock is worked in daylight hours between
0700 and 2200, during the season. The opening
times depend on the tide and are displayed at the
local marinas and in an invaluable booklet available
at the lock. The lock may be closed for more than
one hour at lunch time or close to low water.
Otherwise, it opens on the hour.

The lock is big and crowded and, except close to
high water, quite turbulent. Moor to the vertical
chains and make sure the fenders do not pop out.
Also wait until the turbulence has subsided before
casting off. Fortunately, the lock-keeper manages the
potential chaos with great charm and skill.

BERTHS AND ANCHORAGES

Arzal and Camoël marinas

There is a large marina on the north bank above the
dam at Arzal and a smaller, quieter one at Camoël
on the south side.

Facilities at Arzal

Arzal has all the facilities of a major marina complex
including fuel, all repairs, 15-tonne crane, masting,
haul out, laying up outside or under cover. There are
bars and restaurants, but no shops within 2M. The
dam has a fish pass which is worth seeing.

Camoël marina on the S side is more peaceful, but
has no facilities other than showers and toilets.

⚓ Tréhiguier

Sheltered from S and E but exposed to W and NW,
there is a convenient anchorage near the entrance on
the seaward side of the lock. Anchor outside the
moorings in soft mud. Land at the slip.

The Vilaine below Arzal

There are many places in the river where anchoring
is possible on the edge of the channel. Sound the area
carefully before anchoring because in places the
depths shoal rapidly when the channel is left. Two
anchors may be necessary.

48.3 The control tower of the Arzal Barrier.
If the downstream gates are open then boats can enter and
wait. Boats on the upstream side moor and wait where
they can. If there are many boats waiting expect a bit of a
rush when the gates open

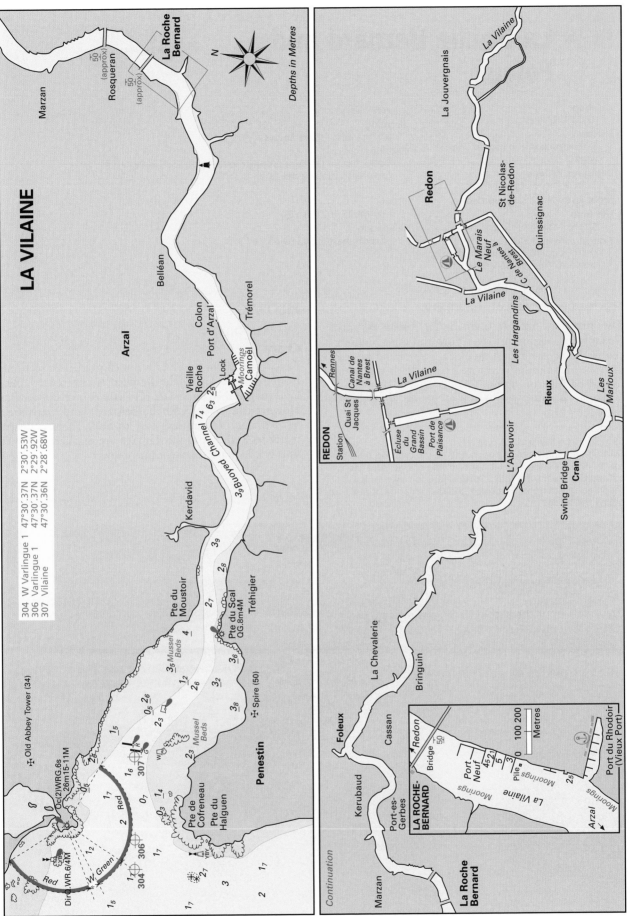

LA VILAINE

Depths in Metres

304	W Varlingue 1	47°30'.37N 2°30'.53W
306	Varlingue 1	47°30'.37N 2°29'.92W
307	Vilaine	47°30'.36N 2°28'.68W

Marzan
Rosqueran
50 (approx)
50 (approx)
La Roche Bernard

Old Abbey Tower (34)
Oc(2)WRG.6s
26m15-11M
DirO.WR.6/4M
Red
W Green
307
306
304
Pte de Cofreneau
Pte du Halguen
Penestin
Mussel Beds
Pte du Scal
QG.8m4M
Tréhigier
Spire (50)
Pte du Moustoir
Mussel Beds
Kerdavid
Buoyed Channel
Trémorel
Camoël
Moorings
Lock
Port d'Arzal
Colon
Vieille Roche
Belléan
Arzal

REDON

Rennes
Canal de Nantes à Brest
La Vilaine
Quai St Jacques
Station
Ecluse du Grand Bassin
Port de Plaisance

La Vilaine
La Jouvergnais
Redon
St Nicolas-de-Redon
Le Marais Neuf
C de Nantes à Brest
Quinssignac
La Vilaine
Les Hargandins
Rieux
Les Marioux
L'Abreuvoir
Swing Bridge
Cran

LA ROCHE-BERNARD

Redon
Bridge
Port Neuf
Pile
Moorings
Moorings
La Vilaine
Arzal
Moorings
Port du Rhodoir (Vieux Port)
0 100 200
Metres

Continuation
Marzan
Foleux
Kerubaud
Port-es-Gerbes
Cassan
La Chevalerie
Bringuin
La Roche Bernard

Plan 48B

49 La Roche Bernard and Foleux

Location
47°31'N 2°19'W

Shelter
Excellent except in very strong SW wind

Depth restrictions
3.0m or more beyond Arzal

Night entry Not recommended

HW time
Above Arzal there is no tide

Tidal stream in the river
There is usually a slight stream to seaward. This can be strong after very heavy rain

Berthing
Marina and visitors' buoys

Facilities
Good marina facilities plus attractive town with shops, cafés and restaurants

Charts
IGN Top25 1022OT (25)

Telephone
Harbourmaster *t* 02 99 90 73 93

The medieval heart of the Vilaine

The attractive holiday town of La Roche Bernard was once an important river port and boat building centre. Today its quaint medieval streets and houses have been beautifully restored to make it the main tourist destination on the Vilaine.

There are two marinas and plenty of visitors' buoys.

49.1 La Roche Bernard looking NE.
Traditionally this town has been one of the crossing places for the River Vilaine. Now it has two fine bridges and the collapsed remains of a third. Port du Rhodoir marina is in the inlet on the right. Port Neuf, the main marina, is just below the bridge

PILOTAGE

(See Plan 48B)

Charts

Beyond the dam, the river is not charted. The section from Arzal to La Roche Bernard is covered by the land map IGN Top25 *1022OT (La Roche Bernard)*. However, beyond La Roche Bernard, land maps are less satisfactory and less easy to find. There is deep water to Redon and the dangers are marked so Plan 48B is adequate for most purposes.

49.2 Port du Rhodoir marina. The first pontoon is the reception pontoon

49.3 Port Neuf marina visitors' pontoon. This is just downstream of the marina and close to the quay

Arzal to La Roche Bernard

Above the dam most of the river has at least 3.0m so it is only necessary to use common sense and not cut the corners.

From Arzal to La Roche Bernard is about 3¾M. There are no hazards and the river is very attractive.

La Roche Bernard to Foleux

From La Roche Bernard to Foleux is about 4¾M. Just N of La Roche Bernard, the river passes under two road bridges (height 50m approx.) and a power cable with unknown but ample clearance. Just before Foleux another power cable crosses the river, again with unknown but ample clearance.

After La Roche Bernard, the river becomes less steep sided but it still winds between wooded hills and is most attractive.

BERTHS AND ANCHORAGES

Port du Rhodoir marina

Port du Rhodoir marina, the Old Port, is in a small inlet on the S side of La Roche Bernard. Local boats mainly use it but the first pontoon is a reception pontoon. The harbourmaster's office is on the quay.

Port Neuf

Port Neuf is the main marina in the river at La Roche Bernard. There is a visitors' pontoon running along the bank downstream of the finger pontoons.

Visitors' moorings

There are many moorings in the river and it is usually possible to borrow one.

Foleux

Foleux has a marina, boatyard and visitors' pontoon. Ashore there are toilets, showers and a restaurant but not much else.

ANCHORAGES IN THE VILAINE

It is possible to anchor almost anywhere in the river except where anchoring is explicitly forbidden. Note that a charge will be made for anchoring in the vicinity of Foleux.

ASHORE IN LA ROCHE BERNARD

The marina can carry out most repairs but there is no chandlery and no fuel berth. Bread can be delivered to yachts each morning.

Ashore, there are cafés, shops and restaurants to suit every taste. The medieval town is well worth exploring. A map showing a recommended walk through the old streets and alleys is available from the tourist office. The maritime museum has models and reconstructions to show what life was like by the Vilaine. Market day is Thursday.

49.4 The bridges at La Roche Bernard

50 Redon

Location
  47°38'N 2°05'W
Shelter
  Excellent in Redon marina
Depth restrictions
  3.0m or more beyond Arzal
Cran bridge opening (local time)
  0900, 1100, 1330, 1530, 1730
  1 April to 31 October
Night entry Not recommended
HW time
  Above Arzal there is no tide
Stream in the river
  There is usually a slight stream to

seaward. This can be strong after very heavy rain
Berthing
  Marina at Foleux and Redon, several riverside pontoons and anchorages
Facilities
  Marina at Foleux, substantial market town at Redon
Radio
  Vilaine navigation VHF 10
  Redon Marina VHF 9
Telephone
  Foleux *t* 02 99 91 80 87
  Redon *t* 02 99 71 35 28

Gateway to the canals

Redon is a pleasant market town and major canal port. It is 26M from the sea and has a completely different atmosphere from most yacht ports. The town is interlaced with canals and locks, and there are many fine buildings that provide evidence of Redon's important role in Breton history.

PILOTAGE

(See Plan 48B)

Foleux to Redon

The swing bridge at Cran

Between April and October the swing bridge at Cran opens at 0900, 1100, 1330, 1530 and 1730 (local time). There is a waiting pontoon on the upstream side and a waiting buoy on the downstream side. The bridge does not open for long and it is important to watch the signals and be ready. Two reds means no passage; one red means get ready; and two greens means go.

By day

From Foleux to Cran is about 7M. The river winds between fields and wooded hills and is most attractive. A nature reserve with a pontoon will be passed in this section. There are no hazards except a power cable just below Cran with 27m headroom.

From Cran bridge to Rieux is just under 3M. Rieux has two visitors' pontoons. Shortly afterwards the vista widens out for the last 3¾M to Redon and the river becomes much more like an inland waterway with junctions and signposts.

The marina is in the old sea lock of the Nantes-Brest canal and it is necessary to follow the signposts to the Port du Redon. The lock gate is permanently open since the barrage at Arzal now maintains the water level.

50.1 The visitors' pontoon and café at Foleux

50.2 Traditional fishing on the Vilaine

50.3 One of the two pontoons at Rieux

50.4 The marina at Redon

50.5 Merchants' houses on the canal

BERTHS AND ANCHORAGES

Redon

The marina is through the lock on the port side. Canal boats use the starboard side. There are no specific visitors' berths and usually the harbourmaster allocates berths. If he is not on duty, find an empty berth and report to the office.

Rieux

There are two visitors' pontoons 2M upstream from Cran close to the village of Rieux.

ANCHORAGES IN THE VILAINE

It is possible to anchor almost anywhere in the river except where anchoring is explicitly forbidden.

ASHORE IN REDON

Redon is a market town and a major port for canal boats so most yachting requirements can be satisfied. The town has a covered market, good shops and restaurants, and an interesting canal museum. There are some fine 15th to 18th century town houses and a surprisingly large abbey church. For a town that has been sacked repeatedly in its history it has all the appearances of a wealthy past.

There are markets every day except Friday and Sunday. The railway station is within easy walking distance of the marina and has direct trains to St Malo.

50.6 Into the canal system. The maximum dimensions for boats using the canal are draught 1.1m, beam 4.5m and air draught 2.5m

51 Piriac-sur-Mer

Location
47°23'N 2°33'W

Shelter
Good in the marina

Depth restrictions
Sill dries 1.0m and opens when there is 2.4m of tide.
The marina has 2.4m

Night entry Lit

HW time
Brest HW+¼ neaps, −½ springs

Mean height of tide (m)

	HWS	HWN	LWN	LWS
St-Nazaire	5.4	4.3	2.0	0.7

Tidal stream in approach
NE – Brest HW–6 to –1 (0.7kts)
SW – Brest HW–1 to –6 (0.7kts)

Berthing
Marina

Fuel
On quay

Facilities
Limited repairs; adequate shops, cafés and restaurants; good market

Charts
BA 2823 (50)
SHOM 7033 (50), 7136 (15)
Imray C39 (78)

Radio VHF 9

Telephone
Harbourmaster *t* 02 40 23 52 32

Delightful holiday resort

Piriac is a delightful place. It is a small 17th century town that has been beautifully renovated as a holiday resort. The town is full of flowers that make the cafés and restaurants seem particularly inviting. For the more adventurous, it is a good base for visiting the Grand Brière or the medieval town of Guérande.

The marina is fairly new and usually has room for visiting yachts up to 12m. It is located in a drying harbour with a sill and a flap gate. The gate opens above half tide and retains the depth in the marina at 2.4m.

PILOTAGE

Approach and entrance to Piriac

Piriac flap gate

The sill dries 1.0m and the gate automatically drops open when the height of tide reaches 2.4m, which gives 1.4m over the sill. The depth gauge alongside the entrance shows the actual depth over the sill.

There is no large-scale chart of the approaches but the channel seems to be deeper than the sill. However, yachts regularly go aground in the approach and just outside the marina entrance so there may be some shallower patches.

By GPS

From the N use
⊕312-Piriac, ⊕313-Piriac 1.

From the W use
⊕314-Rohtrès, ⊕312-Piriac, ⊕313-Piriac 1.

From the SW use
⊕315-Bayonnelles, ⊕314-Rohtrès, ⊕312-Piriac, ⊕313-Piriac 1.

By day

From the N, a distinctive belfry on the seafront identifies Piriac. The approach is rocky so start from a position 100m NE of Grand Norven NCM. Steer about 165° and pass between the green and red beacons to enter the harbour. The line from the red beacon to the harbour is reported to have the deepest water.

From the S or W, avoid the rocks off Pointe du Castelli by keeping outside Les Bayonnelles WCM and Rohtrès NCM and approaching Piriac from the N as above.

The entrance to the marina is to port, immediately inside the breakwaters. It is only about 50 feet wide and is marked by 2 red and 2 green beacons. Red lights indicate that the gate is closed; green lights indicate that it is open.

In the spring of 2004 the drying fishing harbour was dug out to extend the marina, as shown on Plan 51B.

By night

Approach in the white sector of the Inner Mole light and remain in this sector until past the breakwater lights.

51.1 Piriac lock entrance. The visitors' pontoons are on the right of the picture

BERTHS AND ANCHORAGES

Piriac marina

Visitors are normally met by a launch and allocated a berth. If there is no launch, berth on the visitors' pontoon, which is immediately ahead on entering.

⚓ Grand Norven

In settled weather, there is a temporary anchorage, to wait for the tide, E of the Grand Norven beacon in about 2.5m.

⚓ Mine d'Or

Protected from the E, this wide bay is just S of the mouth of the Vilaine. Approach from N of W to avoid the dangers near Ile de Belair. Anchor ½M NE of Ile de Belair where depth permits. A night escape to Piriac or the Vilaine is possible using Penlan light.

⊕308-Mine d'Or (47°28′.16N 2°29′.87W)

⚓ Mesquer

Sheltered from the E, Mesquer is a little harbour and large drying bay 4M NE of Piriac. Approach from a position between Basse Normande NCM′ and Laronesse IDM and steer about 110° towards Mesquer. Enter the harbour between the red and green beacons. At neaps it is possible to anchor E of the jetty. Boats that can take the ground can go further in for better shelter. At neaps, it is also possible to anchor behind Pointe du Bile on the N side of the bay.

⊕310-Mesquer 1 (47°25′.44N 2°28′.20W)

⚓ Ile Dumet

Slightly sheltered from the SW, Ile Dumet is a bird sanctuary 3M WNW of Piriac. There are shallow patches NE and NW of the island so approach with the lighthouse on about 215°. Anchor NE of the lighthouse.

⊕311-Dumet (47°24′.77N 2°36′.94W)

ASHORE IN PIRIAC

Piriac has a fuel pontoon but otherwise it has limited marina facilities. The town is charming. It has a reasonable range of shops and a market on Monday, Wednesday and Saturday. There are many cafés and restaurants.

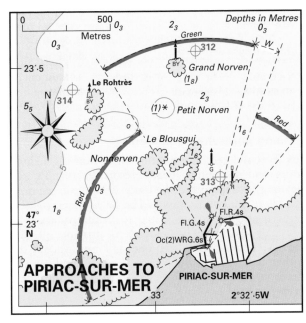

Plan 51A

312 Piriac	47°23′.58N	2°32′.85W
313 Piriac 1	47°23′.17N	2°32′.66W
314 Rohtrès	47°23′.44N	2°33′.45W

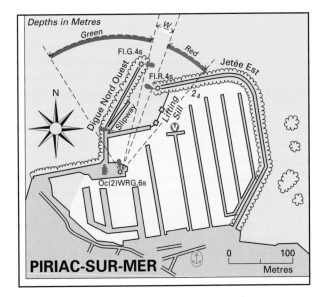

Plan 51B

51.2 Allow some safety margin because it is possible to cross the sill and run aground just outside

52 La Turballe

Location
   47°21'N 2°31'W
Shelter
   Good except from SSW
Depth restrictions
   2.2m in approach
   2.0m in marina
Night entry Lit
HW time
   Brest HW+¼ neaps, –¾ springs
Mean height of tide (m):

	HWS	HWN	LWN	LWS
Le Croisic	5.4	4.3	2.0	0.7

Tidal stream in approach
   N – Brest HW–6 to –1 (0.5kts)
   S – Brest HW–1 to +4 (0.5kts)
   Slack – Brest HW+4 to –6
Berthing Marina
Fuel SW harbour wall
Facilities
   As of a major fishing port
Charts
   BA 2823 (50)
   SHOM 7033 (50), 7145 (25)
   Imray C39 (large scale)
Radio:
   Marina VHF 9
   Must call before entry
Telephone
   Harbourmaster *t* 02 40 23 41 65

Fishing port with large marina

La Turballe is a nice mixture of a working fishing port and a popular beach resort. It is now the leading fishing port in the Loire-Atlantique region.

There are two harbours. The Basin de Garlahy is locked and totally dedicated to fishing boats. The Port de Plaisance is dredged to provide all tide access; fishing boats use one half and yachts the other half. The visitors' area is quite small so the harbourmaster sometimes has to turn visiting boats away.

PILOTAGE

La Turballe approach and entrance

Entry restrictions

Entry is not recommended in strong W wind or swell.

The marina gets very crowded in season and it is necessary to call on VHF 9 before entering. When the marina is full, the harbourmaster may broadcast announcements on VHF 9.

By GPS

Use ⊕316-Turballe, ⊕317-Turballe 1, ⊕318-Turballe 2. A sharp turn to port is required at ⊕317-Turballe 1.

By day

The long white-walled fish market, the water tower at the back of town and the long beach to the S make La Turballe easy to identify from any direction. However, it must only be approached from the SW to avoid the rocky shoals to the N.

Aim for the N end of the beach. When about ¼M S of the harbour, the S facing entrance will open. Make a sharp turn to port to make the final entry on about 005°. Keep towards the W breakwater because rocks extend from the E side. Once past the inner breakwater head, turn sharply to starboard to enter the Port de Plaisance.

By night

Approach in the white sector of the W jetty head light. Enter with the leading lights in line on 007°. After passing the W breakwater head, make a sharp turn to starboard round the green light that marks the entrance to the Port de Plaisance.

52.1 The main harbour is split into two. Fishing vessels are on the N side nearest to the fish market and pleasure boats are on the S side

52.2 The visitors' pontoons form a U-shape beyond the finger pontoons. There is a small aluminium kiosk on the end of the first pontoon. An extra pontoon, without shore access, is sited in the middle of the U

BERTHS AND ANCHORAGES

La Turballe marina

The visitors' pontoons are clearly indicated and are in the SW part of the marina, just past a little aluminium kiosk. Space for berthing and manoeuvring a 12m boat is quite limited.

⚓ S of La Turballe harbour

In offshore winds there is pleasant anchorage off the long sandy beach to the S of the harbour.

ASHORE IN LA TURBALLE

There is a fuel berth on the S breakwater, a 16-tonne crane, a 140-tonne travel-lift and a slipway. All repairs can be undertaken on yachts up to 16m. The town is a lively holiday resort with plenty of restaurants, shops and cafés close to the marina.

A magnificent 2M beach is just S of the marina and there is easy access to the salt mashes to see the wildlife.

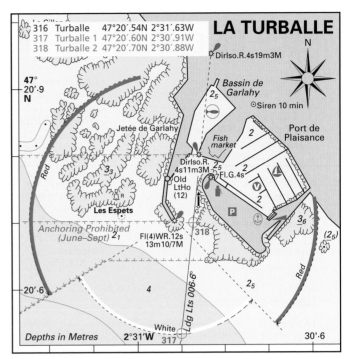

316	Turballe	47°20'.54N 2°31'.63W
317	Turballe 1	47°20'.60N 2°30'.91W
318	Turballe 2	47°20'.70N 2°30'.88W

Plan 52

52.3 La Turballe looking NE.
It is easy to identify La Turballe from the sea as the white wall of the fish market is particularly distinctive. Visitors entering the marina turn to starboard into the main marina. The harbourmaster's office is in the corner of the car park

53 Le Croisic

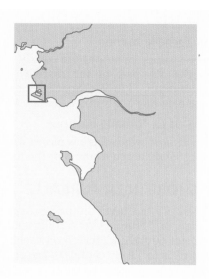

Location
47°18'N 2°31'W

Shelter
Good in drying harbour
Exposed to NW in anchorage

Depth restrictions
0.7m on leading line
Yacht harbour dries 1.7m

Night entry Lit

HW time
Brest HW+¼ neaps, −¾ springs

Mean height of tide (m)

	HWS	HWN	LWN	LWS
Le Croisic	5.4	4.3	2.0	0.7

Tidal stream in entrance
5kts at half-flood and half-ebb

Berthing
Drying harbour and anchorage

Facilities
As of fishing port and holiday resort.

Charts
BA 2823 (50)
SHOM 7395 (50), 7145 (25)
Imray C39 (large scale)

Radio
Marina VHF 9

Telephone
Marina t 02 40 23 10 95

Historic salt port

Le Croisic is a fascinating town. It has been important as a salt port since before the middle ages. The salt was very good for fish curing and Le Croisic had a large sardine fishing fleet. Then in the 19th century it became one of the first swimming resorts.

Today it is a thriving tourist resort and an excellent base from which to visit the salt marshes, the beautiful walled town of Guérande, the salt museum at Batz-sur-Mer or the nearby beaches.

53.1 Le Croisic looking SE.
The largest basin in the foreground is the Grande Chambre, then there are several small, strangely-shaped basins and finally the Port de Plaisance. All the harbours dry.

The harbour is made up of a curious series of islands with drying basins between them. Fishing boats and sailing boats that can take the ground use these. Boats wishing to remain afloat must anchor or borrow a mooring outside the harbour.

PILOTAGE

Le Croisic approach and entrance

Warning
The streams are strong and the flood sets onto the submerged training wall so enter on the last hours of the flood if possible. On the ebb, with strong winds between WSW and N, the entrance is dangerous.

By GPS
From the N or NW use
⊕319-N Croisic, ⊕320-Croisic,
⊕321-Croisic 1.
From the W, with sufficient rise of tide, use
⊕322-W Croisic, ⊕320-Croisic,
⊕321-Croisic 1.

By day
Start from a position about ½M N of Basse Hergo beacon SHM. This can be approached directly from the NW. However, coming from the W, particularly at low water, it is necessary to keep at least 1M off shore to avoid the reef between Basse Castouillet WCM and Basse Hergo SHM.

Le Croisic can be identified by a distinctive belfry in town and a conspicuous hospital at Pen Bron on the E side of the channel. Steer for the belfry on 156°. The leading marks are rather slender light structures with orange tops almost in line with the belfry. Bring them in line on 156° and follow them into the channel. This will leave Basse Hergo SHM and the Jetée du Trehic to starboard.

Follow the transit to the bend in the breakwater. Then steer 174° to follow the second leading marks, which are yellow rectangles each with a vertical green stripe. These marks are located in a bay at the root of the breakwater.

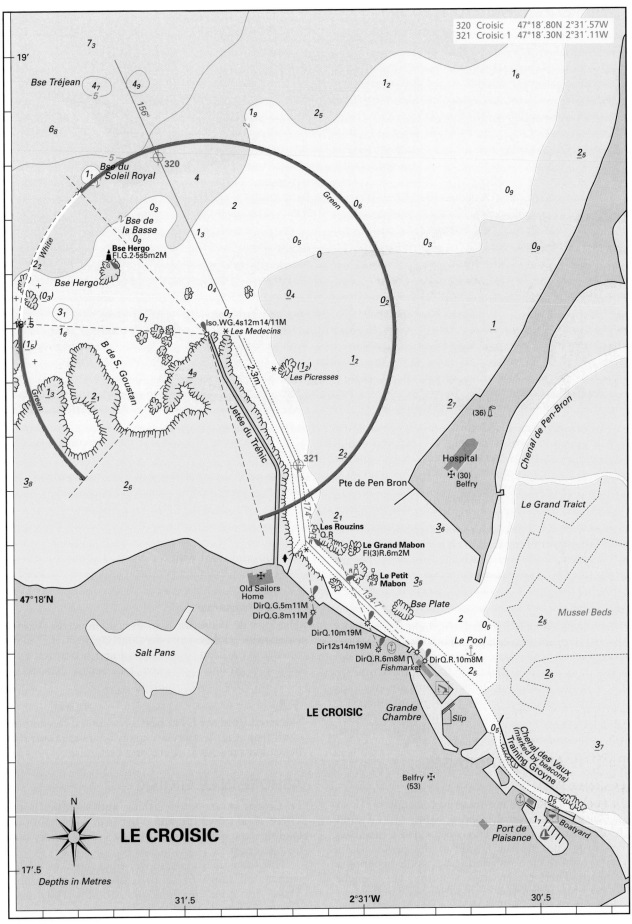

320	Croisic	47°18′.80N 2°31′.57W
321	Croisic 1	47°18′.30N 2°31′.11W

Bse Tréjean

Bse du Soleil Royal

Bse de la Basse

Bse Hergo
Fl.G.2·5s5m2M

Bse Hergo

B de S. Goustan

Iso.WG.4s12m14/11M
✳ Les Medecins

✳ (1₂)
Les Picresses

2·3m

Jetée du Tréhic

Green

White

Green

Pte de Pen Bron

Les Rouzins
Q.R

Le Grand Mabon
Fl(3)R.6m2M

Le Petit Mabon

Hospital
✠ (30)
Belfry

(36) 🕊

Le Grand Traict

Bse Plate

Old Sailors Home
DirQ.G.5m11M
DirQ.G.8m11M

DirQ.10m19M
Dir12s14m19M
DirQ.R.6m8M
Fishmarket

DirQ.R.10m8M

Le Pool

Mussel Beds

Salt Pans

LE CROISIC

Grande Chambre

Slip

Chenal de Pen-Bron

Chenal des Vaux
(marked by beacons)
Training Groyne

Belfry ✠
(53)

Port de Plaisance

Boatyard

N

LE CROISIC

Depths in Metres

Plan 53

At Les Rouzins PHM turn onto 135° and the third transit which is a pair of red and white chequered rectangles on the fish market roof and on the quay in front of the fish market. This channel is buoyed because it moves.

Hold the transit until close to the fishing quay to avoid Basse Plate, drying 2.5m. For the yacht basin, leave the quays about 50m to starboard. Red beacon poles mark a training wall of stakes on the port side of the narrow channel; leave these to port. For an anchorage or mooring, turn to port when the fish market is abeam or to starboard to enter Le Pool.

By night

The white sector of Jetée du Tréhic light clears all the distant dangers, including Le Four and Ile Dumet. However, it leads onto the rocks nearer to the harbour entrance so make the final approach using the E green sector. The three transits are easier to identify by night than by day and it is only necessary to keep on them. The street lighting on the quays is good and there is no difficulty once they are reached.

BERTHS AND ANCHORAGES

Le Croisic Pool

Le Pool is a fair size but moorings occupy much of it. Mussel beds cover the drying banks of Le Grand Traict, but the narrow and steep-sided Chenal de Pen Bron runs up the E side of the peninsula. It contains more moorings and is a possible anchorage at neaps. There are no visitors' buoys, but it might be possible to borrow a mooring in Le Pool or Chenal de Pen Bron. If anchoring, use a trip-line, as

53.2 Le Croisic entrance looking N.
The first transit is followed as far as the bend in the Jetée du Tréhic and the second transits are located at the root of the jetty. The third transits are on the roof of the fish market which is the building on the quay with the long grey roof. The moored boats are in The Pool and the Chenal de Pen-Bron

the bottom is foul with old chain. The ebb runs very hard in the Chenal de Pen Bron and quite hard in Le Pool.

Port de Plaisance

The Port de Plaisance is in the Chambre des Vases. Deep-keel yachts can dry out against the wall outside on a hard, level bottom and boats that can take the ground can enter and secure bow-to a pontoon with a stern mooring.

⚓ Rade de Croisic

Sheltered from the E but horribly exposed to wind or swell from the W, there are many anchorages off the beach between La Turballe and Le Croisic.

ASHORE IN LE CROISIC

Le Croisic is an active fishing and yachting port. There is a travel-lift and boatyard with haul-out facilities, a marine engineer and good chandlery but no fuel berth.

The town is an attractive, busy holiday resort with a full range of shops, cafés and restaurants. There are good markets on Monday (July and August), Thursday and Saturday.

53.3 Le Croisic looking S.
The town has been built on a slender peninsula extending to the W of La Baule. The town on the far coast,
6M S of Le Croisic, is Batz-sur-Mer, the City of Salt. Between the two towns there are many salt pans

54 Le Pouliguen

Location
47°16'N 2°25'W

Shelter
Good except in strong S and SE

Depth restrictions
Entrance dries 1.2m
About 1.3m on visitors' pontoon

Night entry Not recommended

HW time
Brest HW+¼ neaps, −½ springs

Mean height of tide (m)

	HWS	HWN	LWN	LWS
Le Pouliguen	5.4	4.3	2.0	0.7

Tidal stream in river
4kts at half-flood and half-ebb

Berthing
Marina with small visitors' pontoon

Facilities
All marina facilities plus busy and attractive holiday resort

Fuel By visitors' pontoon

Charts
BA 2986 (50)
SHOM 7033 (50), 7145 (25)
Imray C39 (large scale)

Radio
Marina VHF 9

Telephone
Marina *t* 02 40 60 03 50
Harbourmaster *t* 02 40 11 97 97

The genteel marina at La Baule

Le Pouliguen marina is at the W end of the magnificent 5M beach at La Baule. It is ideally situated for the fashionable resorts of La Baule and Le Pouliguen. Unfortunately, there is not much space for visitors so it gets crowded in season and boats over 10m are often turned away.

54.1 Le Pouliguen looking SE.
The marina occupies most of the E side of the river as far as the bridge. The harbourmaster's office is just beyond the bridge on the E side

PILOTAGE

Le Pouliguen approach and entrance

Warning

The approach dries, the sands shift and it is not very well marked, so enter close to high water. Avoid Le Pouliguen altogether if there is strong wind or swell from the SE, particularly on the ebb when the seas break in the shallow water.

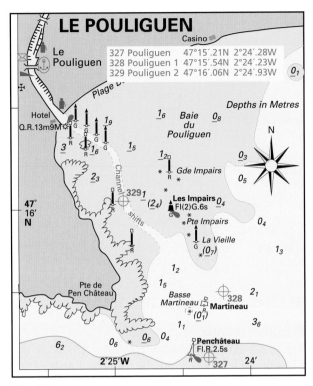

LE POULIGUEN

Casino

Le
Pouliguen

327 Pouliguen	47°15′.21N	2°24′.28W
328 Pouliguen 1	47°15′.54N	2°24′.23W
329 Pouliguen 2	47°16′.06N	2°24′.93W

0_1

Plage D.

Depths in Metres

Hotel
Q.R.13m9M

1_6 Baie 0_8
du
Pouliguen

N

0_3

1_9

3 1_6

1_5

1_2 Gde Impairs
*   R   *

0_5

47°
16′
N

2_3

329_1
(2_4) Les Impairs 0_4
Fl(2)G.6s
G   *Pte Impairs

0_4

$*$ La Vielle
G (0_7)

1_3

1_2

1_5

Pte de
Pen Château

Basse
Martineau 328
(0_1) Martineau

2_1

3_6

1_1

6_2 0_6 0_6 0_4 Penchâteau
Fl.R.2.5s
R 327

2°25′W   24′

Plan 54

By GPS

From the W or S, use
⊕326-W Pornichet, ⊕327-Pouliguen,
⊕328-Pouliguen 1, ⊕329-Pouliguen 2.

From Pornichet use
⊕327-Pouliguen, ⊕328-Pouliguen 1,
⊕329-Pouliguen 2.

By day

The best approach is from the W between
Penchâteau PHM and Les Guérandaises SHM.
Leave Penchâteau PHM to port and steer 020° to
leave Martineau PHM to port. Come round onto
about 320° and steer for a point just E of the second
of the two red beacons. This will leave La Vielle
SHM and Les Petits Impairs beacon SHM well to
starboard.

When the second red beacon is abeam turn to
starboard on about 340° and steer for the channel
marked by the four starboard and two port beacons.
Follow these into the river, if necessary also using the
transit of the church spire between the pier heads.

The channel is quite narrow with high sands on
either side so caution is needed. Also some of the
beacons are quite slender and not very conspicuous.

By night

There are a few lights but night entry is not
recommended. The entry into Pornichet 5M to the E
is well lit.

54.2 The visitors' pontoon just to starboard near the
entrance

54.3 Further up the river the channel is crowded with boats

BERTHS AND ANCHORAGES

Le Pouliguen marina

The visitors' berth is to starboard near the river
entrance. The marina continues upriver and occupies
most of the E side of the river as far as the bridge.
The harbourmaster's office is just beyond the bridge
on the E side of the river.

⚓ Pointe de Penchâteau

If waiting for the tide, there is a temporary
anchorage in about 1m some 400m N of Martineau
buoy.

ASHORE IN LE POULIGUEN

There are all the facilities of a sophisticated yachting
centre with a yard, chandlers and engineers close at
hand. The yacht club is hospitable to visitors and has
showers and toilets. It is a large and clearly labelled
building on the La Baule side above the bridge. Le
Pouliguen is a smart holiday resort with a full range
of shops, restaurants and cafés.

55 Pornichet

Location
47°16'N 2°21'W

Shelter
Excellent

Depth restrictions
2.5m in marina

Night entry Lit

HW time
Brest HW+¼ neaps, −¾ springs

Mean height of tide (m)

	HWS	HWN	LWN	LWS
Pornichet	5.5	4.4	2.1	0.8

Tidal stream in approach
Streams are weak and irregular

Berthing
Large modern marina

Facilities
All marina facilities, town is ½M away

Charts
BA 2986 (50)
SHOM 7033 (50), 7145 (25)
Imray C39 (large scale)

Radio
Marina VHF 9

Telephone
Marina t 02 40 61 03 20
Tourist Office t 02 40 61 33 33

The parking lot at La Baule

Pornichet is a huge modern marina at the E end of the 5M beach at La Baule. It is a long way from the casino and the fashionable part of La Baule but the marina has easier access and much more room than Le Pouliguen.

PILOTAGE

Pornichet approach and entrance

By GPS

From the W use
⊕326-W Pornichet, ⊕330-Pornichet.

From the S or SW by day use
⊕331-SW Pornichet, ⊕330-Pornichet.

From the SE, with a large-scale chart and careful pilotage, it is possible to use
⊕335-Charpentier, ⊕330-Pornichet. However, this is not a safe straight-line route.

By day

From the W, pass between Penchâteau PHM and Guérandaises SHM. Then steer about 085° for the forest of masts at the E end of La Baule. This route passes close N of a SHM buoy.

The marina entrance faces N and the red and green beacons marking the entrance can only be seen on close approach. Pass between the beacons to enter the marina.

From the S and E, the easy route is the W entrance described above. However, with a large-scale chart, there are some more interesting possibilities. A good approach from the SW is to enter the reef between the beacons marking Les Evens and Les Troves and approach the marina on 040°. From the E it is possible to enter the reef between the Grand and the Petit Charpentier but this requires a detailed chart because there are several unmarked rocks

By night

Approach from the W using the white sector of Pornichet pierhead light. Watch out for the unlit SHM buoy ½M E of Penchâteau PHM. The beacons in the entrance are lit.

BERTHS AND ANCHORAGES

Pornichet marina

There are 10 pontoons (A-J) on the S side of the harbour and 4 (K-N) on the N. The heads of all these are allocated to visitors. Also, visitors under 10m can use the whole of pontoon J and the outer side of pontoon I. All the main berths have a depth of 2.8m.

If there are no berths available boats may raft on the large mooring buoy inside the harbour entrance.

⚓ Saint-Marc

Adventurous film buffs may wish to use a large-scale chart to work through the Charpentier reef and visit the pretty holiday resort of Saint-Marc where Jacques Tati made *Monsieur Hulot's holiday*. The anchorage is completely exposed to the S and only suitable as a day anchorage in good weather.

ASHORE IN PORNICHET

Facilities

Pornichet is a well-equipped modern marina. The fuel pontoon is immediately to port on entry and all repairs can be carried out. There is a chandlery, restaurants, cafés and a wine merchant in the marina, but no food shops or bakery.

The marina is about ½M from town, which offers all the delights of a fair-sized beach resort. There is a good market on Wednesday and Saturday.

History

In the late 19th century holiday resorts developed along many of the beautiful French beaches. As soon as the railway arrived at the seaside, developers took the opportunity to build resorts for the new fashion of sea swimming.

This is just how La Baule began. What is particularly interesting is that it became the playground for some of the wealthier families who had more money to invest in holiday homes. During a sixty-year development period architects competed

55.1 The green-topped light marking the entrance to
Pornichet

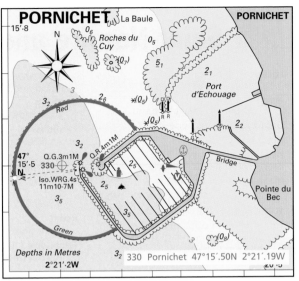

Plan 55

with each other to design something different. A
walk along the promenade and back through the
side streets is fascinating. Every architectural style
has been used, from half-timbered cottages to exotic
Art Deco designs.

55.3 Pornichet marina fuelling pontoon to port of the
entrance

55.2 The marina at Pornichet is built out into the sea and
joined to the land by a causeway. The old drying marina is
just off the beach. The harbourmaster and the shops are at
the landward end. To get to the town and market cross the
causeway and walk in one block from the promenade

56 Saint-Nazaire and Nantes

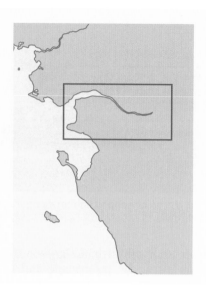

Location
47°16′N 2°12′W

Shelter
Excellent in St-Nazaire basin

Depth restrictions none

Night entry Lit

HW time
Brest HW+½ neaps, −½ springs

Mean height of tide (m)

	HWS	HWN	LWN	LWS
St-Nazaire	5.8	4.6	2.2	0.8

Tidal stream in Loire approaches
Flood – Brest HW–6 to HW
Ebb –Brest HW to –6

Very strong at St-Nazaire at half-flood and half-ebb

Berthing
Alongside in old commercial dock

Facilities
As of a commercial dock

Charts
BA 2986 (50), 2989 (15), 2985
SHOM 7033 (50), 6797 (25), 7396 (15)
Imray C39 (large scale)

Radio
Loire port control VHF 12, 19

Telephone
Harbourmaster *t* 02 40 00 45 20

Busy commercial river

A third of France's maritime trade comes into the Loire but for cruising boats there are only two berthing options. Saint-Nazaire offers visitors a berth in an old commercial dock by the submarine pens. There is a pontoon for organised events but it is not officially available for casual visitors. Nantes has a small, drying marina quite a long way from the centre of town.

The River Loire may, however, be a good route for smaller boats approaching North Biscay through the canals.

PILOTAGE

The Loire to Saint-Nazaire

By GPS

From the W use
⊕335-Charpentier, ⊕337-Loire 1, ⊕339-St Nazaire.

From the S use
⊕336-Loire, ⊕337-Loire 1, ⊕339-St Nazaire.

By day

The approach is straightforward. The big ship channel is well marked by buoys, but it is not necessary to adhere to it until past Pte d'Aiguillon as there is plenty of water either side. There are some isolated dangers outside the channel but they are mostly marked. After Pte d'Aiguillon it is best to keep close to the main channel, although there is generally space to pass outside the buoys if necessary to avoid commercial traffic.

Approach along Chenal de Bonne-Anse leaving the two long breakwaters, which mark the big-ship entrance to the docks, to port. Leave the main channel at this point to pass between the SE Vieux Môle PHM and Basse Sud Nazaire SCM. Turn to port on about 340° until the lock, which lies E/W, will open up to port.

The lock opens for exit on the even hours and for entry about 10 minutes later.

By night

The Passe des Charpentiers leading lights are very conspicuous and lit buoys mark the channel.

Saint-Nazaire to Nantes

Tidal strategy

Leave Saint-Nazaire at low water and expect to carry a fair tide all the way to Nantes. Heading down river, leave Nantes about an hour before high water and expect to encounter some foul tide.

56.1 The two long breakwaters are for the big ship entrance. Leave them and the mole with the white beacon and the PHM to port. The next lock entrance is into Bassin de Saint-Nazaire

56.2 New pontoons have been built next to the submarine pens and museums. Officially these are only for organised events

By day

The channel from St-Nazaire to Nantes is well marked. The river is wide and deep, until Paimbœuf, and a significant sea can build up. Further upstream there can still be a considerable chop in strong winds.

The passage is seldom made by yachts and is interesting but not particularly attractive.

By night

Lit but not recommended.

BERTHS AND ANCHORAGES

Bassin de St-Nazaire

Once through the lock, pass through the swing bridge into the Bassin de St-Nazaire, where yachts berth at the S end, against the wall. The long pontoon on the W side, by the submarine pens, is used by organised events. Visitors are not officially welcomed but the self-sufficient will be tolerated.

There are few facilities but repairs could probably be arranged. The town has all facilities but it is quite a long way away. The main local attraction is the submarine museum in the old submarine pens alongside the dock.

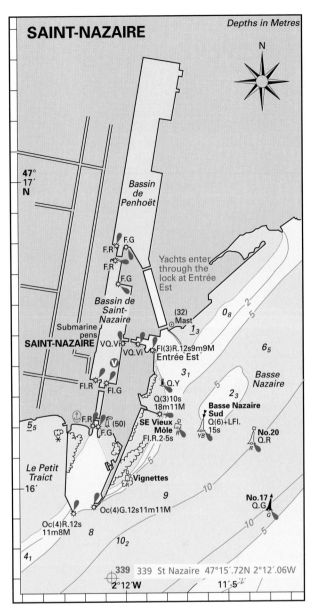

Plan 56A

Trentemoult marina, Nantes

The drying marina at Trentemoult (Plan 56B) lies on the S bank, 1.4M above the only bridge above St-Nazaire. There are few facilities apart from a mobile crane for masting. There are some shops nearby and buses into the city of Nantes.

⌁ Trébézy

Sheltered from W to N, this wide, attractive bay is just N of the Phare de l'Aiguillon. Approach from the SE and anchor where depth permits outside the moorings. There are several more anchorages in the bays between Trébézy and Saint-Nazaire.

⊕338-Trébézy (47°14′.88N 2°15′.33W)

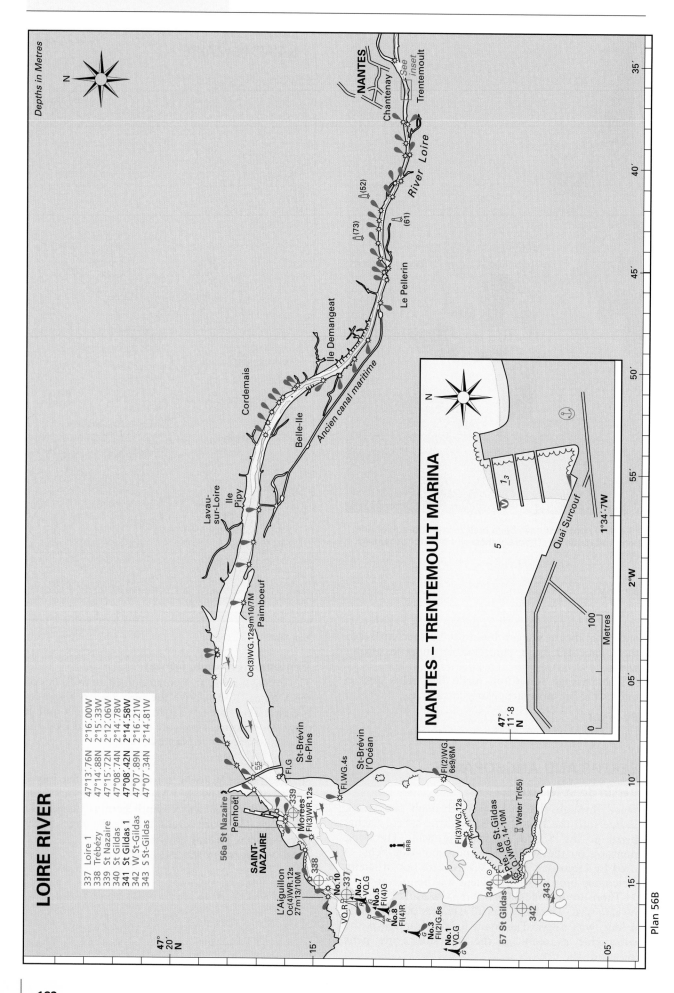

LOIRE RIVER

Depths in Metres

N

337	Loire 1	47°13′.76N	2°16′.00W
338	Trébézy	47°14′.88N	2°15′.33W
339	St Nazaire	47°15′.72N	2°12′.06W
340	St Gildas	47°08′.74N	2°14′.78W
341	**St Gildas 1**	**47°08′.42N**	**2°14′.58W**
342	W St-Gildas	47°07′.89N	2°16′.21W
343	S St-Gildas	47°07′.34N	2°14′.81W

47° 20′ N

NANTES

See inset

Chantenay
Trentemoult

River Loire

(52)

(73)

(61)

Le Pellerin

Ile Demangeat

Cordemais

Belle-Ile

Ancien canal maritime

Lavau-
sur-Loire

Ile
Pipy

Paimboeuf

Oc(3)WG.12s9m10/7M

St-Brévin
le-Pins

St-Brévin
l'Océan

Fl.WG.4s

Fl.G

55

56a St Nazaire

Penhoët

Morées
Fl(3)WR.12s

339

SAINT-
NAZAIRE

L'Aiguillon
Oc(4)WR.12s
27m13/10M

338

No.10

No.7
V.Q.G

337

V.Q.R

No.8
Fl(4)G

No.5
Fl(4)G

No.3
Fl(2)G.6s

No.1
V.Q.G

R
Fl(4)R

15′

BRB

5

Fl(2)WG.
6s9/6M

Fl(3)WG.12s

57 St Gildas

Pte. de St-Gildas
Q.WRG.14-10M

Water Tr(55)

340

343

342

NANTES – TRENTEMOULT MARINA

N

1.3

5

Quai Surcouf

1°34′.7W

2°W

47°
11′.8
N

0   100

Metres

Plan 56B

57 Saint-Gildas

Location
  47°08′N 2°15′W
Shelter
  Good from S, reasonable from W but exposed to N
Depth restrictions
  1.5m on moorings
Night entry Lit
HW time
  Brest HW–¾ neaps, +½ springs
Mean height of tide (m)

	HWS	HWN	LWN	LWS
St-Gildas	5.6	4.4	2.1	0.8

Tidal stream approach
  E – Brest HW–6 to HW (1.0kt)
  W – Brest HW to –6 (1.3kts)
Berthing
  Anchorage and moorings
Facilities
  Limited facilities
Charts
  BA 2986 (50)
  SHOM 7395 (50)
  Imray C40 (109)
Radio
  Harbourmaster VHF 9
Telephone
  Harbourmaster *t* 02 40 21 60 07

Small port and anchorage

Saint-Gildas is a small harbour on the N side of Pointe de Saint-Gildas.

PILOTAGE

St-Gildas approach and entrance

By GPS

From the W or NW use
⊕340-St-Gildas, ⊕341-St-Gildas 1.

From S or SW use
⊕342-W St-Gildas, ⊕340-St-Gildas, ⊕341-St-Gildas 1.

By day

From the N or NW identify St-Gildas lighthouse and a tide gauge near the end of the jetty. Steer for the lighthouse, just left of the tide gauge, on 177°. L'Illot beacon PHM, just N of the harbour, marks a dangerous rock (dries 1.7m). A SHM beacon marks the end of the jetty and in summer there is also a lit SHM buoy.

From the S, avoid the Banc de Kerouars, give Pointe de St-Gildas a wide berth and then follow the N entrance.

57.1 St-Gildas lighthouse, the tide gauge and the SHM beacon

By night

The white sector of Pointe de St-Gildas light leads into the harbour and the breakwater end is lit.

BERTHS AND ANCHORAGES

⚓ Anse du Boucau

This is a crowded, holiday-resort mooring with numerous numbered buoys for small fishing boats. Anchor outside the moorings or dry out on the sandy beach at the head of the harbour.

The bay is sheltered from the S but exposed to the W at HW springs and completely open to the N and NE.

ASHORE IN SAINT-GILDAS

There is a tap at the dinghy pontoon and the usual facilities of a small holiday village.

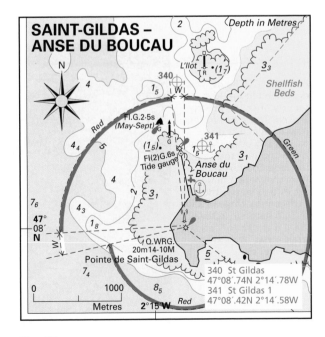

Plan 57

58 Pornic

Location
47°06'N 2°07'W
Shelter
Very good in marina
Depth restrictions
1.0m in approach
Marina dredged 2.0m but silts
Night entry Lit
HW time
Brest HW–¾ neaps, +½ springs
Mean height of tide (m)

	HWS	HWN	LWN	LWS
St-Gildas	5.8	4.6	2.2	0.8

Tidal stream approach
E – Brest HW–6 to HW (1.0kt)
W – Brest HW to –6 (1.0kts)
Berthing Large marina
Facilities
All marina facilities, ¾M to smart
holiday resort
Charts
BA 2986 (50), 2981 (50/15),
SHOM 7395 (50), 7394 (50/15)
Imray C40 (large scale)
Radio
Harbourmaster VHF 9
Telephone
Harbourmaster *t* 02 40 82 05 40

Attractive town with large marina

Pornic is an attractive seaside resort within easy reach of Nantes. It has a delightfully southern feel, with elegant holiday villas set in large gardens. There are numerous pine trees as well as grape vines growing near the marina.

The modern, well-managed marina has excellent road, rail and air communications. It is a pleasant ¾M walk to town past the old drying harbour and Bluebeard's castle. There is a good beach next to the marina.

PILOTAGE

Pornic approach and entrance

By GPS

From N or W use
⊕342-W St Gildas, ⊕343-S St Gildas, ⊕344-Pornic.

From Herbaudière use
⊕347-Herbaudière, ⊕346-N Herbaudière, ⊕344-Pornic. At high water, it is possible to omit ⊕346-N Herbaudière but this route passes close to a 1.1m shallow patch and two rocks that dry 0.7m.

By day

From the N, round Pointe de Saint-Gildas at least ½M off. The long marina wall is distinctive.

From the SW avoid the well-marked dangers NW of Noirmoutier and the dangers off Ile du Pilier that extend 1M to seaward of the lighthouse.

From the S or W, the Banc de Kerouars is a hazard. The unmarked shallow patches are dangerous in rough weather or below half tide.

The marina entrance is at the SE corner and is not visible in the approach. Steer for the fairway buoy and be ready to turn sharply to port between the red and green beacons. Once inside keep clear of the S wall, which is lined with submerged rocks. The E breakwater head is also foul. Pornic entrance silts so assume a depth of 1.0m.

58.1 Pornic marina looking N.
Pornic, like La Baule, was developed in the 19th century after the railway arrived. The green of the pine trees makes it particularly attractive and is the origin of the name, the Jade Coast. A walk from the marina beside the estuary passes the fine 11th century château and the old harbour. In town there is a maze of winding streets that fill with stalls on market day

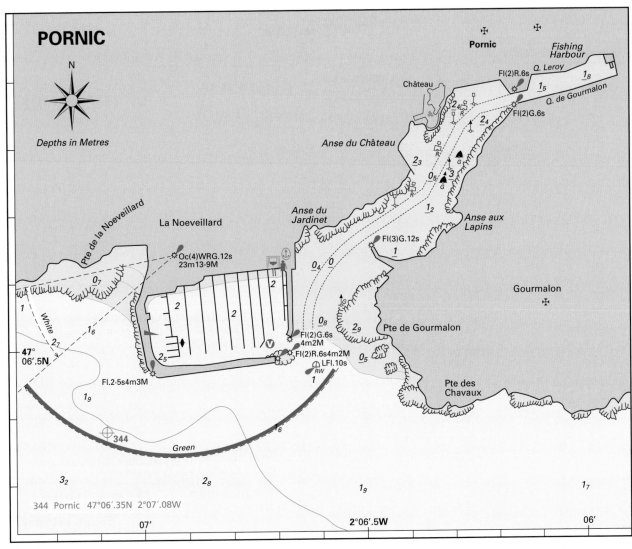

PORNIC

N

Depths in Metres

Pte de la Noeveillard

La Noeveillard

Oc(4)WRG.12s
23m13-9M

White

47°
06'.5N

Fl.2·5s4m3M

344

Green

344 Pornic 47°06'.35N 2°07'.08W

07'   2°06'.5W   06'

Château

Anse du Château

Anse du Jardinet

Anse aux Lapins

Fl(3)G.12s

Fl(2)G.6s 4m2M

Fl(2)R.6s4m2M

LFl.10s RW

Pte de Gourmalon

Gourmalon

Pte des Chavaux

Pornic

Fishing Harbour

Fl(2)R.6s

Q. Leroy

Q. de Gourmalon

Fl(2)G.6s

Plan 58

By night

Approach in the white sector of Pornic light, which clears the Banc de Kerouars and Notre Dame rock. Enter the marina between the entrance lights.

BERTHS AND ANCHORAGES

Pornic marina

The reception berth in the marina is directly ahead on entering and clearly marked.

Drying harbour

Visitors are discouraged from using the old drying harbour. The channel (dries 1.8m) is marked by buoys and beacons. Night entry is not recommended.

ASHORE IN PORNIC

Pornic has all the facilities of a major marina and the marina staff are particularly helpful. The fuel dock is at the base of the narrow first aisle and rather awkward for a 12m yacht.

On the north side of the marina there are cafés, restaurants and chandlers and some of the bars supply bread and croissants in the early morning. It is a ten-minute walk along the riverbank to the town, where there are shops and restaurants and a market four times a week.

58.2 The entrance to Pornic Marina between the red and green beacons

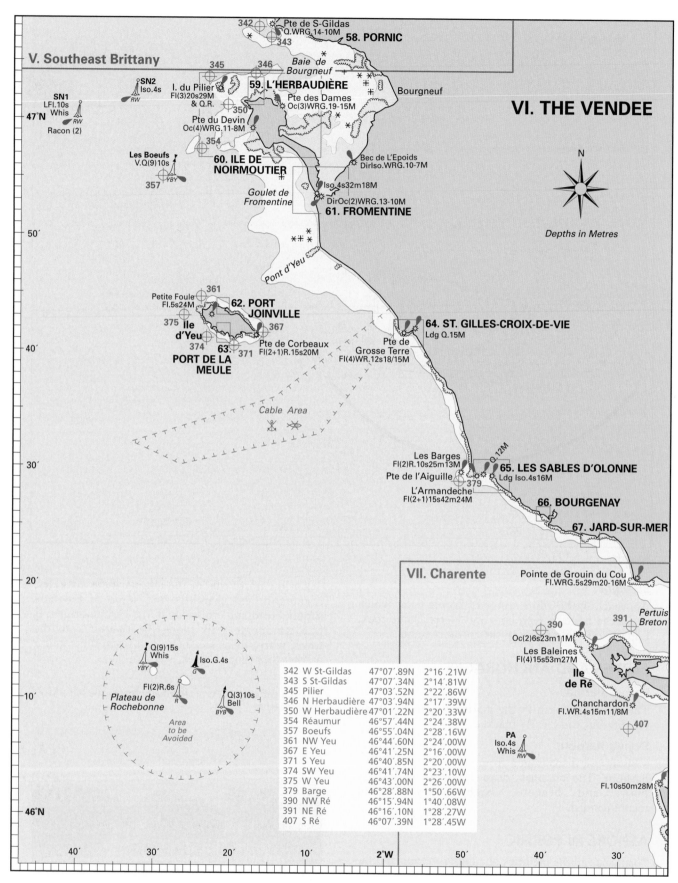

V. Southeast Brittany

58. PORNIC

342 W St-Gildas
Pte de S-Gildas
Q.WRG.14-10M
343

345 346
Baie de
Bourgneuf

59. L'HERBAUDIÈRE
Bourgneuf

SN2
Iso.4s
RW

SN1
LFl.10s
Whis
RW

47°N

Racon (2)

I. du Pilier
Fl(3)20s29M
& Q.R.

350

Pte des Dames
Oc(3)WRG.19-15M

Pte du Devin
Oc(4)WRG.11-8M

354

Bec de L'Epoids
DirIso.WRG.10-7M

Les Boeufs
V.Q(9)10s
YBY

60. ILE DE
NOIRMOUTIER

357

Iso.4s32m18M

Goulet de
Fromentine

DirOc(2)WRG.13-10M

61. FROMENTINE

VI. THE VENDEE

N

Depths in Metres

50′

Pont d'Yeu

Petite Foule
Fl.5s24M

361

62. PORT
JOINVILLE

367

64. ST. GILLES-CROIX-DE-VIE
Ldg Q.15M

375
Ile
d'Yeu

374   63.

371 Pte de Corbeaux
Fl(2+1)R.15s20M

Pte de
Grosse Terre
Fl(4)WR.12s18/15M

PORT DE LA
MEULE

40′

Cable Area

30′

Les Barges
Fl(2)R.10s25m13M

Q.12M

65. LES SABLES D'OLONNE
Ldg Iso.4s16M

Pte de l'Aiguille

379

L'Armandeche
Fl(2+1)15s42m24M

66. BOURGENAY

67. JARD-SUR-MER

20′

VII. Charente

Pointe de Grouin du Cou
Fl.WRG.5s29m20-16M

391
Pertuis
Breton

390
Oc(2)6s23m11M

Q(9)15s
Whis
YBY

Iso.G.4s
G

Les Baleines
Fl(4)15s53m27M

Ile
de Ré

10′

Fl(2)R.6s
R

Q(3)10s
Bell
BYB

Chanchardon
Fl.WR.4s15m11/8M

Plateau de
Rochebonne

407

Area
to be
Avoided

PA
Iso.4s
Whis
RW

342 W St-Gildas	47°07′.89N	2°16′.21W
343 S St-Gildas	47°07′.34N	2°14′.81W
345 Pilier	47°03′.52N	2°22′.86W
346 N Herbaudière	47°03′.94N	2°17′.39W
350 W Herbaudière	47°01′.22N	2°20′.33W
354 Réaumur	46°57′.44N	2°24′.38W
357 Boeufs	46°55′.04N	2°28′.16W
361 NW Yeu	46°44′.60N	2°24′.00W
367 E Yeu	46°41′.25N	2°16′.00W
371 S Yeu	46°40′.85N	2°20′.00W
374 SW Yeu	46°41′.74N	2°23′.10W
375 W Yeu	46°43′.00N	2°26′.00W
379 Barge	46°28′.88N	1°50′.66W
390 NW Ré	46°15′.94N	1°40′.08W
391 NE Ré	46°16′.10N	1°28′.27W
407 S Ré	46°07′.39N	1°28′.45W

Fl.10s50m28M

46°N

40′   30′   20′   10′   2°W   50′   40′   30′

Chart VIA

Lighthouse at Pointe des Corbeaux, Ile d'Yeu

VI. The Vendée

Les Sables d'Olonne

Vendée waiters' race

Ile d'Yeu

Port de la Meule

59 L'Herbaudière

Location
47°02'N 2°18'W
Shelter
Good except from N and NE
Depth restrictions
Entrance dredged 1.5m
Marina 1.5m to 2.0m
Night entry Lit
HW time
Brest HW–¾ neaps, +½ springs
Mean height of tide (m)

	HWS	HWN	LWN	LWS
L'Herbaudière	5.5	4.4	2.1	0.8

Tidal stream in approach
ESE – Brest HW–6 to HW (1.9 kt)
WNW – Brest HW to –6 (1.6 kts)
Berthing
Raft on visitors' pontoon
Facilities All facilities.
Charts
BA 2986 (50), 2981 (50/15),
SHOM 7395 (50), 7394 (50/15)
Imray C40 (large scale)
Radio
Harbourmaster VHF 9
Telephone
Harbourmaster *t* 02 51 39 05 05

The main port on Noirmoutier

Ile de Noirmoutier is well worth visiting. It is about 10M long by about 3M wide, mostly flat and sandy, with much of the N part given over to salt ponds. Bicycles are a perfect way to get about and can be hired in L'Herbaudière.

L'Herbaudière is the only all tide port on Ile de Noirmoutier. It is shared between fishing boats and yachtsmen and has a pleasant genuine atmosphere. Unfortunately, the visitors' pontoon is not very large and is a bit exposed to the N.

PILOTAGE

(See also Plan 60)

L'Herbaudière approach and entrance

By GPS

From the NW and NE use
⊕346-N Herbaudière, ⊕347-Herbaudière, ⊕349-Herbaudière 2. This route passes close W of several shallow patches in the outer approaches.

From the W and SW via Chenal de la Grise use ⊕350-W Herbaudière, ⊕348-Herbaudière 1, ⊕349-Herbaudière 2. This passage is quite narrow and the tide runs very strongly but the dangers are well marked.

By day

From the N, L'Herbaudière can be identified by a 40m radio mast to the W and the stone breakwater.

Start from a position about ½M W of Basse du Martroger beacon NCM but do not approach the beacon from due N because there are several shallow patches. From this position, steer for the harbour on 190° keeping the breakwaters just open. The last ¼M is marked by buoys and beacons and, if visibility is poor, the leading lights are switched on.

The harbour entrance faces E so it is necessary to round the W breakwater and turn fairly sharply to starboard.

From the SW, use the Chenal de la Grise. Start S of Passe de la Grise SCM. Then steer 058° towards Basse de Martroger beacon NCM. About ¼M before Matroger, when the harbour bears 190°, turn onto this course and enter the harbour as described above. Note that the tide runs very strongly in the Passe de la Grise.

By night

From N, approach in either of the two N white sectors of Basse du Martroger light. Then use the white sector of L'Herbaudière breakwater light on 188°. Identify the leading lights on 188° and follow this transit into the harbour, leaving the red and green lit buoys to port and starboard.

From the S, through the Chenal de la Grise, use the white sector of Basse du Martroger light, bearing between 055° and 060°. When the breakwater head light turns white, steer 188° and proceed as above.

59.1 L'Herbaudière harbour looking S.
The harbour entrance faces E so turn sharply to starboard after rounding the W breakwater. The fishing docks are to starboard and the visitors' pontoon is to port

59.2 L'Herbaudière has a distinctly southern feel

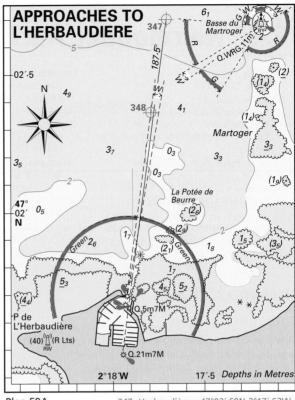

Plan 59A

347 Herbaudière   47°02′.69N 2°17′.62W
348 Herbaudière 1 47°02′.36N 2°17′.69W

59.3 The NE *vente solaire* can blow straight into the harbour entrance and onto the visitors rafted to the pontoon, on the right of the picture

BERTHS

L'Herbaudière marina

Visitors' berth on the pontoon directly in front of the entrance and must expect to be rafted during the season. This berth is exposed and may be uncomfortable if the wind is from the N or NE.

ASHORE IN L'HERBAUDIERE

L'Herbaudière has all the facilities of a yacht and fishing port. There is a fuel berth, a 30-tonne travel-lift, chandlers and all repairs. The town is small but has a good range of shops, cafés and restaurants.

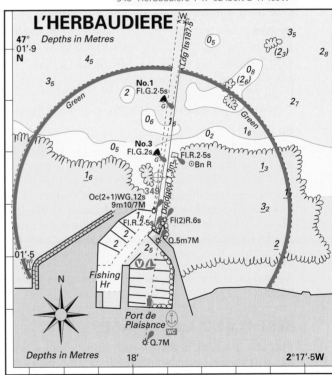

Plan 59B

349 Herbaudière 2 47°01′.67N 2°17′.83W

Fresh fish can be bought near the fish market. Bicycles can be hired and provide an excellent way to see the island. The local beaches, the saltpans and the main town of Noirmoutier-en-Ile are all worth visiting. If time and tide permit, the causeway to the mainland is also interesting, if only to see the scale and diligence of the *pêche à pied*.

60 Noirmoutier Anchorages

Location
47°01'N 2°13'W

Depth restrictions
Noirmoutier dries 2.5m
Bois de la Chaise about 1.0m
Port Morin pool 1.0m, harbour dries

Night entry
Lit to Boise de la Chaise and Port Morin

HW time
Brest HW–¾ neaps, +½ springs

Mean height of tide (m)

	HWS	HWN	LWN	LWS
L'Herbaudière	5.5	4.4	2.1	0.8

Facilities
Noirmoutier has good shops, Boise de la Chaise has a few shops, Port Morin only has a good beach

Charts
BA 2981 (50/15)
SHOM 7394 (50/15)

Telephone
Noirmoutier HM *t* 02 51 39 08 39

BOIS DE LA CHAISE

Attractive anchorage

Sheltered from W and S and to some extent from N and E, this attractive anchorage is on the NE corner of the island, near Pointe des Dames.

PILOTAGE

Bois de la Chaise approach and entrance

By GPS

From Pornic use
⊕352-Chaise but watch out for the rocks that extend SE of Notre-Dame IDM.
From L'Herbaudière use
⊕346-N Herbaudière, ⊕351-Pères, ⊕352-Chaise.

By day

From the NW, keep outside Banc de la Blanche NCM and Basse des Pères ECM. Then steer 150° for La Chaise SWM. The headland is steep and tree covered and only the lighthouse top is visible.

From Herbaudière, stay inside Banc de la Blanche using a back transit of the red and white radio tower in line with Martroger tower on 035°.

By night

Approach in the white sector of Pointe de Dames light.

BERTHS AND ANCHORAGES

This is a popular holiday beach and sailing school base with a large number of small craft moorings for the summer visitors. There is room to anchor inshore of the RW buoy.

There are a few shops and restaurants in Bois de la Chaise but Noirmoutier-en-Ile is only 1M away. There is a big campsite with a shop just to the S.

NOIRMOUTIER-EN-ILE

Busy drying port

Noirmoutier-en-Ile is a nice place but best visited by bicycle. It dries 2.5m leaving steeply sloping, unstable mud. Rafting is normally necessary and rafted boats may tip and cross masts, or fall outwards into the scoured channel.

PILOTAGE

Noirmoutier approach and entrance

By GPS

The entrance requires careful visual pilotage, ⊕352-Chaise, ⊕353-Noirmoutier may help in the approach.

By day

From the Bois de la Chaise anchorage, keep about 400m offshore, inside the mussel bed. There is a line of green beacons along the shore. Follow them into the entrance and continue up the marked channel to town. The best water at the entrance is on the S side near the training wall.

60.1 Moored in the soft mud at Noirmoutier-en-Ile

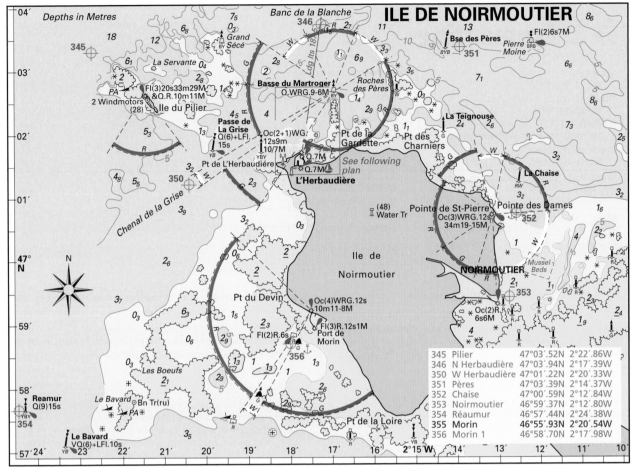

Plan 60

BERTHS AND ANCHORAGES

Moor to the first quay on the starboard side, just before the crane. Further up, the quays are shallower. The mud is very soft so, with luck, the keel may sink in, leaving the boat upright.

ASHORE IN NOIRMOUTIER-EN-ILE

Noirmoutier has all facilities. It is a pleasant market town and well worth visiting. Markets are held on Tuesday, Friday and Sunday, in season.

PORT DE MORIN

Drying harbour and anchorage

This new drying harbour is on the W of the island. There is a pool outside the harbour where deep draught yachts can anchor in good weather.

PILOTAGE

Port de Morin approach and entrance

By GPS

Use ⊕355-Morin, ⊕356-Morin 1.

By day

Starting from ⊕355-Morin, steer 032° towards the masts and the harbour. There are buoys about 1M apart. The route crosses a shallow patch (dries 1.3m), with deeper water to starboard.

The entrance channel is marked by a red and a green buoy. Pass between them and steer for the end of the breakwater. The anchorage is SE of the red and green buoys.

ASHORE IN PORT DE MORIN

There are very few facilities apart from a magnificent beach.

60.2 Port de Morin drying harbour looking SE

61 Fromentine

Location
46°54'N 2°10'W
Shelter
Fairly exposed
Hazards
Shifting bar with very strong tides
Depth restrictions
Bar dries 1.5m
Night entry Lit but not recommended
HW time
Brest HW—¾ neaps, +¼ springs
Mean height of tide (m)

	HWS	HWN	LWN	LWS
Fromentine	5.5	4.4	2.1	0.8

Tidal stream in entrance
Flood – Brest HW—6 to –2 (5kt)
Ebb – Brest HW–2 to –6 (8kts)
Berthing
Anchorage
Facilities
All facilities of small holiday resort
Charts
BA 2981 (50)
SHOM 7394 (50)
Imray C40 (large scale)
Telephone
Harbourmaster *t* 02 51 39 05 05

Small resort with challenging access

The Goulet de Fromentine is the passage between the S end of Ile de Noirmoutier and the mainland. The streams are very strong, the sand bar shifts and the anchorage is uncomfortable. Although Fromentine is a pleasant holiday resort, a visit is probably not worth the effort.

PILOTAGE

Warning

The adventurous may wish to use the Goulet de Fromentine as a shortcut to Pornic or Herbaudière by crossing the causeway. The combination of very shallow water and very strong tides make this passage unsafe for deep draught yachts. It is not described in this volume but in the French pilot *Quiberon – La Rochelle* by Alain Rondeau (*Pilote Cotier 5B*).

Tidal strategy

The tide ebbs for 8 hours and floods for 4 and the streams, particularly on the ebb, are very strong. Only attempt to enter in the last hours of the flood and do not attempt to enter if there is strong SW wind or swell.

Fromentine approach and entrance

By GPS

The sand shifts and the buoys are moved to reflect this. The following waypoints only provide a general indication of the channel.
⊕358-Fromentine, ⊕359-Fromentine 1,
⊕360-Fromentine 2.

By day

The Goulet can be identified by a conspicuous water tower on Noirmoutier and Notre-Dame-de-Monts lighthouse. Start well offshore at L'Aigle SCM and steer 050° for Fromentine fairway buoy. Be prepared for some S stream. From the fairway buoy, follow the channel buoys to the red and white beacons that mark the entrance. Passing between the beacons, the

channel deepens and a SHM buoy indicates the course to the navigation arch of the bridge (clearance 27m). After the bridge, a PHM buoy marks the channel to Fromentine pier. N of this buoy are two wrecks, exposed at LW.

61.1 Fromentine approach and the bridge joining Ile de Noirmoutier to the mainland looking E.
The anchorage at Pointe de la Fosse is just visible on the left of the picture. Opposite is the Fromentine ferry jetty

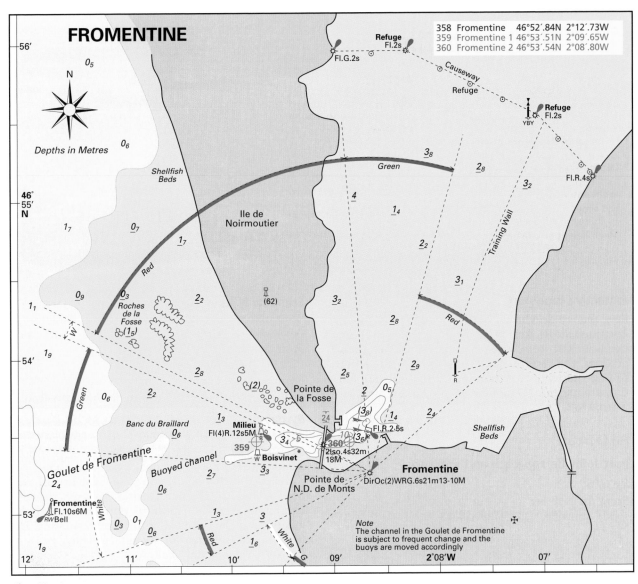

FROMENTINE

358	Fromentine	46°52'.84N 2°12'.73W
359	Fromentine 1	46°53'.51N 2°09'.65W
360	Fromentine 2	46°53'.54N 2°08'.80W

Plan 61

BERTHS AND ANCHORAGES

⚓ Fromentine and Pointe de la Fosse

Depending on draught, anchor off the jetty on the Noirmoutier side at Pte de la Fosse, with less tidal stream, or just W of the Fromentine ferry jetty and just E of the cable area. The streams in the fairway are very strong, about 5kts, but they moderate towards the shore. Anchor as far in as draught and tide allow.

Owing to the strength of the tide it is said to be unwise to leave a yacht unattended while at anchor, and this would certainly be true at the top of springs. If going in to the Pte de la Fosse side, beware of the wrecks just N of the channel; they lie between the first and second red buoys after the bridge, so turn in either before the first red buoy or after the second. It is not practical to row across the stream to Fromentine in the dinghy.

ASHORE IN FROMENTINE

Water can be obtained from the ferry jetty. Fromentine is a small holiday resort with typical facilities, including a ferry to Ile d'Yeu.

61.2 The causeway joins Ile de Noirmoutier to the mainland. It dries 3m and is used as a road during low water

62 Port-Joinville

Location
46°44'N 2°21'W

Shelter
Good in marina

Hazards
Entrance dangerous in strong N and E winds

Depth restrictions
Entrance 1.2m, marina 1.5m to 2.5m

Night entry Lit

HW time
Brest HW–½ neaps, +¼ springs

Mean height of tide (m)

	HWS	HWN	LWN	LWS
Joinville	5.2	4.1	2.0	0.8

Berthing
Marina

Fuel
At entrance to marina

Facilities
All facilities

Charts
BA 3640 (10)
SHOM 7410 (20/10)
Imray C40 (large scale)

Radio
Harbourmaster VHF 9

Telephone
Harbourmaster *t* 02 51 58 38 11

Attractive tuna port

Ile d'Yeu is a delightful island and well worth a visit. Port-Joinville is the only safe harbour and is an excellent base from which to explore. The marina is modern and welcoming. The town is an active fishing and ferry port with lots of shops, cafés and restaurants; the fishmonger alone makes the visit worthwhile.

PILOTAGE

Port-Joinville approach and entrance

By GPS

From the NW use
⊕364-Joinville, ⊕365-Joinville1.

From the N use
⊕357-Boeufs to clear the dangers W of Ile de Noirmoutier.

From St-Gilles use
⊕366-E Joinville, ⊕365-Joinville1.

From Sables-d'Olonne or further S use
⊕367-E Yeu, ⊕366-E Joinville, ⊕365-Joinville1.

By day

Port-Joinville is easy to locate from seaward and steering 224° for the conspicuous water tower behind the town leads straight into the harbour.

Enter the harbour leaving the NW breakwater head 50m to starboard. After passing the old lighthouse (see 62.2) bear to port and round the inner end of the breakwater to enter the marina. Do not stray to starboard in the outer harbour because the SW corner is very shallow.

62.1 Port-Joinville looking SE.
The marina has plenty of space for visitors on pontoons located just inside the entrance and close to the Bureau du Port. Smaller, local boats are moored at the far end of the marina.
The remainder of this large harbour is devoted to deep-sea fishing boats and ferries coming from the mainland

62.2 Port-Joinville lighthouse is half way along the NW breakwater

By night

Approach in either of the white sectors of the NW breakwater light and enter the harbour with the leading lights in line on 219°. Remember to avoid the drying patch in the SW corner of the outer harbour.

BERTHS AND ANCHORAGES

Port-Joinville Marina

Visiting boats berth in the marina according to size. Pontoons A, B and the W side of C, D and E are available. To reach the reception pontoon follow the inside of the breakwater and turn to starboard at the end of B pontoon in front of the harbourmaster's office. At busy times, visiting yachts are met by a launch and directed to a vacant berth.

⚓ Anse de Ker Châlon

Sheltered from S and W but exposed to the N, there is a convenient bay ½M E of Joinville harbour. There are rocky outcrops on either side and some rocks close inshore so it is best to anchor quite well out.

ASHORE IN JOINVILLE

Joinville has all marine facilities including a big chandler and a fuel berth. In the town there is a full range of shops, cafés and restaurants, two good supermarkets and an outstanding fishmonger selling tuna straight from the fishing boats.

Bicycle hire is easy and very popular with the hundreds of visitors. Those who enjoy walking may prefer to visit the magnificent S coast on foot because the footpath and bicycle path are mostly separate and the bicycle path is a bit of a racetrack. Cars can also be hired and the island is just about large enough to make this worthwhile. Maps are available from the harbourmaster's office.

There is a regular ferry service to Fromentine and, in summer, to St Gilles and, less frequently, Les Sables-d'Olonne.

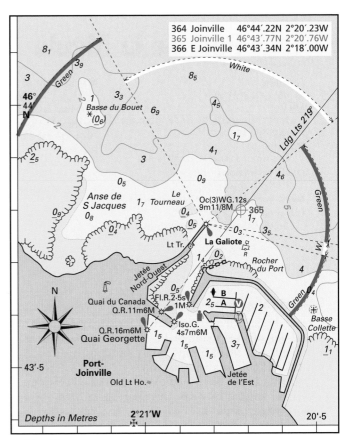

364 Joinville	46°44′.22N	2°20′.23W
365 Joinville 1	46°43′.77N	2°20′.76W
366 E Joinville	46°43′.34N	2°18′.00W

Plan 62

62.3 A typical Ile d'Yeu cottage

62.4 The waterfront at Port-Joinville

63 Port de la Meule

Location
46°42′N 2°21′W

Shelter
Moderate from the N, dangerously exposed to S

Hazard
Unsafe in S wind or swell

Depth restrictions
Harbour dries

Night entry Lit but not recommended

HW time
Brest HW−½ neaps, +¼ springs

Mean height of tide (m)

	HWS	HWN	LWN	LWS
Joinville	5.2	4.1	2.0	0.8

Berthing
Anchorage outside tiny harbour

Facilities
Restaurants

Charts
SHOM 7410 (20)

Tiny fishing harbour

Port de la Meule is a tiny, picturesque fishing harbour on the S side of Ile d'Yeu. The harbour is packed with small fishing boats and mostly dries so it is necessary to anchor outside.

If you do not have the time or the settled offshore weather to visit by boat, then Port de la Meule is a worthwhile walk or bike ride. A round trip to include the Vieux Château (see 63.3) and the coast path works very well.

63.1 Port de la Meule and the rocky W coast of Ile d'Yeu looking E.
The path along the cliffs is for walkers while the large path inland is for cyclists

PILOTAGE

Port de la Meule approach and entrance

By GPS

From Joinville via the E
⊕366-E Joinville, ⊕367-E Yeu, ⊕368-SE Yeu, ⊕371-S Yeu, ⊕373-Meule 1. This route does not enter Port de Meule by the normal transit and the harbour will only open when the final waypoint is reached.

From Joinville via the W use
⊕364-Joinville, ⊕361-NW Yeu, ⊕375-W Yeu, ⊕374-SW Yeu, ⊕372-Meule, ⊕373-Meule 1.

63.2 The tiny fishing harbour of Port de la Meule

By day

Port de la Meule is between Pointe du Châtelet, with its distinctive white stone cross, and Pointe de la Tranche with a conspicuous white semaphore tower and a red and white radio mast. The entrance can only be identified from almost due S when the lighthouse and white chapel become visible.

The bay is clear of off-lying rocks so it is safe to steer for the lighthouse on 022°. On close approach, keep clear of the headland on the W side, which has rocks projecting to the SE. These can usually be seen but it is best to keep towards the starboard side of the channel. Once inside, the reef is normally marked by PHM lobster pots.

If proceeding to the quay, keep towards the port side to avoid some rocks close to the E side of the entrance and be prepared to turn sharply to port into the harbour.

The harbour is sheltered in winds from W through N to E but in S winds, the swell surges right into the harbour.

By night

The entrance is lit but night entry is not recommended.

BERTHS AND ANCHORAGES

Port de la Meule

The harbour dries but in settled offshore winds it is possible to anchor in the entrance, though some swell enters even in NE winds. The bottom is rocky and there is little swinging room, so two anchors are necessary. There is not really room in the harbour for a boat to dry out but it might be possible with advice from the local fishermen.

⚓ Anse des Vieilles

Sheltered from the N, this attractive sandy bay is just over 1M E of Port de la Meule. It should be approached from the SE to avoid the Ours des Vieilles reef that extends nearly ½M SE of Pointe des Vieilles. Anchor in about 3m in the centre of the bay.
⊕370-Vieilles 1 (46°41′.53N 2°18′.70W)

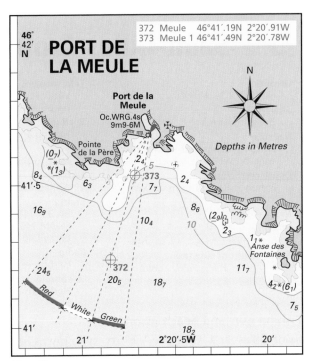

Plan 63

⚓ Anse des Broches

Sheltered from SW through S to E, this fair-weather anchorage is on the NW coast of Ile d'Yeu.

Approach with the Petit Foule lighthouse bearing 145°. There are drying and above-water rocks on both sides of the bay but this approach passes well clear of them. When Les Chiens Perrins WCM bear about 225° turn to port onto 125° and go in as far as depth and draught allow. Anchor on sand, with Petit Foule bearing about 155° and the lighthouse about 250°. The GPS route is more direct.
⊕363-Broches 1 (46°43′.85N 2°23′.50W)

ASHORE IN PORT DE LA MEULE

There are three restaurants, but almost no other facilities. The cliff walks to E and W are magnificent and there is an interesting ruined castle about 1M to the W.

63.3 The Vieux Château, built in the 11th century, is thought to have been a pirates' lair at some time in its history

64 Saint-Gilles-Croix-de-Vie

Location
46°41'N 1°56'W

Shelter
Good in marina

Hazards
Entrance dangerous in strong SW wind or swell

Depth restrictions
Entrance 1.5m but silts to 0.8m
Visitors' berth 1.5m

Night entry Lit

HW time
Brest HW–½ neaps, +¼ springs

Mean height of tide (m)

	HWS	HWN	LWN	LWS
Saint-Gilles	5.1	4.1	2.0	0.7

Tidal streams
Weak in the bay but 6kts on ebb in harbour, much affected by rain

Berthing
Marina and visitors' buoys

Fuel
Next to the visitors' berth

Facilities
All facilities

Charts
BA 3640 (10),
SHOM 7402 (50/10)
Imray C40 (large scale)

Radio
Harbourmaster VHF 9

Telephone
Harbourmaster *t* 02 51 55 30 83

Fishing port and beach resort

Saint-Gilles and Croix-de-Vie are two towns on opposite side of the Vie River. Saint-Gilles, on the S, is a beach resort whereas Croix-de-Vie is an important fishing port and sizeable town. The river separating them has a fishing harbour and a large marina. The combination of resort and bustling river gives the place a very pleasant atmosphere.

PILOTAGE

Saint-Gilles approach and entrance

Warning

The entrance is shallow and exposed to winds from the SW; the ebb runs at up to 6 knots. Entry is therefore dangerous in strong wind against tide conditions. Even in moderate conditions it is better to enter and leave on the last of the flood.

By GPS

From the NW or W use
⊕376-St Gilles, ⊕377-St Gilles 1.

From the S use
⊕377-St Gilles 1.

From E of S use ⊕378-SE St Gilles,
⊕377-St Gilles 1 to avoid getting too close to Roche Bonneau (depth 0.2m).

By day

The entrance can be located by the low rocky headland of Grosse Terre, to the N, and the high lighthouse of Croix-de-Vie. On closer approach, Pill' Hours island can be seen in front of the harbour entrance and the red-topped leading lighthouses.

The approach should be made shortly before high water, with the leading lighthouses in line on 043°. This leaves Pill'Hours SCM to port and leads between the breakwater heads into the buoyed channel. The stream runs very hard and the buoys

64.1 Croix-de-Vie and Sainte-Gilles looking NE. Croix-de-Vie on the bend in the river is the largest fishing town in the Vendée. Sainte-Gilles, on the opposite bank, is a holiday resort. The marina is up river past the fishing harbour on the Croix-de-Vie side.
The ebb runs very strongly in the river and the exposed entrance can be rough

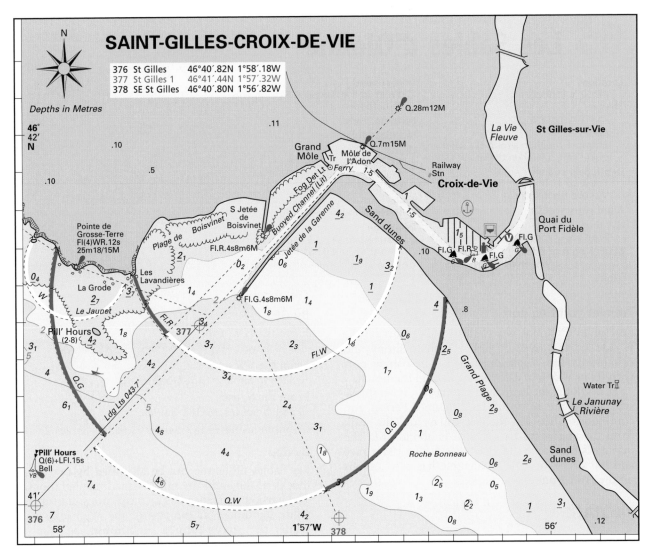

SAINT-GILLES-CROIX-DE-VIE

376	St Gilles	46°40'.82N 1°58'.18W
377	St Gilles 1	46°41'.44N 1°57'.32W
378	SE St Gilles	46°40'.80N 1°56'.82W

Plan 64

should be given a good berth as they are moored on the high ground beside the channel.

After a 90° turn to starboard, the channel passes the fishing-boat basins to reach the marina. The reception berth lies at the far end, beyond the fuel berth and round the bend to port. There is not much room to manoeuvre near the pontoon. Beware of the shallow water marked by green buoys and the strong stream.

Departure should be made before high water, as the strong ebb quickly raises a sea at the entrance.

By night

The entrance is well lit. Get the leading lights in line before passing Pill'Hours SCM. Once the SE breakwater head is reached, follow the lit channel buoys. Unless conditions are ideal, borrow a vacant berth in the main part of the marina rather than attempt to berth on the visitors' pontoon in the dark.

BERTHS AND ANCHORAGES

Saint-Gilles Marina

The visitors' pontoon is often crowded and marina staff may direct yachts, particularly those over 10m, to a vacant berth in the main part of the marina.

ASHORE IN SAINT-GILLES

The marina has all facilities including a fuel berth near the visitors' pontoon. St-Gilles and Croix-de-Vie have a full range of cafés, restaurants and shops with a good supermarket over the bridge in St-Gilles. There are connections by rail to Nantes.

64.2 The red-topped lighthouse is one of a pair marking the leading line on 043°. The green-topped lighthouse is on the N jetty in the harbour entrance at the start of the buoyed channel

65 Les Sables d'Olonne

Location
46°30'N 1°48'W
Shelter
Good in marina
Hazards
Entrance rough in strong SW wind or swell, particularly on the ebb
Depth restrictions
Entrance 1.1
Visitors' berth 2.0m
Night entry Well lit
HW time
Brest HW–½ neaps, +¼ springs
Mean height of tide (m)

	HWS	HWN	LWN	LWS
Sables	5.2	4.1	2.0	0.7

Tidal streams
Weak in the bay but 2.5kts on ebb in harbour
Berthing Marina
Facilities All facilities
Charts
BA 3640 (10), 3638 (10)
SHOM 7411 (10)
Imray C40 (large scale)
Radio
Harbourmaster VHF 9, 16
Telephone
Marina *t* 02 51 32 51 16
Tourist office *t* 02 51 96 85 85

Premier yachting port

Les Sables d'Olonne is a sophisticated resort on the E side of the river. It has a casino, shops and restaurants and a splendid beach. The fishing port with its market and cafés is just behind the beach.

Port Olona, the large modern marina, is on the W side above the town of La Chaume. Ferries run continuously between the two towns and the walk from the marina to La Chaume is about ½M. The marina is the home of the *Vendée Globe* yacht race and has every facility. La Chaume has cafés, shops on the river front and a market.

PILOTAGE

Sables d'Olonne approach and entrance

Warning

Entry under sail is prohibited.

The approach can be very rough and even dangerous in strong SE, S or SW winds, especially if there is any swell. Avoid entering or leaving in these conditions. In bad weather, the SE approach is reported to be safer.

By GPS

From the NW, use
⊕379-Barge, ⊕380-W Sables, ⊕381-Sables.
From the SW use
⊕380-W Sables, ⊕381-Sables.
From the S, use
⊕384-E Sables, ⊕381-Sables.
Continue using ⊕382-Sables 1, ⊕383-Sables 2.

By day

Les Sables d'Olonne can be identified by two large blocks of flats and the tall L'Armadèche lighthouse. The harbour entrance has a conspicuous red-topped white lighthouse at the end of the W breakwater, while the green-topped lighthouse on the E breakwater is less easy to spot.

From the SE, use the transit of the green-topped breakwater light with the crenellated, white-topped, La Chaume lighthouse on 320°. This leaves all the shoals to port and the water is deep until within 400m of the harbour entrance. This approach should always be used in bad weather.

65.1 Sables d'Olonne looking S.
Port Olona marina is in the foreground. The Port de Commerce is in the middle and the fishing harbour is closest to town.

65.2 The capitainerie at Port Olona. Visitors must secure to the and report to the office to be given a berth

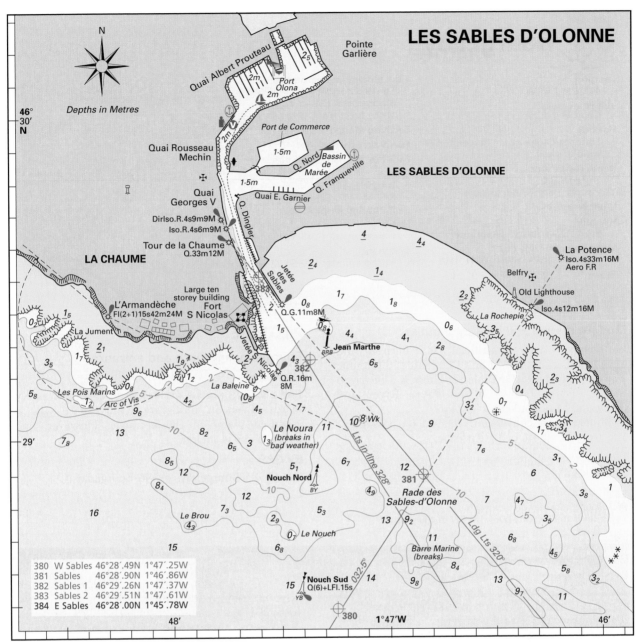

LES SABLES D'OLONNE

Depths in Metres

Quai Albert Prouteau

Port Olona

Pointe Garlière

Quai Rousseau Mechin

Port de Commerce

Q. Nord *Bassin de Marée*

LES SABLES D'OLONNE

Quai Georges V

Quai E. Garnier

Q. Franqueville

DirIso.R.4s9m9M

Iso.R.4s6m9M

Tour de la Chaume
Q.33m12M

LA CHAUME

La Potence
Iso.4s33m16M
Aero F.R

Belfry

Old Lighthouse
Iso.4s12m16M

La Rochepie

L'Armandèche
Fl(2+1)15s42m24M

Fort S Nicolas

Large ten storey building

La Jument

Q.G.11m8M

Jean Marthe

Les Pois Marins

Arc of Vis

La Baleine

382
Q.R.16m 8M

Le Noura
(breaks in bad weather)

Wk

Nouch Nord

Le Brou

Le Nouch

Le Noura

381

Rade des Sables-d'Olonne

Barre Marine (breaks)

Nouch Sud
Q(6)+LFl.15s

380	W Sables	46°28′.49N	1°47′.25W
381	Sables	46°28′.90N	1°46′.86W
382	Sables 1	46°29′.26N	1°47′.37W
383	Sables 2	46°29′.51N	1°47′.61W
384	**E Sables**	**46°28′.00N**	**1°45′.78W**

380

1°47′W

Plan 65

From the N or NW, start close to La Petite Barge SCM and make good 100° to leave Nouch Sud SCM to port. Turn onto 033° and identify the harbour entrance. The leading line on the left of the beach front is between the belfry and two blocks of flats. The front light is above a red board on the beach.

Near LW, after passing the end of the W breakwater, alter to port to bring the red panels on the starboard side in transit on 328°. Above half tide the dangers are covered and the transit need not be followed precisely.

By night

The harbour is well lit. Follow the leading lights on 320° until the W breakwater light is abeam to port. Then turn to port to get the leading lights into line on 328°.

BERTHS

Port Olona

The reception pontoon is on the port side just before the fuel berth and the marina basin. The ebb runs hard here. Visitors must secure and visit the capitainerie to be allocated a berth.

ASHORE IN LES SABLES D'OLONNE

The marina has all facilities including a 28-tonne travel-lift, two slips and all repair facilities. The fuel berth is near the reception pontoon and there are some shops, cafés and restaurants in the marina complex. The shops of La Chaume are nearby and the delights of Les Sables can be reached by ferry from La Chaume or from the marina in high season. There is a large car park and excellent communications by train, bus and air.

66 Bourgenay

Location
46°26′N 1°41′W

Shelter
Good in marina

Hazards
Entrance dangerous in moderate SW wind or swell

Depth restrictions
Entrance 1.0
Visitors' berths 1.0m to 2.0m

Night entry Lit

HW time
Brest HW–½ neaps, +¼ springs

Mean height of tide (m)

	HWS	HWN	LWN	LWS
Sables	5.2	4.1	2.0	0.7

Tidal streams in approaches
SE – Brest HW–5½ to +½ (0.9kts)
Slack – Brest HW +½ to +1½
NW – Brest HW+1½ to –5½ (1.3kts)

Berthing Marina

Fuel S breakwater

Facilities All marina facilities

Charts
BA 2998 (50)
SHOM 7403 (50)
Imray C40 (large scale)

Radio
Harbourmaster VHF 9, 16

Telephone
Harbourmaster t 02 51 22 20 36

Modern marina and holiday complex

Bourgenay is a large, artificial yacht harbour and marina village about 6M SE of Les Sables d'Olonne. The nearest town is 2M inland. There is a beach to the S, oyster farms on the Payré River and pinewoods and marshes to explore.

Bourgenay is conveniently placed on passage to and from Ile de Ré or La Rochelle.

PILOTAGE

Bourgenay approach and entrance

Warning

Entry should not be attempted in strong W or SW winds. Even in moderate winds there will be confused water in the entrance. However, once inside, there is shelter.

By GPS

Use ⊕385-Bourgenay, ⊕386-Bourgenay 1.

66.1 Bourgenay marina looking N.
The inset is the Fairway buoy 1M SW of the marina

66.2 The green panels in line with the low point of the white roofs

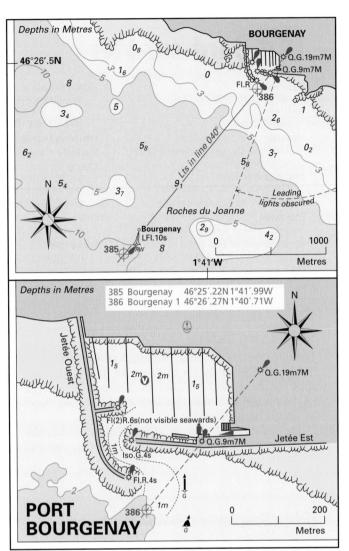

Plan 66A and 66B

66.3 The visitors' pontoon at Bourgenay

By day

Bourgenay is identified by the sandy beach at the mouth of the Payre River to the S and the white roofs of the two marina buildings.

Locate the fairway buoy 1M SW of the marina. The leading marks on 040° are green panels with the rear one on a tall white column. This column can be seen easily and it is sufficient to keep this on 040° at the low point between the two white roofs until the front mark is seen.

On close approach leave a green buoy and a green beacon to starboard; then make a 90° turn to port followed by a 90° turn to starboard to enter the marina. Fluorescent red and white chevrons indicate this latter turn.

By night

Follow the leading lights until the entrance is reached. The breakwater heads are lit but the green buoy and beacon are not.

BERTHS

Bourgenay Marina

The reception pontoon is marked E. Visitors should secure to it unless met by a marina launch and shown to a berth. There are 110 berths for visitors; maximum length 20m.

ASHORE IN BOURGENAY

There is a fuel berth on the S breakwater, a grid, a slip, a 15-tonne travel-lift, a chandlery and engineers. There are cafés, a few small shops and bicycle hire in the marina complex. Up the hill is a supermarket and a post office but all other shops are about 2 miles away in Talmont-St Hilaire.

67 Jard-sur-Mer

Location
46°24′N 1°35′W

Shelter
Good in marina

Hazards
Entrance dangerous in strong SW wind or swell

Depth restrictions
Entrance dries, access HW±2

Night entry Not recommended

HW time
Brest HW−½ neaps, +¼ springs

Mean height of tide (m)

	HWS	HWN	LWN	LWS
Sables	5.2	4.1	2.0	0.7

Tidal streams in approaches
SE – Brest HW−5½ to +½ (1.0kts)
Slack – Brest HW+½ to +1½
NW – Brest HW+1½ to −5½ (1.4kts)

Berthing Drying harbour

Facilities Limited

Charts
BA 2998 (50)
SHOM 7403 (50)
Imray C40 (large scale)

Radio
Harbourmaster VHF 9

Telephone
Harbourmaster *t* 02 51 33 90 61

Small drying harbour

Jard-sur-Mer is a small drying harbour that lies about 10M N of the tip of Ile de Ré. It is a pleasant spot for those who can take the ground. The village of Jard-sur-Mer has reasonable facilities and there are good beaches nearby.

In offshore weather at neaps a deeper draught yacht could find a pleasant day anchorage off the harbour.

67.1 The drying harbour of Jard-sur-Mer looking SE. Jard-sur-Mer is a small holiday resort with miles of sandy beaches. The sea bed is flat, shallow rock and any swell is magnified

PILOTAGE

Jard-sur-Mer approach and entrance

By GPS

⊕387-Jard, ⊕388-Jard 1, ⊕389-Jard 2.

By day

Jard is easy to identify as it is the only town on this stretch of coast. However, there are offlying dangers so it is best to start from ⊕387-Jard or identify the PHM and SHM buoys that mark the entrance.

From the buoys, it should be possible to identify two white beacons set in the sand dunes on 038°. Follow this transit towards the shore. The course appears to be quite a long way E of the harbour. This

67.2 Jard-sur-Mer is mainly used by small fishing boats

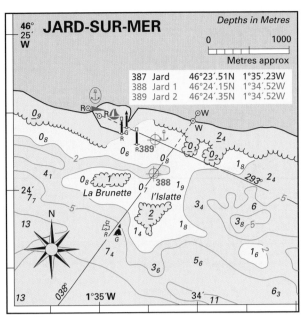

Plan 67

is necessary to avoid a shallow patch (dries 1.0m) SE of the harbour.

Once the harbour opens, turn to port to enter. The transit is two red boards with a white stripe on 293° but it is sufficient to follow the line of the breakwater. There are also some beacons to indicate the deepest water.

BERTHS AND ANCHORAGES

Jard-sur-Mer harbour

The harbour dries but boats that can take the ground may dry out alongside the little quay on outer breakwater, or borrow a mooring. It is also possible to anchor clear of the moorings but bow and stern anchors should be used.

⚓ Outside the harbour

Deep-keeled yachts can anchor outside in settled weather. The best spot is between the harbour mouth and the two white beacons at neaps or further out at springs. This spot is untenable in any wind or swell from the W and it would be difficult to leave at night.

ASHORE IN JARD-SUR-MER

There are showers and toilets at the capitainerie and modest shops in the village, which is a short walk away. There are good beaches nearby.

67.3 It is possible to dry out alongside the little quay on the outer breakwater

67.4 The entrance to Jard-sur-Mer harbour as the tide goes out

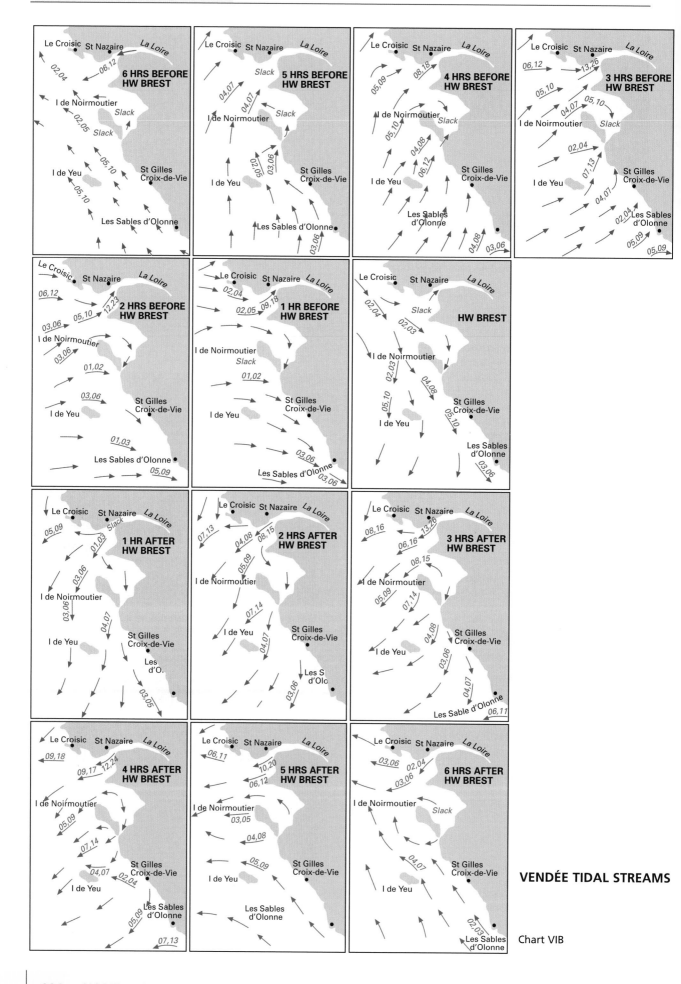

VENDÉE TIDAL STREAMS

Chart VIB

Ré Bridge

VII. Charente

St Martin, Ile de Ré

Ile d'Aix

Marennes

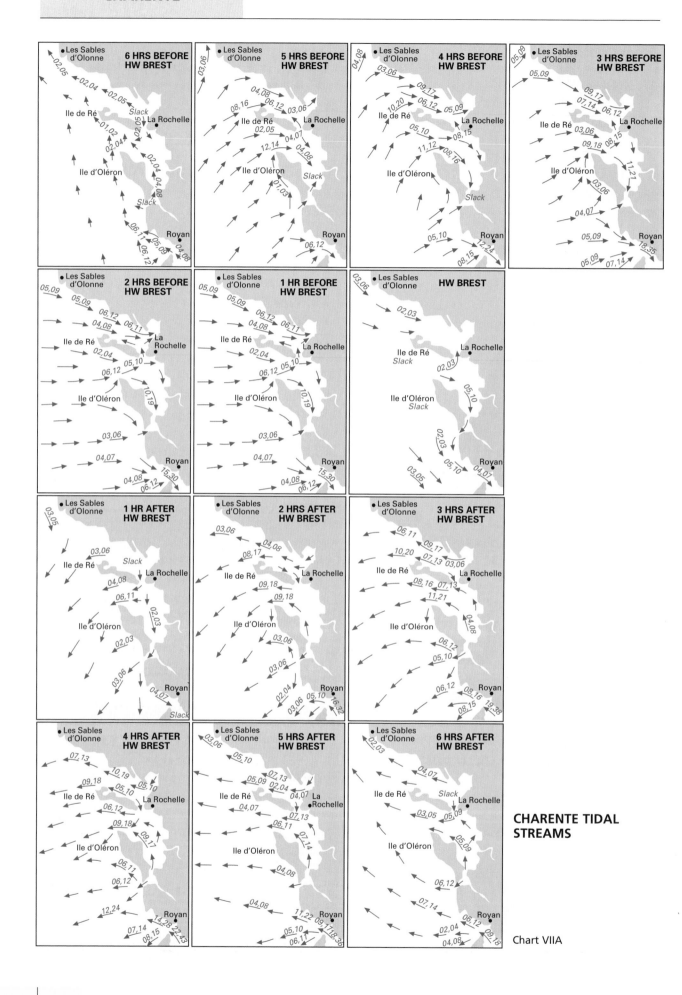

CHARENTE TIDAL STREAMS

Chart VIIA

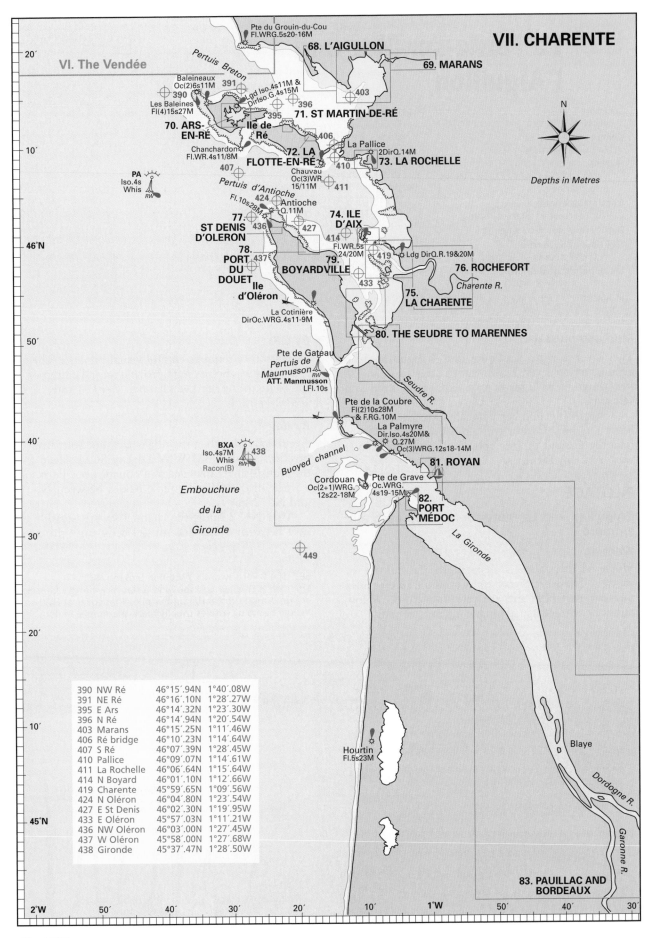

VI. The Vendée

VII. CHARENTE

Pte du Grouin-du-Cou
Fl.WRG.5s20-16M

68. L'AIGULLON

69. MARANS

Pertuis Breton

Baleineaux
Oc(2)6s11M
391
390
Les Baleines
Fl(4)15s27M

Lgd Iso.4s11M &
DirIso.G.4s15M
395
396

403

71. ST MARTIN-DE-RÉ

Ile de
Ré

**70. ARS-
EN-RÉ**

406

La Pallice
2DirQ.14M

**72. LA
FLOTTE-EN-RÉ**

410

73. LA ROCHELLE

Chancardon
Fl.WR.4s11/8M

407

Chauvau
Oc(3)WR.
15/11M

411

PA
Iso.4s
Whis
RW

Pertuis d'Antioche

424
Fl.10s28M

Antioche
Q.11M

**74. ILE
D'AIX**

**77.
ST DENIS
D'OLERON**

436

427

414
Fl.WR.5s
24/20M

Ldg DirQ.R.19&20M

419

76. ROCHEFORT

**78.
PORT
DU
DOUET**

437

**79.
BOYARDVILLE**

Ile
d'Oléron

433

**75.
LA CHARENTE**

Charente R.

La Cotinière
DirOc.WRG.4s11-9M

80. THE SEUDRE TO MARENNES

Pte de Gateau
Pertuis de
Maumusson
RW

Seudre R.

ATT. Manmusson
LFl.10s

Pte de la Coubre
Fl(2)10s28M
& F.RG.10M

La Palmyre
Dir.Iso.4s20M&
Q.27M
Oc(3)WRG.12s18-14M

BXA
Iso.4s7M
Whis
Racon(B)
RW
438

Buoyed channel

81. ROYAN

Embouchure

Cordouan
Oc(2+1)WRG.
12s22-18M

Pte de Grave
Oc.WRG.
4s19-15M

de la

**82.
PORT
MÉDOC**

Gironde

La Gironde

449

Blaye

Hourtin
Fl.5s23M

Dordogne R.

N

Depths in Metres

Garonne R.

**83. PAUILLAC AND
BORDEAUX**

390	NW Ré	46°15′.94N	1°40′.08W
391	NE Ré	46°16′.10N	1°28′.27W
395	E Ars	46°14′.32N	1°23′.30W
396	N Ré	46°14′.94N	1°20′.54W
403	Marans	46°15′.25N	1°11′.46W
406	Ré bridge	46°10′.23N	1°14′.64W
407	S Ré	46°07′.39N	1°28′.45W
410	Pallice	46°09′.07N	1°14′.61W
411	La Rochelle	46°06′.64N	1°15′.64W
414	N Boyard	46°01′.10N	1°12′.66W
419	Charente	45°59′.65N	1°09′.56W
424	N Oléron	46°04′.80N	1°23′.54W
427	E St Denis	46°02′.30N	1°19′.95W
433	E Oléron	45°57′.03N	1°11′.21W
436	NW Oléron	46°03′.00N	1°27′.45W
437	W Oléron	45°58′.00N	1°27′.68W
438	Gironde	45°37′.47N	1°28′.50W

Chart VIIB

68 La Faute-sur-Mer and l'Aiguillon

Location
46°16'N 1°16'W

Shelter
Fair weather only

Hazards
Timber piles of mussel beds extend into channel.

Depth restrictions
Approach dries 1.6m or more

Night entry Not recommended

HW time at St-Martin
PdG HW neaps, −½ springs

Mean height of tide (m)

	HWS	HWN	LWN	LWS
St-Martin	5.9	4.7	2.3	0.9

Tidal stream in approach
Flood – PdG HW–5½ to –½ (1.3kts)
Slack – PdG HW–½ to +1½
Ebb — PdG HW +½ to +5½ (1.0kts)
Slack – PdG HW+5½ to –5½
1.5kts in river

Berthing
Drying jetty, moorings and anchorage

Facilities Limited

Charts
BA 2999 (50)
SHOM 7404 (50)
Imray C41 (109)

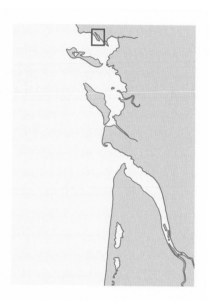

Mud and mussels

The River Lay to La-Faute and L'Aiguillon is a genuine oyster river. The entrance dries 1.6m and at low water there is just a vast expanse of mud and salt grass.

A surprising number of yachts are based in the River Lay but a visitor will almost certainly have to take the ground in very soft mud, probably a long way from any facilities.

PILOTAGE

L'Aiguillon and La Faute-sur-Mer approach and entrance

Warning

Much of the shore is devoted to the culture of mussels. These are grown on substantial timber piles that cover at HW and are very dangerous. Yellow buoys or withies usually mark the mussel beds.

By GPS

The entrance requires careful visual pilotage. The following waypoints may provide an indication of the route to the marked channel. ⊕401-Faute, ⊕402-Faute 1.

By day

Approach only when the tide is well up. Start from a position about 0.3M W of Le Lay SCM. Head for the transformer, adjacent to a conspicuous barn, on a track of 035°. This course passes between No. 1 and No. 2 buoys.

After No. 2 buoy, the channel swings steadily to port between oyster and mussel beds, until the river

---

68.1 The River Lay and L'Aiguillon looking NE.
The river is shallow and the land is flat 'dry marsh'. Mussels are grown on substantial timber piles that cover at HW. Yellow buoys or withies usually mark the mussel beds

opens up and the distant town of L'Aiguillon, with the prominent water tower of Bel Air, can be seen ahead. From there, beacons mark the channel.

At Banc des Marsouins, the channel splits. Both channels are very narrow but the N one is preferred. The river then turns sharply to starboard and runs NW to Faute-sur-Mar and L'Aiguillon.

BERTHS AND ANCHORAGES

La Faute-sur-Mer

On the west bank about two-thirds of the way up to the bridge, is a landing slip marked by two posts with orange tops. Just upstream of the slip is the Yacht Club jetty (drying), where visitors may secure.

L'Aiguillon

Continuing up to L'Aiguillon, the river is full of fishing boat moorings and wooden jetties line the E bank. It may be possible to anchor or borrow a mooring in the pool below the bridge at L'Aiguillon. Depths are uncertain due to silting and the river can almost dry on any tide. Moorings are generally for shallow-draught fishing boats.

ASHORE IN L'AIGUILLON AND FAUTE-SUR-MER

There is a boat-yard and slipway but no fuel at L'Aiguillon. There are shops, cafés and restaurants in both L'Aiguillon and La Faute and a good beach at La Faute. There are markets in La Faute on Thursday and Sunday and in L'Aiguillon on Tuesday and Friday.

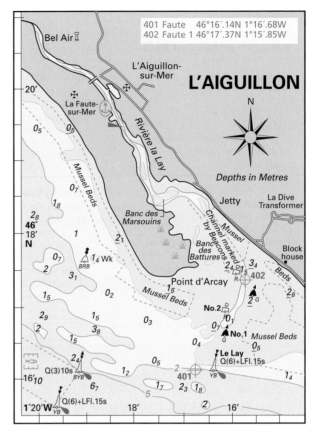

Plan 68

68.2 L'Aiguillon drying marina is built from piles embedded in the mud. There are no visitors' berths. Anchor or borrow a mooring in the pool below the bridge. Depths are uncertain and the river can dry on any tide

69 Marans

Location
46°17′N 1°10′W

Shelter
Good in Marans

Hazards
Shallow approach with strong streams; can be rough

Depth restrictions
Approach dries 0.1m
2.0m in canal to Marans

Brault lock times
Entry – Brault HW
Exit – Brault HW –1

Night entry Not recommended

HW time at Brault lock
PdG HW +½ neaps, –¼ springs

Mean height of tide (m)

	HWS	HWN	LWN	LWS
St-Martin	5.9	4.7	2.3	0.9

Tidal stream in approach
Flood – PdG HW–5½ to –½ (1.3kts)
Slack – PdG HW–½ to +1½
Ebb – PdG HW +½ to +5½ (1.0kts)
Slack – PdG HW+5½ to –5½
4kts in river

Berthing Town quay and marina

Facilities All facilities

Charts
BA 2999 (50)
SHOM 7404 (50)
Imray C41 (109)

Telephone
Lock *t* 05 46 01 53 77

Gateway to the Marais Poitevin

The Marais Poitevin is a huge marshland conservation area that extends from the sea to Niort. The coastal part, W of Marans, has been drained to form the 'dry marsh' of flat fields and salt marsh. The 'wet marsh' extends from Marans to Niort and is a mass of canals that wind through the lush landscape.

The 9M passage to Marans provides a wonderful opportunity to see the rich wildlife of the 'dry marsh' and, in Marans, it is possible to hire a canal boat to visit the 'wet marsh'. Marans is a pleasant market town where visiting boats are completely sheltered in an old canal.

PILOTAGE

Marans approach and entrance

Warning

Much of the shore is devoted to the culture of mussels. These are grown on substantial timber piles that cover at HW and are very dangerous. Yellow buoys or withies usually mark the mussel beds.

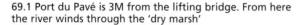

69.1 Port du Pavé is 3M from the lifting bridge. From here the river winds through the 'dry marsh'

69.2 The lifting bridge opens for waiting boats in time for them to arrive at the lock at local HW. From the bridge it is ½M to the lock

Tidal strategy

Telephone the lock-keeper in good time to advise him of your arrival. The lock opens for entry at local HW, which is approximately 20 minutes after La Rochelle HW. The lifting bridge is ½M before the lock and about 5½M from L'Aiguillon SWM so it is best to start well before La Rochelle HW and wait at the bridge. The tide will still be flooding quite strongly.

By GPS

From the NW, use
⊕396-N Ré to avoid the mussel farm N of St-Martin. Use ⊕403-Marans, ⊕404-Marans 1, ⊕405-Marans 2 to cross the Anse l'Aiguillon and enter the river.

By day

Start at L'Aiguillon SWM. Make good 035° for the second SWM. Try to hold the track accurately to avoid the mussel beds on either side. At the second SWM, follow the beacons on about 045° towards

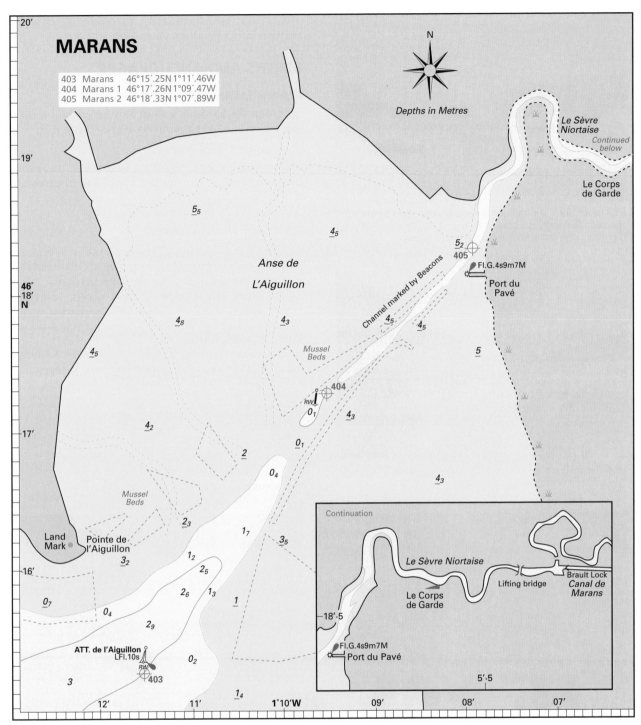

MARANS

403	Marans	46°15'.25N 1°11'.46W
404	Marans 1	46°17'.26N 1°09'.47W
405	Marans 2	46°18'.33N 1°07'.89W

Depths in Metres

Anse de L'Aiguillon

Channel marked by Beacons

Port du Pavé

Fl.G.4s9m7M

Mussel Beds

RW 404

Mussel Beds

Land Mark

Pointe de l'Aiguillon

ATT. de l'Aiguillon LFl.10s

403

Continuation

Le Sèvre Niortaise

Le Corps de Garde

Lifting bridge

Brault Lock
Canal de Marans

Port du Pavé

Fl.G.4s9m7M

Le Sèvre Niortaise

Le Corps de Garde

Plan 69

the SHM on Port du Pavé jetty.

Beyond Port du Pavé, the river is constrained by banks. The plan indicates the deepest water but in general, stay in the middle but watch out for buoys that mark shoals on the bends.

The lifting bridge is about 3M beyond Port de Pavé. There are two waiting buoys on the starboard side before the bridge. Do not lie to these on a falling tide with a strong W wind because they are very close to shallow water.

The lock-keeper operates the bridge using TV cameras to observe the road and river traffic. If boats are waiting, the bridge is opened so they can enter the lock at local HW. On the way back, remember that the departure opening is one hour before local HW.

The lock is enormous with gently sloping banks and a short pontoon on the port-hand side that can be used while the lock is operated. A swing road bridge, at the upper end of the lock, gives access to the Marans canal.

The attractive tree-lined canal runs straight for about 3M to Marans. Towards the end, it appears to come to a dead end, but the channel to Marans

69.3 Brault lock and the swing road bridge open to give access to the Marans Canal. A notice at the lock says that it is going to be restored but no dates are given

69.4 The straight tree-lined canal leads for 3M to Marans. The bird life is very rich and varied

opens up to starboard, through a pair of permanently open lock gates.

BERTHS AND ANCHORAGES

Marans Marina
Secure to the harbour wall or another yacht on the S side or to one of the pontoon berths further up.

⚓ Anse de L'Aiguillon
Sheltered from NW to NE, it is possible to anchor between the two RW buoys. Go as far towards the second as depth permits.

ASHORE IN MARANS

Marans has all marina facilities and is a popular place to over-winter. However, fuel is only available in cans from the garage by the supermarket.

The town has a good range of shops, cafés and restaurants. There is an excellent supermarket on the main road out of town and markets are held on Tuesday and Saturday.

Hire boats for the Marais Poitevin are found at the end of the marina, beyond the road bridge.

69.5 Boats moored in the canal at Marans

70 Ars-en-Ré

Location
46°13′N 1°30′W

Shelter
Good in either marina

Hazards
Shifting very shallow approach. Easy to get neaped

Depth restrictions
Channel dries 3.4m
Marinas have 1.5m or more

Night entry Lit but not recommended

HW time
PdG HW neaps, −½ springs

Mean height of tide (m)

	HWS	HWN	LWN	LWS
St-Martin	5.9	4.7	2.3	0.9

Tidal stream in approach
Slack – PdG HW−½ to +½
W – PdG HW+½ to +5½ (1.2kts)
E – PdG HW+5½ to −½ (1.3kts)

Berthing Two marinas

Facilities Marina facilities plus small town

Charts
BA 2999 (50)
SHOM 7404 (50), 7412 (15)
Imray C41 (large scale)

Radio VHF 9

Telephone
Harbourmaster *t* 05 46 29 25 10

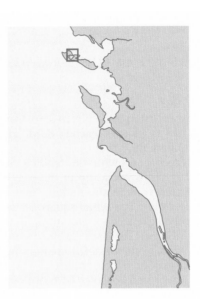

Large drying natural harbour

Le Fier d'Ars is a large drying harbour on the NW coast of Ile de Ré. It is well sheltered and, despite only having access near HW, the two marinas have become the principal sailing centre for the island. The village is small but Ars-en-Ré is an excellent base for exploring the island by bicycle.

70.1 Le Fier d'Ars at low water looking N.
The moorings off Point du Fier are visible at the top of the picture. The marina is Bassin de la Criée. Note that the channel dries 3.4m where it narrows for the final approach

PILOTAGE

Le Fier d'Ars approach and entrance

Warning

The very shallow bar in the final approach (dries 3.4m) makes it extremely easy to get neaped. Occasionally the sluices are opened at LW to scour the channel. This is seldom done in season but when it occurs, access to the harbour is restricted.

By GPS

The entrance shifts and the channel buoys are moved so the waypoints only provide an indication of the correct route.

From the W and NW use
⊕391-NE Ré, ⊕392-Ars, ⊕393-Ars 1,
⊕394-Ars 2.
From the E use ⊕395-E Ars, ⊕392-Ars, ⊕393-Ars
1, ⊕394-Ars 2.

By day

The easiest approach is to start from a position close N of Les Islattes beacon NCM. This is about 1M E of Pointe du Grouin.

Steer 266° with the leading marks in line (see 70.2). Look for a dip in the tree line with a black, pointed roof in the middle, that looks like a lone tree. Below is a white square at the top of the wide sandy beach. The rear mark is to the left of the lighthouse. The Banc du Bucheron tends to move S, so watch out for SHM channel buoys and beacons that may be off the transit.

At the red beacon ¼M E of Pointe du Fier turn to port and steer 231° for the black-topped Ars church spire (see 70.3). The official leading marks on 232° (see 70.4) are not easy to see by day.

If proceeding to the harbour, follow the buoyed channel, which dries 3.4m.

By night

(See plan 70B)

Both transits are lit but night entry is not recommended for a first visit.

BERTHS AND ANCHORAGES

Bassin de la Criée

This is the outer locked marina and the gate opens local HW±3; the sill dries 2.5m. The marina is a short walk from the village and close to the excellent daily market. It is probably the best and most comfortable base for exploring Ile de Ré by bicycle.

Bassin de la Prée

This is the inner harbour at Ars-en-Ré. It is in the centre of the attractive village and has a small visitors' pontoon just inside the entrance to starboard. The gate opens local HW±2½; the sill dries 3m. There are drying berths immediately outside the gates to La Prée but they are mainly used by fishing boats.

⚓ Les Portes

Sheltered from the SW, there are visitors' buoys and an anchorage NE of Les Portes.

⚓ Pointe du Fier

Sheltered except from the NE, there is an anchorage and some moorings just outside the channel near Pointe du Fier. Anchor outside the moorings in 1.5m to 2.0m. There is also an anchorage further E in a pool in the channel, however it is rather exposed and cannot be recommended.

ASHORE IN ARS-EN-RE

Ars-en-Ré has all the facilities of a small fishing, yachting and holiday town. There are basic marina facilities, including fuel at the entrance to the Bassin de La Prée. The small town is attractive and has shops, restaurants, cafés and, most important, bicycle hire. There is an excellent market every day during the season.

70.4 The official leading marks on 232° are less easy to see than the spire in 70.3

70.2 The Pointe du Fier leading marks on 266°

70.3 The distinctive black-topped spire of Ars church

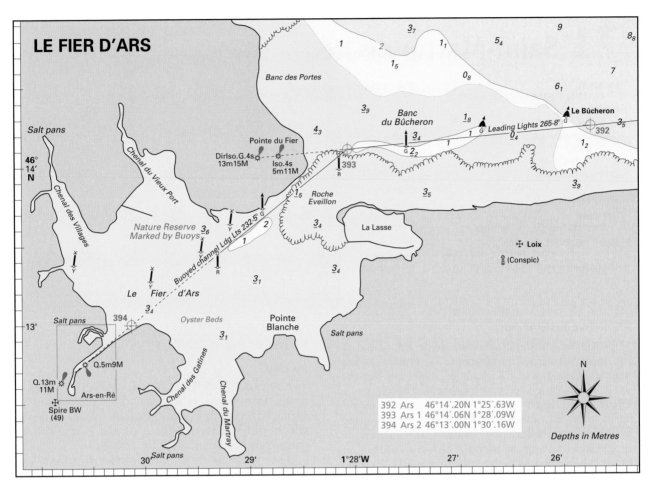

LE FIER D'ARS

Salt pans

Banc des Portes

Banc du Bûcheron

Le Bûcheron

Pointe du Fier

DirIso.G.4s
13m15M

Iso.4s
5m11M

Leading Lights 265·8°

392

393

R

Chenal du Vieux Port

Salt pans

Chenal des Villages

46°
14'
N

Nature Reserve
Marked by Buoys

Roche
Eveillon

Buoyed channel Ldg Lts 232·5°

La Lasse

Loix

(Conspic)

Le   Fier   d'Ars

13'

394

Salt pans

Oyster Beds

Pointe
Blanche

Salt pans

Q.5m9M

Q.13m
11M

Ars-en-Ré

Spire BW
(49)

Chenal des Gatines

Chenal du Martray

N

392	Ars	46°14'.20N 1°25'.63W
393	Ars 1	46°14'.06N 1°28'.09W
394	Ars 2	46°13'.00N 1°30'.16W

Depths in Metres

30   Salt pans   29'   1°28'W   27'   26'

Plan 70A

70.5 The canal approaching Bassin de la Prée

70.6 The visitors' pontoon at Bassin de la Criée

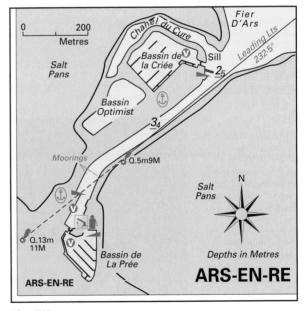

0   200
Metres

Chenal du Cure

Fier
D'Ars

Salt
Pans

Bassin de
la Criée

Sill

Leading Lts 232·5°

2₅

Bassin
Optimist

3₄

Moorings

Q.5m9M

Salt
Pans

N

Q.13m
11M

Bassin de
La Prée

Depths in Metres

ARS-EN-RE

ARS-EN-RE

Plan 70B

71 Saint-Martin-de-Ré

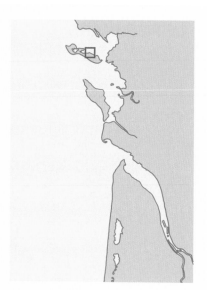

Location
46°12′N 1°22′W
Shelter
Good in wet dock
Depth restrictions
Entrance dries 1.5m
Wet dock has 3.0m
Other restrictions
Wet dock gets very crowded
Night entry Lit
HW time
PdG HW neaps, −½ springs
Mean height of tide (m)

	HWS	HWN	LWN	LWS
St-Martin	5.9	4.7	2.3	0.9

Tidal stream in approach
Slack – PdG HW−½ to ½
W – PdG HW+½ to +5½ (1.2kts)
E – PdG HW +5½ to −½ (1.3kts)
Berthing
Drying harbour and wet dock
Facilities
All facilities in a very attractive town
Charts
BA 2999 (50)
SHOM 7404 (50), 7412 (15)
Imray C41 (large scale)
Radio VHF 9
Telephone
Harbourmaster *t* 05 46 09 26 69

Attractive historic port

Saint-Martin, on the N coast of Ile de Ré, is one of the most attractive harbours in W France and a magnet for visitors. It is crowded in season but the lively atmosphere is part of its appeal. The yachts lie afloat in the heart of the town, with smart shops, cafés and restaurants nearby. Energetic crew members can explore the Vaubin fortifications or hire bicycles to tour the island. The less energetic can enjoy their boats being photographed by the hundreds of visitors.

PILOTAGE

St-Martin approach and entrance

By GPS

From the W or SW use
⊕391-NE Ré, ⊕395-E Ars, ⊕397-St Martin, ⊕398-St Martin 1.

From Marans or the Ré bridge use ⊕397-St Martin, ⊕398-St Martin 1.

By day

The entrance dries 1.6m so entry is only possible at neaps from local HW−2 to +1½; a bit more at springs. During this period, the outer rocks to the W will be safely covered; those on the E will still be dangerous but are marked by a NCM.

The harbour and Vaubin fortifications are distinctive. Start from a position about 1M away, with the harbour bearing 200°. Then approach with the square church tower in line with the light at the end of the Grand Mole on 201°. Try to follow the transit accurately and particularly avoid drifting off course to the E by ensuring that the large, red-topped lighthouse is left of the church tower.

On arrival at the harbour, leave the wave breaker close to port and the mole head very close to starboard. The waiting pontoon in the outer

71.1 Saint-Martin-de-Ré looking NE. When entering the harbour leave the wave breaker close to port and the mole head very close to starboard. Wait alongside the pontoon in the harbour for the lock to open. Once inside visitors raft in the N corner

71.2 The drying E harbour. The square church tower and the ruined church are distinctive from the sea

71.3 The narrow lock gates leading to the Bassin à Flot. Visitors moor just inside the entrance

harbour is to starboard and, beyond that, the channel to the dock gates is also to starboard.

Approaching from the E, keep well to the N of the NCM beacon on the Couronneau rocks and do not confuse the citadel, to the E, with St-Martin itself.

By night

Approach in the white sector of St-Martin light bearing 200°. On close approach alter to starboard to bring the mole light onto 195° and enter leaving the light, marking the NW end of the wave breaker, close to port and the mole light close to starboard.

BERTHS AND ANCHORAGES

Outer harbour

In the summer months a long pontoon is arranged along the Grand Môle with a section dredged to 2m along its length. This is initially dredged 16m wide

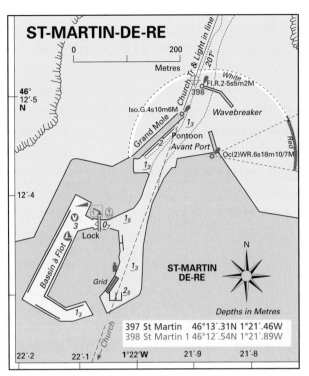

Plan 71

to allow boats to raft alongside the pontoon, but it quickly silts up with soft mud, into which the keels of deep-draught yachts sink. In N winds a swell enters round the wave breaker, causing the pontoon to pitch.

Drying harbour

There are quays on the E side that dry 1.5m. Vessels should not berth along the inner half of the W quay because there is a fuelling berth and a large grid.

Wet dock

The wet dock gates are opened about HW–3 to +2½, less at neaps, between 0630 to 2200. Exact times are posted at the harbourmaster's office and other harbours in the area.

To get a place inside, it is usually necessary to arrive early and wait in the outer harbour for the dock. Once inside, berth as directed by the harbour staff. There is not much room and visitors are likely to be rafted.

Rade de St-Martin

There are four white visitors' buoys off the entrance and it is possible to anchor nearby. There is also an anchorage, sheltered from the W through S to SE, inshore of La Rocha NCM.

ASHORE IN ST-MARTIN

The harbour has all facilities including a fuel berth on the W side of the drying harbour. The town is a sophisticated holiday resort with a good range of shops, cafés and restaurants. There is a market on Tuesday, Thursday and Saturday.

72 La-Flotte-en-Ré

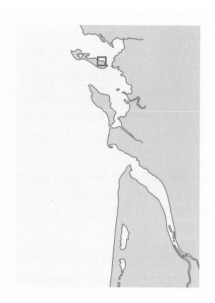

Location
46°11'N 1°19'W
Shelter
La Flotte, good except from N
Depth restrictions
La Flotte-en-Ré dries
Martray is shallow near the beach
Night entry La Flotte-en-Ré is lit
HW time
PdG HW neaps, −½ springs
Mean height of tide (m)

	HWS	HWN	LWN	LWS
St-Martin	5.9	4.7	2.3	0.9

Tidal stream in approach
E – PdG HW–5½ to –1½ (0.9kts)
Slack – PdG–1½ to +½
W – PdG HW+½ to +5½ (0.9kts)
Slack – PdG HW +5½ to –5½
Berthing
Anchorages and drying harbour
Facilities Limited
Charts
BA 2999 (50)
SHOM 7404 (50)
Imray C41 (large scale)
Radio VHF 9
Telephone
La Flotte HM *t* 05 46 09 67 66

Attractive drying harbour

The drying harbour of La Flotte, 2M SE of St-Martin, was once a fishing port, famous for its lobsters, shrimps and sole. Today it is a quiet, attractive leisure port with narrow streets, white painted houses and a beautiful church. The anchorage and visitors' buoys are well sheltered except from the N so La Flotte provides a good alternative to the bustle of St-Martin.

72.1 The attractive curved wall of the drying harbour at La-Flotte-en-Ré

PILOTAGE

La-Flotte-en-Ré approach and entrance

By GPS

Use ⊕399-La Flotte, ⊕400-La Flotte 1.

By day

La Flotte is easy to identify by the curved breakwater with the green-topped lighthouse on the end but the approach requires care. The channel through the sand dries 2.0m. On both sides are ledges of rock, and oyster beds marked by yellow beacons.

Start from a position about 1M offshore and steer 215° for the lighthouse on the end of the breakwater. This leaves the Pointe des Barres NCM well to port. A moiré fringe panel on a post to the left of the lighthouse will be visible day and night. This ingenious device displays vertical black and orange stripes on the correct course of 215° but, on incorrect courses, it changes to one or more arrowheads pointing in the direction to steer.

To enter the harbour, leave the breakwater head to starboard and steer for the narrow entrance between the jetty heads.

72.2 The lighthouse and moiré fringe panel at the end of the breakwater

By night

Approach on 215° in the white sector of the breakwater light.

BERTHS AND ANCHORAGES

Visitors' moorings

Deep-draught yachts can anchor or use the five white mooring buoys some ¾M offshore in 2m.

Outer harbour

Visitors may be able to secure to the ends of the pontoons on the inside of the outer breakwater where they will dry out in the mud.

Inner harbour

The inner harbour dries 2m. Pontoons for local boats are installed in the inner half of the basin. Space for visitors is limited but they may dry out against the inner side of the Jetée Nord.

⚓ Anse du Martray (S coast)

Sheltered in light NW to NE wind, Anse du Martray is a sandy bay on the W end of the S coast. Start from a position ½M E of Chanchardon octagonal black-topped white tower. Steer 350° past the white mooring buoy into the bay. There are reefs less than ½M either side of the approach so it is important to hold the course fairly accurately. Anchor where depth permits but note that a deep-draught yacht will not be able to get very close to the beach. It is possible to land at the sea wall and walk to Ars-en-Ré through the salt pans or along the coast road to Martray.

⊕409-Martray 1 (46°11′.56N 1°28′.02W)

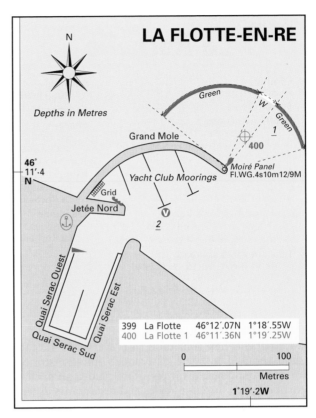

Plan 72

ASHORE IN LA FLOTTE

Water is on the quay and there are shops, cafés and restaurants in town. Markets are held every day.

72.3 Visitors may be able to secure to the ends of the pontoons in the Outer Harbour

72.4 The Inner Harbour at La Flotte-en-Ré looking SW

73 La Rochelle

Location
46°09'N 1°10'W
Shelter Good
Depth restrictions
Approach 0.5m; Minimes 2.0m
Old port 1.0m with very soft mud
Bassin à Flot 3.0m, sill 1.2m
Night entry Well lit
HW time
PdG HW +¼ neaps, −½ springs
Mean height of tide (m)

	HWS	HWN	LWN	LWS
La Rochelle	6.0	4.9	2.4	0.9

Tidal stream in approach
E – PdG HW–5½ to –½ (1.9kts)
Slack – PdG–½ to +½
W – PdG HW+½ to –5½ (2.3kts)

Berthing
Huge marina and old port
Facilities All facilities
Charts
BA 2999 (50), 2743 (15)
SHOM 7404 (50), 7413 (15)
Imray C41 (large scale)
Radio
Port des Minimes VHF 9
La Rochelle VHF 9
Telephone
Minimes *t* 05 46 44 41 20
La Rochelle HM *t* 06 03 54 00 57

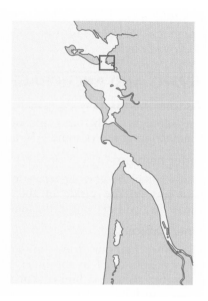

Fascinating historic city

La Rochelle has something for everyone. Elegant shops housed in some of France's finest historical arcaded buildings; a variety of museums; an ancient fortified port; dozens of cafés and restaurants as well as the best food market in North Biscay. In summer, street entertainers and musicians perform on the waterfront.

La Rochelle is so lively that wherever you moor expect to hear the sounds of music and of people enjoying themselves

PILOTAGE

La Rochelle from the W or S

By GPS

From the W use
⊕407-S Ré, ⊕411-La Rochelle,
⊕413-La Rochelle 2.

From the S use
⊕412-La Rochelle 1, ⊕413-La Rochelle 2.

By day

Start from a position between Chauveau SCM and Roche du Sud WCM. Steer 059° towards the distinctive red Tour Richelieu and the two famous stone towers. The transit is two lighthouses in line on 059°. The front one is striped red and white; the rear one is white with a green top. They are very distinctive because they show bright white lights by day (Fl.4s). Follow the transit to Tour Richelieu and follow the buoyed channel to the Vieux Port.

Port des Minimes is just past Tour Richelieu to starboard. The entrance is buoyed but be sure not to cut the corner; go all the way to the beacon WCM before turning into the channel.

By night

The leading lights on 059° make a night entrance very easy. However, note that N of the transit the stone towers may obscure the lights.

73.1 La Rochelle looking SW towards the vast Minimes marina.
In La Rochelle there are three ports. From left to right: Basin des Chalutiers is the L-shaped dock. The small, locked Bassin à Flot is in the middle and on the right is the Vieux Port

To enter Minimes marina, turn to starboard 200m past Tour Richelieu. The beacon WCM and two PHM buoys are unlit, but there is normally plenty of background light.

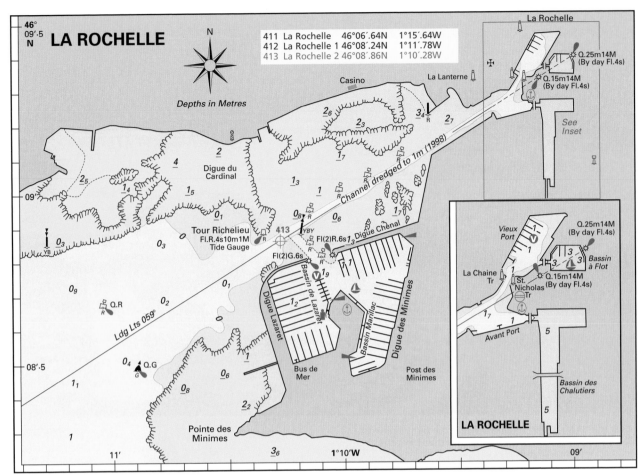

411	La Rochelle	46°06′.64N	1°15′.64W
412	La Rochelle 1	46°08′.24N	1°11′.78W
413	La Rochelle 2	46°08′.86N	1°10′.28W

Plan 73

La Rochelle via the Ré bridge

By GPS

From the N via the Ré bridge use
⊕406-Ré bridge, ⊕410-Pallice,
⊕412-La Rochelle 1, ⊕413-La Rochelle 2. This route has a least depth of 2.5m and passes close S of a shallow patch (dries 0.1m) near Pointe de Chef-de-Baie.

By day

The navigable part of the Ré bridge is clearly marked by buoys and on the pillars. The clearance is 30m. One arch is used for S-going boats and another for N-bound. After passing under the bridge, leave the outer breakwaters of the commercial harbour and the fishing harbour to port. Then follow the coastline, about ½M off, until the Tour Richelieu is sighted.

The final approach is the same as from the W or S. However, be sure to keep to the leading line for the final approach because there is a shallow patch just W of Tour Richelieu.

By night

The navigable section of the bridge, the commercial harbour and the fishing harbour are all well lit. However, the shortcut inside Plateau du Lavardin is not lit.

BERTHS AND ANCHORAGES

Port des Minimes

Port des Minimes is a 3,000-berth marina about 1M from the centre of La Rochelle. The reception pontoon is opposite the entrance and the fuel pontoon is nearby. Tie up at reception to be allocated a berth.

There are excellent marina facilities and some local shops. It is a long walk to town but there is a regular water-bus from the SW corner of the marina.

73.2 The fuel berth and the pontoon outside the harbourmaster's office at Minimes marina

73.3 The Bassin à Flot is approached from the Vieux Port. The picture also shows the lighthouses that form the leading line into La Rochelle

Le Vieux Port

Le Vieux Port is in the centre of the liveliest part of the town and is the place to be if you want to enjoy the atmosphere. Pass through the towers and bear to port. The visitors' pontoons are straight ahead beyond the ferry pontoons. They only have depth of 1.0m but the mud is soft so deep-draught yachts remain upright. The pontoons have water and electricity and there are showers and toilets in the capitainerie at the Bassin des Chalutiers.

The Bassin à Flot

This may be preferable for boats over 12m, or for those staying a few days. The lock gate is to starboard just inside Le Vieux Port. Access is from 2 hours before to ½ hour after HW by day. Call the harbourmaster to ask for space and for the lock gate to be opened.

Bassin des Chalutiers

The Bassin des Chalutiers is used for special events but, space permitting, it is also available for visitors. It is particularly suitable for larger boats. Contact the harbourmaster to arrange for a berth and for the lifting bridge to be opened.

⚓ Anse l'Oubye

Sheltered from the W, there is a wide bay at the E end of Ile de Ré, between Pointe de Chauveau and the bridge. Approach from the SE and anchor in 2m on sand and mud. There are two large visitors' buoys.

73.4 The lifting bridge into the Bassin des Chalutiers is to starboard just before the entrance to the Vieux Port. Access must be cleared with the harbourmaster before arrival

ASHORE IN LA ROCHELLE

La Rochelle has every imaginable yachting facility. There are boat builders, chandlers, engineers and sail makers. Most major marine manufacturers have agencies.

In town there is so much to do that a guidebook or a visit to the tourist office (Le Gabut, S of the Bassin à Flot) is the best approach. Try to visit the museums early as they can become crowded later in the day.

The covered market is open every day and the street market fills the surrounding streets twice a week.

73.5 Looking SE out of the Vieux Port. Tour de la Chaine on the right was built in the 14th century. At that time a chain was stretched across the harbour mouth at night to close it to shipping. Tour St-Nicolas was built as a fortress and dedicated to the patron saint of sailors. Both towers are now museums

73.6 The Vieux Port and the city of La Rochelle.

74 Ile d'Aix

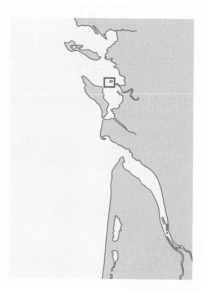

Location
46°01'N 1°11'W

Shelter
Fair weather only

Depth restrictions
Visitors' buoys 2.0m

Night entry Approaches well lit

HW time
PdG HW +¼ neaps, −¾ springs

Mean height of tide (m)

	HWS	HWN	LWN	LWS
Ile d'Aix	6.1	4.9	2.4	0.9

Tidal stream in approach
SE – PdG HW–5½ to +½ (2.1kts)
Slack – PdG+½ to +1½
NW – PdG HW+1½ to –5½ (1.7kts)

Berthing
Anchorages and visitors' buoys

Facilities
A few shops, restaurants and cafés

Charts
BA 3000(50), 2747 (20)
SHOM 7405 (50), 7415 (20)
Imray C41 (109)

Small island with history

Ile d'Aix is a small island surrounded by beaches. There are pretty white houses with multi-coloured hollyhocks, no cars, good walking or biking and two museums.

The island is about 8M S of La Rochelle and is a good stopover on the way to Rochefort or a good day trip from La Rochelle. There are some visitors' buoys and several anchorages.

PILOTAGE

Ile d'Aix approach and entrance

By GPS

Use ⊕415-SW Aix or ⊕416-SE Aix or ⊕418-NE Aix as destination waypoints.

By day

The approach is simple from any direction. Avoid the reef, marked by two WCM buoys, that extends ½M to the NW. Also avoid the oyster beds, marked by a yellow buoy, that extend ¾M to the SE.

By night

From the NW, keep in the white sector of the Ile d'Aix light until Chauveau light turns from red to white, bearing 342°. Steer 162° down this boundary, passing through the red sector of Ile d'Aix light. When it turns white again, use the Charente leading lights bearing 115°. When Ile d'Aix light bears N steer 020° and anchor in 3m, or pick up a mooring.

The passage E of Ile d'Aix

By GPS

From the N use ⊕417-E Aix, ⊕419-Charente.

By day

Fosse d'Enet is a narrow channel between Ile d'Aix and the mainland.

From the N, leave the E point of the Ile d'Aix at least ¼M to starboard to avoid a rocky spur. Steer

195° toward the WCM buoy just W of the conspicuous Fort d'Enet. A yellow buoy marks the dangers SE of Ile d'Aix.

BERTHS AND ANCHORAGES

⚓ SE of Pointe Sainte-Cathérine

Well sheltered from N and NW with some shelter from other directions, there is an anchorage withvisitors' buoys off the SE tip of Ile d'Aix. Look for mooring buoys with a green band. Approach from the SE and go in as far as depth allows. The mud is very soft so the holding is poor. The area is so well lit that it would be easy to leave at night and move to La Rochelle.

⊕416-SE Aix (46°00'.26N 1°10'.18W)

⚓ NW of Pointe Sainte-Cathérine

Sheltered from the E and partially sheltered from the SE, there is an anchorage with four mooring buoys NW of Fort de la Rade.

⊕415-SW Aix (46°00'.70N 1°11'.04W)

⚓ Bébé-Plage

Sheltered from the SW, Bébé-Plage off the NE coast makes a pleasant fine weather anchorage. Night departure to La Rochelle would be very easy. There are three visitors' buoys.

⊕418-NE Aix (46°01'.38N 1°09'.35W)

ASHORE IN ILE D'AIX

The village has modest shops and some cafés and restaurants. Bicycles and horse drawn carriages are also available for a tour of the island. A walk round the island will take about 2½ hours. There are two museums and two forts.

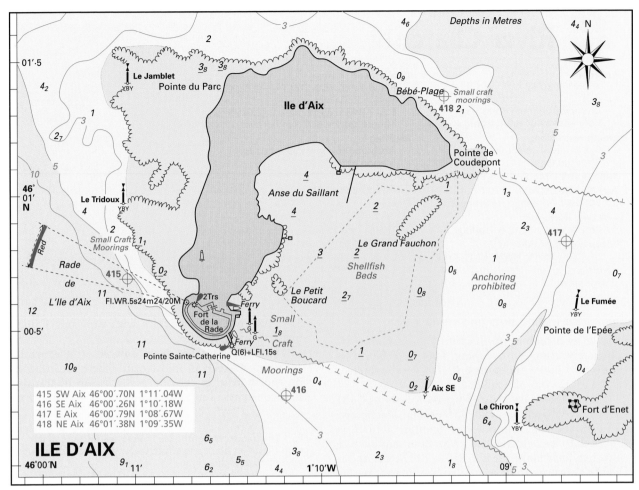

Depths in Metres

Le Jamblet YBY
Pointe du Parc
Ile d'Aix
Bébé-Plage *Small craft moorings* 418 2₁
Pointe de Coudepont
Le Tridoux YBY
Anse du Saillant
Le Grand Fauchon
Shellfish Beds
Small Craft Moorings
Le Tridoux
Rade de L'Ile d'Aix
415
Fl.WR.5s24m24/20M
2Trs
Fort de la Rade
Ferry
Le Petit Boucard
Anchoring prohibited
417
Le Fumée YBY
Pointe de l'Epée
Ferry
Q(6)+LFl.15s
Pointe Sainte-Catherine
Small Craft Moorings
416
Aix SE Y
Le Chiron YBY
Fort d'Enet

415	SW Aix	46°00′.70N	1°11′.04W
416	SE Aix	46°00′.26N	1°10′.18W
417	E Aix	46°00′.79N	1°08′.67W
418	NE Aix	46°01′.38N	1°09′.35W

ILE D'AIX
46°00′N

Plan 74

74.1 Ile d'Aix is a small, flat island with two conspicuous lighthouses on the SW side

74.2 Fort Boyard can be sailed round but not visited

74.3 In Anse du Saillant, shellfish are raised on numerous wooden posts. These cover at high tide.

75 River Charente

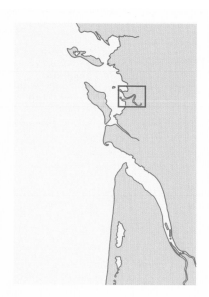

Location
   45°59′N 1°07′W
Hazard
   Dangerous bar at Fouras
   Bore above Rochefort at big springs
Depth restrictions
   Bar at entrance has 0.8m
   River has 0.8m
Night entry Lit to Port-des-Barques
HW time Ile d'Aix
   PdG HW +¼ neaps, −¾ springs
HW time Rochefort
   PdG HW +½ neaps, −¼ springs
Mean height of tide (m)

	HWS	HWN	LWN	LWS
Ile d'Aix	6.1	4.9	2.4	0.9
Rochefort	6.5	5.3	2.2	0.8

Tidal stream in river
   Flood – PdG HW–5½ to +½ (2.0kts)
   Slack – PdG+½ to +1½
   Ebb – PdG HW+1½ to –5½ (2.0kts)
   Stream can be 4.0kts in narrows
Berthing
   Anchorages and visitors' buoys
   Marina at Rochefort
Facilities
   All facilities at Rochefort
Charts
   BA 2747 (20)
   SHOM 7415 (20)
   Imray C41 (109)

River with fishing huts and sunflowers

Despite its proximity to Rochefort, the Charente is completely rural with fishing huts and fields of sunflowers lining the banks. It is a very attractive river with masses of wildlife.

It is navigable for masted yachts for about 16M to Tonnay-Charente, about 3M beyond Rochefort. Motorboats can continue to Saintes, which is reported to be a delightful trip. Even quite large ships regularly make the passage to Rochefort and it is quite a surprise to be overtaken by a coaster in this idyllic rural setting.

Older charts show a lifting bridge below Rochefort. This has been removed and replaced by a bridge with 32m of headroom.

PILOTAGE

The Charente to Tonnay-Charente

Warning

There is a dangerous bar at the mouth of the river, near Fouras. Seas break heavily on the ebb in wind against tide conditions so it is best to cross the bar as close to HW as possible on the flood if the wind is from W or NW.

By GPS

The Charente requires visual pilotage; the following waypoints may help in the entrance.
⊕419-Charente, ⊕420-Charente 1,
⊕421-Charente 2, ⊕422-Charente 3,
⊕423-Charente 4.

By day

Start from a position S of Ile d'Aix and close N of Les Palles NCM. The first transit is beyond Royan. It is a very tall red-topped white lighthouse in line with a stubby red-topped white lighthouse on 115°. There is a tall radio mast nearby. The second transit is two lighthouses in Port-des-Barques in line on 135°. The rear lighthouse has a black, pointed roof and the front light is white with ears and a small black window.

Once the river has been entered it is generally sufficient to keep in midstream. There are beacons on the shore that provide a succession of transits. Each one carries a conspicuous letter, running from

75.1 The low front lighthouse in Port-des-Barques in line with the taller black and white tower. Note the conspicuous white house on the right

75.2 The A transit near Rochefort. The letter transits are really only for use by ships

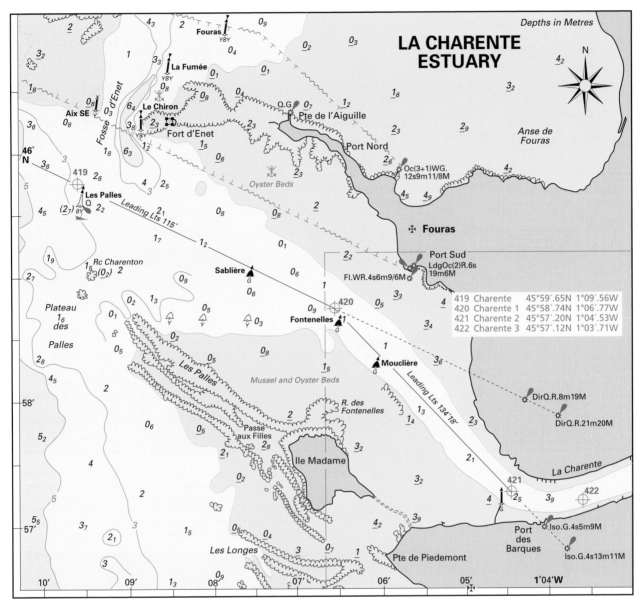

Plan 75A

T at Port-des-Barques to A, just below Rochefort. These are fun to follow but they are only really necessary for the coasters.

By night

The leading lines are lit as far as Port-des-Barques. Night passage beyond there is not permitted for small craft.

BERTHS AND ANCHORAGES

Port-des-Barques

Sheltered, except from the NW, there is an anchorage at Port-des-Barques, just upstream from the village in 2–3m.

Soubise

Soubise has a visitors' pontoon and some visitors' moorings. Alternatively, anchor on the S side of the river as near to the bank as possible. Soubise is an attractive village with a range of shops.

The Yacht Club de Rochefort

The Yacht Club de Rochefort is on the E bank downstream of Soubise. It has landing facilities and a number of moorings along the opposite bank.

Rochefort

(See Chapter 76)

Tonnay-Charente

Tonnay-Charente is 3M beyond Rochefort at the limit of masted navigation. It has a modern pontoon that may be available for visitors but the depth is unknown. There are shops, cafés and restaurants and a splendid, historic suspension bridge.

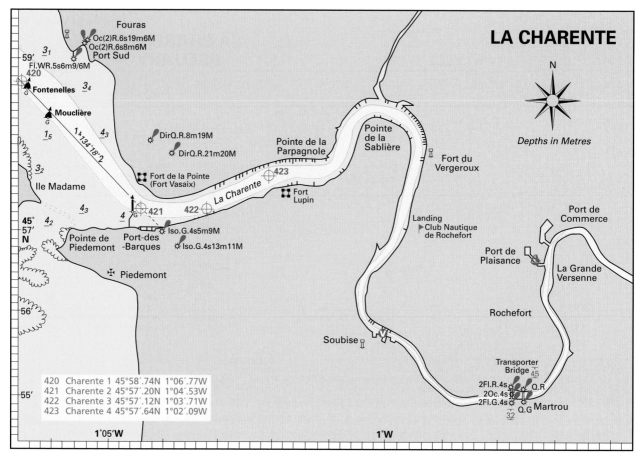

Plan 75B

75.3 The Transbordeur is just a few miles below Rochefort. It is one of five that were built in France at the beginning of the 20th century. Apart from being a fine example of industrial art, it was built to allow large masted ships to pass up and down the river. The bridge is 164 feet (50 metres) high and is now used as a tourist attraction

75.4 Fort Lupin

75.5 Surprisingly large ships go to Rochefort commercial docks

75.6 Just above Port des Barques the banks are lined with
fishing huts built on long walkways

76 Rochefort

Location
45°57'N 0°57'W
Shelter
Good in Rochefort marina
Depth restrictions
River has 0.8m
Marina has 1.8m or more
Rochefort lock and bridge opening
Rochefort HW–¼ to +¼ (approx)
Night entry Forbidden.
HW time Rochefort
PdG HW +½ neaps, –¼ springs
Mean height of tide (m)

	HWS	HWN	LWN	LWS
Rochefort	6.5	5.3	2.2	0.8

Tidal stream in river
Flood – PdG HW–5½ to +½ (2.0kts)
Slack – PdG+½ to +1½
Ebb – PdG HW+1½ to –5½ (2.0kts)
Stream can be 4.0kts in narrows
Berthing
Marina at Rochefort
Facilities
Marina facilities, good shops,
restaurants and museums.
Charts
BA 2748 (20)
SHOM 7415 (20)
Imray C41 (109)
Radio VHF 9
Telephone
Harbourmaster *t* 05 46 83 99 96
or *t* 06 86 01 64 29

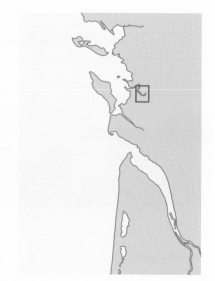

Historic naval shipyard

Rochefort is a delight. It was created by Colbert in the 17th century as a naval arsenal to rival Toulon. The dignified architecture from that period is still largely preserved. The original ropewalk is particularly fine and has been made into a rope museum. Alongside the museum, craftsmen are building a replica of the 1779 frigate *L'Hermione* using traditional methods.

Rochefort has all the facilities of a regional centre, including excellent communications. This and the good facilities for yachtsmen, helpful marina staff and reasonable prices make it a good place to keep a yacht.

PILOTAGE

See Chapter 75

BERTHS

Rochefort Port de Plaisance

The lock to the marina usually opens at about HW La Rochelle and remains open for between ½ hr and 1½ hr. The exact times are given in a booklet *Le Guide de la Plaisance Rochefortaise* that is given away in port offices throughout the region. Alternatively call the port on 06 86 01 64 29 to find the lock times or to book a space.

The entrance to the marina requires a sharp turn to port just after the splendid 17th-century ropewalk. There is a waiting pontoon in the river outside and another at the entrance to the lock. The outside pontoon may be used for up to 24 hours. It dries but the bottom is soft mud.

When the lock opens, the two inner bridges open at the same time. Visitors are directed to a berth. Those staying longer than one night normally go into the second basin, Bassin Bougainville.

The berths are not well labelled and there is often a queue of boats entering when the lock opens, so

76.1 Bassin No. 1 at Rochefort has fine 17th-century buildings along one side

manoeuvring can be interesting. It is best to leave as much space as possible behind the boat in front and be prepared to secure temporarily to the wall or another boat.

ASHORE IN ROCHEFORT

The marina has all facilities except a fuel berth. There are chandlers, engineers and repairs. The marina has a small crane for masting and mobile cranes are used for lift out. They also have storage afloat or ashore.

Rochefort is a wealthy town with an excellent range of shops, cafés and restaurants. There is a supermarket upstream on the road by the river and an excellent street market in town on Tuesday, Thursday and Saturday. Car hire is by the marina and the railway station is within walking distance.

76.2 Bassin No. 2 has a Mediterranean atmosphere

The ropewalk, maritime museum and dry-dock, where the replica frigate *L'Hermione* is being rebuilt, are all close to the marina and well worth visiting.

The old transporter bridge is a couple of miles S of the marina. It was restored in 1994 and takes cyclists and pedestrians across the river.

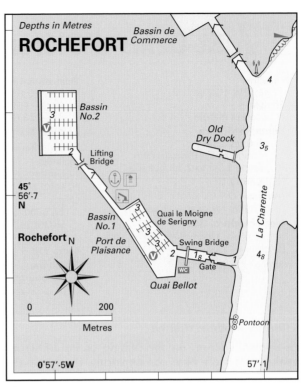

Plan 76

76.3 The River Charente and Rochefort looking N. The waiting pontoon in the river can be seen just downstream of the lock entrance. Bassin No.2 is entered through the narrow canal with a lifting bridge at the end

77 St-Denis-d'Oléron

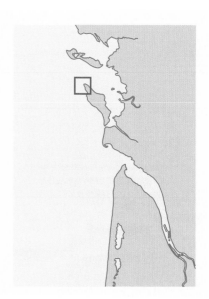

Location
46°02′N 1°22′W

Shelter
Good in marina

Depth restrictions
Sill dries 1.5m
Waiting buoys 0.7m to 1.0m
Marina 1.5m to 2.5m but silts

Night entry Lit

HW time
PdG HW +¼ neaps, −¾ springs

Mean height of tide (m)

	HWS	HWN	LWN	LWS
Ile d'Aix	6.5	5.3	2.2	0.8

Tidal stream in approach
E – PdG HW–5½ to –½ (1.9kts)
Slack – PdG–½ to +½
W – PdG HW+½ to –5½ (2.3kts)

Berthing Marina

Fuel Marina entrance

Facilities
Limited repairs but good shops,
cafés and restaurants

Charts
BA 3000 (50)
SHOM 7405 (50)
Imray C41 (large scale)

Radio VHF 9

Telephone
Harbourmaster *t* 05 46 47 97 97

Friendly modern marina

St-Denis-d'Oléron, on the NE tip of Ile d'Oléron, makes a perfect base for exploring the N of the island. There are sheltered family beaches nearby and the wilder beaches of the windward W side are not far away. Ile d'Oléron is particularly well set up for cyclists and bikes can be hired near the marina.

The marina is modern and purpose built and offers good shelter and good facilities. The attractive village is about ¼M away.

PILOTAGE

St-Denis approach and entrance

By GPS

From the W and NW use ⊕424-N Oléron, ⊕425-St Denis, ⊕426-St Denis 1.

From NE and E use ⊕425-St Denis, ⊕426-St Denis 1.

From the SE use ⊕427-E St Denis, ⊕426-St Denis 1. This route passes over rocks that dry 0.6m but be careful not to stray further S because there are some much shallower rocks.

By day

Avoid the shoals N of the island and start the approach from a position quite well E of the town (⊕427-E St Denis). Approach with the church spire in line with the green beacon pole on 260°. In the final approach, leave the green beacon 100m to starboard and alter course to starboard to leave the red beacon well to port. In the season the channel is marked with small red and green buoys.

By night

Start from a position about 2M NNE of the harbour. Approach in the narrow white sector of the directional light on 205°. On entering the white sector of the E breakwater light, alter to starboard to enter the marina. Leave the E breakwater 40m to starboard to avoid an outcrop of sand and stones encroaching on the channel.

77.1 The visitors' pontoon is to port just beyond the fuel dock. Larger boats raft alongside but there may be finger pontoons for smaller boats

77.2 St-Denis d'Oléron looking S. The marina has been dug out of the sand and has a sill at the entrance. At low water the bay outside the marina dries

BERTHS

St-Denis Marina

The visitors' pontoon is to port just beyond the fuel dock. The marina silts so note the depth at the sill to be able to calculate the depth of water in the marina when the sill dries.

There are three waiting buoys 1M ENE of the entrance.

ASHORE IN ST-DENIS D'OLERON

The marina has a fuel berth at the entrance but there are no repair facilities on site. The bike hire shops are in the road just outside the marina. Further along is the village with shops, including a good supermarket and a daily market.

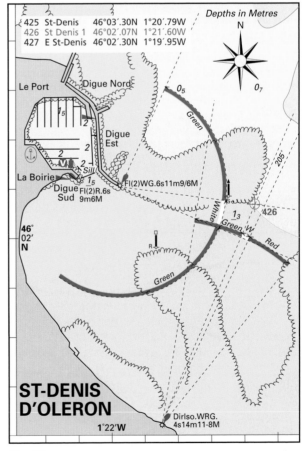

Plan 77

78 Port du Douhet

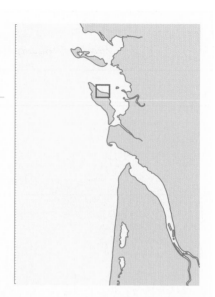

Location
46°00′N 1°19′W
Shelter
Good in marina
Hazard
Overfalls in entrance in NE wind
against ebb
Depth restrictions
Entrance dredged 1.0m
Sill dries 1.8m
Visitors' pontoon 1.5m
Night entry Not lit
HW time
PdG HW +¼ neaps, −¾ springs

Mean height of tide (m)

	HWS	HWN	LWN	LWS
Ile d'Aix	6.5	5.3	2.2	0.8

Tidal stream in approach
SE – PdG HW–5½ to +½ (2.0kts)
Slack – PdG+½ to +1½
NW – PdG HW+1½ to –5½ (2.0kts)
Berthing Marina
Facilities Limited facilities
Charts
BA 3000 (50)
SHOM 7405 (50)
Imray C41 (large scale)
Radio VHF 9
Telephone
Harbourmaster *t* 05 46 47 10 28

Quiet marina with good beaches

Port du Douhet is about 3M SE of St-Denis-d'Oléron. It is quiet, well sheltered and attractively set amongst pine trees. There are good beaches nearby but it is a long way from town.

PILOTAGE

Port du Douhet approach and entrance

Warning

The entrance is a narrow dredged channel across ½M of sand and rock that dries 2.5m or more. It must be positively identified before attempting an entrance. Note that the channel can be quite rough in N and E winds.

By GPS

The channel into Douhet shifts so the following waypoints only provide an indication of the route ⊕428-Douhet, ⊕429-Douhet 1.

By day

Coming from the N, keep at least 2M offshore. Start the approach from Douhet NCM (⊕428-Douhet). Steer 250° towards the marina and locate the red and green buoys that mark the channel. Follow the

78.1 Port du Douhet looking N.
Unlike the E coast of Ile d'Oléron where mussel and oyster farming predominates, the N coast is mainly given over to tourism. The beaches are wonderful and there are miles of bicycle tracks

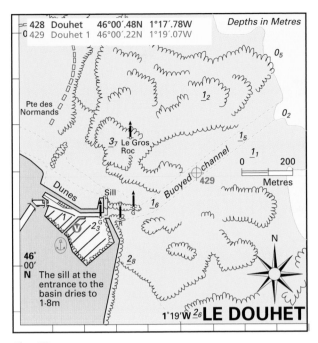

Plan 78

78.2 The buoyed channel to Le Douhet marina at low water

buoyed channel past two beacon SHMs into the marina.

Once inside, turn sharply to port into the first basin. The visitors' pontoon is in the NW of the basin.

ASHORE IN LE DOUHET

The marina has limited facilities and no fuel berth. There are a few small shops, including a baker and bike hire. Otherwise, the nearest shops are at La Brée les Bains (3km) or St Georges d'Oléron (4km).

Douhet is well placed for visiting the safe family beaches and pine forests between Douhet and Boyardville.

78.3 Once inside the rocky breakwater turn sharply to port in front of the yellow post, which will only just be sticking up out of the water. Turn to starboard to reach the visitors' pontoon at D. There is not much room for manoeuvring

79 Boyardville

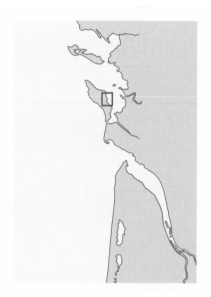

Location
45°58'N 1°14'W
Shelter
Good in marina
Depth restrictions
Entrance dries 2.0m
Sill dries 1.8m
Visitors' pontoon 1.5m
Night entry partially lit
HW time
PdG HW +¼ neaps, –¾ springs
Mean height of tide (m)

	HWS	HWN	LWN	LWS
Ile d'Aix	6.5	5.3	2.2	0.8

Tidal stream in approach
As Ile d'Aix
2kts in river
Berthing Marina
Fuel
Opposite marina entrance
Facilities All facilities
Charts
BA 3000 (50)
SHOM 7405 (50)
Imray C41 (large scale)
Radio VHF 9
Telephone
Harbourmaster *t* 05 46 47 23 71

Small marina in a pleasant fishing town

Boyardville has a small marina in a locked basin accessed by tidal river. The basin is perfectly sheltered, in the centre of town, surrounded by shops and cafés. The ambience is pleasant but it does become busy in season.

On the weekend after 14 July a spectacular firework display takes place at Fort Boyard, 2M off the port. This can be watched from the beach, N of the town or from a boat at anchor off the beach.

PILOTAGE

Boyardville approach and entrance

By GPS

From the NW use ⊕430-W Boyard, ⊕431-Boyardville, ⊕432-Boyardville 1.
From the Charente or La Rochelle via Fosse d'Enet use
⊕419-Charente, ⊕431-Boyardville, ⊕432-Boyardville 1.

By day

Start from a position close to La Perrotine SHM, which is about 2M S of the conspicuous Fort Boyard

79.1 Boyardville marina and the river entrance looking NE.
On the W side of the marina are a row of cafés and shops. The car park to the S is used for the market. The marshes are close by for walking or cycling and on Ile d'Oléron a beach is never far away

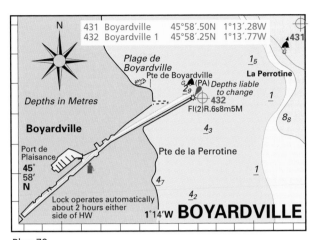

Plan 79

79.2 Once in the river look for the fuel berth and get ready for a sharp turn to starboard.

(see 74.2). Steer about 260° towards the breakwater and the second SHM buoy close to the breakwater. The channel shifts so watch the depth and be prepared to follow the deepest water. Once past the breakwater head, the best water is usually on the S side of the channel.

Continue into the river entrance and be prepared for a very sharp turn to starboard into the marina. The turn comes just after the fuel berth and it is important not to cut the corner: almost go past the entrance before turning.

The gates into the wet basin are automatically operated by the water level. They generally open HW±1 hour at neaps and HW±2½ hours at springs.

By night
The mole head is lit but night entry is not recommended.

BERTHS AND ANCHORAGES

Port du Boyardville
Visitors' berth on the pontoon to starboard of the entrance or on a pontoon berth as directed by the harbourmaster.

Drying out, alongside one of the quays in the river, may be possible but the bottom is uneven in places so check with the harbourmaster first.

Visitors' moorings
About ½M NNW of La Perrotine SHM there are six visitors' buoys and a large number of small craft moorings. Boyardville charges for their use and, in return, provides a taxi service to the beach. Alternatively, anchor nearby but note that the bottom shoals rapidly.

ASHORE IN BOYARDVILLE

The marina has all facilities including a fuel berth on the riverbank opposite the marina entrance.

Boyardville is a small town with a full range of shops close to the marina. It is a good base for exploring the coast by bicycle. The Atlantic beaches are spectacular and run for miles along most of the W coast. The SE coast is devoted to oyster and mussel farming, which is operated out of picturesque shacks in muddy creeks.

79.3 The lock gate is before the aluminium walkway and around the boats moored on the corner. Almost go past the entrance before turning

79.4 Visitors moor to starboard just inside the lock gate

80 The Seudre to Marennes

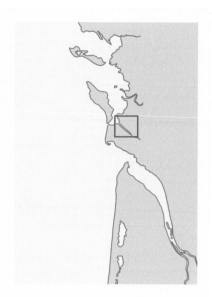

Location
45°49'N 1°10'W

Shelter
Excellent in Marennes marina

Hazard
Pertuis Maumusson is not advised in any conditions

Depth restrictions
Entrance dries 1.0m
Marennes canal dries 2.5m

Height restriction
Road bridge 15m

Night entry Not lit

HW time La Cayenne (R. Seudre)
PdG HW +½ neaps, −¼ springs

Mean height of tide (m)

	HWS	HWN	LWN	LWS
La Cayenne	5.6	4.6	2.4	1.0

Tidal stream in N approach
S – PdG HW−5¾ to +1¼ (2.1kts)
N – PdG HW+1¼ to −5¾ (1.7kts)
Complex at mouth of Seudre
4kts in Seudre

Berthing
Marina

Facilities
Basic facilities, good supermarket

Charts
BA 3000 (50)
SHOM 7405 (50), 7414 (25)

Telephone
Marennes marina t 05 46 85 02 68

Oyster capital of France

Marennes is the centre of a huge area of marshes and tidal mud flats that stretch from Rochefort to Royan and include much of the E side of Ile d'Oléron. The water is mostly shallow, the tides are strong and the area is dedicated to the culture of the renowned Marennes-Oléron oyster. Visiting boats are neither appropriate nor particularly welcome. Nevertheless, it is a fascinating area with outstanding seafood and can be visited in suitable conditions. There are several anchorages and a small marina at Marennes.

PILOTAGE

Pertuis de Maumusson

Warning

The Pertuis de Maumusson is the passage S of Ile d'Oléron. It has a very dangerous bar that moves

80.1 Marennes Canal.
The tall spire of Marennes church is visible for miles in this flat landscape

and may be shallower than shown on the chart. The strong tide over this bar causes breaking seas even in good weather. Royan lifeboat coxswain advises visitors not to attempt the passage, even in perfect weather.

The Seudre River from the N

By GPS

The passage requires careful visual pilotage; the following waypoints may help in the approach to Charret beacon: ⊕433-E Oléron, ⊕434-Charret.

By day

The channel is intricate and the pilotage is mostly buoy hopping so an up to date version of the large-scale chart SHOM 7414 is recommended. Note that the direction of buoyage is from the S.

Start from a position close to ⊕433-E Oléron. Steer 157° with Marennes church spire in line with the Juliar beacon ECM. Leave Juliar beacon to starboard and continue on the same course using the Charret beacon (black rectangle with a white circle on a tall pole) in line with Marennes church, still on 157°. About ½M from the Charret beacon (⊕434-Charret) turn to starboard and steer about 220° to leave Agnas SHM to starboard (i.e. the wrong side going S) and follow the buoys round the S side of Bank d'Agnas to the bridge.

The two preferred routes under the bridge (height 15m) are marked with either a red square or a green triangle on a white square. The SE route is easier and has deeper water but the NW one is believed to have more headroom. Pass under the bridge, taking care to avoid the wreck S of the bridge, and follow the buoys to Bry NE SHM. Turn sharply back to port and steer 115° towards Soumaille NW PHM, which is the start of the River Seudre. Follow the buoys up the river and under the road bridge (height 18m) to La Cayenne at the entrance to the Marennes canal.

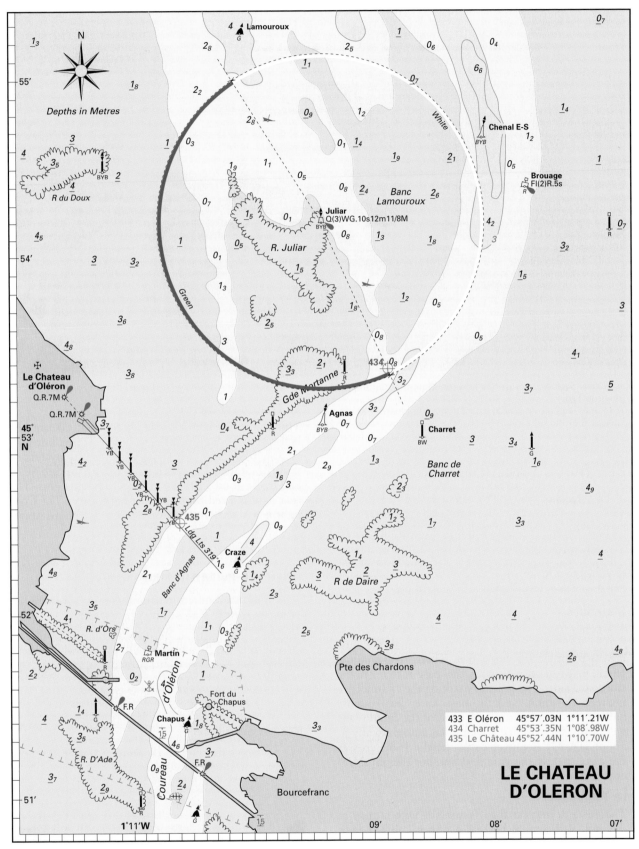

N

Depths in Metres

R du Doux

55'

54'

45°
53'
N

52'

51'

Le Chateau
d'Oléron
Q.R.7M
Q.R.7M

Lamouroux

Chenal E-S

Brouage
Fl(2)R.5s

Banc
Lamouroux

Juliar
Q(3)WG.10s12m11/8M

R. Juliar

White

Green

Gde Mortanne

434

Agnas

Charret

Banc de
Charret

435

Craze

Banc d'Agnas

Ldg Lts 319

R de Daire

R. d'Ors

Martin

d'Oléron

Pte des Chardons

Fort du
Chapus

Chapus

R. D'Ade

Coureau

Bourcefranc

1°11'W

09'

08'

07'

433	E Oléron	45°57'.03N	1°11'.21W
434	Charret	45°53'.35N	1°08'.98W
435	Le Château	45°52'.44N	1°10'.70W

LE CHATEAU
D'OLERON

Plan 80A

80.2 River Seudre, La Cayenne and the Marennes Canal looking NW.
The canal leads from La Cayenne to the small marina at Port de Marennes

BERTHS AND ANCHORAGES

⚓ La Cayenne

The best anchorages are near the disused ferry slips at La Cayenne (N bank) and at the entrance to La Tremblade canal about ½M upstream on the S bank. Anchor near the side of the river and land at the ferry slip. Above the entrance to the Tremblade canal is a wreck, marked by a green buoy.

Marennes

Marennes has a small marina in an old dock.

The entrance to the Marennes canal lies just downstream of the ferry pier. There is a shallow patch in the entrance with the best water on the starboard side. The perches marking the channel are high on the mud, and the best water lies roughly halfway between them. At the end of the canal is the wet basin, the gates of which open automatically at about HW±1. A power cable (height 16m) crosses the canal below the gate and another (height 24m) crosses the dock.

La Tremblade

There is a drying canal to Tremblade with a quay at the end of the canal beyond a power cable (height 15m), but there is very little room for visitors. It is very attractive with much oyster farming activity, but best visited by dinghy.

La Tremblade is a small market town with a boatyard, marine repair facilities and a range of shops and restaurants.

Le Château d'Oléron

This is an oyster port on the E coast of Oléron just before the bridge. Yachts are not welcome but may be able to secure for a short while to buy oysters or visit the citadel. Approach from Mortagne Sud SCM and make good 319° towards the leading lights. The rear light is a red-topped white light tower. The front light is a squat white tower with a red board above it.

⊕435-Le Château (45°52′.44N 1°10′.70W)

ASHORE IN MARENNES

Marennes has limited marina facilities but there are modest shops, cafés and restaurants. A large hypermarket is at the rear of the post office a few minutes' walk through the municipal gardens. There are markets on Tuesdays, Thursdays and Saturdays. The church tower can be visited to see the panoramic view of the marshes.

80.3 Port de Marennes

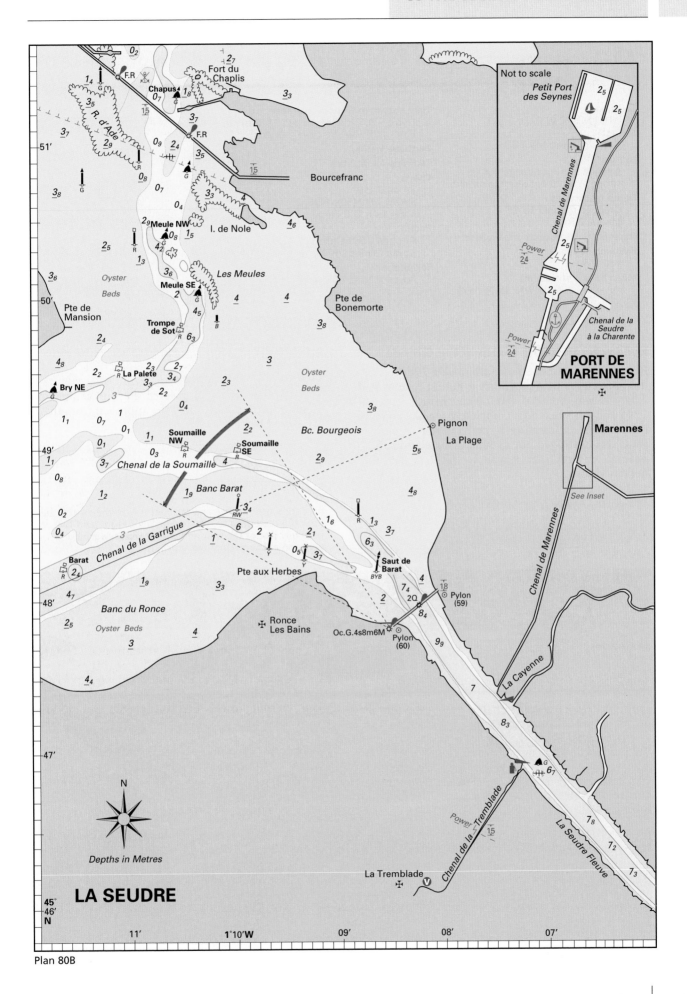

Not to scale

Petit Port des Seynes

2_5
2_5

Chenal de Marennes

Power 2_4

2_5

Power 2_4

2_5

Chenal de la Seudre à la Charente

PORT DE MARENNES

Marennes

See Inset

Fort du Chaplis

0_2

2_7

1_4

F.R

Chapus 1_8
0_7

3_5

R. d'Ade

1_5

3_3

3_7

2_9

F.R

0_9 2_4

3_5

51'

3_7

0_8

1_5

Bourcefranc

3_8

0_7

3_3

0_4

4_6

2_9 **Meule NW**
0_8 1_5

I. de Nole

2_5

4_2

1_3

Les Meules

3_6

Pte de Bonemorte

3_6

Meule SE
2

Oyster Beds

4

4

50'

Pte de Mansion

4_5

3_8

Trompe de Sot
6_3

2_4

3

4_8

2_3 2_7

Oyster

2_2 **La Palete** 3_4

3_3

Beds

Bry NE
3

2_2

0_4

2_3

1_1 0_7 1

3_8

Pignon

49'

0_1

1_1

Soumaille NW 2_2

Bc. Bourgeois

La Plage

1_1

0_3 4 **Soumaille SE**

2_9

5_5

1_1

3_7

Chenal de la Soumaille

0_8

4_8

1_2

1_9 **Banc Barat**

0_2

3_4

1_6

1_3

RW

0_4

6 2 2_1

3_7

6_3

Barat
2_4

Chenal de la Garrigue 1

0_5 3_7

Saut de Barat
BYB

4

1_9

Pte aux Herbes

2

7_4
2Q

4

1_8
Pylon (59)

4_7

Banc du Ronce

3_3

8_4

48'

2_5

Oyster Beds

Ronce Les Bains

2

9_9

3

4

Oc.G.4s8m6M

Pylon (60)

4_4

7

Chenal de Marennes

8_3

La Cayenne

47'

6_7

N

La Seudre Fleuve

Power 1_5

7_8

Chenal de la Tremblade

7_2

Depths in Metres

7_3

45°
46'
N

LA SEUDRE

La Tremblade

11'

1°10'W

09'

08'

07'

Plan 80B

81 Royan

Location
45°37′N 1°02′W
Shelter
Good in Royan Marina
Hazard
Gironde entrance dangerous in strong W wind or swell against ebb
Depth restrictions
Dredged channel 1.7m
Marina 2.5m
Night entry Lit to outer breakwater
HW time Royan
PdG HW
Mean height of tide (m)

	HWS	HWN	LWN	LWS
Royan	5.1	4.2	2.1	1.0

Tidal stream in Gironde entrance
Flood – PdG HW–5½ to +1½ (1.3kts)
Ebb – PdG HW+1½ to –5½ (2.2kts)
Berthing Marina
Facilities All facilities
Charts
BA 3057 (50)
SHOM 7028 (50), 7425 (25)
Imray C41, C42 (large scale)
Radio
Gironde tide height VHF 17
Royan Marina VHF 9, 16
Telephone
Royan Marina *t* 05 46 38 72 22

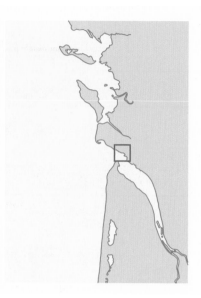

Holiday resort at the mouth of the Gironde

Royan was one of the most fashionable 19th century holiday resorts with magnificent hotels, casinos and villas. It was bombed flat by the British in April 1945 and has since been completely rebuilt. Some of the modern architecture is perhaps not as fine as what was destroyed but its mild climate and superb position ensures that Royan is still a fashionable holiday resort.

PILOTAGE

Coverage of the Gironde

The Gironde is fully covered in the companion volume *South Biscay*. Only the approach from the N is covered here.

81.1 Royan marina looking W.
The fishing harbour is to port of the entrance. The harbourmaster's office and facilities are on the central spur opposite the entrance. The reception pontoon and fuel are on the N side of the spur and visitors moor to a long pontoon at the back of the spur

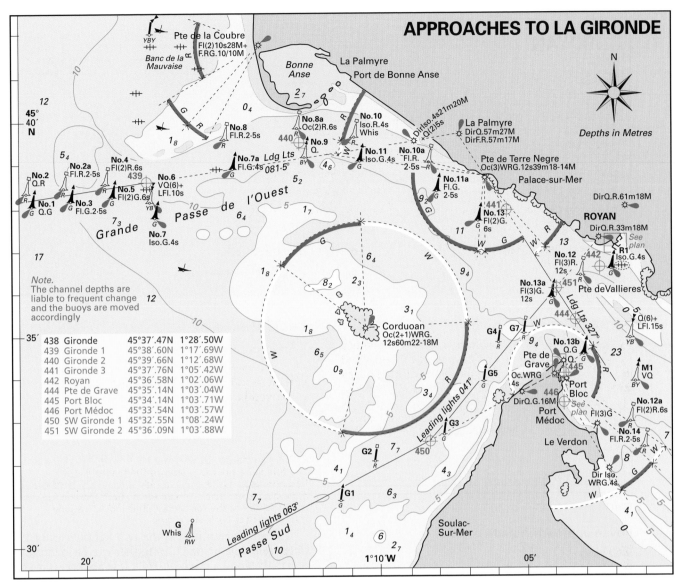

APPROACHES TO LA GIRONDE

Plan 81A

Depths in Metres

Pte de la Coubre
Fl(2)10s28M+
F.RG.10/10M

Banc de la
Mauvaise

Bonne
Anse

La Palmyre
Port de Bonne Anse

DirIso.4s21m20M
+Q(2)5s

La Palmyre
DirQ.57m27M
DirF.R.57m17M

No.8a
Oc(2)R.6s

No.10
Iso.R.4s
Whis

Pte de Terre Negre
Oc(3)WRG.12s39m18-14M

Palace-sur-Mer

DirQ.R.61m18M

ROYAN
DirQ.R.33m18M

See plan

R1
Iso.G.4s

Pte de Vallieres

Q(6)+
LFl.15s

No.8
Fl.R.2·5s

440

No.9
Q.

No.7a
Fl.G.4s

Ldg Lts
081·5°

No.11
Iso.G.4s

No.10a
Fl.R.
2·5s

No.11a
Fl.G.
2·5s

441
No.13
Fl(2)G.
6s

442

No.12
Fl(3)R.
12s

451

No.13a
Fl(3)G.
12s

444

Ldg Lts 327°

No.2a
Fl.R.2·5s

No.4
Fl(2)R.6s

439

No.6
VQ(6)+
LFl.10s

Passe de l'Ouest

Grande

No.2
Q.R

No.1
Q.G

No.3
Fl.G.2·5s

No.5
Fl(2)G.6s

No.7
Iso.G.4s

Corduoan
Oc(2+1)WRG.
12s60m22-18M

G4

G7

W

M1
VQ

No.13b
Q.G

Pte de
Grave
Q.G

445

Port
Bloc

See plan

No.12a
Fl(2)R.6s

G5

Leading lights 041°

Port
Médoc
DirQ.G.16M

Port
Médoc

No.14
Fl.R.2·5s

Le Verdon

Dir Iso.
WRG.4s

W

Note.
The channel depths are
liable to frequent change
and the buoys are moved
accordingly

G3

G2

450

438	Gironde	45°37'.47N	1°28'.50W
439	Gironde 1	45°38'.60N	1°17'.69W
440	Gironde 2	45°39'.66N	1°12'.68W
441	Gironde 3	45°37'.76N	1°05'.42W
442	Royan	45°36'.58N	1°02'.06W
444	Pte de Grave	45°35'.14N	1°03'.04W
445	Port Bloc	45°34'.14N	1°03'.71W
446	Port Médoc	45°33'.54N	1°03'.57W
450	SW Gironde 1	45°32'.55N	1°08'.24W
451	SW Gironde 2	45°36'.09N	1°03'.88W

G1

G
Whis

Leading lights 063°

Passe Sud

Soulac-
Sur-Mer

81.2 Pointe de la Coubre lighthouse and the coastguard
tower looking NE

81.3 The entrance transit is the two lighthouses of La
Palmyre in line on 081°

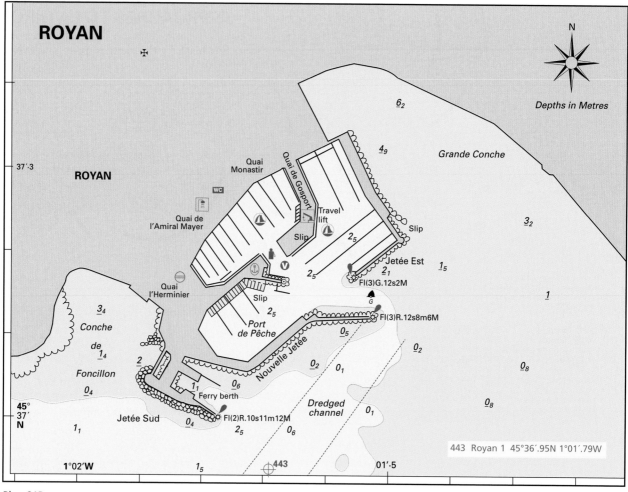

ROYAN

Depths in Metres

Grande Conche

ROYAN

Quai
Monastir

WC

Quai de
l'Amiral Mayer

Travel
lift

Slip

Slip

Jetée Est

Fl(3)G.12s2M

Quai
l'Herminier

Slip

Fl(3)R.12s8m6M

Conche
de

Foncillon

Slip

Port
de Pêche

Nouvelle Jetée

Dredged
channel

Ferry berth

Jetée Sud

Fl(2)R.10s11m12M

443 Royan 1 45°36'.95N 1°01'.79W

Plan 81B

Royan approach from N

Warning

In the mouth of the Gironde, between No. 3 and No. 9 buoys, wind against tide conditions generate very steep seas. In strong W winds against the ebb, the seas are dangerous and may break right across the channel.

In light weather, reliable auxiliary power is necessary to keep out of the breakers on the banks.

Tidal strategy

The best time to enter the Gironde is on the first of the flood. Outward bound, Royan should be left well before HW to be well clear of the channel before the ebb sets in.

By GPS

Use ⊕438-Gironde, ⊕439-Gironde 1, ⊕440-Gironde 2, ⊕441-Gironde 3, ⊕442-Royan, ⊕443-Royan 1.

Note that the channel moves so follow the buoyed channel.

By day

The coast immediately N of the entrance has few conspicuous features. It is essential to keep at least 5M off the land to avoid the dangerous Banc de la Mauvaise. Do not cut the corner and be sure to start the entrance from BXA SWM.

The entrance transit is the two lighthouses of La Palmyre in line on 081°. Until they can be identified, just make good a track of 081°. It is not necessary to follow the transit precisely but it is best to keep in the buoyed channel.

At No. 9 buoy, make good 110° to No.13 Buoy. Leave the main channel at No.13 but continue on the same track to R1 SHM. Just before arriving at R1 SHM, turn to port, for the harbour entrance. Leave the Nouvelle Jetée close to port.

By night

Start in the vicinity of BXA buoy and identify the first pair of leading lights on 081°. As the channel buoys are reached, Pte de La Coubre light turns from red to green. All the channel buoys are lit so follow them to Royan R1 as by day. The three outer breakwaters are lit but the marina breakwaters are not lit.

BERTHS

Royan Marina

The reception berth is on the N side of the central spur to the left of the inner harbour entrance directly below the harbourmaster's office. Secure here unless met by the harbour launch in the entrance.

81.4 Royan visitors' pontoon

ASHORE IN ROYAN

Royan has all the facilities of a major marina including a fuel berth by the visitors' pontoon. It is a good place for de-masting prior to entering the Canal du Midi.

There are some shops, restaurants and cafés at the marina and plenty of shops in town. Royan has an interesting modern covered market.

There are few tourist attractions in the town since Royan is chiefly famous for its beaches, known locally as *conches*. Conche Foncillon is the small, family-friendly beach near the marina. The largest, longest and most famous beach is the Grande Conche.

81.5 Leave the Nouvelle Jetée at Royan to port when entering the marina. Beyond is the wide curve of the Grande Conche beach

82 Port Médoc

Location
45°34'N 1°04'W

Shelter
Good in Port Médoc

Hazard
Gironde entrance dangerous in strong W wind or swell against ebb

Depth restrictions
2.0m to 3.0m in marina

Night entry Not known

HW time Pte de Grave
PdG HW

Mean height of tide (m)

	HWS	HWN	LWN	LWS
Pte de Grave	5.4	4.4	2.1	1.0

Tidal stream at Pte de Grave
Flood – PdG HW–5½ to +1½ (3.6kts)
Ebb – PdG HW+1½ to –5½ (3.8kts)

Berthing Marina

Facilities
Not known but ¾M to shops

Charts
BA 3057 (50)
SHOM 7028 (50), 7425 (25)
Imray C41, C42 (large scale)

Radio
Gironde tide height VHF 17

Telephone
Port Medoc Marina *t* 05 56 09 69 75

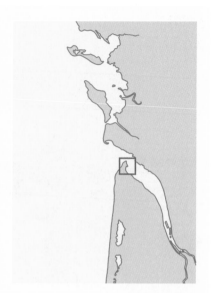

New marina near Port Bloc

Port Médoc is a new 800-berth marina that opened in July 2004. When complete it will have all the equipment and services you would expect from a modern port.

PILOTAGE

Coverage of the Gironde

The Gironde is fully covered in the companion volume *South Biscay*. Only the approach from the N is covered here.

Port Médoc approach from N

(See Plan 81A)

Warning

In the mouth of the Gironde between No. 3 and No. 9 buoys, wind against tide conditions generate very steep seas. In strong W winds against the ebb, the seas are dangerous and may break right across the channel.

In light weather, reliable auxiliary power is necessary to keep out of the breakers on the banks.

Tidal strategy

The best time to enter is on the first of the flood.

Outward bound, Port Médoc should be left well before HW to be clear of the channel before the ebb sets in.

By GPS

Use ⊕438-Gironde, ⊕439-Gironde 1, ⊕440-Gironde 2, ⊕441-Gironde 3, ⊕444-Pte de Grave, ⊕446-Port Médoc.

Note that the channel moves so follow the buoyed channed.

By day

The coast immediately N of the Gironde entrance has few conspicuous features. It is essential to keep at least 5M off the land to avoid the dangerous Banc de la Mauvaise. Do not cut the corner and be sure to start the entrance from BXA SWM.

The entrance transit is the two lighthouse of La Palmyre in line on 081°. Until they can be identified, just make good a track of 081°. It is not necessary to follow the transit precisely but it is best to keep in the buoyed channel.

At No. 9 buoy, make good 110° to No.13 Buoy. When close to it, turn onto 140° towards the Pointe de Grave. The back transit is La Palmyre lighthouse in line with Pointe de Terre-Negre lighthouse on 327°. This need not be followed accurately but the stream can be very strong so the transit provides a useful check. When close to No.13b buoy, turn onto 215° to enter Port Médoc, again allow for the possibility of a very strong stream.

By night

Start in the vicinity of BXA buoy and identify the first pair of leading lights on 081°. As the channel buoys are reached, Pte de La Coubre light turns from red to green. All the channel buoys are lit so follow them until La Palmyre comes in transit with Pointe de Terre-Negre on 327°. Use this as a back transit to enter the river. When Pointe de Grave light turns from white to red alter course to 215° to approach Port Médoc. It is presumed that Port Médoc entrance will be lit but the lights are not yet known.

BERTHS

Port Médoc Marina

The reception berth is to starboard just inside the entrance.

Port Bloc

Port Bloc is a busy ferry port just N of Port Médoc. It does not welcome visiting boats and boats may not enter without prior approval of the harbour authority on VHF 9.

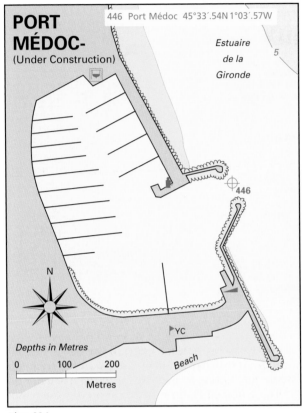

PORT MÉDOC-
(Under Construction)

446 Port Médoc 45°33′.54N 1°03′.57W

Estuaire de la Gironde

N

Depths in Metres

0   100   200

Metres

YC

Beach

Plan 82A

ASHORE IN PORT MEDOC

Port Médoc is expected to have all the facilities of a major marina as well as shops, bars and restuarants. It is in an isolated location about 1M from Le Verdon-sur-Mer but only about 1M from the ferry port of Port Bloc from where regular ferries run to Royan.

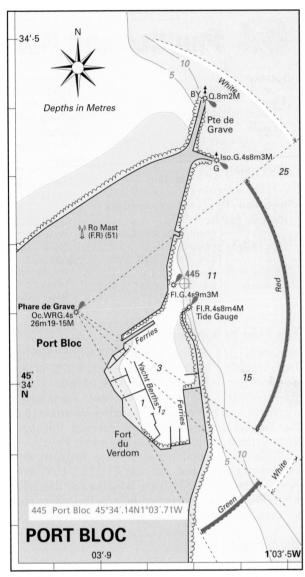

N

Depths in Metres

34′.5

White

BY Q.8m2M

Pte de Grave

Iso.G.4s8m3M

G

25

Red

Ro Mast (F.R) (51)

445 11

Fl.G.4s9m3M

Fl.R.4s8m4M
Tide Gauge

Phare de Grave
Oc.WRG.4s
26m19-15M

Port Bloc

Ferries

Yacht Berths

3

15

1   1₂

Ferries

45°
34′
N

Fort du Verdom

10

5

White

Green

445 Port Bloc 45°34′.14N1°03′.71W

PORT BLOC

03′.9

1°03′.5W

Plan 82B

82.1 Port Bloc and Point de Grave looking N.
Port Médoc is just S of Port Bloc

82.2 The ferry port and marina at Port Bloc. A regular ferry runs from Port Bloc across the Gironde to Royan

83 Pauillac and Bordeaux

Location
45°12′N 0°43′W

Shelter
Good in Pauillac marina

Hazards
Do not enter Pauillac on the ebb and only manoeuvre at slack water

Depth restrictions
2.0m to 3.0m in marina
1.0m in entrance

Night entry Lit but not recommended

HW time Pauillac
PdG HW+2 neaps, +2½ springs

Mean height of tide (m)

	HWS	HWN	LWN	LWS
Pauillac	5.3	4.4	1.1	0.5
Bordeaux	5.3	4.2	0,.4	0.0

Tidal stream at Pte de Grave
Flood – PdG HW–6 to –1 (3.1kts)
Ebb – PdG HW–1 to –6 (4.2kts)

Berthing Marina

Facilities
All facilities, excellent wine

Charts
BA 2916 (50)
SHOM 7427 (52)
Imray C42 (large scale)

Radio
Gironde tide height VHF 17
Pauillac marina VHF 9
Halte nautique VHF 9

Telephone
Pauillac marina *t* 05 46 38 72 22
Lormont YC *t* 05 56 31 50 10
Bassin No 2 *t* 05 56 90 59 57

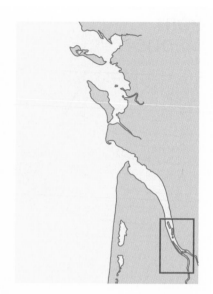

The River to Bordeaux

Bordeaux is a fine city and well worth visiting. Unfortunately, masted yachts must berth in the outskirts, a long way from the tourist sights. Furthermore, the estuary is not particularly attractive and becomes increasingly industrialised as the city is approached. Unless entering the canal system, the 55M journey may not justify the effort.

There are several places to stop between Port Medoc and Bordeaux, but only Pauillac, 27M from Port Médoc and 25M from Bordeaux is described here. The estuary is covered fully in the companion volume *South Biscay*.

PILOTAGE

Royan to Bordeaux

Leaving Royan or Port Médoc at low water, and maintaining 5 knots, it is possible to reach Bordeaux on a single tide. In the same way, leaving Bordeaux well before high water, it is possible to carry the ebb all the way to Port Médoc or Royan.

The river is well marked by buoys and beacons and the passage presents no navigational problems. As far as Pauillac, it can be quite rough so a mast carried on deck must be very well secured. If the river is in spate, there is a considerable amount of debris and whole trees may be encountered.

There are no height restrictions before Pont de Pierre in Bordeaux (3.9m). Power cables (height 48m) cross the river above Bordeaux and the Pont d'Aquitaine (height 51m) crosses just before Lormont Yacht Club.

BERTHS AND ANCHORAGES

Pauillac marina

Pauillac marina is on the W bank about halfway between Royan and Bordeaux. The streams are strong in the approach and in the marina so it is best to arrive or leave at slack water. If the tide is running strongly, it is better to anchor and wait for slack tide before attempting to manoeuvre in the marina.

The entrance is close to the shore on the S side and distinctively marked by a 4m lighthouse in the shape of a wine bottle. Approach from the E allowing for the stream. At LW, the entrance is quite narrow and it is necessary to leave the outer breakwater close to starboard. A night entry is not recommended for a first visit.

Berths for visitors are on the first two pontoons to starboard inside the entrance.

⚓ Pauillac

Anchorage is prohibited 200m S of the entrance and it is better to anchor N of the harbour while waiting for daylight or slack water. A waiting buoy is sometimes places S of the entrance.

⊕448-Pauillac (45°11′.86N 0°44′.44W)

83.1 Pauillac marina looking E.
Visitors' berths are on the first two pontoons to starboard near the entrance

83.2 The entrance to Pauillac marina. Mud builds up on the bank on the port side. Keep the outer breakwater close to starboard

83.4 Pont d'Aquitaine and the pontoons at Point du Jour looking SE. Lormont Yacht Club usually has a few visitors' berths available.

83.3 Pauillac marina at LW looking upriver towards Bordeaux

83.5 Basin No. 2, Bordeaux, looking SE

Lormont Yacht Club Bordeaux

Just beyond Pont d'Aquitaine on the W side there are a three pontoons administered by Lormont Yacht Club. Visitors are welcome and there are usually a few available berths. There are some wharves nearby but these are not recommended because of the very strong currents.

Berth alongside and report to the Yacht Club. There are special berthing arms to hold yachts off the pontoon, as there is considerable wash from passing vessels.

Basin No. 2 Bordeaux

It is possible to lock into Basin No. 2 by prior agreement.

ASHORE IN PAUILLAC AND BORDEAUX

Pauillac

Pauillac marina is helpful and welcoming, with good facilities including a small crane for masting.

Pauillac is a pleasant riverside town in the heart of the Médoc wine region. It has a full range of shops, restaurants and cafés. Wine lovers will enjoy sampling the local produce and perhaps visiting some of the great Médoc châteaux. Visits can be arranged through the tourist office.

Lormont Yacht Club

Facilities are limited but there is a small crane that can be used to remove deck-stepped masts of up to 12m. The process is precarious except at slack water and it is better to de-mast at one of the larger marinas downstream.

POINT DU JOUR

Halte nautique

PAUILLAC

La Gironde

Fl.G.4s

Q.R

Q.G

0°44'·5W

45°12'N

100 Metres

442	Royan	45°36'·58N	1°02'·06W
444	Pte de Grave	45°35'·14N	1°03'·04W
445	Port Bloc	45°34'·14N	1°03'·71W
446	Port Médoc	45°33'·54N	1°03'·57W
447	Gironde 4	45°31'·35N	0°59'·52W
448	Pauillac	45°11'·86N	0°44'·44W
451	SW Gironde 2	45°36'·09N	1°03'·88W

Depths in Metres

La Gironde

Pyramide de Beaumont (66)

Port Maubert
F.R.9m5M
F.R.5m5M

Leading Lts 024·5°

Digue de Valeyrac

La Rive

No.26 Fl.R.2·5s

No.24 Q.R.

No.27 Fl.G.2·5s

No.25 Q.G

Banc de Richard

No.22 Fl(2)R.6s

No.23 Fl(2)G.6s

Pile(4)

Tide gauge

No.20 Iso.R.4s

No.21 Iso.G.4s

(Disused) Lt Ho (17)

Oyster Beds

No.18 Fl(2)R.

No.19 Q.G

11

16 Fl.R.2·5s

15 Iso.G.4s 447

Banc des Marguerites

Banc de Talais

Pte de Meschers

Mast (14) 5 Wk

Pyramide de la Garde (52)

Pte aux Oiseaux

Oyster Beds

Fl(2)6s BRB

Q(6)+ LFl.15s

M1 V.Q.

14 Fl.R. 2·5s

13b Q.G

12a Fl(2)R.6s

13a Fl(2)G.6s

13 Fl(3)G.2M Fl.G.3M

Dir.Iso.WRG. 4s12·8M+ Fl.G.2·5s

ROYAN
See plan

DirQ.R. 33m18M

R1 Fl(2)R

Iso.G.4s 442

12 Fl(3)R.12s 451

Pte du Chay

Pte de Grave Oc.WRG.4s19-15M See plan

Dir.QG 22m16M

Port Bloc
Port-Médoc

Q. Fl.G 445

444 Iso.G.4s 446

Ségonzac

Fort (43)

BLAYE
Fl(2)G (96)

Gasworks

Oil Refinery Fl.G.4s

Ile Verte Q.G

Ile Nouvelle

Q(3)R.5s

Fl.G.4s

Ile Nouvelle

Fort Médoc

45°30'N

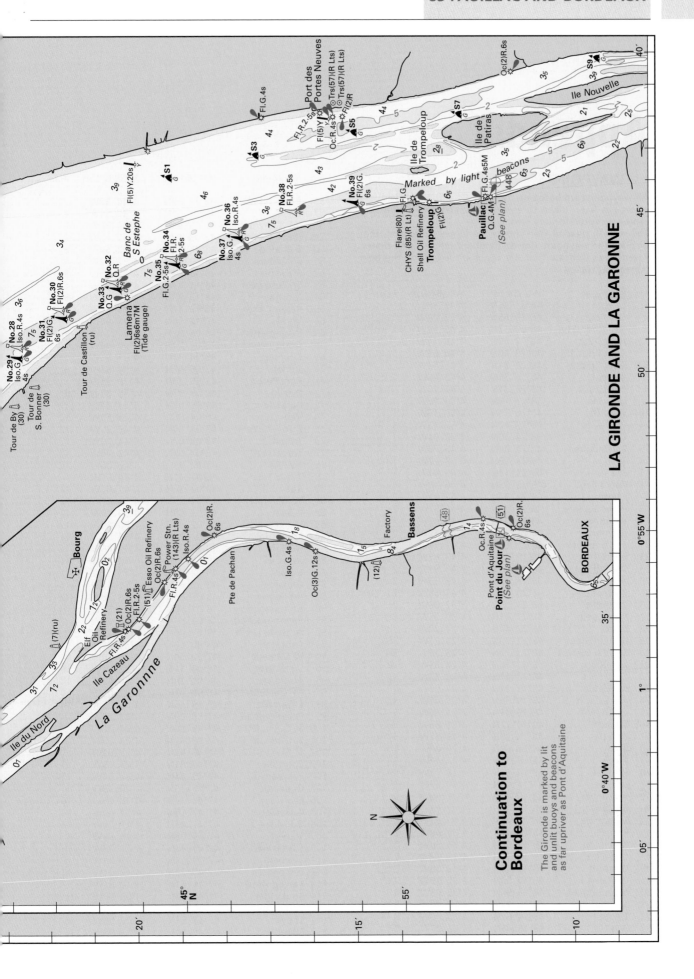

LA GIRONDE AND LA GARONNE

Tour de By (30)
Tour de S. Bonner (30)

No.29 Iso.G.4s
No.28 Iso.R.4s
No.31 Fl(2)G.6s
No.30 Fl(2)R.6s

Tour de Castillon (ru)

Lamena Fl(2)6s6m7M (Tide gauge)

Banc de S Estephe

No.33 Q.G.4 **No.32** Q.R
No.35 Fl.G.2.5s **No.34** Fl.R.2.5s
No.37 Iso.G.4s **No.36** Iso.R.4s

S1 G
S3 G

Fl(5)Y.20s Y

No.38 Fl.R.2.5s
No.39 Fl(2)G.6s

Flare(80) Fl.G.
CHYS (85)IR Lt) Fl.G.
Shell Oil Refinery
Trompeloup Fl(2)G.

Pauillac Q.G.4M Fl.G.4s5M
448 (See plan)

Marked by light beacons

Ile de Trompeloup
Ile de Patiras
Ile Nouvelle

Oc.R.4s
Fl.R.2.5s
Fl(5)Y
Port des Portes Neuves
Fl.G.4s
© Trs(57)/R Lts
© Trs(57)/R Lts
Fl(2)R
S5 G
S7 G
S9 G
Oc(2)R.6s

Continuation to Bordeaux

La Garonnne

Ile du Nord
Ile Cazeau

Bourg

Elf Oil Refinery
Fl.R.4s
(7)(ru)
(21) Oc(2)R.6s
Esso Oil Refinery Oc(2)R.6s
(51) Fl.R.2.5s
Power Stn. (143)/R Lts
Fl.R.4s
Iso.R.4s
Oc(2)R.6s

Pte de Pachan

Iso.G.4s
Oc(3)G.12s

Factory
Bassens
(12)
(48)

Oc.R.4s
Pont d'Aquitaine
Point du Jour (See plan)
Oc(2)R.6s
(51)

BORDEAUX

The Gironde is marked by lit and unlit buoys and beacons as far upriver as Pont d'Aquitaine

45° N
55'

0°55'W   0°40'W   1°   35'   05'

20'
15'
10'

Appendix

⊕ **WAYPOINTS**

All waypoints are based on the WGS 84 datum. While every effort has been taken to ensure their accuracy, no liability can be accepted for any errors.

The column headed *Plan* shows the largest-scale plan that displays the waypoint. Roman numbers indicate area charts. Parentheses indicate that the waypoint is outside the plan but referenced on it.

No	WP Name	WGS84 Lat	WGS84 Lon	Plan
1	Le Four	48°31′.36N	4°49′.38W	1
2	NW Four	48°29′.63N	4°52′.08W	1
3	NW Aber Ildut	48°29′.37N	4°49′.68W	
4	Aber Ildut	48°28′.09N	4°48′.14W	
5	Aber Ildut 1	48°28′.20N	4°46′.65W	
6	Aber Ildut 2	48°28′.21N	4°45′.83W	
7	Porspaul	48°26′.58N	4°48′.08W	
8	Porspaul 1	48°26′.61N	4°47′.26W	
9	Luronne	48°27′.18N	4°54′.80W	1
10	Valbelle	48°26′.39N	4°50′.16W	1
11	Plâtresses	48°25′.22N	4°52′.15W	1
12	Corsen	48°24′.30N	4°48′.91W	1
13	Porsmoguer	48°24′.09N	4°46′.78W	1
14	Taboga	48°23′.18N	4°48′.27W	1
15	St-Pierre	48°23′.13N	4°49′.01W	1
16	Porz-Illien	48°22′.95N	4°46′.18W	1
17	L'Ilette	48°22′.37N	4°47′.37W	2
18	Blanc Sablons	48°22′.27N	4°46′.27W	2
19	Vinotière	48°21′.94N	4°48′.67W	2
20	Kermorven	48°21′.86N	4°47′.72W	2
21	Le Conquet	48°21′.60N	4°47′.11W	2
22	Fourmi	48°19′.25N	4°47′.85W	2
23	St-Mathieu	48°18′.98N	4°46′.97W	2
24	Martel	48°18′.72N	4°42′.33W	2
25	Bertheaume	48°20′.38N	4°41′.58W	2
26	Ste-Anne	48°21′.53N	4°32′.88W	2
27	Pénoupèle	48°21′.41N	4°30′.51W	5
28	Elorn	48°22′.42N	4°27′.28W	3B
29	Moulin Blanc	48°22′.79N	4°25′.86W	3B
30	Moulin Blanc 1	48°23′.22N	4°25′.78W	3A
31	Kéralliou	48°23′.16N	4°24′.83W	3B
32	Camfrout	48°23′.41N	4°23′.63W	4
33	Ile Ronde	48°19′.21N	4°27′.96W	5
34	Auberlac'h	48°19′.55N	4°25′.48W	5
35	La Chèvre	48°19′.41N	4°21′.89W	5
36	Tinduff	48°20′.27N	4°21′.85W	5
37	Daoulas	48°19′.99N	4°19′.57W	5
38	Bindy	48°18′.69N	4°20′.64W	5
39	Aulne	48°18′.33N	4°22′.17W	5
40	Hôpital	48°18′.63N	4°18′.72W	5
41	Le Fret	48°17′.12N	4°30′.17W	5
42	Roscanvel	48°19′.41N	4°31′.58W	5
43	Roscanvel 1	48°18′.81N	4°32′.62W	5
44	Espagnols	48°20′.76N	4°31′.62W	5
45	Robert	48°20′.41N	4°33′.40W	2
46	Kerviniou	48°19′.59N	4°34′.90W	2
47	Capucins	48°19′.10N	4°35′.17W	2
48	Camaret	48°17′.44N	4°36′.08W	7
49	Camaret 1	48°16′.92N	4°35′.19W	7
50	N Toulinguet	48°16′.94N	4°38′.08W	8
51	S Toulinguet	48°16′.13N	4°38′.20W	8
52	Tas de Pois	48°14′.82N	4°38′.40W	8
53	Pen-Hir	48°15′.45N	4°36′.97W	8
54	Dinan	48°15′.04N	4°33′.87W	8
55	Vandrée	48°15′.22N	4°48′.55W	IB
56	Basse du Lis	48°12′.99N	4°44′.58W	
57	Bouc	48°11′.51N	4°37′.51W	8
58	SW Chèvre	48°09′.64N	4°34′.78W	8
59	Basse Vielle	48°08′.12N	4°35′.28W	8
60	S Chèvre	48°08′.44N	4°32′.58W	8
61	SE Chèvre	48°09′.43N	4°32′.32W	8
62	St-Nicolas	48°10′.74N	4°32′.20W	8
63	St-Norgard	48°11′.77N	4°30′.92W	8
64	Morgat	48°13′.39N	4°29′.18W	9
65	Ile de l'Aber	48°13′.42N	4°25′.81W	
66	Verrès	48°12′.56N	4°25′.90W	
67	Douarnenez	48°06′.82N	4°21′.24W	IB
68	Douarnenez 1	48°06′.14N	4°20′.44W	10
69	Coulinec	48°06′.32N	4°21′.05W	
70	Jument	48°06′.62N	4°24′.88W	IB
71	Porz Péron	48°05′.38N	4°29′.35W	
72	Duellou	48°05′.37N	4°35′.83W	IB
73	Basse Jaune	48°05′.01N	4°42′.44W	12
74	Van	48°04′.06N	4°44′.58W	12
75	E Tévennec	48°03′.90N	4°46′.25W	12
76	Trépassés	48°03′.07N	4°44′.19W	12
77	Trépassés 1	48°02′.87N	4°42′.78W	12
78	NW Raz	48°02′.91N	4°46′.26W	12
79	Trouz Yar	48°02′.41N	4°44′.65W	
80	Raz	48°02′.37N	4°45′.86W	12
81	W Tévennec	48°04′.29N	4°50′.47W	12
82	N Sein	48°03′.68N	4°50′.70W	11
83	Vouzerez	48°02′.61N	4°50′.89W	11
84	Men Brial	48°02′.36N	4°50′.85W	11
85	NE Sein	48°03′.30N	4°49′.45W	11
86	Nerroth	48°02′.61N	4°50′.47W	11
87	E Sein	48°02′.61N	4°48′.57W	11
88	Ganaloc	48°02′.61N	4°51′.57W	11
89	SW Raz	48°01′.83N	4°45′.78W	12
90	Koummoudog	48°01′.50N	4°43′.31W	
91	Fuenteun-Aod	48°01′.54N	4°41′.60W	
92	Anse du Loc'h	48°01′.44N	4°38′.29W	
93	Cabestan	48°00′.56N	4°35′.91W	
94	W Gamelle	47°59′.54N	4°33′.00W	14
95	Ste Evette	48°00′.31N	4°32′.87W	14
96	Audierne	48°00′.50N	4°32′.41W	14
97	NE Gamelle	48°00′.07N	4°32′.05W	14
98	E Gamelle	47°59′.46N	4°31′.55W	14
99	Pors-Poulhan	47°59′.00N	4°27′.80W	
100	St Guénolé	47°48′.80N	4°24′.20W	
101	St Guénolé 1	47°48′.41N	4°23′.33W	
102	St Guénolé 2	47°48′.59N	4°22′.99W	
103	Eckmühl	47°46′.81N	4°23′.88W	11
104	Penmarc'h	47°45′.94N	4°25′.08W	11
105	Guilvinec	47°45′.79N	4°20′.33W	II
106	Guilvinec 1	47°46′.72N	4°18′.28W	16
107	Guilvinec 2	47°47′.16N	4°17′.60W	16
108	Guilvinec 3	47°47′.41N	4°17′.22W	16
109	Spineg	47°45′.08N	4°18′.89W	II
110	S Guilvinec	47°45′.42N	4°17′.28W	(16)
111	Lesconil	47°47′.62N	4°12′.51W	17
112	Lesconil 1	47°47′.73N	4°12′.21W	17
113	Karreg Kreiz	47°46′.01N	4°10′.84W	II
114	Boulanger	47°47′.33N	4°08′.98W	II
115	Roustolou	47°46′.48N	4°06′.86W	II
116	Malvic	47°48′.51N	4°06′.88W	II
117	Bilien	47°49′.10N	4°07′.95W	II
118	Loctudy	47°49′.70N	4°07′.58W	II
119	Loctudy 1	47°50′.08N	4°09′.21W	18

No	WP Name	WGS84 Lat	WGS84 Lon	Plan	No	WP Name	WGS84 Lat	WGS84 Lon	Plan
120	Loctudy 2	47°50′.20N	4°09′.70W	18	194	Commerce	47°44′.56N	3°20′.92W	30
121	Loctudy 3	47°50′.19N	4°10′.21W	18	195	Port Louis	47°42′.78N	3°21′.45W	30
122	Bénodet	47°51′.55N	4°06′.42W	19	196	Anéno	47°43′.18N	3°21′.41W	30
123	Bénodet 1	47°52′.19N	4°06′.66W	19	197	Ste-Catherine	47°43′.53N	3°21′.12W	30
124	Astrolabe	47°47′.84N	4°04′.48W	II	198	Blavet	47°44′.29N	3°20′.17W	30
125	La Voleuse	47°49′.32N	4°03′.15W		199	Port Tudy	47°38′.96N	3°26′.46W	32
126	Mousterlin	47°48′.56N	4°02′.48W	II	200	Mélite	47°38′.94N	3°25′.38W	33C
127	Men Vras	47°49′.62N	4°01′.56W		201	Pte de la Croix	47°38′.14N	3°24′.87W	33C
128	Porceaux	47°45′.84N	3°59′.73W	II	202	Cougy	47°37′.96N	3°23′.77W	33C
129	La Pie	47°43′.94N	3°59′.74W	21	203	SE Chats	47°35′.64N	3°23′.42W	33C
130	Bananec	47°43′.24N	3°59′.10W	21	204	Les Chats	47°36′.09N	3°25′.08W	33C
131	Chambre	47°43′.20N	3°59′.56W	21	205	Locmaria	47°36′.54N	3°26′.19W	33C
132	N Penfret	47°43′.94N	3°56′.91W	21	206	Locmaria 1	47°37′.36N	3°26′.39W	33A
133	W Penfret	47°43′.06N	3°57′.93W	21	207	St-Nicolas	47°37′.74N	3°29′.59W	33B
134	E Penfret	47°43′.07N	3°56′.83W	21	208	Etel	47°38′.03N	3°13′.04W	34
135	Ruolh	47°40′.97N	3°54′.89W	II	209	Etel 1	47°38′.65N	3°12′.70W	34
136	Ruolh 1	47°41′.14N	3°56′.36W	21	210	Chiviguete	47°35′.29N	3°13′.93W	III
137	S Glénan	47°38′.52N	4°01′.37W	II	211	W Birvideaux	47°29′.14N	3°18′.91W	III
138	Brilimec	47°39′.14N	3°59′.64W	(21)	212	S Birvideaux	47°27′.44N	3°17′.48W	III
139	Brilimec 1	47°42′.04N	3°57′.90W	21	213	SW Quiberon	47°27′.82N	3°08′.35W	38
140	Brilimec 2	47°42′.46N	3°58′.62W	21	214	Port Maria	47°27′.84N	3°07′.43W	38
141	Bluiniers	47°43′.23N	4°04′.12W	21	215	Port Maria 1	47°28′.49N	3°07′.32W	
142	Broc'h	47°43′.26N	4°01′.38W	21	216	Poulains	47°23′.94N	3°14′.88W	IV
143	SE Beg-Meil	47°50′.73N	3°57′.23W	II	217	Sauzon	47°22′.80N	3°12′.81W	37B
144	Laouen Pod	47°51′.22N	3°57′.96W	II	218	Sauzon 1	47°22′.61N	3°12′.95W	35
145	Beg Meil	47°51′.87N	3°58′.53W		219	Port Jean	47°21′.94N	3°11′.29W	37B
146	Cap Coz	47°52′.81N	3°58′.80W	22	220	Taillefer	47°22′.03N	3°09′.28W	37B
147	La-Forêt	47°53′.39N	3°58′.18W	22	221	Le Palais	47°20′.84N	3°08′.98W	36
148	Vas Hir	47°51′.67N	3°56′.66W		222	Salio	47°19′.84N	3°08′.19W	37B
149	Concarneau	47°51′.35N	3°55′.73W	23	223	Yorc'h	47°19′.65N	3°07′.23W	37B
150	Concarneau 1	47°51′.84N	3°55′.34W	23	224	Port Maria Bl	47°17′.56N	3°04′.38W	37B
151	Kersos	47°51′.83N	3°54′.72W	23	225	Pouldon	47°17′.29N	3°08′.58W	37B
152	Kersos 1	47°51′.56N	3°54′.46W	23	226	Herlin	47°17′.94N	3°10′.39W	37B
153	Concarneau 2	47°51′.99N	3°54′.76W	23	227	Kerel	47°17′.79N	3°12′.22W	37B
154	Concarneau 3	47°52′.22N	3°54′.76W	23	228	Goulphar	47°17′.51N	3°14′.10W	37B
155	Pouldohan	47°50′.47N	3°54′.96W		229	Goulphar 1	47°17′.99N	3°13′.92W	37B
156	Pouldohan 1	47°50′.81N	3°54′.08W		230	Goulphar 2	47°18′.11N	3°13′.72W	(37B)
157	An Houarnou	47°49′.70N	3°54′.27W	II	231	Stêr-Wenn	47°22′.62N	3°15′.82W	37A
158	W Trévignon	47°46′.94N	3°54′.08W	II	232	Stêr-Wenn 1	47°22′.40N	3°15′.15W	37A
159	SW Trévignon	47°46′.40N	3°52′.56W	II	233	S Goué Vas	47°25′.44N	3°04′.87W	38
160	E Glénan	47°42′.54N	3°49′.50W	III	234	E Goué Vas	47°26′.28N	3°03′.98W	38
161	SE Trévignon	47°45′.74N	3°49′.75W	III	235	Teignouse	47°27′.54N	3°02′.30W	38
162	Kersidan	47°46′.93N	3°49′.53W		236	E Teignouse	47°27′.02N	3°01′.26W	38
163	Kersidan 1	47°47′.62N	3°49′.45W		237	S Beniguet	47°23′.67N	3°00′.70W	39
164	Ile Verte	47°45′.98N	3°48′.14W	III	238	Rouleau	47°23′.79N	3°00′.36W	39
165	Raguénez	47°46′.70N	3°47′.71W	III	239	Béniguet	47°23′.79N	2°59′.62W	39
166	Aven & Belon	47°47′.66N	3°43′.91W	24	240	N Béniguet	47°24′.55N	2°59′.97W	39
167	Port Manec'h	47°48′.10N	3°44′.26W	24	241	Portz Ler	47°24′.02N	2°59′.26W	39
168	Belon	47°48′.37N	3°43′.31W	24	242	Hastellic	47°23′.89N	2°58′.74W	39
169	W Brigneau	47°46′.08N	3°40′.09W	26A	243	Portz Navallo	47°23′.76N	2°58′.42W	39
170	Brigneau	47°46′.31N	3°39′.71W	26A	244	St-Gildas	47°23′.61N	2°57′.26W	39
171	Brigneau 1	47°46′.76N	3°40′.09W	26A	245	Er Jeneteu	47°23′.94N	2°56′.51W	39
172	Merrien	47°46′.20N	3°39′.06W	26B	246	En Tal	47°23′.61N	2°56′.08W	39
173	Merrien 1	47°46′.60N	3°39′.02W	26B	247	Er Yoc'h	47°23′.27N	2°56′.08W	39
174	Doëlan	47°45′.70N	3°36′.75W	27	248	E Houat	47°23′.19N	2°55′.17W	39
175	Doëlan 1	47°46′.14N	3°36′.57W	27	249	Gourhed	47°23′.17N	2°56′.99W	39
176	Pouldu	47°45′.17N	3°32′.44W	(28)	250	Houteliguet	47°22′.54N	2°56′.48W	39
177	Pouldu 1	47°45′.74N	3°32′.20W	28	251	Beg Pell	47°22′.03N	2°56′.63W	39
178	Kerroc'h	47°41′.66N	3°28′.09W	29B	252	SE Houat	47°21′.52N	2°56′.08W	39
179	Kerroc'h 1	47°42′.18N	3°28′.09W	29B	253	Chevaux	47°21′.65N	2°58′.23W	39
180	Pérello	47°41′.69N	3°26′.40W	29B	254	Gadoérec	47°22′.24N	2°57′.68W	39
181	Loméner	47°41′.29N	3°25′.58W	29A	255	Chubéguez	47°22′.64N	2°57′.68W	39
182	Loméner 1	47°41′.99N	3°25′.63W	29A	256	Salus	47°22′.81N	2°57′.50W	39
183	W Lorient	47°40′.81N	3°24′.85W	30	257	SW Houat	47°22′.52N	2°59′.08W	39
184	Lorient	47°41′.93N	3°22′.30W	30	258	S Soeurs	47°20′.15N	2°55′.36W	40
185	Lorient 1	47°42′.30N	3°22′.13W	30	259	N Soeurs	47°21′.22N	2°54′.82W	40
186	Larmor Plage	47°42′.29N	3°22′.74W	30	260	NW Hoedic	47°21′.38N	2°53′.50W	40
187	S Lorient	47°40′.67N	3°22′.42W	30	261	Argol	47°20′.74N	2°52′.50W	40
188	Goeland	47°41′.65N	3°22′.21W	30	262	N Hoëdic	47°21′.14N	2°52′.25W	40
189	Cabon	47°42′.10N	3°21′.58W	30	263	NE Hoëdic	47°21′.25N	2°51′.58W	40
190	Souris	47°42′.20N	3°21′.57W	30	264	Gurannic'h	47°20′.79N	2°50′.41W	40
191	Cochon	47°42′.81N	3°21′.95W	30	265	Lannegui	47°20′.30N	2°51′.16W	40
192	Kernéval	47°43′.32N	3°21′.98W	30	266	Lannegui 1	47°20′.35N	2°51′.67W	40
193	Pen Mané	47°44′.24N	3°20′.96W	30	267	SE Hoëdic	47°18′.74N	2°50′.34W	40

No	WP Name	WGS84 Lat	WGS84 Lon	Plan	No	WP Name	WGS84 Lat	WGS84 Lon	Plan
268	Madavoar	47°19′.62N	2°51′.47W	40	342	W St-Gildas	47°07′.89N	2°16′.21W	56B
269	La Croix	47°19′.91N	2°52′.08W	40	343	S St-Gildas	47°07′.34N	2°14′.81W	56B
270	S Hoëdic	47°18′.80N	2°53′.06W	40	344	Pornic	47°06′.35N	2°07′.08W	58
271	Haliguen	47°29′.39N	3°05′.88W	41	345	Pilier	47°03′.52N	2°22′.86W	60
272	Orange	47°31′.32N	3°07′.37W		346	N Herbaudière	47°03′.94N	2°17′.39W	60
273	Colomban	47°33′.79N	3°05′.93W		347	Herbaudière	47°02′.69N	2°17′.62W	59A
274	W Carnac	47°33′.86N	3°04′.40W		348	Herbaudière 1	47°02′.36N	2°17′.69W	59A
275	E Carnac	47°33′.92N	3°03′.32W		349	Herbaudière 2	47°01′.67N	2°17′.83W	59B
276	Trinité	47°33′.48N	3°00′.46W	42	350	W Herbaudière	47°01′.22N	2°20′.33W	60
277	Trinité 1	47°34′.90N	3°00′.95W	42	351	Pères	47°03′.39N	2°14′.37W	60
278	E Trinité	47°32′.59N	2°59′.86W	IVB	352	Chaise	47°00′.59N	2°12′.84W	60
279	Philibert	47°33′.27N	2°58′.94W		353	Noirmoutier	46°59′.37N	2°12′.80W	60
280	Philibert 1	47°33′.76N	2°58′.90W		354	Réaumur	46°57′.44N	2°24′.38W	60
281	Meaban	47°31′.20N	2°57′.86W	IVB	355	Morin	46°55′.93N	2°20′.54W	(60)
282	SW Crouesty	47°30′.68N	2°55′.32W	IVB	356	Morin 1	46°58′.70N	2°17′.98W	60
283	Crouesty	47°32′.19N	2°54′.77W	45	357	Boeufs	46°55′.04N	2°28′.16W	VIA
284	NE Crouesty	47°32′.51N	2°55′.28W	45	358	Fromentine	46°52′.84N	2°12′.73W	(61)
285	Kerpenhir	47°33′.21N	2°55′.27W	43	359	Fromentine 1	46°53′.51N	2°09′.65W	61
286	Grégan	47°33′.74N	2°55′.04W	43	360	Fromentine 2	46°53′.54N	2°08′.80W	61
287	Huernic	47°34′.87N	2°56′.02W	43	361	NW Yeu	46°44′.60N	2°24′.00W	VIA
288	Creizig	47°34′.92N	2°52′.01W	43	362	Broches	46°44′.27N	2°24′.41W	
289	Fogeo	47°32′.04N	2°53′.26W		363	Broches 1	46°43′.85N	2°23′.50W	
290	Cornault	47°30′.86N	2°51′.37W		364	Joinville	46°44′.22N	2°20′.23W	(62)
291	Chimère	47°28′.76N	2°54′.08W	IVB	365	Joinville 1	46°43′.77N	2°20′.76W	62
292	Recherche	47°25′.73N	2°47′.58W	IVB	366	E Joinville	46°43′.34N	2°18′.00W	(62)
293	St-Jacques	47°28′.09N	2°47′.38W	IVB	367	E Yeu	46°41′.25N	2°16′.00W	VIA
294	St-Jacques 1	47°28′.97N	2°47′.08W		368	SE Yeu	46°40′.95N	2°17′.18W	
295	Suscinio	47°28′.63N	2°43′.78W		369	Vieilles	46°41′.17N	2°18′.30W	
296	Suscinio 1	47°29′.94N	2°43′.38W		370	Vieilles 1	46°41′.53N	2°18′.70W	
297	Penerf	47°28′.94N	2°38′.91W	47	371	S Yeu	46°40′.85N	2°20′.00W	VIA
298	Penerf 1	47°30′.01N	2°38′.88W	47	372	Meule	46°41′.19N	2°20′.91W	63
299	E Penerf	47°29′.11N	2°38′.48W	47	373	Meule 1	46°41′.49N	2°20′.78W	63
300	E Penerf 1	47°29′.89N	2°38′.63W	47	374	SW Yeu	46°41′.74N	2°23′.10W	VIA
301	Accroche	47°28′.96N	2°33′.88W	48A	375	W Yeu	46°43′.00N	2°26′.00W	VIA
302	Accroche 1	47°30′.37N	2°31′.27W	48A	376	St Gilles	46°40′.82N	1°58′.18W	(64)
303	W Varlingue	47°28′.31N	2°31′.98W	48A	377	St Gilles 1	46°41′.44N	1°57′.32W	64
304	W Varlingue 1	47°30′.37N	2°30′.53W	48A	378	SE St Gilles	46°40′.80N	1°56′.82W	(64)
305	Varlingue	47°28′.23N	2°31′.26W	48A	379	Barge	46°28′.88N	1°50′.66W	VIA
306	Varlingue 1	47°30′.37N	2°29′.92W	48A	380	W Sables	46°28′.49N	1°47′.25W	65
307	Vilaine	47°30′.36N	2°28′.68W	48A	381	Sables	46°28′.90N	1°46′.86W	65
308	Mine d'Or	47°28′.16N	2°29′.87W		382	Sables 1	46°29′.26N	1°47′.37W	65
309	Mesquer	47°25′.59N	2°29′.88W		383	Sables 2	46°29′.51N	1°47′.61W	65
310	Mesquer 1	47°25′.44N	2°28′.20W		384	E Sables	46°28′.00N	1°45′.78W	(65)
311	Dumet	47°24′.77N	2°36′.94W		385	Bourgenay	46°25′.22N	1°41′.99W	66A
312	Piriac	47°23′.58N	2°32′.85W	51A	386	Bourgenay 1	46°26′.27N	1°40′.71W	66B
313	Piriac 1	47°23′.17N	2°32′.66W	51A	387	Jard	46°23′.51N	1°35′.23W	(67)
314	Rohtrès	47°23′.44N	2°33′.45W	51A	388	Jard 1	46°24′.15N	1°34′.52W	67
315	Bayonnelles	47°22′.68N	2°35′.38W	V	389	Jard 2	46°24′.35N	1°34′.52W	67
316	Turballe	47°20′.54N	2°31′.63W	(52)	390	NW Ré	46°15′.94N	1°40′.08W	VIIB
317	Turballe 1	47°20′.60N	2°30′.91W	52	391	NE Ré	46°16′.10N	1°28′.27W	VIIB
318	Turballe 2	47°20′.70N	2°30′.88W	52	392	Ars	46°14′.20N	1°25′.63W	70A
319	N Croisic	47°19′.43N	2°31′.98W	V	393	Ars 1	46°14′.06N	1°28′.09W	70A
320	Croisic	47°18′.80N	2°31′.57W	53	394	Ars 2	46°13′.00N	1°30′.16W	70A
321	Croisic 1	47°18′.25N	2°31′.11W	53	395	E Ars	46°14′.32N	1°23′.30W	VIIB
322	W Croisic	47°18′.11N	2°34′.76W	V	396	N Ré	46°14′.94N	1°20′.54W	VIIB
323	SW Croisic	47°17′.07N	2°33′.28W	V	397	St Martin	46°13′.31N	1°21′.46W	VIIB
324	Basse Capella	47°15′.64N	2°42′.39W		398	St Martin 1	46°12′.54N	1°21′.89W	71
325	Batz	47°15′.65N	2°29′.48W	V	399	La Flotte	46°12′.07N	1°18′.55W	(72)
326	W Pornichet	47°15′.14N	2°25′.08W	V	400	La Flotte 1	46°11′.36N	1°19′.25W	72
327	Pouliguen	47°15′.21N	2°24′.28W	54	401	Faute	46°16′.14N	1°16′.68W	68
328	Pouliguen 1	47°15′.54N	2°24′.23W	54	402	Faute 1	46°17′.37N	1°15′.85W	68
329	Pouliguen 2	47°16′.06N	2°24′.93W	54	403	Marans	46°15′.25N	1°11′.46W	69
330	Pornichet	47°15′.50N	2°21′.19W	55	404	Marans 1	46°17′.26N	1°09′.47W	69
331	SW Pornichet	47°14′.13N	2°22′.63W	V	405	Marans 2	46°18′.33N	1°07′.89W	69
332	Banche	47°09′.94N	2°28′.58W	V	406	Ré bridge	46°10′.23N	1°14′.64W	VIIB
333	N Lambarde	47°11′.34N	2°21′.65W	V	407	S Ré	46°07′.39N	1°28′.45W	VIIB
334	SW Lambarde	47°10′.33N	2°23′.28W	V	408	Martray	46°09′.72N	1°27′.48W	
335	Charpentier	47°12′.62N	2°19′.13W	V	409	Martray 1	46°11′.56N	1°28′.02W	
336	Loire	47°11′.24N	2°17′.73W	V	410	Pallice	46°09′.07N	1°14′.61W	VIIB
337	Loire 1	47°13′.76N	2°16′.00W	56B	411	La Rochelle	46°06′.64N	1°15′.64W	VIIB
338	Trébézy	47°14′.88N	2°15′.33W	56B	412	La Rochelle 1	46°08′.24N	1°11′.78W	(73)
339	St Nazaire	47°15′.72N	2°12′.06W	56A	413	La Rochelle 2	46°08′.86N	1°10′.28W	73
340	St Gildas	47°08′.74N	2°14′.78W	57	414	N Boyard	46°01′.10N	1°12′.66W	VIIB
341	St Gildas 1	47°08′.42N	2°14′.58W	57	415	SW Aix	46°00′.70N	1°11′.04W	74

No	WP Name	WGS84 Lat	WGS84 Lon	Plan
416	SE Aix	46°00′.26N	1°10′.18W	74
417	E Aix	46°00′.79N	1°08′.67W	74
418	NE Aix	46°01′.38N	1°09′.35W	74
419	Charente	45°59′.65N	1°09′.56W	75A
420	Charente 1	45°58′.74N	1°06′.77W	75A
421	Charente 2	45°57′.20N	1°04′.53W	75A
422	Charente 3	45°57′.12N	1°03′.71W	75A
423	Charente 4	45°57′.64N	1°02′.09W	75B
424	N Oléron	46°04′.80N	1°23′.54W	VIIB
425	St-Denis	46°03′.30N	1°20′.79W	(77)
426	St-Denis 1	46°02′.07N	1°21′.60W	77
427	E St-Denis	46°02′.30N	1°19′.95W	(77)
428	Douhet	46°00′.48N	1°17′.78W	(78)
429	Douhet 1	46°00′.22N	1°19′.07W	78
430	W Boyard	46°00′.22N	1°15′.00W	
431	Boyardville	45°58′.50N	1°13′.28W	79
432	Boyardville 1	45°58′.25N	1°13′.77W	79
433	E Oléron	45°57′.03N	1°11′.21W	(80A)
434	Charret	45°53′.35N	1°08′.98W	80A
435	Le Château	45°52′.44N	1°10′.70W	80A
436	NW Oléron	46°03′.00N	1°27′.45W	VIIB
437	W Oléron	45°58′.00N	1°27′.68W	VIIB
438	Gironde	45°37′.47N	1°28′.50W	VIIB
439	Gironde 1	45°38′.60N	1°17′.69W	81A
440	Gironde 2	45°39′.66N	1°12′.68W	81A
441	Gironde 3	45°37′.76N	1°05′.42W	81A
442	Royan	45°36′.58N	1°02′.06W	81A
443	Royan 1	45°36′.95N	1°01′.79W	81B
444	Pte de Grave	45°35′.14N	1°03′.04W	81A
445	Port Bloc	45°34′.14N	1°03′.71W	82B
446	Port Médoc	45°33′.54N	1°03′.57W	82A
447	Gironde 4	45°31′.35N	0°59′.52W	83
448	Pauillac	45°11′.86N	0°44′.44W	83
449	SW Gironde	45°28′.29N	1°20′.08W	VIIB
450	SW Gironde 1	45°32′.55N	1°08′.24W	81A
451	SW Gironde 2	45°36′.09N	1°03′.88W	81A

LIGHTS

I WEST BRITTANY

1 Chenal de Four
Chenal du Four
A **Le Four** 48°31′.4N 4°48′.3W Fl(5)15s28m18M Horn(3+2)60s Grey tower
Ldg Lts 158·5°
B *Front* **Kermorvan** 48°21′.7N 4°47′.4W Fl.5s20m22M Horn 60s White square tower
C *Rear* **Saint Mathieu** 48°19′.8N 4°46′.3W Fl.15s56m29M & DirF.54m28M 157·5°-intens-159·5° White tower, red top
D **Les Plâtresses** 48°26′.3N 4°50′.9W Fl.RG.4s17m6M 343°-R-153°-G-333° White octagonal tower
E **Valbelle buoy (port)** 48°26′.4N 4°50′.0W Fl(2)R.6s5M Whis
F **Basse St Paul buoy (port)** 48°24′.8N 4°49′.2W Oc(2)R.6s
Chenal de la Helle
Ldg Lts 138°
G *Front* **Kermorvan** 48°21′.7N 4°47′.4W Fl.5s20m22M Horn 60s White square tower
H *Rear* **Lochrist** 48°20′.6N 4°45′.6W DirOc(3)12s49m22M 135°-intens-140° Octagonal white tower, red top
Ldd Lts 293°
I *Front* **Le Faix** 48°25′.7N 4°53′.9W VQ.16m8M Tower (N card)
J *Rear* **Le Stiff** 48°28′.5N 5°03′.4W Fl(2)R.20s85m24M Two white towers, side by side
K **Pourceaux buoy (NCM)** 48°24′.0N 4°51′.3W Q
Both channels
L **Corsen** 48°24′.9N 4°47′.6W DirQ.WRG.33m12-8M 008°-R-012°-W-015°-G-021° White hut
M **La Grande Vinotière** 48°21′.9N 4°48′.4W LFl.R.10s15m5M

Octagonal red tower
N **Le Rouget buoy (starboard)** 48°22′.1N 4°48′.9W Fl.G.4s Whis
O **St Mathieu auxiliary** 54m at 291° from main tower Q.WRG.26m14-11M 085°-G-107°-W-116°-R-134° White tower
P **Tournant et Lochrist buoy (port)** 48°20′.6N 4°48′.1W Iso.R.4s
Q **Les Vieux Moines** 48°19′.3N 4°46′.6W Fl.R.4s16m5M 280°-vis-133° Octagonal red tower
Leading lights 007°
R *Front* **Kermorvan** 48°21′.7N 4°47′.4W Fl.5s20m22M Horn 60s White square tower
S *Rear* **Trézien** 48°25′.4N 4°46′.7W DirOc(2)6s84m20M 003°-intens-011° Grey tower, white towards south

2 Goulet de Brest
A **Pointe du Petit Minou** 48°20′.2N 4°36′.9W Fl(2)WR.6s32m19/15M Horn 60s shore-R-252°-W-260°-R-307°-W(unintens)-015°-W-065·5° 070·5°-W-shore Grey round tower, W on SW side, red top
Ldg Lts 068°
Front DirQ.30m23M 067·3°-intens-068·8° Same structure
B **Pointe du Portzic** 48°21′.5N 4°32′.1W Oc(2)WR.12s56m19/15M 219°-R-259°-W-338°-R-000°-W-065·5° 070·5°-W-219° 041°-vis-069° when W of Goulet Grey 8-sided tower
Ldg Lts 068°
Rear DirQ.54m22M 065°-intens-071° Same structure
For Passe Sud DirQ(6)+LFl.15s54m24M 045°-intens-050° Same structure
C **Basse du Charles Martel buoy (port)** 48°18′.9N 4°42′.2W Fl(4)R.15s Whis
D **Fillettes buoy (WCM)** 48°19′.8N 4°35′.7W VQ(9)10s Whis
E **Roche Mengam** 48°20′.3N 4°34′.6W Fl(3)WR.12s10m11/8M 034°-R-054°-W-034° RBR beacon tower

3 Brest
L'Elorn river
A **Pénoupèle buoy (port)** 48°21′.5N 4°30′.5W Fl(3)R.12s
B **R2 buoy (port)** 48°22′.1N 4°28′.7W Fl(2)R.6s
C **R1 buoy (starboard)** 48°21′.8N 4°28′.3W Fl.G.4s
D **R4 buoy (port)** 48°22′.2N 4°28′.1W LFl.R.10s
E **R3 buoy (NCM)** 48°22′.5N 4°28′.1W Q(6)+LFl.15s (to be left to port)
F **Beacon** 48°22′.7N 4°26·5W Fl(4)R.15s2M red pile
G **Moulin Blanc buoy (port)** 48°22′.8N 4°26′.0W Fl(3)R.12s
H. **Starboard** and port buoys MB1 Fl.G.2s MB2 Fl.R.2s
I **Marina entrance beacons** Fl.G.2s & Fl.R.2s &
J **MBA Beacon ECM** 48°23′.5N 4°25′.8W Q(3)10s E card beacon

7 Camaret-sur-Mer
A **North mole head** 48°16′.9N 4°35′.3W Iso.WG.4s7m12/9M135°-W-182°-G-027° White pylon, green top
B **South mole head** 48°16′.6N 4°35′.3W Fl(2)R.6s9m5M Red pylon

8 The Crozon Peninsula
A **Pointe du Toulinguet** 48°16′.8N 4°37′.7W Oc(3)WR.12s49m15/11M shore-W-028°-R-090°-W-shore White square tower on building
B **Pointe du Petit Minou** 48°20′.2N 4°36′.9W Fl(2)WR.6s32m19/15M shore-R-252°-W-260°-R-307°-W(unintens)-015°-W-065·5°, 070·5°-W-shore Grey round tower white on SW side, red top
C **Pointe du Portzic** 48°21′.5N 4°32′.1W Oc(2)WR.12s56m19/15M 219°-R-259°-W-338°-R-000°-W-065·5°, 070·5°-W-219° Grey 8-sided tower
D **Le Bouc buoy (WCM)** 48°11′.5N 4°37′.4W Q(9)15s

9 Morgat
A **Basse Vieille buoy (IDM)** 48°08′.2N 4°35′.8W Fl(2)6s8m7M Whis
B **Pointe du Millier** 48°05′.9N 4°27′.9W Oc(2)WRG.6s34m16-11M 080°-G-087°-W-113°-R-120°-W-

129°-G-148°-W-251°-R-258° White house

C **Pointe de Morgat** 48°13′·2N 4°29′·8W
Oc(4)WRG.12s77m15-10M shore-W-281°-G-301°-W-021°-R-043° White square tower, red top, white house

D **Morgat buoy (port)** 48°13′·6N 4°29′·7W 48°13′·7N 4°29′·6W Fl.R.4s

E **Morgat mole head** 48°13′·5N 4°30′·0W
Oc(2)WR.6s8m9/6M 007°-W-257°-R-007° White and red metal framework tower
Entrance between wave-breakers

F **Port** Fl.R.4s

G **Starboard** Fl.G.4s

10 Douarnenez

A **Ile Tristan** 48°06′·1N 4°20′·3W Oc(3)WR.12s35m13/10M
shore-W-138°-R-153°-W-shore Grey tower, white band, black top

B **Pointe Biron head** 48°06′·1N 4°20′·5W Q.G.7m6M White column, green top

C **Port-Rhu Dir Lt** 48°05′·4N 4°19·8W DirFl(5)WRG.20s16m5-4M 154°-G-156°-W-158°-R-160° Lantern on bridge

D **Barrage Ls** 48°05′·7N 4°20·1W Fl.G.5s & Fl.R.5s either side of gate.

11 Ile de Sein

A **Ile de Sein, main Lt** 48°02′·6N 4°52′·1W Fl(4)25s49m29M
White tower, black top

B **Men Brial** 48°02′·3N 4°51′·0W Oc(2)WRG.6s16m12-7M
149°-G-186°-W-192°-R-221°-W-227°-G-254° Green and white tower

C **Cornoc an Ar Braden buoy (starboard)** 48°03′·2N 4°50′·9W Fl.G.4s Whis

D **Tévennec** 48°04′·3N 4°47′·8W Q.WR.28m9/6M 090°-W-345°-R-090° White tower and dwelling
DirFl.4s24m12M 324°-intens-332° same structure

E **Le Chat** 48°01′·4N 4°48′·9W Fl(2)WRG.6s27m9-6M 096°-G-215°-W-230°-R-271°-G-286°-R-096° S card tower

12 Raz du Sein

A **Tévennec** 48°04′·3N 4°47′·8W Q.WR.28m9/6M 090°-W-345°-R-090° White tower and dwelling
DirFl.4s24m12M 324°-intens-332° same structure

B **La Vieille** 48°02′·4N 4°45′·4W Oc(2+1)WRG.12s33m18-13M Horn(2+1)60s 290°-W-298°-R-325°-W-355°-G-017°-W-035°-G-105°-W-123°-R-158°-W-205° Grey square tower, black top

C **La Plate** 48°02′·4N 4°45′·6W VQ(9)10s19m8M W card tower

13 Sainte Evette

A **Pointe de Lervilly** 48°00′·0N 4°33′·9W
Fl(3)WR.12s20m14/11M 236°-W-269°-R-294°-W-087°-R-109° White round tower, red top

B **Jetée de Ste Evette head** 48°00′·3N 4°33′·1W
Oc(2)R.6s2m7M Red column

Passe de l'Est. Ldg Lts 331°

C *Front* **Jetée de Raoulic head** 48°00′·5N 4°32′·5W
Fl.3WG.12s11m14/9M shore-W-034°-G-shore, but may show W 037°-055° White tower

D *Rear* **Kergadec** 48°01′·0N 4°32′·8W DirF.R.44m9M 321°-intens-341°White 8-sided tower, red lantern

E **Pors Poulhan** W side of entrance 47°59′·1N 4°27′·9W
Q.R.14m9M White square tower, red top

14 Audierne

As 13 Sainte Evette.

II BENODET BAY

15 Pointe de Penmarc'h

A **Eckmühl** 47°47′·9N 4°22′·4W Fl.5s60m23M Horn 60sGrey 8-sided tower

B **Men Hir** 47°47′·7N 4°24′·0W Fl(2)WG.6s19m7/4M 135°-G-315°-W-135° White tower, black band

C **Locarec** 47°47′·3N 4°20′·3W Iso.WRG.4s11m9/6M 063°-G-068°-R-271°-W-285°-R-298°-G-340°-R-063° Metal column on rock

D **Lost Moan** 47°47′·0N 4°16′·8W Fl(3)WRG.12s8m9/6M
327°-R-014°-G-065°-R-140°-W-160°-R-268°-W-273°-G-317°-W-327° White tower, red top

E **Cap Caval buoy (WCM)** 47°46′·5N 4°22′·7W Q(9)15s Whis

F **Spinec buoy (SCM)** 46°45′·2N 4°18′·9W Q(6)+LFl.15s Whis

G **Karreg Kreiz (ECM)** 47°46′·0N 4°11′·4W Q(3)10s Whis

16 Le Guilvinec

A **Névez buoy (starboard)** 47°45′·8N 4°20′·1W Fl.G.2·5s

B **Spinec Buoy (SCM)** 46°45′·2N 4°18′·9W Q(6)+LFl.15s Whis

C **Lost Moan** 47°47′·0N 4°16′·8W Fl(3)WRG.12s8m9/6M
327°-R-014°-G-065°-R-140°-W-160°-R-268°-W-273°-G-317°-W-327° White tower, red top

D **Locarec** 47°47′·3N 4°20′·3W Iso.WRG.4s11m9/6M 063°-G-068°-R-271°-W-285°-R-298°-G-340°-R-063° Metal column on rock

Ldg Lts 053° Synchronised

E *Front* 47°47′·4N 4°17′·1W Q.7m8M 233°-vis-066° White pylon on starboard mole spur
Middle 210m from front Q.WG.12m14/11M 006°-W-293°-G-006° Red square on white column
Rear 1085m from front DirQ.26m8M 051·5°-vis-054·5° Red square on white tower, red stripe

F **Capelan buoy (starboard)** 47°47′·1N 4°17′·6W Fl(2)G.6s

I **S mole head** 47°47′·5N 4°17′·2W Fl.G.4s5m7M Round white hut, green top

17 Lesconil

A **Karreg Kreiz (ECM)** 47°46′·0N 4°11′·4W Q(3)10s Whis

B **Men-ar-Groas** 47°47′·8N 4°12′·7W Fl(3)WRG.12s14m10-7M 268°-G-313°-W-333°-R-050° White tower, green top

C **E breakwater head** 47°47′·7N 4°12′·7W Q.G.5m5M Green tower

D **S breakwater head** 47°47′·7N 4°12′·7W Oc.R.4s5m6M White pylon, red top

18 Loctudy

A **Pointe de Langoz** 47°49′·9N 4°09′·6W
Fl(4)WRG.12s12m15-11M 115°-W-257°-G-284°-W-295°-R-318°-W-328°-R-025° White tower, red top

B **Ile aux Moutons** 47°46′·5N 4°01′·7W Oc(2)WRG.6s18m15-11M 035°-W-050°-G-063°-W-081°-R-141°-W-292°-R-035° White tower and dwelling
Auxiliary Lt DirOc(2)6s17m16M 278·5°-intens-283·5° Synchronised with main light, same structure
Bénodet Ldg Lts 000·5°

C *Front* **Pte de Combrit** 47°51′·9N 4°06′·8W
Oc(3+1)WR.12s19m12-9M 325°-W-017°-R-325° White square tower grey corners

D *Rear* **Pyramide** 340m from front Oc(2+1)12s48m11M White tower, green top

E **Bilien buoy (ECM)** 47°49′·1N 4°08′·1W VQ(3)5s Whis

F **Karek-Saoz** 47°50′·0N 4°09′·4W Fl.R.2.5s3m1M Red truncated tower

G **Le Blas** 47°50′·3N 4°10′·2W Fl(4)G.15s5m1M Green truncated column

19 Bénodet and Sainte Marine

A **Pointe de Langoz** 47°49′·9N 4°09′·6W
Fl(4)WRG.12s12m15-11M 115°-W-257°-G-284°-W-295°-R-318°-W-328°-R-025° White tower, red top

B **Ile aux Moutons** 47°46′·5N 4°01′·7W Oc(2)WRG.6s18m15-11M 035°-W-050°-G-063°-W-081°-R-141°-W-292°-R-035° White tower and dwelling
Auxiliary Lt DirOc(2)6s17m16M 278·5°-intens-283·5° Synchronised with main light, same structure
Ldg Lts 000·5°

C *Front* **Pte de Combrit** 47°51′·9N 4°06′·8W
Oc(3+1)WR.12s19m12-9M 325°-W-017°-R-325° White square tower grey corners

D *Rear* **Pyramide** 340m from front Oc(2+1)12s48m11M White tower, green top

Ldg Lts 345·5°

F *Front* **Pte du Coq** 47°52′·3N 4°06′·7W
DirOc(2+1)G.12s11m17M 345°-intens-347°White round tower, vertical green stripe
Rear **Pyramide** 1180m from front. Oc(2+1)12s48m11M White tower, green top

G **Pte du Toulgoët** 47°52′·3N 4°06′·9W Fl.R.2.5s2m1M Red mast

21 Iles de Glénan

A **Ile aux Moutons** 47°46′·5N 4°01′·7W Oc(2)WRG.6s18m15-11M 035°-W-050°-G-063°-W-081°-R-141°-W-292°-R-035° White tower and dwelling
Auxiliary Light DirOc(2)6s17m24M 278·5°-intens-283·5° Synchronised with main light, same structure

B **Penfret** 47°43′·3N 3°57′·2W Fl.R.5s36m21M White square tower, red top
Auxiliary light DirQ.34m12M 295°-vis-315° Same structure

C **La Pie** 47°43′·8N 3°59′·8W Fl(2)6s9m3M Isolated danger beacon

22 Port-La-Fôret

A **Cap-Coz (west) mole head** 47°53′·5N 3°58′·3W Fl(2)WRG.6s5m7-5M shore-R-335°-G-340°-W-346°-R-shore Red lantern on grey post, white hut

B **Kerleven (east) mole head** 47°53′·6N 3°58′·4W Fl.G.4s8m1M Green lantern on grey mast, white hut

C **Marina mole head** 47°53′·9N 3°58′·6W Iso.G.4s5m1M Green lantern on grey mast, white hut

D **Buoys marking entrance of channel** – Fl(2)G.2·5s & port Fl.R.2·5s

23 Concarneau

A **Le Cochon** 47°51′·5N 3°55′·5W Fl(3)WRG.12s5m9-6M 048°-G-205°-R-352°-W-048° Green tower

B **Basse du Chenal buoy (port)** 47°51′·6N 3°55′·6W Q.R

C **Men Fall buoy (starboard)** 47°51′·8N 3°55′·3W Fl.G.4s

Ldg Lts 028·5°

D *Front* **La Croix** 47°52′·2N 3°55′·1W Oc(3)12s14m13M 006·5°-vis-093° Red and white tower

E *Rear* **Beuzec** 47°53′·4N 3°54′·0W 1·34M from front DirQ.87m23M 026·5°-intens-030·5° Belfry

F **Lanriec** 47°52′·0N 3°54′·6W Q.G.13m8M 063°-vis-078° Green window in white gable

G **La Médée** 47°52′·1N 3°54′·8W Fl.R.2·5s9m4M Red tower

H **Ville-Close** 47°52′·3N 3°54′·7W Oc(2)WR.6s4m9-6M 209°-R-354°-W-007°-R-018° Red tower below wall of La Ville Close

I **East side (No. 1) Beacon** 47°52′·2N 3°54′·6W Fl.G.4s4m5M Green round tower

J **Entrance to Marina** 47°52′·2N 3°54′·7W Fl(3)R.12s3m1M Red post on N end of wavebreaker

III GROIX AND THE RIAS

24 The Aven River and Port Manec'h

A **Port Manec'h (Pointe de Beg-ar-Véchen)** 47°48′·0N 3°44′·4W Oc(4)WRG.12s38m10-7M 050°-W(unintens)-140°-W-296°-G-303°-W-311°-R-328°-W-050° Obscd by Pointe de Beg-Moreg when bearing less than 299° White and red tower

26 Merrien

A **Brigneau mole head** 47°46′·9N 3°40′·2W Oc(2)WRG.6s7m12-9M 280°-G-329°-W-339°-R-034° White column, red top

B **Merrien** 47°47′·1N 3°39′·0W Q.R.26m7M 004°-vis-009° White square tower, red top

27 Doëlan

Ldg Lts 013.8°

A *Front* 47°46′·5N 3°36′·5W Oc(3)WG.12s20m13/10M shore-305°-G-314°-W-shore White tower, green band and top

B *Rear* 47°46′·5N 3°36′·3W 326m from front Q.R.27m9M White tower, red band and top

29 Lomçner

A **Anse de Stole** 47°42′·3N 3°25′·6W DirQ.WRG.13m10-8M 349·2°-G-355·2°-W-359·2°-R-005·2° White tower, red top

B **Kerroc'h** 47°42′·0N 3°27′·7W Oc(2)WRG.6s22m11-8M 096·5°-R-112·5°-G-132°-R-302°-W-096·5° White truncated tower, red top

30 Lorient

Passe de l'Ouest
Ldg Lts 057°

A *Front* **Les Soeurs** 47°42′·1N 3°21′·8W DirQ.11m13M 042·5°-intens-058·5° Red tower, white bands

B *Rear* **Port Louis** 47°42′·4N 3°21′·3W 740m from front DirQ.22m18M White daymark on building, red bands

C **Les Trois Pierres** 47°41′·5N 3°22′·5W Q.RG.11m6M 060°-G-196°-R-002° Black tower, white bands

Passe de la Sud
Ldg Lts 008·5°

D *Front* **Fish Market** 47°43′·8N 3°21′·2W DirQ.R.16m17M 006°-intens-011°Red square with green bands on grey metal framework tower

E *Rear* **Kergroise-La Perrière** 47°44′·1N 3°21′·6W 515m from front DirQ.R.34m16M 006°-intens-011° Synchronised with front Red square with white stripe on grey metal framework tower

Entrance
Ile Saint-Michel Ldg Lts 016·5°

F *Front* 47°43′·5N 3°21′·6W DirOc(3)G.12s8m16M 014·5°-intens-017·5° Grey tower, green top

G *Rear* 47°43′·7N 3°21′·5W 306m from front DirOc(3)G.12s14m16M 014·5°-intens-017·5° Synchronised with front grey tower, green top

H **La Citadelle** 47°42′·6N 3°21′·9W Oc.G.4s6m6M 009°-vis-193° Green concrete tower. Destroyed; VQ.G 2·3M on green spar, 012°-vis-192° (T) 2003

I **La Petite Jument** 47°42′·6N 3°22′·1W Oc.R.4s5m6M 182°-vis-024° Red concrete tower

K **Le Cochon** 47°42′·8N 3°22′·0W Fl.R.4s5m5M Red tower, green band

Harbour
Kéroman Submarine Base Ldg Lts 350°

L *Front* 47°43′·6N 3°22′·0W DirOc(2)R.6s25m15M Red house, white bands

M *Rear* 95m from front DirOc(2)R.6s31m15M 349°-intens-351° Synchronised with front red and white topmark on grey pylon, red top

Kernével Ldg Lts 217°

N *Front* 47°43′·0N 3°22′·3W DirQ.R.10m15M 215°-intens-219° Red truncated cone on red and white metal framework tower

O *Rear* 47°42′·9N 3°22′·4W DirQ.R.18m15M 215°-intens-219° White square tower, red top

P **Pte de L'Espérance** 47°44′·5N 3°20′·76W DirQ.WRG.8m10-8M 034·2°-G-036·7°-W-037·2°-R-047·2° (White sector covers Kernével Ldg Lts 14, 15) White tower, green top

Q **Fishing harbour entrance, E side** 47°43′·6N 3°21′·9W Fl.RG.4s7m6M 000°-G-235°-R-000° White truncated tower, green top

R **Pengarne** 47°43′·9N 3°21′·2W Fl.G.2·5s3m3M Green tower

S **Ro Ro terminal jetty head** 47°44′·4N 3°21′·0W Oc(2)R.6s7m6M Red structure

Kernével

T **South basin, E Breakwater head** 47°43′·2N 3°21′·9W Fl.Y.2·5s4m2M

U **North basin entrance E side (buoy)** 47°43′·5N 3°22′·0W Fl.Y.2·5s Conical yellow buoy, can topmark

V **North basin entrance W side (buoy)** 47°43′·5N 3°22′·0W Fl(4)Y.15s Conical yellow buoy, triangle topmark

Locmiquélic (Ste Catherine)

W **Breakwater head (S side of entrance)** 47°43′·6N 3°21′·0W Q.G.5m2M Green post

X **N side (buoy)** 47°43′·5N 3°21′·1W Q.R Red can buoy, can topmark

Port de Commerce

Y **Entrance, S side (No. 8 buoy)** 47°44′·6N 3°21′·0W Fl.R.2·5s Red can buoy, can topmark

31 Port Louis and Locmalo

A **Ile aux Souris** 47°42′·2N 3°21′·5W DirQ.WG.6m3/2M

041·5°-W-043·5°-G-041·5° Green framework tower

B **Port Louis jetty head** 47°42'·7N 3°21'·2W Iso.G.4s7m6M 043°-vis-301° White tower, green top

32 Port Tudy

A **East mole head** 47°38'·7N 3°26'·8W Fl(2)R.6s11m7M 112°-vis-226° White round tower, red top

B **North mole head** 47°38'·7N 3°26'·7W Iso.G.4s12m7M White tower, green top

33 Locmaria

A **Pen Men** 47°38'·9N 3°30'·5W Fl(4)25s60m29M 309°-vis-275° White square tower, black top

B **Pointe des Chats** 47°37'·2N 3°25'·3W Fl.R.5s16m19M White square tower and dwelling

C **Les Chats buoy (SCM)** 47°35'·7N 3°23'·6W Q(6)+LFl.15s

D **Pointe de la Croix** 47°38'·0N 3°25'·0W Oc.WR.4s16m12-9M 169°-W-336°-R-345°-W-353° White pedestal, red lantern

34 Etel

A **Plateau des Brivideaux** 47°29'·1N 3°17'·5W Fl(2)6s24m10M Black tower, red bands

B **West side of entrance** 47°38'·7N 3°12'·9W Oc(2)WRG.6s13m9-6M 022°-W-064°-R-123°-W-330°-G-022° Red metal framework tower

C **Epi de Plouhinec head** 47°38'·7N 3°12'·8W Fl.R.2·5s7m2M Red structure

IV QUIBERON BAY

35 Sauzon

A **West jetty** 47°22'·4N 3°13'·1W Q.G.9m5M 194°-vis-045° White tower, green top

B **NW jetty head** 47°22'·5N 3°13'·1W Fl.G.4s8m8M White tower, green top

C **SE jetty head** 47°22'·4N 3°13'·1W Fl.R.4s8m8M White truncated tower, red top

36 Le Palais

A **South jetty head** 47°20'·8N 3°09'·1W Oc(2)R.6s8m11M White round tower, red lantern

B **North jetty head** 47°20'·8N 3°09'·1W Fl(2+1)G.12s8m7M White tower, green top

37 Belle-Ile Anchorages

A **Goulphar** 47°18'·6N 3°13'·7W Fl(2)10s87m27M Grey tower, red lamp

B **Pointe des Poulains** 47°23'·3N 3°15'·2W Fl.5s34m23M White square tower and dwelling, red lamp

C **Pointe de Kerdonis** 47°18'·6N 3°03'·6W Fl(3)R.15s35m15M White square tower, red top and white dwelling

38 Teignouse Passage

A **Port Maria main light** 47°28'·8N 3°07'·5W Q.WRG.28m14-10M 246°-W-252°, 291°-W-297°-G-340°-W-017°-R-051°-W-081°-G-098°-W-143° White tower, green lantern

B **La Teignouse** 47°27'·5N 3°02'·8W Fl.WR.4s20m15/11M 033°-W-039°-R-033° White round tower, red top

C **Goué Vaz Sud buoy (SCM)** 47°25'·8N 3°04'·9W Q(6)+LFl.15s Whis

D **Basse du Milieu buoy (starboard)** 47°25'·9N 3°04'·1W Fl(2)G.6s9m2M Green triangle on green HFPB

E **Goué Vaz E buoy (port)** 47°26'·2N 3°04'·3W Fl(3)R.12s

F **NE Teignouse buoy (starboard)** 47°26'·6N 3°01'·9W Fl(3)G.12s

G **Basse Nouvelle buoy (port)** 47°27'·0N 3°02'·0W Fl.R.2·5s

H **Port Haliguen, E breakwater head** 47°29'·3N 3°06'·0W Oc(2)WR.6s10m11-8M 233°-W-240·5°-R-299°-W-306°-R-233° White tower, red top

39 Ile Houat

A **Port St Gildas N mole** 47°23'·6N 2°57'·3W Fl(2)WG.6s8m9-6M 168°-W-198°-G-210°-W-240°-G-168° White tower, green top

40 Ile Hoëdic

A **Port de l'Argol breakwater head** 47°20'·7N 2°52'·6W Fl.WG.4s10m9-6M 143°-W-163°-G-183°-W-194°-G-143° White tower, green top

B **Grouguéguez (Les Grands Cardinaux)** 47°19'·3N 2°50'·1W Fl(4)15s28m13M Red tower, white band

41 Port Haliguen

A **Port Maria main Lt** 47°28'·8N 3°07'·5W Q.WRG.28m14-10M 246°-W-252°, 291°-W-297°-G-340°-W-017°-R-051°-W-081°-G-098°-W-143° White tower, green lantern

B **Marina, new breakwater head** 47°29'·3N 3°06'·0W Oc(2)WR.6s10m11-8M 233°-W-240·5°-R-299°-W-306°-R-233° White tower, red top

C **Old breakwater elbow** 47°29'·3N 3°06'·0W Fl.R.4s10m5M 322°-vis-206° White tower, red top

D **NW mole head** 47°29'·4N 3°06'·1W Fl.G.2·5s9m6M White column, green top

E **Pier head** 49°29'·3N 3°06'·0W Fl.Vi.2·5s5m Purple column

42 La Trinité

La Trinité Ldg Lts 347°

A *Front* 47°34'·1N 3°00'·4W Q.WRG.11m10-7M 321°-G-345°-W-013·5°-R-080° White tower, green top

B *Rear* 560m from front DirQ.21m15M 337°-intens-357° Synchronised with front White round tower, green top

C **La Trinité-sur-mer** Dir Lt 347° 47°35'·0N 3°01'·0W DirOc.WRG.4s9m13-11M 345°-G-346°-W-348°-R-349° White tower

D **Le Petit Trého buoy (port)** 47°33'·5N 3°00'·7W Fl(4)R.15s

E **S pier head** 47°35'·1N 3°01'·5W Oc(2)WR.6s6m9/6M 090°-R-293·5°-W-300·5°-R-329° White tower, red top

F **Marina pierhead** 47°35'·3N 3°01'·5W Iso.R.4s8m5M White framework tower, red top

43 River Auray

A **Port Navalo** 47°32'·9N 2°55'·1W Oc(3)WRG.12s32m15-11M 155°-W-220°, 317°-G-359°-W-015°-R-105° White tower and dwelling

B **Le Grand Mouton beacon (starboard)** 47°33'·7N 2°54'·9W Q.G.4m3M Green tripod

C **Grégan** 47°33'·9N 2°55'·1W Q(6)+LFl.15s3m7M Black beacon, yellow top

44 Vannes

As 43 The Auray River and Auray

V SOUTHEAST BRITTANY

47 Pénerf

A **Le Pignon** 47°30'·0N 2°38'·9W Fl(3)WR.12s6m9-6M 028·5°-R-167°-W-175°-R-349·5°-W-028·5° Red square on tower

48 The Vilaine to Arzal

A **Basse de Kervoyal** 47°30'·4N 2°32'·6W DirQ.WR.6-4M 269°-W-271°-R-269° S card beacon tower

B **Basse Bertrand** 47°31'·1N 2°30'·7W Iso.WG.4s6m9-6M 040°-W-054°-G-227°-W-234°-G-040° Green tower

C **Penlan** 47°31'·0N 2°30'·1W Oc(2)WRG.6s26m15-11M 292·5°-R-025°-G-052°-W-060°-R-138°-G-180° White tower, red bands

D **Pointe du Scal** 47°29'·7N 2°26'·8W Q.G.8m4M White square tower, green top

51 Piriac-sur-Mer

A **Inner Mole Head** 47°22'·9N 2°32'·7W Oc(2)WRG.6s8m10-7M 066°-R-148°-G-194°-W-201°-R-221° White column

B **East Breakwater head** 47°23'·0N 2°32'·7W Fl.R.4s4m5M White structure, red top

52 La Turballe

A **Jetée de Garlahy (W breakwater head)** 47°20'·7N 2°30'·9W Fl(4)WR.12s13m10-7M 060°-R-315°-W-060° White pylon, red top

Ldg Lts 006·5°

B *Front* 47°20'·8N 2°30'·9W DirIso.R.4s11m3M 004°-intens-009° Metal mast, orange top

C *Rear* 280m from front DirIso.R.4s19m8M 004°-intens-009° Metal mast, orange top

53 Le Croisic

A **Jetée du Tréhic head** 47°18'·5N 2°31'·4W Iso.WG.4s12m14-11M 042°-G-093°-W-145°-G-345° Grey tower, green top

B **Basse Hergo tower** 47°18'·6N 2°31'·7W Fl.G.2·5s5m2M Green beacon tower

First Ldg Lts 156°

C *Front* 47°18'·0N 2°31'·0W DirQ.10m19M 154°-intens-158° Orange topmark on white metal framework tower

D *Rear* 116m from front DirQ.14m19M 154°-intens-158° Synchronised with front Orange topmark on white metal framework tower

Second Ldg Lts 174°

E *Front* 47°18'·1N 2°31'·1W DirQ.G.5m11M 171°-vis-177° Yellow can topmark, green stripe on green and white pylon

F *Rear* 48m from front DirQ.G.8m11M 171°-vis-177° Yellow can topmark, green stripe on green and white pylon

G **Le Grand Mabon** 47°18'·0N 2°31'·0W Fl(3)R.12s6m2M Red framework structure and pedestal

Third Ldg lights 134·7°

H *Front* 47°17'·9N 2°30'·8W DirQ.R.6m8M 125·5°-intens-143·5° Red and white chequered rectangle on white pylon, red top

I *Rear* 52m from front DirQ.R.10m8M 125·5°-intens-143·5° Synchronised with front Red and white chequered rectangle on pylon, on fish market roof

54 Le Pouliguen

A **Les Guérandaises buoy** 47°15'·0N 2°24'·3W Fl.G.2·5s Starboard-hand pillar buoy

B **Penchâteau buoy** 47°15'·2N 2°24'·4W Fl.R.2·5s Port-hand pillar buoy

C **Petits Impairs** 47°16'·0N 2°24'·6W Fl(2)G.6s6m2M Green triangle on tower

D **Le Pouliguen, S jetty** 47°16'·4N 2°25'·4W Q.R.13m9M 171°-vis-081° White column, red lantern

55 Pornichet

A **Les Guérandaises buoy** 47°15'·0N 2°24'·3W Fl.G.2·5s Starboard-hand pillar buoy

B **Penchâteau buoy** 47°15'·2N 2°24'·4W Fl.R.2·5s Port-hand pillar buoy

C **Pornichet, S breakwater head** 47°15'·5N 2°21'·2W Iso.WRG.4s11m10/7M 303°-G-081°-W-084°-R-180° White tower

D **Pornichet entrance west** 47°15'·5N 2°21'·1W Q.G.3m1M

E **Pornichet entrance east** 47°15'·5N 2°21'·1W Q.R.4m1M

56 Saint-Nazaire and Nantes

A **La Banche** 47°10'·6N 2°28'·1W Fl(2)WR.6s22m15-11M 266°-R-280°-W-266° Black tower, white bands

B **Ile du Pilier** 47°02'·6N 2°21'·6W Fl(3)20s33m29M Grey pyramidal tower
Auxiliary light Q.R.10m11M 321°-vis-034° same structure

C **Le Grand Charpentier** 47°12'·8N 2°19'·2W Q.WRG.22m14-10M 020°-G-054°-W-062°-R-092°-W-111°-R-310°-W-020° Grey tower, green lantern

D **Pointe de St-Gildas** 47°08'·2N 2°14'·8W Q.WRG.20m14-10M 264°-R-308°-G-078°-W-088°-R-174°-W-180°-G-264° Metal framework tower on white house

E **Pointe d'Aiguillon** 47°14'·5N 2°15'·8W Oc(3)WR.12s27m13-10M 207°-R-233°-W-293°, 297°-W-300°-R-327°-W-023°-R-069° White tower

Ldg lights 025·5°

F *Front* 47°15'·2N 2°15'·0W DirQ.6m22M 024·7°-intens-026·2° White column on dolphin

G *Rear* 0.75M from front DirQ.36m24M 024°-intens-027° Synchronised with front, shown throughout 24 hours Black square, white stripe on metal tower

H **Villè-es-Martin, jetty head** 47°15'·3N 2°13'·7W Fl(2)6s10m10M White tower, red top

I **Morées** 47°15'·0N 2°13'·0W Fl(3)WR.12s12m6-4M 058°-W-224°, 300°-R-058° Green truncated tower

J **St-Nazaire, W Jetty** 47°16'·0N 2°12'·3W Oc(4)R.12s11m8M White tower, red top

K **St-Nazaire E Jetty** 47°16'·0N 2°12'·1W Oc(4)G.12s11m11M White tower, green top

M **Basse Nazaire Sud buoy** 47°16'·2N 2°11'·6W Q(6)+LFl.15s S card pillar buoy

N **Old mole head** 47°16'·3N 2°11'·8W Q(3)10s18m11M White tower, red top

57 Saint-Gildas

A **Pointe de St-Gildas** 47°08'·2N 2°14'·8W Q.WRG.20m14-10M 264°-R-308°-G-078°-W-088°-R-174°-W-180°-G-264° Metal framework tower on white house

B **Breakwater head** 47°08'·5N 2°14'·7W Fl(2)G.6s3M Metal post

58 Pornic

A **Pointe de St-Gildas** 47°08'·2N 2°14'·8W Q.WRG.20m14-10M 264°-R-308°-G-078°-W-088°-R-174°-W-180°-G-264° Metal framework tower on white house

B **Pointe de Noëveillard** 47°06'·6N 2°06'·9W Oc(4)WRG.12s23m13-9M shore-G-051°-W-079°-R-shore White square tower, green top, white dwelling

C **Marina elbow** 47°06'·4N 2°07'·0W Fl.2.5s4m3M Grey structure

D **Marina entrance, S side** 47°06'·5N 2°06'·7W Fl(2)R.6s4m2M Black column, red top

E **Marina entrance, N side** 47°06'·5N 2°06'·7W Fl(2).G.6s4m2M Black column, green top

F **Fairway buoy** 47°06'·5N 2°06'·6W LFl.10s Red and white buoy

VI VENDÉE

59 Herbaudière

A **Ile du Pilier** 47°02'·6N 2°21'·6W Fl(3)20s33m29M Grey pyramidal tower
Auxiliary Lt Q.R.10m11M 321°-vis-034° same structure

B **Basse du Martroger** 47°02'·6N 2°17'·1W Q.WRG.11m9-6M 033°-G-055°-W-060°-R-095°-G-124°-W-153°-R-201°-W-240°-R-033° N card beacon tower

C **Passe de la Grise SCM** 47°01'·7N 2°20'·0W Q(6)+LFl.15s

D **Pierre Moine** 47°03'·4N 2°12'·4W Fl(2)6s14m7M Isolated danger tower

L'Herbaudière

I **West jetty** 47°01'·6N 2°17'·9W Oc(2+1)WG.12s9m10/7M 187·5°-W-190°-G-187·5° White column and hut, green top

Ldg Lts 187·5°

J *Front* 47°01'·6N 2°17'·9W Q.5m7M 098°-vis-278° Grey mast

K *Rear* 310m from front Q.21m7M 098°-vis-278°Grey mast

L. **East jetty head** 47°01'·7N 2°17'·7W Fl(2)R.6s8m4M Red tripod

60 Noirmoutier Anchorages

A **Pointe du Devin (Port Morin)** 46°59'·1N 2°17'·6W Oc(4)WRG.12s10m11-8M 314°-G-028°-W-035°-R-134° White column and hut, green top

B **Basse du Martroger** 47°02'·6N 2°17'·1W Q.WRG.11m9-6M 033°-G-055°-W-060°-R-095°-G-124°-W-153°-R-201°-W-240°-R-033° N card beacon tower

C **Pierre Moine** 47°03'·4N 2°12'·4W Fl(2)6s14m7M Isolated danger tower

D **Pointe des Dames** 47°00'·7N 2°13'·3W Oc(3)WRG.12s34m19-15M 016·5°-G-057°-R-124°-G-165°-W-191°-R-267°-W-357°-R-016·5° White square tower

E **Port de Noirmoutier jetty** 46°59'·3N 2°13'·1W Oc(2)R.6s6m6M White column, red top.

62 Port-Joinville

A **Petite Foule (main light)** 46°43'·1N 2°23'·0W Fl.5s56m24M Square white tower green lantern

B **Les Chiens Perrins** 46°43'·6N 2°24'·6W Q(9)WG.15s16m7-4M 330°-G-350°-W-200° W card beacon tower

C **Pointe des Corbeaux** 46°41′·4N 2°17′·1W
Fl(2+1)R.15s25m20M White square tower, red top
D **Port Joinville NW jetty head** 46°43′·8N 2°20′·8W
Oc(3)WG.12s6m11-8M shore-G-150°-W-232°-G-279°-W-285°-G-shore White octagonal tower, green top
Quai du Canada Ldg Lts 219°
F *Front* 46°43′·6N 2°21′·0W Q.R.11m6M 169°-vis-269° Pylon
G *Rear* 85m from front Q.R.16m6M 169°-vis-269° Pylon

63 Port de la Meule

A **Port de la Meule** 46°41′·7N 2°20′·8W Oc.WRG.4s9m9-6M
007·5°-G-018°-W-027·5°-R-041·5° Grey square tower, red top

64 Saint-Gilles-Croix-de-Vie

A **Pointe de Grosse Terre** 46°41′·5N 1°57′·9W
Fl(4)WR.12s25m18-15M 290°-R-339°-W-125°-R-145°
White truncated conical tower
Ldg Lts 043·7°
B *Front* 46°41′·9N 1°56′·7W Q.7m15M 033·5°-intens-053·5°
White square tower, red top
C *Rear* 260m from front Q.28m15M 033·5°-intens-053·5°
Synchronised with front White square tower, red top
D **Pill'Hours buoy (SCM)** 46°41′·0N 1°58′·1W Q(6)+ LFl.15s
E **NW jetty head** 46°41′·6N 1°57′·2W Fl.R.4s8m6M Red
column on white hut
F **SE jetty head** 46°41′·5N 1°57′·3W Fl.G.4s8m6M White
structure, green top

65 Les Sables d'Olonne

A **L'Armandèche** 46°29′·4N 1°48′·3W Fl(2+1)15s42m24M
295°-vis-130° White 6-sided tower, red top
B **Les Barges** 46°29′·7N 1°50′·5W Fl(2)R.10s25m13M Grey
tower
C **Petite Barge buoy (SCM)** 46°28′·9N 1°50′·6W
Q(6)+LFl.15s3M Whis
Passe du SW Ldg Lts 032·5°
D *Front* 46°29′·4N 1°46′·4W Iso.4s12m16M Shown
throughout 24hrs Metal mast
E *Rear* 330m from front Iso.4s33m16M Shown throughout
24hrs White square masonry tower
F **Nouch Sud buoy (SCM)** 46°28′·6N 1°47′·4W Q(6)+LFl.15s.
Passe du SE Ldg Lts 320°
G *Front* **Jetée des Sables** 46°29′·4N 1°47′·5W Q.G.11m8M
White tower, green top
H *Rear* **Tour d'Arundel** 465m from front Q.33m12M Large
grey square tower surmounted by white turret
I **Jetée Saint Nicolas head** 46°29′·2N 1°47′·5W Q.R.16m8M
143°-vis-094° White tower, red top
Entrance Ldg Lts 328·1°
J *Front* 46°29′·7N 1°47′·8W Iso.R.4s6m9M Red square on
white hut
K *Rear* 65m from front DirIso.R.4s9m9M 324°-vis-330° Red
square on white hut

66 Bourgenay

A **Fairway buoy** 46°25′·3N 1°41′·9W LFl.10s Red and white
striped pillar buoy
Ldg Lts 040°
B *Front* 46°26′·4N 1°40′·6W Q.G.9m7M 020°-vis-060° Green
rectangle on white tower
C *Rear* 162m from front Q.G.19m7M 010°-vis-070° Green
rectangle on white tower
D **W breakwater head** 46°26′·3N 1°40′·5W Fl.R.4s8m9M
Red structure

VII CHARENTE

70 Ars-en-Ré

A **Pointe du Grouin du Cou (mainland)** 46°20′·7N 1°27′·8W
Fl.WRG.5s29m20-16M 034°-R-061°-W-117°-G-138°-W-034°
White 8-sided tower, black lantern
B **Les Baleineaux** 46°15′·8N 1°35′·2W Oc(2)6s23m11M Pink
tower, red top
C **Les Baleines** 46°14′·6N 1°33′·7W Fl(4)15s53m27M Grey 8-sided tower, red lantern
Le Fier d'Ars Ldg Lts 265·8°
D *Front* 46°14′·1N 1°28′·6W Iso.4s5m11M 141°-vis-025°
White rectangle on grey framework
E *Rear* 370m from front DirIso.G.4s13m15M 264°-intens-266° Synchronised with front Green square tower on
dwelling
Ars-en-Ré Ldg Lts 232·5°
F *Front* 46°12′·8N 1°30′·6W Q.5m9M White rectangular
hut, red lantern
G *Rear* 370m from front Q.13m11M 142°-vis-322° Black
rectangle on white framework tower, green top

71 Saint-Martin-de-Ré

A **Ramparts E of entrance** 46°12′·4N 1°21′·9W
Oc(2)WR.6s18m10-7M shore-W-245°-R-281°-shore White
tower, red top
B **Mole head** 46°12′·5N 1°21′·9W Iso.G.4s10m6M White
tripod, green top
C **W end of breakwater** 46°12′·5N 1°21′·9W Fl.R.2·5s5m2M
White post, red top

72 La-Flotte-en-Ré

A **La Flotte-en-Ré** 46°11′·3N 1°19′·3W Fl.WG.4s10m12-9M
130°-G-205°-W-220°-G-257° Moiré effect Dir Lt 212·5°
White round tower, green top

73 La Rochelle

A **Le Lavardin** 46°08′·1N 1°14′·5W Fl(2)WG.6s14m11-8M
160°-G-169°-W-160° Black tower, red band
B **Tour Richelieu** 46°08′·9N 1°10′·4W Fl.R.4s10m7M Red 8-sided tower
Ldg Lts 059°
C *Front* 46°09′·4N 1°09′·2W DirQ.15m14M 056°-intens-062°Red round tower, white bands (By day Fl.4s)
D *Rear* 235m from front Q.25m14M 044°-vis-074°, 061°-obscd-065° Synchronised with front White 8-sided tower,
green top (By day Fl.4s)
E **Port de Minimes W mole head** 46°08′·9N 1°10′·1W
Fl(2)G.6s9m5M White tower, green top
F **Port de Minimes E mole head** 46°08′·9N 1°10′·0W
Fl(2)R.6s6m5M White tower, red top

74 Ile d'Aix

A **Chauveau (SE of Ile de Ré)** 46°08′·0N 1°16′·4W
Oc(3)WR.12s27m15-11M 057°-W-094°-R-104°-W-342°-R-057° White round tower, red top
B **Fort Boyard** 46°00′·0N 1°12′·9W Q(9)15s Fort
C **Ile d'Aix** 46°00′·6N 1°10′·7W Fl.WR.5s24m24-20M 103°-R-118°-W-103° Two white round towers, red tops
La Charente river entrance Ldg Lts 115°
D *Front* 45°58′·0N 1°04′·4W DirQ.R.8m19M 113°-intens-117° White square tower, red top
E *Rear* 600m from front DirQ.R.21m20M 113°-intens-117°
White square tower, red top
Auxiliary Q.R.21m8M same structure

75 River Charente

Ldg Lts 115°
D *Front* 45°58′·0N 1°04′·4W DirQ.R.8m19M 113°-intens-117° White square tower, red top
E *Rear* 600m from front DirQ.R.21m20M 113°-intens-117°
White square tower, red top
Auxiliary Q.R.21m8M same structure
Port-des-Barques Ldg Lts 134·3°
C *Front* 45°57′·0N 1°04′·2W Iso.G.4s5m9M125°-intens-145°
White square tower
D *Rear* 490m from front Iso.G.4s13m11M 125°-intens-145°
Synchronised with front White square tower with black

band on W side

77 St-Denis-d'Oléron

A **Pointe de Chassiron** 46°02′·8N 1°24′·7W Fl.10s50m28M White round tower, black bands

B **Rocher d'Antioche** 46°03·9′N 1°24′·7W Q.20m11M NCM tower, surrounded by above-water wrecks.

St-Denis

C **Dir Ldg Lt 205°** 46°01′·6N 1°22′·0W Dir Iso.WRG.4s14m11-8M 190°-G-204°-W-206°-R-220° White concrete mast

D **East breakwater head** 46°02′·1N 1°22′·1W Fl(2)WG.6s6m9-6M 205°-G-277°-W-292°-G-165° Square masonry hut with pole

E **South breakwater head** 46°02′·1N 1°22′·2W Fl(2)R.6s3m6M Square masonry hut

79 Boyardville

A **Mole head** 45°58′·2N 1°13′·9W Fl(2)R.6s8m5M White metal framework tower, red top

80 The Seudre to Marennes

A Tourelle Juliar 45°54′·2N 1°09′·4W Q(3)WG.10s12m11-8M 147°-W-336°-G-147° E card beacon tower

Le Château Ldg Lts 319°

B *Front* 45°53′·1N 1°11′·4W Q.R.11m7M 191°-vis-087° Red rectangle on low white tower

C *Rear* 240m from front Q.R.24m7M Synchronised with front White tower, red top

81 Royan

A **BXA light buoy (SWM)** 45°37′·5N 1°28′·7W Iso.4s7M

B **La Coubre** 45°41′·8N 1°14′·0W Fl(2)10s64m28M White tower, red top
Auxiliary light F.RG.42m12-10M 030°-R-043°-G-060°-R-110° Same structure

C **Cordouan** 43°35′·2N 1°10′·4W Oc(2+1)WRG.12s60m22-18M 014°-W-126°-G-178·5°-W-250°-W(unintens)-267°-R(unintens)-294·5°-R-014° White conical tower, dark grey band and top, dark grey base

Ldg Lts 081·5°

D *Front* 45°39′·6N 1°08′·7W DirIso.4s21m20M 080·5°-intens-082·5° White pylon on dolphin
Auxiliary Q(2)5s10m2M Same structure

E *Rear* **La Palmyre** 45°39′·7N 1°07′·2W 1·1M from front DirQ.57m27M 080·7°-intens-082·2° White radar tower
Auxiliary DirF.R.57m17M 325·7°-intens-328·2° Same structure

Ldg Lts 327°

F *Front* **Terre Nègre** 45°38′·8N 1°06′·3W Oc(3)WRG.12s39m18-14M 304°-R-319°-W-327°-G-000°-W-004°-G-097°-W-104°-R-116° White tower, red top on W side

G *Rear* **La Palmyre** 45°39′·7N 1°07′·2W 1·1M from front DirQ.57m27M 080·7°-intens-082·2° White radar tower

Passe Sud Ldg Lts 063°

H *Front* **St Nicholas** 45°33′·7N 1°05′·0W DirQ.G.22m16M 061·5°-intens-064·5° White square tower

I *Rear* **Pointe de Grave** 45°34′·2N 1°03′·9W 0·84M from front Oc.WRG.4s26m19-15M 033°-W(unintens)-054°-W-233·5°-R-303°-W-312°-G-330°-W-341°-W(unintens)-025° White square tower, black corners and top

Leading Lights 041°

J *Front* **Le Chay** 45°37·3N 1°02′·4W DirQ.R.33m18M 039·5°-intens-042·5° White tower, red top

K *Rear* **Saint Pierre** 45°38′·1N 1°01′·4W 0·97M from front DirQ.R.61m18M 039°-intens-043° Red water tower

Royan entrance

L **South jetty head** 45°37′·0N 1°01′·8W Fl.(2)R10s11m12M White tower, red brick base

M **W jetty** 45°37′·2N 1°01′·6W Fl(3)R.12s8m6M White mast, red top

N **East jetty head** 45°37′·2N 1°01′·5W Fl(3)G.12s2m6M 311°-vis-151° White post, green top

82 Port Médoc

A **Pointe de Grave** 45°34′·2N 1°03′·9W Oc.WRG.4s26m19-15M 033°-W(unintens)-054°-W-233·5°-R-303°-W-312°-G-330°-W-341°-W(unintens)-025° White square tower, black corners and top

B **Pointe de Grave N jetty head** 45°34′·4N 1°03′·7W Q.8m2M N card beacon

C **Pointe de Grave N jetty spur** 45°34′·3N 1°03′·7W Iso.G.4s8m3M 190°-vis-045° Green triangle on green mast

D **Port Bloc entrance, N side** 45°34′·1N 1°03′·7W Fl.G.4s9m3M White metal framework tower, green top lit by day in fog

E **Port Bloc entrance, S side** 45°34′·1N 1°03′·7W F.R.4s8m4M White tower, red top lit by day in fog

83 Pauillac and Bordeaux

A **Pauillac Breakwater elbow** 45°12′·0N 0°44′·6W Fl.G.4s7m5M Green mast

B **Pauillac Breakwater head** 45°11′·9N 0°44′·6W Q.G.7m4M Green mast

C **Pauillac Mole head** 45°11′·9N 0°44′·5W Q.R.4m2M 320°-vis-050° Large wine bottle

Index